Created and Directed by Hans Höfer

INSIGHT GUIDES

SOUTHERN SPAIN

Edited by Andrew Eames
Editorial Director: Brian Bell

APA PUBLICATIONS

SOUTHERN SPAIN

First Edition (2nd Reprint)
© 1992 APA PUBLICATIONS (HK) LTD
All Rights Reserved
Printed in Singapore by Höfer Press Pte. Ltd

ABOUT THIS BOOK

Insight Guide: *Southern Spain* is the fifth book on Spain by the Insight team, following hard on the heels of Insight *Spain*, the island titles *Mallorca and the Balearics, Tenerife and the Western Canaries* and *Gran Canaria and the Eastern Canaries*. Although *Southern Spain* is one of the first books to come out of Apa Publications' new London office, the experience that went into the production of this volume is tried and tested.

Southern Spain's editor is **Andrew Eames**, who edited three of the previous Spain books, as well as Apa's *Cityguide: London*. Eames is managing editor with special responsibility for the new batch of Spanish titles, which also include books on *Catalonia, Barcelona* and *Madrid*.

Eames first became interested in Insight Guides while working as a young journalist in South-east Asia. Since then he has published his travel autobiography, *Crossing the Shadow Line*, and is currently working on a book of his experiences in Scotland. His newspaper work in London includes a spell on the *Times* and a regular series in the *Independent*; his magazine experience includes the editorship of *Business Traveller* and freelance magazine consultancy.

People and Legends

One of the key writers Eames recruited at an early stage in the book's production was **David Baird**, the author of *Inside Andalusia*. Baird has lived in Andalucía since 1971, and in the pages of this Insight Guide he brings together his years of observations in chapters about the people, legends, cultural influ-ences and fiestas of Southern Spain. He says there's a special quality about the people and region of Andalucía which keeps him there. Baird also compiled the comprehensive Travel Tips section with the able assistance of **Penny Ward**.

For a historical perspective on Andalucía, Eames called on **Jan Read**, the author of—amongst 23 other titles—a history of the Moorish influence in Spain. Read is one of those multi-talented people who has pursued a great many careers in his lifetime. Born in Australia, but brought up and now resident in Scotland with his Spanish wife, he was first a film director and script writer (including for the BBC TV series *Dr Finlay's Casebook*) before turning to books. His consuming passion is wine in Spain, about which he has written several recent books.

Thomas Hinde first visited Spain for his six-week honeymoon in 1951. Since then he has revisited the country on numerous occasions and in 1963 he published *Spain*, an anthology of writing about the country. In 1975 he and his family and two donkeys set out to walk from Spain to Turkey, the story of which is told in *The Great Donkey Walk*, which he wrote with his wife, the biographer Susan Chitty. Hinde is a prolific novelist (16 so far) and has also published a dozen other books on varied subjects. In this book he writes about Gibraltar and the province of Málaga.

Alastair Boyd (Lord Kilmarnock), who writes on the white towns and on Ronda, is well known to any Hispanophile. His books on Catalonia and Madrid are essential reading for those who want to be well-informed. Boyd lived in Spain from 1957 to 1975, and still maintains a house in Andalucía.

Janet Mendel is an American journalist

Eames

Baird

Read

Boyd

who has lived in Andalucía for the past 20 years. She is the author of *Cooking in Spain;* in these pages she is responsible for the chapters on food and Córdoba, about which she says: "It's so familiar; I think I lived there in a former lifetime."

Another American contributor is **Jan McGirk**, a Californian who has lived in Morocco, Andalucía and Madrid. McGirk is the author of a guidebook to rural Spain, as well as the chapters on Morocco and wild Andalucía in this book. A graduate in cultural anthropology from the University of California, she attributes her wanderlust to a misspent youth in Adventureland, her favourite section of Disneyland, which is half an hour's drive from her parents' house.

Mike Eddy, who wrote the chapters on Cádiz and Huelva, is an English anthropologist living and working in the Canary Islands, who contributed extensively to Apa's books on that archipelago. Columbus sailed from Huelva to the Canaries on the way to his discoveries; Eddy flew back the other way to do his research.

Geraldine Mitchell, an Irish journalist who spends much of her year commuting between Barcelona and Granada, wrote the chapters on Granada and the Alhambra.

The chapters on the gossip of the Costa and the strangers in the Alpujarras were written by **Nigel Bowden,** a long-time resident of the Costa and something of a specialist in behind-the-scenes articles on southern Spain. Also a specialist is **Muriel Feiner,** a Madrid-based American who came to live in Madrid after graduate school, founded the International Bullfight Organisation and married a bullfighter. Feiner is one of two acknowledged foreign experts on bullfighting resident in Spain. **Harry Debelius**, veteran Spanish correspondent for the *Times*, wrote the chapter on the sherry dynasties.

Borrowed from the team for Insight Guide*: Mallorca* were **Vicky Hayward** (who writes on Almería and Jaén) and **Robin Neillands**, who recounts his journey across Andalucía on foot. Since writing for Insight Guides, Hayward has gone to live in Madrid. The chapter on flamenco is the work of **Philip Sweeney**, a musicologist and editor of Apa's guide to *The Gambia & Senegal.*

The photographs in this book reflect the combined talents of **Bill Wassman**, a New York based photographer who has completed many assignments for Insight Guides—particularly those with a Spanish connection—and of **Jean Dominique Dallet**, a Frenchmen who was born in Morocco but now lives on the Costa del Sol. Dallet is a regular photographer for *Lookout* magazine, *Geo* and London's *Sunday Times* magazine.

An Expert Team

Particular thanks are due to **Javier Baselga Lej** and his assistants at the Junta de Andalucía in Seville, without whom this book would not, as they say, have been possible; to **Chris Fisher** and the public relations team at Expo'92; to **Mark Little** at *Lookout* magazine for his advice; and to **Air Europe**, who carried visiting journalists safely—and extremely comfortably—backwards and forwards to Southern Spain via Gibraltar.

They also served who only stayed at home, of course. **Jill Anderson** marshalled the book skilfully through a variety of Macintosh computers; **Berndtson & Berndtson** drew the maps; proof-reading and indexing were expertly handled by **Kate Owen**.

Mendel   *Eddy*   *Hayward*

CONTENTS

HISTORY AND FEATURES

PLACES

TRAVEL TIPS

THE SOUL OF SPAIN

Southern Spain is the source of Spanish cliché, of sherry, of flamenco, of *machismo*, of bullfighting and of coastal resorts crammed with ice-cream eating foreigners. It is Spain *par excellence,* paradoxically and simultaneously exuberant and desolate, crowded and quiet, original and tacky.

For package tourists the cathedrals of the Costas are Torremolinos, Marbella and Fuengirola and the miles of clubs, bars, cafés, golf clubs and urbanisations that line what was once a rocky, unwanted coast. To cultural visitors its highlights are the cities of Seville, Córdoba and Granada with their monuments the Giralda, Mezquita and Alhambra. For businessmen it is the site of the 1992 world fair, Expo'92; for wildlife enthusiasts it has some of the highest mountains in Europe (including Europe's southernmost skiing resort) and marshlands crowded with flamingos and camels.

Other than on the coast, very little has changed in Andalucía in hundreds of years. There have been only two major periods in the region's history. The first was the era of the Moors, who dominated the southern end of the peninsula for 800 years until 1492 and who have left their stamp on its cities and its landscape. The year of their downfall heralded the second period of Andalucía's glory, when Christopher Columbus set off from Huelva in search of America. The riches from the New World flowed back across the Atlantic, up the Guadalquivir and into Seville, turning it into one of the richest cities in Europe.

In the long centuries of decline since then the gradual acceleration of life elsewhere has drawn many of the original *andaluz* away from their homeland. They left to populate the new colonies of Latin America (who today speak Spanish with an Andalucían accent), and to work in the factories of northern Spain. On the edge of Europe between the Third World and the First, Andalucía went into limbo economically and culturally.

The limbo is still there, but it has been recreated for foreigners: the Costa del Sol is a political and social limbo of its own dedicated to the spending of money, legally or illegally, wisely or unwisely, in the pursuit of a good time.

Recent years of change—following the death of Franco and the joining of the European Community—are at last penetrating over the Sierra Morena and into Andalucía. Spain is bonding itself together for the next century—including the unwilling donkey of the south. Life is speeding up, imperceptibly but surely, in the *pueblos*; Andalucía is poised for change. These pages are a testament to this moment in time, recalling the past, portraying the present, and predicting the future.

Preceding pages: rolling hills on the road to Granada; tropical gardens of the Alhambra; the white face of Alcalá de los Gazules; Seville town houses beside the Giralda. Left, modern example of a rich and exuberant culture.

José Ortega y Gasset, the shrewd Spanish writer, once wrote an essay on *The Theory of Andalucía* in which he commented on the Andalucían stereotypes of bullfighting, flamenco and Carmen with a rose in her mouth. He maintained that such self-miming and narcissism is the product of long civilisation; and although Andalucía takes its name from al-Andalus, as it was called by the Moors who invaded it in AD 711, it is in fact one of Western Europe's oldest civilisations and trading communities.

Ortega y Gasset makes the further point that over the centuries Andalucía has been invaded by most of the most warlike peoples of the Mediterranean, but that, like the Chinese, the Andalucíans have in the end "conquered" all their invaders by inculcating in them their own life-style and culture.

Mythical beginnings: The south of Spain was originally settled by the Iberians, a Mediterranean race of uncertain origin. However, the first inhabitants of whom there is historical evidence were the Tartessians of the Bronze Age in the second millennium BC. Their land, known to the ancient Greeks as Tartessos and to the Hebrews as Tarshish, lay near Hades at the edge of the world where the sun sinks into the ocean and where Hercules was sent to fetch the fabled cattle of King Geryon.

On his arrival Hercules first planted a couple of pillars on either side of the strait between Africa and Europe, before shooting the three-headed, three-bodied Geryon sideways through all three bodies with a single arrow and making off with his herd.

The German archaeologist Adolph Schulten spent much of his time between 1925 and 1945 in studying ancient sources and excavating the marshy Coto Doñana at the mouth of the River Guadalquivir in an attempt to discover the lost city of Tartessos, but without success; unlike Troy, this city has never been found. Nevertheless, quite by accident in 1957, Mata Carriazo, Professor of Archaeology at the University of Seville, picked up the bronze of a fertility goddess in a

Seville junk shop, and was able to identify it as being of Tartessian origin.

This was followed by the discovery of a sculpture, *The Mask of Tharsis*, when a mining company opened up the galleries, unworked for centuries, of a mine near Huelva; and in 1961, during construction work at the Seville Pigeon Shooting Club in the hills across the river from the city, a workman's pick struck a metallic object. It proved to be only one of a hoard of Tartessian plates, bracelets and necklaces.

During recent years archaeologists have unearthed thousands of other artefacts—pottery, sculpture, jewellery and objects of silver and gold—testifying to a knowledge of mining, industry and agriculture at a very early date and even bearing out the Greeks' description of Tartessos as a veritable El Dorado and the comment of the geographer Strabo (63 BC–*circa* AD 19) that the people of Turdetania (as he knew Tartessos) were "using silver feeding troughs and wine jars".

Aegean sailors were trading with Tartessos for copper, scarce in the Eastern Mediterranean, during the second millennium, long before the reign of King Solomon (*circa* 950

Left, the writings of Hernan Cortes, in safe hands in a Seville convent. **Right**, Tartessian mask.

BC), of whom the Bible (Second Chronicles 9.21) reports that "the king's ships went to Tarshish with the servants of Hiram (King of Tyre); once every three years came the ships of Tarshish bringing gold, and silver, ivory, and apes, and peacocks." (Nearby Gibraltar is, of course, still wellknown for its apes to this day.)

A custom which still survives and is known as the *almadraba*, the fishing for tuna during their spawning run into the Mediterranean through the Straits of Gibraltar, almost certainly dates from Tartessian times. It is vividly described by the classical poet Oppian: "First a skilful Tunny-watcher ascends a steep high hill, who remarks the various shoals, their kind and size, and informs his comrades. Then straightaway all the nets are set in the waves like a city, and the net has gate-warders and gates withal and inner courts. And swiftly the Tunnies speed on in line… Without end they pour within the nets, so long as they desire and as the net can receive the throng of them; and rich and excellent is the spoil."

Trading places: The Tartessians ventured much further afield, fishing along the Atlantic coast and around the Canaries, and their sailors are reliably said to have sailed the "tin route" to Galicia and possibly as far as Cornwall. Strabo has a story of a Phoenician captain from Gadir (Cádiz) who kept the secret of the "tin islands" from a Roman ship that was shadowing him by purposely running his own ship aground, for which he was rewarded by his government. It was largely because of the abundance of tuna—Tyrian salted fish was famous—and the availability of tin, used in making bronze, and of other metals from the mines of Huelva that the Tartessians' trading partners and allies, the seafaring Phoenicians, established a factory at Gadir about 1100 BC.

There was peaceful competition from the Phocaean Greeks, who founded a trading post at Mainake near Málaga, and Tartessos was at its most prosperous in the 6th century BC during the long and peaceful reign of King Arganthonius, but suffered an abrupt change of fortune after the Battle of Alalia *circa* 535 BC.

Tartessos's allies, the Phocaeans, had established a colony at Alalia in Corsica and had inflicted enormous losses on the Carthaginians and Etruscans by pirating their ships. The battle was fought off Alalia with 60 Phocaean ships facing double the number of Carthaginian and Etruscan. The Phocaeans claimed victory, but lost 40 of their ships for 60 of the enemy's, while the remainder suffered major damage to their bows and rams. As a result the Carthaginians were able to close the whole Western Mediterranean to all but their own ships.

From then on Carthage, founded in the first place as a North African colony of Tyre, had a free hand in Spain and supplanted the Phoenicians. The kingdom of Tartessos disintegrated, and in the 3rd century BC, in a bloody campaign which cost the life of their commander, Hamilcar Barca, father of Hannibal, Carthaginian forces unified most of greater Andalucía by force.

The Romans, now the emergent power in the Mediterranean, watched events in Spain with anxiety. They had made a pact with the Carthaginians that they should not advance north of the River Ebro.

Hannibal's attack on the city of Saguntum, which was south of the Ebro but under Roman protection, led to the outbreak of the Second Punic War (218–201 BC). Rome was now mistress of the seas and relied on a counter-attack in Spain, but was foiled by the speed of Hannibal's famous crossing of the Alps and invasion of Italy itself, in which he destroyed one Roman army after another. Slowly the Romans fought back. Under Publius and Gnaeus Scipio they were defeated in Spain by Hannibal's brother Hasdrubal in 211 BC, but a new Roman commander, Publius Cornelius Scipio, was sent to Spain in 209 BC. He succeeded in seizing the Carthaginian base of Carthago Nova (Cartagena) by a surprise attack, and by 201 BC had driven the last of the Carthaginians from the country.

Roman rule: It took long campaigning, especially in the north, for the Roman legions to subdue the native tribes of Hispania, and there was also fierce fighting between the Romans themselves. The long-standing feud between Julius Caesar and Pompey came to its bitter end when Caesar annihilated the forces of Pompey's sons, Gnaeus and Sextus, at Munda, now Montilla of the famous wine in Córdoba province, on 17 March 45 BC.

The Roman occupation of Spain was to last for some seven centuries, during which agriculture was reorganised; bridges, roads and aqueducts were built, and the Roman legal system was introduced. The influence of the Romans cannot be underestimated, since it was to pervade the Spain of the Visigoths and profoundly to modify the Arabic civilisation of the Moors.

During the reign of Caesar's successor, Augustus (63 BC–AD 14), the country was divided into three provinces, of which the most southerly, Baetica, corresponded very largely to present-day Andalucía. Hispania, and especially Baetica with its flourishing agriculture and mineral resources, was to become one of the richest provinces of the Empire. The Romans greatly expanded the garum, a product of the tuna fishing industry. This paste, made by marinating the belly meat, as expensive as caviar today and synonymous with high life in Rome, was believed by some, like the elder Pliny, to have curative powers, though Martial, Spanish-born as he was, complained of its poisonous odour. A garum rather different from that of the Romans, in the form of a smooth paste of anchovies, black olives, capers and herbs, is still available in Catalonia; and a product more like the original is a household word, under the name of ñnoc-man, in Vietnam and southeast Asia and may be bought in food-stores selling oriental products.

Salt and sensuality: Martial was, in fact,

Above, Roman sarcophagus in the Alcázar museum in Córdoba.

production of wheat, olives and wine. It was they who introduced the large earthenware jars or *orcae*, still used in Montilla for fermenting and storing wine, and it has been estimated that by the 2nd century AD some 20 million amphorae of Spanish wine had been shipped to Rome, proof of which is the extraordinary artificial mountain of broken vessels from Monte Testaccio, still bearing their seals of origin.

Another export, from Cádiz (renamed Gades by the Romans), was the costly more interested in a different export of Cádiz, its sensual delights. The early 19th-century traveller Richard Ford, who remains the most lucid and intuitive of all writers on Spain, describes Cádiz as "the centre of sensual civilisation, the purveyor of gastronomy etc." and adds that "It is quite clear that Cádiz was the eldest daughter of Tyre, and her daughters (i.e. descendants of settlers from Sidon) have inherited the Sidonian 'stretching forth of necks, wanton eyes, walking and mincing as they go' (Book of Isaiah iii.16)."

Dancers from Cádiz, the *puellae Gaditanae*, Byron's "black-eyed maids of

Heaven formed for all the witching arts of love", were much in demand at entertainments in classical Rome, and Martial in particular returns to them time and again in his verses. So he writes about his mistress, the ravishing Telethusa: "She who was cunning to show wanton gestures to the sound of Baetic castanets and to frolic to the tunes of Gades, she who could have roused passion in palsied Pelias, and have stirred Hecuba's spouse even by Hector's pyre—Telethusa burns and racks with love her former master. He sold her as his maid, now he buys her back as mistress."

Richard Ford put forward good reasons for identifying the famous statue of *Aphrodite*

Pliny's description of Martial's pointed and salty style, comments that "This mixture of salt and gall is most peculiar to the satirical Sevillians, whose tongues flay their victims alive".

Many other illustrious Roman writers, among them Lucan, the Sénecas and Columella, who in his *De Re Rustica* wrote about the sherry-like wines from his native Cádiz, were in fact born in Andalucía, and even more famous were the Emperors Trajan and Hadrian, both born in Italica (Santiponce, near Seville).

Baetica was famous for the culture of its cities, either, like Hispalis (Seville), developed from an existing settlement, or, like the

Kallipygos (the Venus of the shapely buttocks) in the Naples Archaeological Museum as Telethusa in person, and there is another representation in the Villa Item in Pompeii of a naked *puella Gaditana*, with upraised arms and castanets in the act of dancing, startlingly like a flamenco dancer of today.

It seems beyond doubt that there is a strong historical connection between flamenco and these dances. Flamenco as we know it today has also been influenced by the Moors and by the gypsies who arrived in Andalucía from India during the 15th century.

Famous sons: Ford, commenting on

splendid Italica of which only the ruins remain, founded to house the retired legionnaires, administrators, colonists and merchants from abroad. Roman cities the length and breadth of the Empire, from Britain to Africa, were built to a pattern, and many of those in Andalucía preserve the remains of their temples, forums, aqueducts, bridges, theatres and circuses.

So bridges survive at Córdoba (Roman name Corduba) and Espejo (Ucubi); aqueducts at Seville (Hispalis) and Almuñecar (Sexi); theatres at Málaga (Malaca) and Casas de la Reina (Regina); an amphitheatre at Ecija (Astigi); a temple and baths at Santiponce (Italica); while at Bolonia near Gibraltar the ruins of Baelo overlooking the sea comprise a fortified precinct, streets with columns, a forum and fountain, temples with statues, an amphitheatre and the remains of numerous houses and even premises for salting fish.

These Roman cities were not large by modern standards, but their size belies their importance as the centres of power and culture. It has, for example, been estimated that the area of Roman Córdoba was 172 acres (70 hectares) and that of Carmo (Carmona), then a place of importance, only 50 acres (20 hectares). Hispalis (Seville) probably ran to rather more than 247 acres (100 hectares), but its boundaries have not been accurately established.

The wealthy *bourgeoisie* often owned *villae* on the outskirts of the towns with extensive gardens and orchards, and beyond these lay the large estates or *latifundia*, worked by slave labour in Roman times. In modified form, these have survived over the centuries and have differentiated the rural economy and social patterns of Andalucía from those of northern Spain.

Decline and fall: With the decay of the Roman Empire the first "barbarians" entered Spain via the Pyrenees during AD 407–409, but left little mark on the south. They were shortly followed by the Visigoths, a Germanic people, theoretically auxiliaries of the tottering Empire. This fiction persisted until 468, when their king, Euric, broke with Rome. They met with little resistance in the south; the Andalucíans were in Livy's phrase "*Omnium Hispanorum maxime imbelles*" (Of all the Spaniards, the least warlike), and the Hispano-Roman nobility, dependent on a slave society, soon came to terms with the new rulers.

After the conversion of Visigothic King Reccared to Christianity in 568, the Church played an important role in unifying the country, but a fundamental weakness of the Visigothic kingdom, especially in Andalucía, was the division into haves and have nots, a situation which has largely persisted since then. The Visigothic aristocracy and Hispano-Roman nobility, with their large estates, exerted unchecked authority over

Left, Italica (Santiponce), the centre of Roman rule. Right, the medieval caves of Antequera.

the serfs, slaves and freed men, who formed the mass of the population.

Further instability arose from the lack of a law of succession of the king by his son; of the 33 Visigothic kings, who ruled Hispania from 414 to 711, three were deposed, 11 assassinated and only 19 died a natural death. So weak was the central authority that King Wamba resorted to calling up the clergy for service in his army; they took a grotesque revenge by conspiring with the nobles, trapping him and shaving his head as the mark of a slave.

Roderick, the last of the Visigothic kings, assumed power in 710 after bitter wrangling. Legend has it that one of his enemies, Count

Julián, sent his daughter Florinda to court at Toledo to receive the education befitting a princess, but that Roderick was so carried away with the girl that he seduced her, thus earning Count Julián's undying hatred and inducing him to conspire with the Berbers in North Africa.

Whatever the truth of this picturesque yarn, the Visigoths with their deeply divided leadership and lack of popular support had been lulled into a sense of false security by the apparent absence of any threat from the north or from Africa, and when invasion came they were almost totally unprepared to meet it.

In AD 711 Tariq ibn-Ziyad, Governor of Tangier, a far-flung outpost of the Damascus Caliphate, crossed the Straits of Gibraltar with some 7,000 men and established himself on the flanks of Mount Calpe (subsequently to be known as Gibraltar, from the Arabic *Jabal Tariq*, "the mountain of Tariq"). His arrival caught King Roderick, the last Visigothic king, by surprise. Roderick nevertheless massed a large army and launched a frontal attack on the Moors, now reinforced and in a strong position near present-day Algeciras. The Visigothic king, at the centre, fought bravely, but the flanks of his army, commanded by renegades, treacherously turned tail. Roderick was either killed or took flight, never to reappear.

The advance into Spain marked the tip of an Arab thrust along the North African coast which had begun with the annexation of Egypt in AD 642 by the second of the Umayyad caliphs of Damascus and was to be halted only in France by Charles Martel at the Battle of Tours in 732.

During the 30 years following the first incursion, Moslem governors of al-Andalus followed thick and fast and pressed northwards until al-Andalus, as the Moorish-occupied part of Spain became known, covered virtually the whole of modern Spain and Portugal apart from pockets of resistance in the far northwest and the Basque country. The invaders were, however, split into different factions: the Qaysites and Kalbites of pure Arabian descent and also the North African Berbers, on whom Tariq and his successors largely relied in the conquest of the country. Al-Andalus was finally united by the establishment of the Umayyad dynasty of Córdoba which was to control its destiny for some 300 years.

First of the line: Andalucía's founder, Abd-al-Rahman I (The Immigrant), was barely 20 when in January 750 the Umayyads in Syria were irrevocably overthrown. The results were far-reaching. Abu al-Abbas, the founder of the Abbasids, was determined to

root out and destroy every representative of the fallen Umayyads everywhere in the world. Abd-al-Rahman was hunted from pillar to post, but with his brother succeeded in reaching the Euphrates, their pursuers hard on their heels.

A contemporary chronicle, the *Akhbar Majmua*, describes what then ensued in the prince's own words: "We managed to reach the river ahead of them and threw ourselves into the water. When we got to the bank they began shouting: 'Come back; you have noth-

ing to fear.' I swam and my brother swam; I was a little ahead of him. Half way across, I turned to encourage him; but on hearing their promises he had turned back, afraid of drowning. I shouted to him, 'Come back, beloved'; but God did not will that he heard me. I swam on to the opposite bank. Then I saw that some of the soldiers were undressing to swim after me. They stopped, caught the boy and cut off his head in front of me. He was 13 years old."

Abd-al-Rahman's mother, Rah, was a Berber, and he succeeded in making his way along the North African coast to the family's ancestral home at Nakur in Morocco, from

Preceding pages: Moorish riches. Left, in the Córdoba mosque. Right, Mozarabic miniature of the fight between David and Goliath.

where he began negotiations with the Moslem leaders in Spain, eventually sailing with a few supporters to Almuñecar, near Málaga. In the event, the Moslem leaders in al-Andalus had second thoughts about a Umayyad restoration in Spain, but Abd-al-Rahman was meanwhile gathering support on all sides and in 756 decisively defeated his opponents near Córdoba.

Abd-al-Rahman I was 26 when he became Emir of al-Andalus. He is described in the *Bayan al-Mughrib* of the 13th-century Moorish chronicler Ibn-Idhari as being "tall, fair, one-eyed (this without further explanation), with shrunken cheeks and a mole on his forehead and wore his hair in two long

ians or Jews, far less to put them to the sword for a refusal to be converted.

In granting a large degree of religious freedom the invaders were not as disinterested as might appear at first sight. Some were desert nomads with little bent for cultivating the lands which they had seized, who preferred to move on to fresh conquests and quick booty. Others settled in the cities, leaving agriculture to the original owners. Always provided that they were People of the Book (i.e. Christians or Jews and not polytheists and worshippers of idols), the conquered people enjoyed local autonomy and freedom to pursue their own religion, subject to the payment of tax or tribute. The

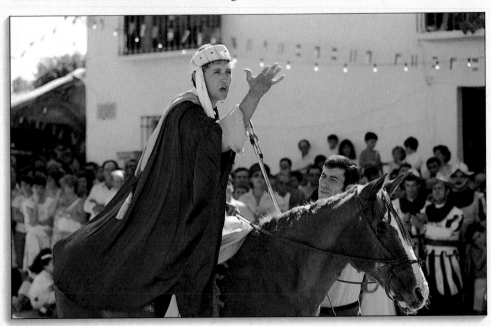

ringlets." Something of the bitterness of his early struggles comes out in a poem which he wrote at the time:

I, and I alone, driven by a consuming anger, bared a two-edged sword,
Crossed the desert and furrowed the sea, mastering waves and wasteland.
I won a kingdom, gave it strength, and built a mosque for prayer.

The new regime: It has been argued that the Moslem invasion of Spain was a *jihad* or holy war. In truth, at no point, either at the time of the first invasion or subsequently, did the victorious Moslems display any great enthusiasm to convert the indigenous Christ-

levying of tribute from converts to Islam was not permissible, so had there been conversions on a large scale the invaders would have suffered severe loss of income.

In all probability no more than 40,000 Arabs had crossed into Spain with the invading armies. As time went on they married with the local women, and because of this intermingling of race the later Umayyads were more Spanish than Arab. However, the lustre of their royal origin survived and they remained fiercely proud of their Arab descent; this was to prove a two-edged weapon, since in the eyes of both Christians and Berbers they remained a foreign dynasty.

However, vivid testimony to their success in fostering a feeling if not an appearance of a national identity emerges from the *Indiculus luminosus* of 854, quoted by T. W. Arnold in *The Preaching of Islam*: "Our Christian young men, with their elegant airs and fluent speech, are showy in their dress and carriage, and are famed for the learning of the gentiles; intoxicated with Arab eloquence they greedily handle, eagerly devour and zealously discuss the books of the Chaldeans (i.e. Muhammadans), and make them known with every flourish of rhetoric… looking down with contempt on the streams of the Church that flow forth from Paradise."

The centre: The capital and heart of Islamic

horseshoe arch, so typical of Moorish Spain, is in fact of Visigothic origin. As if emphasising the lack of distinction between moral and civil law, the great hall of the Mosque was also used for teaching and the administration of justice.

Around the Mosque and schools the market sprang up, whose shops numbered 80,000 at the height of the city's prosperity. A good idea of its layout can be gained from the old Jewish quarter of the city (the Judería) as it still exists today, with its narrow alleys criss-crossing and running at random, so providing shade from the beating heat of the sun and opening into small tree-lined squares; its white-washed houses with

Spain was Córdoba—at its apogee it housed more than 100,000 inhabitants, many more than the London or Paris of the period, and was the foremost city of Europe.

At the heart of Córdoba was its Great Mosque, reconstructed by Abd-al-Rahman I from 785. Although the central portion has been vandalised by its conversion to a Christian cathedral, its vast spaces resemble nothing so much as a cool grove of palm trees. The double tiers of arches were probably suggested by Roman aqueducts, and the

Left, re-enactment of the Moorish invasion in a fiesta near Granada and **above**, in Baeza.

wrought-iron grilles over the windows; its secret flowered patios; and the sudden snatch of flamenco coming from one of its cool *tabernas*.

The workshops of the tailors, shoemakers, leather-workers, jewellers, weavers, dyers, smiths and armourers were situated in the market itself; other craftsmen, like potters and tanners, who required more space for their kilns and pits, worked on the outskirts of the town.

The kings: Abd-al-Rahman and his successors, notably Abd-al-Rahman II (822–852), were lavish patrons of poets, musicians, scientists and philosophers, of whom one of the most colourful was Abu al-Hasan Ali ibn-Nafi, known for short as Ziryab because of his dark complexion; the Arabic word, appropriately enough, signifies a bird with black plumage. The most gifted singer and musician of his age, he so delighted the Caliph of Baghdad, Haroun al-Rashid, as to excite the jealousy of the Master of Music at the court. Ziryab had to seek refuge with Abd-al-Rahman II in fear of his life.

Ziryab is credited with the introduction to al-Andalus of the five-stringed lute and influenced the whole subsequent development of popular music and dance in Spain by introducing musical forms from Persia.

More than a musician, he became the fashionable arbiter of taste in Córdoba. He instituted styles for the different seasons of the year—light silk robes and vivid colours for spring and quilted robes or furs for winter—and also introduced toothpaste and short haircuts.

Ziryab revolutionised the cuisine with recipes from Baghdad and from his time, food was no longer served *en masse*, but as separate courses. Even today Andalucía owes many of its best and most typical dishes to the Moors, including the cold soups or *gazpachos*; the meat and vegetable stews or *ollas*; and the multiplicity of small cakes and sweetmeats, often made with egg yolks and almonds. Ironically enough, these latter are made today by the Christian nuns in their convents to help swell the revenues of the religious orders.

Abd-al-Rahman II was, in the elegant French of the great Arabist Lévi-Provençal, *un grand amateur des femmes*, and according to the chronicler Ibn-Idhari his numerous wives and concubines presented him with 45 sons and 42 daughters. The management of this extensive harem was entrusted to one Nasr, who became so powerful as to be described as "the proconsul of the keys, who administers the whole of Hispania".

Nasr finally overstepped himself and at the behest of one of the Emir's wives offered a poisoned draught to Abd-al-Rahman in the guise of a medicine. However, the doctor who had been blackmailed into preparing it warned another wife, the charming and devoted Fakr. Nasr was forthwith bidden to drink the poison himself and at once expired.

Glorious era: Al-Andalus reached its zenith under Abd-al-Rahman III (912–961). He found it on his accession in a disturbed and rebellious state, but soon settled accounts with dissidents within al-Andalus and then directed equally forceful operations against the Christians of the Marches to the north. Only on one occasion did he suffer a reverse, at the hands of the resolute Ramiro II of León—a defeat attributed by the Christians to the appearance of St James (Santiago) on the field of battle at Simancas.

Having successfully pacified his kingdom and secured its borders, Abd-al-Rahman III took the important step in 929 of declaring himself Caliph, so asserting his rights, inherited from his Umayyad forebears, as an absolute sovereign.

As a symbol of his new status, in 936 he embarked upon a palace of unparalleled magnificence on the outskirts of Córdoba. The construction of Madinat al-Zahra (now known as Medina Azahara) involved "10,000 to 12,000 workmen; 15,000 mules and 4,000 camels transported the materials; and each day the works called for 6,000 items of dressed stone and 11,000 loads of lime and sand, without counting bricks and gravel" (Henri Terasse, *Islam d'Espagne*). The centrepiece of the great pillared reception hall was a pool of quicksilver, reflecting a quivering light over the whole interior and giving an exhilarating overall impression of constant movement.

Extensive excavation has begun to reveal the full extent of the palace (5 miles/8 km west of Córdoba by the C-431), which was destroyed stone by stone by the Berbers only 70 years after it was finished. It lay on three levels, a mosque on the lowest, above it gardens and above them the palace proper. Two of its pavilions, with their beautiful stonework carved in floral patterns, are in the course of reconstruction.

The mystic Ibn-al-Arabi describes the pomp and ritual of Madinat al-Zahra at its peak. To impress an embassy of Christians from the north of Spain, the Caliph had mats unrolled for a distance of three miles from the gates of Córdoba to the entrance of the palace and a double rank of soldiers was stationed along the route, their naked swords meeting at the tips like the rafters of a roof.

Ibn-al-Arabi also says that, inside the palace "the caliph had the ground covered with brocades. At regular intervals he placed dignitaries whom they took for kings, for they were seated on splendid chairs and arrayed in brocades and silk. Each time the ambassadors saw one of these dignitaries they prostrated themselves before him, imagining him to be the caliph, whereupon they were told, 'Raise your heads! This is but a slave of his slaves!' At last they entered a courtyard strewn with sand. At the centre was the caliph. His clothes were coarse and short: what he was wearing was not worth four dirhems. He was seated on the ground, his head bent; in front of him was a Koran, a sword and fire. 'Behold the ruler', the ambassadors were told."

The economy: The overflowing riches of al-Andalus and its ruler originated within the country and were dependent on agriculture and the exploitation of mineral resources rather than on foreign trade. The most important crops, as in Roman times, were cereals, beans and peas of various types, olives and vines; it was the Moors who were responsible for the vineyards of Jerez.

Wine was openly drunk even by the emirs and caliphs, though in deference to the Koranic prohibition on consumption of alcohol it was usually made and sold by Christians.

Left, painting was one of the courtly skills. **Right**, ornate window in the Seville Alcázar.

So al-Mu'tamid (1040–95), the poet king of Seville, could write:

*As I was passing by
A vine, its tendrils tugged my sleeve.
"Do you design", said I,
"My body so to grieve?"*

*"Why do you pass", the vine
Replied, "and never greeting make?
It took this blood of mine
Your thirsting bones to slake."*

The Arabs introduced a variety of new crops, herbs and fruits to Spain, notably bitter oranges and lemons, grown as they still are around Seville, and almonds, saffron, nutmeg and black pepper. They also planted

a profusion of semi-tropical crops in the *vegas* and *huertas*—pomegranates, sugar cane, bananas, coconut palms, maize and rice among others—and these depended on efficient irrigation, for which the Moors took over and greatly extended existing works instituted by the Romans.

Water held the same fascination for the Moors as for their Spanish descendants, who still refer to *agua muy rica* (very rich water), and they took infinite delight in its decorative use as in the plashing fountains of the Alhambra and Generalife gardens in Granada or the Alcázar in Seville.

Gold, silver, copper, mercury, lead and

iron had all been worked by the Romans, but the mines had largely fallen into disuse during the Visigothic period. They were reopened by the Moors, who also mined cinnabar at Almadén near Córdoba in workings operated by a thousand men, divided into separate gangs for the different operations of producing mercury.

It was from here that al-Nasir ("defender of the faith", as Abd-al-Rahman was known after assuming the title of Caliph) obtained the quicksilver for the pool at Madinat al-Zahra, and Almadén later supplied the mercury shipped to the Conquistadores for the refining of Peruvian silver.

For all its brilliance, the Caliphate suffer-

gothic kingdom. But before the final cataclysm there was one last outburst.

Intrigue: Abd-al-Rahman III's successor, the bookish al-Hakam II, was an efficient enough ruler, but he fathered a sickly and incompetent successor, Hisham, the son of a Basque concubine, Subh. His tutor, Ibn-Abi Amir, was a young man of boundless ambition and took the first step on the ladder to fame and power by making Subh his mistress. Soon he had made himself controller of the Mint and administrator of the prince's finances, and the one obstacle to his becoming virtual dictator was the army commander, General Ghalib.

Ibn-Abi Amir thereupon abandoned Subh

ed from an infrastructure which was to lead to disintegration and downfall. As time went on, the inhabitants of al-Andalus, in their enjoyment of an increasing prosperity, preferred to pay mercenaries rather than defend themselves against the increasingly belligerent Christians of the north.

The sharp division of social classes into the monied and influential and an amorphous proletariat subject to the least whim of the caliph and his deputies resulted in a passivity and lack of initiative amongst the mass of the population—a state of affairs of which the Arabs had themselves taken advantage in over-running the earlier Visi-

and married Ghalib's daughter, the talented and intelligent Asma. This did not placate the loyal old soldier, who took up arms on behalf of his Umayyad master and joined battle with Ibn-Abi Amir at San Vicente near Atienza in July 981. The gallant Ghalib spurred into the melée to encourage his soldiers, his red scarf streaming from his golden helmet, but, as Ibn Hazam relates, was thrown from his horse. His hand was cut off and, with the ring still on his finger, delivered with his head to "the accursed hunchback".

Ghalib's death removed the last check to Ibn-Abi Amir's ambitions. Without actually deposing the caliph, he had him confined to the palace of Madinat al-Zahra and himself assumed the title of al-Mansur bi'llah ("victor with the help of Allah") or Almanzor in Spanish form.

Whatever his faults, al-Mansur was a superb soldier and is credited with no less than 57 successful expeditions against the Christians of the north and west. Among the most important were those of 985 against Barcelona; of 998 against Vermudo II of León, during which Coimbra, Zamora and León itself were occupied; and of 994 against Sancho García of Castile.

However, of all al-Mansur's successes, the most spectacular was the great expedition of 997, undertaken by way of Oporto, which struck at the very heart of Christian Spain and destroyed the church of Santiago de Compostela. It was a disaster for the Christians which resounded far beyond the peninsula, for Santiago (St James) was the patron saint of Spain and his shrine in the far northwest of Spain was one of the most celebrated of medieval Christendom, and the popular goal of a multitude of pilgrims from all over Europe.

The city and its cathedral were razed to the ground, only the actual tomb of St James being left intact at the express command of al-Mansur. The army marched back to Córdoba through Lamego, carrying with it an enormous booty, which included the bells and doors of the cathedral. These were carried by Christian captives and used to embellish the Great Mosque.

Later, when Córdoba fell to the Christians, the bells were carried back to Santiago, this time by Moorish prisoners.

Poisoned fruit: When al-Mansur died in 1002, with Hisham II still titularly caliph, he was for all practical purposes succeeded by a younger son Abd-al-Malik, who had already proved his worth as a soldier in North Africa. Things went well enough for six years until, on the way back to Córdoba after a successful campaign against Sancho García of Castile, Abd-al-Malik complained of pains in the chest and died. It was suspected that he had been poisoned by his own younger brother Sanchuelo, who, according to one story, offered to share an apple with

him and cut it with a knife which had been smeared with poison on one side.

The vain and pleasure-loving Sanchuelo was no soldier or administrator like his dead brother. His debauched parties with his boon companion Hisham II became the byword of Córdoba, and it was not long before he was deposed and executed in a palace revolution.

The sorry events of the next two decades have been eloquently summarised by Lévi-Provençal in his masterly *Histoire de l'Espagne musulmane*:

"In the whole history of Moslem Spain, no period was more troubled or tragic. Córdoba raised the flag of revolt; the civil war soon spread to the provinces and the more distant parts of the Marches. At the beck and call of rival factions, sovereigns came and went, in almost every case ending in bloodshed and lasting more often for months rather than years. At times these ephemeral monarchs disappeared into the shadows, only to reappear. In brief, this was chaos which engulfed and irretrievably wrecked the patient work of the great princes of the dynasty and ended the political unity they had made so many efforts to achieve."

The disintegration of the caliphate, abolished by a council of ministers in 1031, marks a turning point in the history of Moorish Spain, though it was to be more than another four centuries before Granada, the last of the independent kingdoms into which it broke up, fell to the Christians.

Towards the end it was undoubtedly the presence of large numbers of restless and warlike Berbers, who had no scruples about pillaging a country in which many were still strangers, which led to the ruin of the caliphate. And ironically enough, it was the all-conquering al-Mansur, with his massive new infusion of Berbers into the army, who paved the way for the final and irrevocable disaster that befell the empire.

Weep for the splendour of Córdoba, for disaster has overtaken her.
Fortune made her a creditor and demanded payment of the debt.
She was at the height of her beauty; life was gracious and sweet
Until all was overthrown and today no two people are happy in her streets.
Then bid her goodbye, and let go in peace since depart she must.
— from the *Bayan al-Mughrib* of Ibn-Idhari.

By the end of the caliphate al-Andalus had disintegrated into some 30 small principalities governed by so-called *reyes de taífas* or "party kings". In the east the Slavs (mercenaries from northern Europe) and the eunuchs of the palace guard carved out their kingdoms for themselves in Valencia and the Balearics; Granada and Málaga were taken over by Berbers; while in the western heartland of Seville and Córdoba, Moslems of both Arab and Spanish descent held sway.

Meanwhile the Christians of the north, inspired by a new religious zeal, began making inroads into al-Andalus under leaders such as Ferdinand I of León-Castile, his son Alfonso VI of León-Castile and that scourge of the Moors, the freebooting El Cid. The most brilliant soldier of his generation, El Cid, having quarrelled with his liege lord Alfonso VI, began his private campaign against the Moors, culminating in the capture of Valencia in 1094.

Christian comeback: In a sudden reversal of roles as the reconquest got underway, it was increasingly the Moslems who became tributaries of the Christian kings. Impoverished as they were and unable to repopulate their new territories, these kings were, to begin with, only too pleased to accept this arrangement. The adjustment seems to have been made without much difficulty, since Moslems and Christians had for centuries been used to living side by side and pursuing their different religions. And in any case the caliphate had evolved a civilisation and customs of its own, and the large majority of its people thought of themselves first and foremost as belonging to al-Andalus, rather than Africa.

Of all the *taífas*, the Abbadid kingdom of Seville most nearly approached the fallen caliphate in the extent of its territories and the splendours of its court. Its founder, al-Mu'tadid (1042–69), extended his realm as far as southern Portugal. Ruthless, cruel and sensual, he planted flowers in the skulls of his decapitated enemies, using them to decorate the palace gardens, and had his first son

put to death on suspicion of plotting against him.

He was succeeded by the gifted and intellectual al-Mu'tamid, under whom 11th-century Seville saw a remarkable flowering of culture, in poetry at least even surpassing the achievements of the caliphate. His vizier, Ibn-Ammar, was one of the most accomplished poets of his time, and it was through him that al-Mu'tamid met the captivating and wilful Rumaykiyya.

It happened that the king was one evening walking by the banks of the Guadalquivir, when, struck by the appearance of the water in the light breeze, he improvised the following couplet:

The wind scuffs the river
And makes it chain mail...

He turned to Ibn-Ammar to complete the verse, but for once the poet was unable to oblige. A passing slave-girl then broke in:

Chain mail for fighting
Could water avail

So impressed was al-Mu'tamid with the girl's wit and appearance that he sent a eunuch to bring her to the palace and asked her who she was.

"My name is I'timad," she said, "but I'm usually called Rumaykiyya, because I am the slave of Rumayk and drive mules for him."

"Are you married?" he asked.

"No, your Majesty."

"Good," said he, "I shall buy you and marry you."

Al-Mu'tamid remained in love with her until their last tragic banishment to Africa, but, as the Dutch Arabist Reinhardt Dozy relates, she was a creature of caprice. One day in February, looking out from a window of the palace at Córdoba, she saw the whole plain covered with a sparkling white mantle of snow and forthwith turned to her husband, reproaching him that he never took her to the countries of the north where she could see it more often. Al-Mu'tamid promised to grant her wish and planted the whole Córdoban plain with almond trees, so that she could enjoy the sheets of blossom each spring.

Crumbling empire: The idyll was not to last. Al-Mu'tamid, who had added to his domains by the capture of Córdoba, might be as a lion to the rulers of the other *taífas*, but was no match for Alfonso VI of León-Castile. There is a picturesque story that when Alfonso first advanced on Seville in 1078, he was tricked by Ibn-Ammar, who had a magnificent chess set constructed with pieces made of ebony, aloe and sandalwood and inlaid with gold. The king was so enamoured of it that Ibn-Ammar challenged him to a game, promising him the set if he won. If, on the other hand, Alfonso lost, he must grant a wish. Ibn-Ammar won with ease and promptly demanded the raising of the siege; Alfonso kept to his word, but doubled the tribute.

However, Alfonso captured Toledo in 1085, declared himself Emperor of Spain and issued a peremptory demand for the surrender of Córdoba. The writing was on the wall, and with much heart-searching al-Mu'tamid took the momentous step of summoning aid from the fanatical Yusuf ibn-Tashufin, leader of the Almoravids in North Africa. In his own words from the chronicle *Al-holal al-mawshiya*: "I do not want a curse to be levelled against me in all the mosques of Islam; and faced with the choice, I would rather drive the camels of the Almoravids than be a swineherd among the Christians."

Men of war: The Almoravids, a warlike and puritanical sect devoted to a return to the original purity of the Koran, had swept across half of North Africa. Their leader, Ibn-Tashufin, already 70 years old, is described as thin-faced with beetling eyebrows and a straggling beard, dark-complexioned and high-pitched in voice. He dressed in wool; partook only of barley bread, milk and the flesh of the camel; and viewed with repugnance the wine-imbibing, the music and culture of al-Andalus.

Caught unawares by the landing of the Almoravids in June 1086, Alfonso marched to meet the invading army, swelled by the forces of al-Mu'tamid and other party kings, at Sagrajas near Badajóz. Here, for the first time, the Christians faced the tactic of compact and well-ordered bodies of infantry, supported by lines of Turkish archers and manoeuvring as a unit to the command of thunderous rolls from the massed tambours of the Moors.

Used as they were to single combat, where personal valour counted above all, the Christians broke and fell into confusion. Only 500 horsemen, most of them wounded, survived, among them Alfonso.

Defeat for all: The battle of Sagrajas set back the cause of reconquest in al-Andalus for some 60 years, but the rulers of the *taífas*, soon to be expelled from their kingdoms, were equal losers. All al-Mu'tamid's misgivings about Ibn-Tashufin were justified. In September 1091, after heroic resistance and a desperate plea for help from the erstwhile enemy Alfonso VI, Seville was overrun by the Almoravids. Al-Mu'tamid and Rumaykiyya were exiled to Aghmat in the Atlas Mountains and lived in penury until the end of their lives. In the words of Ibn-al-Labbana's moving epitaph:

Chameleon-coloured fortune
Shows many a varied face.
We are chessmen in her hands
And the king may fall to a lowly pawn.

Under the puritanical Almoravids, Seville was shorn of its former glories. The common people at first welcomed their new rulers, but soon found that they had exchanged the flamboyant liberalism of the Arabo-Andalucían aristocrats of the *taífas* for the sterile rules of Moslem theologians, the *faqihs*. It was now the Christian kingdoms of the north which tolerated a symbiosis of religions and cultures; and although the Christians and Jews were the worst sufferers, poets, philosophers and scientists soon felt the full force of a religious inquisition.

In spite of a publicly proclaimed austerity, even the Almoravids, and particularly the officials charged with the everyday conduct of affairs, fell victims to the easy lifestyle of al-Andalus. A new Christian champion had meanwhile arisen in the shape of Alfonso *El Batallador* (The Fighter) of Aragón, who in 1125 struck deep into the south, reaching the Mediterranean near Málaga.

The Moorish chronicler Ibn al-Athir said of *El Batallador* that "he slept in his armour and scorned a mattress, and when asked why he did not bed with the daughters of Moorish potentates he had made captive, he replied: 'A true soldier ought to live only with men and not with women.' With his death [in 1134] Allah allowed the faithful to breathe again, free from his hammer blows."

By now the power of the Almoravids was effectively spent; once more al-Andalus seemed ripe for reoccupation by the Christians, but yet again they were to be cheated for another long century. The Almoravid empire in North Africa was overwhelmed in 1145 by that of the Almohads, also religious in inspiration but with a broader interpretation of Islam and bitterly opposed to the narrow doctrines of the Almoravids.

It was not until 1171 that Abu-Ya'qub Yusuf embarked on the systematic subjugation of al-Andalus. The rulers of a second generation of *reyes de taífas*, who had filled the vacuum left by the downfall of the Almoravids, trimmed their sails to the wind and swore allegiance to the new Almohad caliph, one of whose lasting achievements was the building of the Great Mosque of Seville, of which the minaret, the Giralda,

light", according to the *Crónica Latina*.

Nothing daunted, Alfonso VIII, the lion-hearted king of Castile, worked tirelessly with the Archbishop of Toledo to cement a grand alliance, and his efforts were recognised by Pope Innocent III, who in 1211 declared a crusade against the Moors. By May of that year Alfonso VIII had assembled a huge army, swelled by some 60,000 crusaders from beyond the Pyrenees, and in July he faced the Moors under Muhammad al-Nasir strongly positioned at Las Navas de Tolosa in the Sierra Morena.

It was a fiercely fought battle. According to one account, the caliph had a premonition of disaster and his negro guard were hemmed

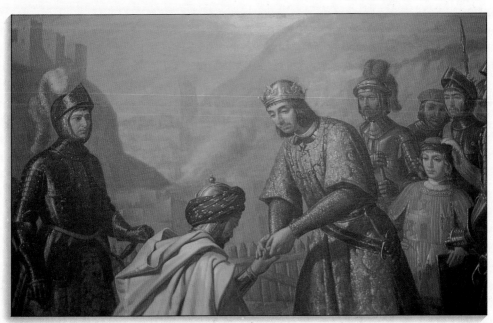

305 ft (93 metres) high and containing a ramp wide enough to make the ascent on horseback, still survives.

Holy war: Al-Andalus, extended by the conquest of most of present-day Portugal, remained firmly in Almohad hands for the rest of the century. In 1195 at Alarcos the Christians suffered one of their worst defeats in the history of the reconquest. "Both sides fought fiercely and the day ended in a blood-bath, the Moors descending to hell and the Christians being received into palaces of

Above, the Moors in defeat. Granada was the last kingdom to fall.

around him with iron chains. At the end of the day the Moors were routed, the plucky Archbishop Arnold of Narbonne who took part putting their dead at 60,000 or more, for the loss of 40,000 Christians. Las Navas de Tolosa was more than an episode in a war: it presaged the overthrow of the Almohad empire and the final disintegration of Moorish al-Andalus.

The greatest triumph of the Almohads was posthumous and lay in the achievements of the 12th and 13th-century Toledo school of translators in transmitting to Western Europe the work, not only of Andalucían scholars and scientists, like Averroës

(1126–98), but also, via Arabic translations, that of Euclid and Aristotle. Another event of major importance was the introduction of Arabic numerals (which we still use) in place of the clumsy Roman system.

During the 13th century Moorish resistance in al-Andalus crumbled under the hammer blows of James the Conqueror of Aragón, of Ferdinand III of Castile and of his son Alfonso X (The Wise). Baeza and Ubeda in the east were taken in 1233, Córdoba in 1236, Jaén in 1245 and Seville in 1248.

New rulers: The lands retaken from the Moors were made over to the knights and barons who had fought beside the kings. Many of these land grants were small or

have beset Andalucía until the present day.

The Guzmáns, probably of German origin, had distinguished themselves at the battle of Las Navas de Tolosa and in the capture of Seville. Don Alfonso Pérez de Guzmán (El Bueno, the good) is famous for his heroic defence of Tarifa in 1294. His son was captured by the Moors during the siege; faced by the Moors with a demand for surrender, failing which the boy would be killed, he defiantly tossed down a dagger from the walls—which they promptly used to kill his son.

It is to the credit of the new Christian rulers that, initially, they reverted to the tolerant policies of the earlier Moorish regimes,

medium-sized; for example, in Jerez de la Frontera, recaptured by Alfonso X in 1264, 40 councillors and knights were each allocated six *aranzadas* or about seven acres, half of it vineyard, and were enjoined to plant the other half with vines. Among them were Don Fernán Yanez Palomino and Don Alonso Valdespino, ancestors of the famous sherry families of today.

Vast tracts of land were, however, also ceded to families such as the Guzmáns, forebears of the Dukes of Medina Sidonia; and these huge *latifundios*, akin to the *latifundia* of Roman and Visigothic times, were to be the cause of the agrarian problems which

Moslems and Jews remaining free to practise their religions, subject to a capitation tax. Mudéjars (Moslems living in the reconquered Christian areas, as distinct from Moriscos or Christian converts) formed the preponderance of agricultural workers, and estates were taken over by their new Christian owners without changing the pattern of country life.

As artisans and craftsmen the Mudéjars were unrivalled, especially in such skilled techniques as decorative plaster work, marquetry, wood carving, and the construction of ornate ceilings from jointed pieces of wood (the so-called *artesanado* work).

Above all, they excelled in the manufacture of ceramics and tiles—the *azulejos*, which are the glory of buildings such as the Alhambra in Granada and the Alcázar in Seville, reconstructed by Pedro the Cruel (1364–66) in Mudéjar style a century after the fall of the city to the Christians.

By the time the Catholic Monarchs, Isabella and Ferdinand, became joint rulers of Spain in 1479, the sole remaining Moorish enclave in the country was the Kingdom of Granada. Apart from Granada itself, with its magnificent Alhambra crouched below the snow-capped Sierra Nevada, the kingdom also comprised Málaga and Ronda. At its peak it extended only 112 miles (180 km)

from east to west and 50 miles (80 km) from the sea to its inland border. Towards the end of the Moorish rule as many as 100,000 people crowded into this small area.

Last bastion: That Granada lasted so long was because Ibn-al-Ahmar, the founder of its Nasrid dynasty, had become a vassal of Ferdinand III of Castile and had actually assisted in the capture of Seville in 1248. When Ferdinand died in 1252, his funeral was attended by a hundred knights from Granada, and Ibn-al-Ahmar further helped

Left, Ferdinand and Isabella. **Above**, the Christians drove the Moors back into Africa.

his successor, Alfonso X, to overthrow the remaining emirates in the south, those of Jerez, Lebrija, Arcos, Medina Sidonia and Niebla.

Thereafter the Nasrids cleverly played off their North African Marinid allies against the Castilians and, by keeping a low profile and by the unwilling payment of tribute, staved off a frontal attack. Ibn-al-Ahmar nevertheless took the precaution of constructing a chain of watchtowers along the mountainous borders of his kingdom and outlying castles.

One of the key defences was the castle of al-Hamah, taken in a surprise attack by the Marquis of Cádiz in 1482 and thereafter the scene of bitter fighting between Christians and Moors. Though little remains of these defences, the picturesque village of Alhama de Granada on a by-road from Granada to Málaga (C-340) is still worth a visit.

The fall of Granada in 1492 cannot be explained simply by internal weaknesses or by the feud between its leaders which left it a prey to the advancing Christians. By the beginning of the 14th century signs of religious and racial conflict began to appear, which grew increasingly bitter during the reign of the Catholic Monarchs.

Racial conflict: The Christians in the reoccupied territories were uneasily aware of the abilities of the Mudéjars as workmen and artisans, and of the Jews as administrators, doctors and merchants. From this it was a short step to postulate that such employment was unworthy of a Christian, who was held to be specially fitted for soldiering, priesthood or government; and any attempt by the Jew or Mudéjar to better his status was fiercely resented. As early as 1391 the Jewish quarters of Córdoba and Seville suffered mob violence and thousands of their inhabitants were killed.

Once the doctrine of *limpieza de sangre* (purity of blood) had been declared, it became a disgrace for any convert to Christianity to be even remotely tainted by the Jewish blood of his ancestors. Only those who could claim complete purity of blood were admitted to positions of public authority (although, in fact, even Ferdinand the Catholic was of Jewish blood on his mother's side and Torquemada, the first Inquisitor General, was a New Christian of Jewish descent).

Starting with the setting up of the Inquisition and the first *auto de fé*—the pronouncement of sentence on heretics and their burning at the stake—in Seville in 1481, the Catholic monarchs issued a decree in March 1492, giving Jews a choice between baptism or expulsion and allowing unbaptised Jews four months to liquidate their property and possessions.

When it became apparent that the Jews were emigrating *en masse*, even the harsh conditions of the decree were dishonoured and many of the emigrés were stripped of their possessions and had to leave the country destitute. It was, in fact, only a matter of time before the Moriscos were to suffer the same fate as the Jews. Apart from the enormous human suffering inflicted by the expulsions, Spain was at the same time deprived of the services of its best doctors, administrators and financiers, who were Jewish, large numbers of skilled Morisco artisans and a sizeable part of its agrarian labour force.

It is difficult to tell whether the rulers of Granada in their isolated mountain fastness understood the full significance of these events or realised that, once Christian Spain had absorbed the idea of nationhood bound by a single religion, the traditional multi-religious co-existence was no longer possible. By 1482 the Catholic monarchs began to make concerted plans for the overthrow of Granada and another crusade was declared by the co-operative Pope.

Meanwhile a bitter family feud had broken out in Granada itself. The emir, Abu'l-Hasan, was to return from a military expedition to find that the garrison of the Alhambra had revolted and declared in favour of his son, Muhammad Abu-Abd-Allah. Boabdil, as he is better known, and his mother A'isha intensely resented Abu'l-Hasan's open partiality for his sons by a Christian concubine. In the circumstances Abu'l-Hasan was forced to take refuge with his brother, Muhammad al-Zaghal, governor of Málaga, and the only member of his family still loyal.

The campaign against Granada began disastrously for the Christians. So confident were they of success that their large army under the Marquises of Santiago and Cádiz was accompanied by a train of merchants anxious to profit in the anticipated spoils.

In the event the invading force was routed in March 1483 by al-Zaghal on the mountainous approaches to Málaga, and the merchants spent their gold in buying their own freedom.

Unlucky king: Boabdil was less successful; his reign began as disastrously as it was to end—not for nothing was he named The Unlucky by his subjects. Over-reaching himself in an attack on the Christians, he was taken captive and released by King Ferdinand only on condition that he acknowledged vasselage to Castile and took the part of the Christians against his father and his uncle, al-Zaghal.

During the next 10 years Ferdinand's forces moved in relentlessly on Granada. Málaga was taken after an epic resistance in 1487, and Ferdinand decided to make an example of it. The town's citizens were deported *en masse* to other parts of Spain and those unable to pay crippling ransoms were sold into slavery. Boabdil had been living under the delusion that he would be left in possession of Granada, but after the final defeat of al-Zaghal was peremptorily bidden to deliver up the city. This caused an immediate public outcry and Boabdil belatedly decided to fight.

In 1491 a Christian army of 40,000 foot-soldiers and 10,000 cavalry invaded the lush *vega* below the city. They were beaten off by the gallant Moorish general Musa ibn-Abu l-Ghazan and Ferdinand then decided to sit it out and set up the huge tented encampment of Santa Fé outside the city.

The Christians suffered a major reverse when the tent occupied by Queen Isabella caught fire and the conflagration swept through the camp, but it was only a matter of time before the besieged town was starved into submission. After prolonged negotiations the capitulation, generous in its terms in view of Boabdil's double-dealing, was signed on 25 November 1491.

So, in a minor key, almost 800 years of Moorish rule in the peninsula came to an end. Boabdil had surrendered the last outpost without a fight to the end, and the bitter reproach of his mother A'isha rings down the centuries as his epitaph as he fled the city: "Weep like a woman for what you could not defend like a man."

Right, the treaty which agreed the surrender of Granada, with the signatures of Ferdinand and Isabella, the victorious monarchs.

    & 575

In January 1492, with the surrender of Granada signed and the Christian army about to enter the city, Christopher Columbus, a lonely and Quixotic-looking figure on a mule, rode into the encampment of Santa Fé. It had been six years since he first petitioned Queen Isabella for support in his project for reaching the Indies by sailing to the west. The project had been ridiculed and rejected by a commission of enquiry; Columbus was in despair and was staying at the monastery of La Rábida near Huelva before taking ship for France.

While there, he discussed his hopes with one of the friars, Juan Pérez, who had been the Queen's confessor. Pérez wrote to Isabella; what he said has not been preserved, but it was of such consequence that Columbus was immediately sent money to return to court and seven months later his three ships set forth from the small port of Palos on their epic voyage of discovery.

Andalucía was thus associated from the outset with the discovery of the New World. The three little ships were crewed mainly with sailors from Palos, Moguer and Huelva; many of the Conquistadores and most of the first colonists were from Andalucía or neighbouring Extremadura; and in 1503, within 11 years of Columbus's first voyage, Seville was playing such a central role in trade with America that Queen Isabella established a *Casa de Contratación* there to regulate all trade with the New World. Its functions included the furnishing of embarkation permits; the inspection of ships and provision of escorts; the supplying of the mercury needed for refining silver; the registration of merchandise and the handling of the gold, silver and pearls destined for the royal exchequer. It further administered justice, saw to the despatch of missionaries, and served as a centre for navigational studies.

Gateway to a new world: Seville (and later Cádiz in 1717, when the Guadalquivir river silted up and was no longer navigable for large ships) thus acquired a virtual mono-

poly of the trade with America. This was not, as is often thought, simply a matter of the Catholic monarchs and their successors exploiting its position. The ships of the time were limited in range, and depended on the trade winds and a staging post in the Canaries to make the voyage at all; the Andalucían ports were therefore much better placed than those of the north or the Mediterranean.

J. Vicen Vives, for example, in his *Moments crucials de la historia de Catalunya*,

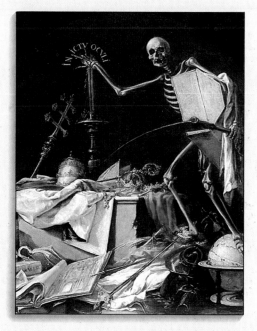

has cogently put the technical reasons for the absence of Catalan shipping on the Atlantic route: "It was not feasible for a caravel to make the passage of the Strait of Gibraltar from west to east, against current and winds, without losing much time and risking men and ships. It required the nautical revolution of the early 18th century, especially the introduction of sails known as *focs*, and an enlarged cruising range before the Mediterranean peoples could hope to participate in the American trade. Málaga, an important part of the Kingdom of Granada, with a hinterland rich in wheat, wines and silk, did not take part in commerce with America

Preceding pages: Defeat of the Spanish Armada. Left, Seville prospered after Columbus. Right, In the blink of an eye, by Seville artist Valdés Leal.

until 1778, although expressly awarded the privilege of free trade by Charles V in 1529."

Another compelling reason for routing shipping through Seville or Cádiz was to organise convoys. To begin with, ships sailed singly or in groups unguarded; but as buccaneers and pirates began preying on the treasure ships of the Spanish Main, fleets were assembled at Seville, Cádiz or Sanlúcar de Barrameda and sailed under the protection of heavily armed galleons. The practice survived until the mid-18th century, when even eight or ten galleons could no longer protect the fleets against the depredations of the British Navy.

British piracy: The attacks on Spanish ship-

with supplies for the Armada, which was assembling in Lisbon. Drake's fleet, flying no colours so as to avoid identification, burst into the outer haven and within 24 hours had destroyed or captured some 24 ships. But for the prompt arrival of the Duke of Medina Sidonia with reinforcements, it would probably have captured the city.

The immediate result of the raid and the subsequent destruction of shipping and supplies along the Portuguese coast was to delay the sailing of the Armada for a year. Another and more unexpected outcome was that by seizing some 2,900 pipes of sherry, or "sack" as it was then known, and releasing it on the English market just at the point when it was

ping by Sir John Hawkins and Sir Francis Drake during the 1570s and 1580s contributed to Philip II of Spain's decision to embark on the ill-fated invasion of England with his massive Armada. Andalucía was the first to feel the effects when Drake made his pre-emptive strike on Cádiz. Such is the terror he inspired that mothers in that part of Spain still frighten rebellious children by saying, "El Draque will get you if you don't behave."

In April 1587 the harbour of Cádiz was jammed with some 60 vessels, from hulks and coasters to the tuna fishing fleet and large merchantmen, many of them laden

scarce and becoming popular, Drake contributed to a lasting demand for the drink.

When the Armada finally did sail in May 1588, it was under the command of Don Alfonso Pérez de Guzmán, Duke of Medina Sidonia, Andalucía's premier noble. The fleet included a strong squadron of 11 ships from Andalucía with a complement of 780 seamen and 2,325 soldiers under the command of Don Pedro de Valdés. His flagship, *Nuestra Señora del Rosario*, was one of the most heavily-gunned in the Armada and was therefore assigned the role of "troubleshooter" charged with the defence of slower moving and more vulnerable craft. By ill luck the vessel was an early casualty of the first clash in the English Channel, when, having gone to the aid of another ship, she was disabled in a collision with the *Santa Catalina*, also of the Andalucían squadron, and captured by Drake.

The Armada's losses were appalling. After a battering in the Channel by the English fleet, the survivors were driven by gales up the North Sea and round the north of Scotland; of the 130 ships which had sailed for England, only 60 made the return journey to Spain. Medina Sidonia survived the disaster, sick in body and spirit, with a flagship that limped into Santander near to foundering.

Rivers of gold: During the early years of the

trade with the Americas, "rivers of gold" poured into Seville; it has been said that the emeralds from Colombia and pearls from Darien were traded around the cathedral in the same sacks used for chick-peas. There was ostentatious spending on public works, palatial houses and on building and adorning churches. Perhaps the most grandiose project was the construction during the late 16th and early 17th centuries of the *Lonja de Mercaderes* or exchange, now the Archive of the Indies, which was financed with a

Above, *The Victory being towed into Gibraltar with the body of Nelson,* **by Clarkson Stanfield.**

quarter of a percent of the silver arriving from the Americas.

Another source of wealth was the export to the colonies of olive oil and wine; in return, Andalucía received new plants and foodstuffs, such as maize, potatoes, peppers, tomatoes, tobacco, chocolate and quinine. Many of these plants, introduced to Western Europe through Spain, were brought over soon after the first voyages of Columbus. Their planting and exploitation were patchy, taking place mostly around Seville and in western Andalucía.

Andalucían writers, such as Antonio Domínguez Ortíz in his *Andalucía ayer y hoy,* comment on a similar failure to grasp the enormous opportunities afforded by Seville's near trading monopoly during the early period. This has been put down to a number of causes, in particular to the lack of industry, except on a small artisan scale—for example, the manufacture of textiles and tiles. The textile industry could not, however, compete with northern Europe, and though much has been made of Seville's monopoly, most of the textiles exported to the Americas through Seville were made in England and the Low Countries.

Shipbuilding too would have seemed an obvious opportunity; but, because of their poor quality, ships built in Andalucían yards were prohibited by royal decree from being used on Atlantic routes. There was a wide-open opportunity for Seville to establish itself as the banking centre of the Western world; but, perhaps because of the ill-judged expulsion of the Jews, all attempts to establish a viable banking system collapsed, with disastrous repercussions on the mercantile community.

By the time of Philip IV (1621–65), because of the decision of the Count Duke of Olivares to squander American silver and human resources on a fruitless war in Flanders, inflation was rampant. Trade had declined and the most valuable export that Andalucía could offer was that of its people.

Thanks to the meticulous rules of the *Casa de Contratación* which required each and every emigrant to register, there is now in the Archive of the Indies a list of 150,000 signatures of persons who sailed for the Americas. Soldiers and sailors were not required to register, and there were huge numbers of clandestine emigrants, so that it is entirely possible that the real figure was double.

Emigration from Andalucía and neighbouring Extremadura for the period 1493–1600 is reliably put at 40 percent and 16.4 percent of the total. The result is a prevalence of Andalucían customs in South America and the resemblance of Spanish as spoken in Latin America to Andalucían.

Debating point: The issue of Gibraltar at the southernmost tip of Andalucía has now for almost three centuries soured relationships between Spain and Britain. The dispute dates from the War of the Spanish Succession (1701–13), when Charles II of Spain died without heir and the choice of a successor lay between the Archduke Charles of

Austria and Philip of Anjou. After Philip was crowned with the support of Louis XIV, war broke out between Spain and France on the one side and Austria on the other, supported by Britain, Holland and Portugal.

In 1704 the allies decided to open a new front by seizing Gibraltar. The Spanish garrison was hopelessly outnumbered and outgunned by an Anglo-Dutch fleet under the command of Admiral Rooke, and after a siege of only three days the governor surrendered to Prince George of Hesse as the representative of the Archduke Charles.

Gibraltar was ceded to Britain in 1713 as part of the Treaty of Utrecht, by which the war was brought to an end. The Spanish were soon to question Britain's right to its possession. During 1779–83, at the time of the American War of Independence, it underwent one of the famous sieges of history, when it was beset both by sea and land by the armies and fleets of Spain and France. It was, however, well prepared, with storage galleries cut into the rock and the latest types of artillery capable of raking the attackers at low angle; and a desperate shortage of food and supplies was made good when Admiral Rodney broke the blockade.

The siege culminated with the French throwing in 10 floating batteries "fortified 6 or 7 ft thick… with green timber bolted with iron, cork and raw hides; which were to carry guns of heavy metal and be bomb-proof on the top with a descent for the shells to slide off." The British found an answer to them in firing off red-hot cannon balls; and after subjecting the defenders to a tremendous hammering, all 10 of the platforms caught fire and sank or blew up.

The argument over Gibraltar rumbles on, with Spaniards naturally resenting the presence of a foreign enclave on Spanish soil and some regarding the polyglot and fiercely anglophile population as little better than a gang of smugglers, while the British government finds itself in a cleft stick when every referendum results in a near 100 percent preference for the status quo.

Bonaparte's attack: During the next major conflict on Spanish soil, the British were for once allies instead of enemies. In writing about the Peninsular War of 1807–14, during which Napoleon's armies overran the whole of Spain and Portugal, Richard Ford remarks: "The Spanish have two objects: one to detail the ill-usage which they have sustained from the invaders; the second to blink as much as possible the assistance afforded by England." A fair statement of what happened is that the British troops would have had no chance of beating Bonaparte and the French in open battle but for the relentless resistance of the Spanish, especially the guerrillas, any more than the Spanish could have continued the fight without the inspiration of Wellington's victories.

The French assault on Andalucía began in January 1810 after a series of disastrous Spanish defeats. Marshal Soult and Joseph Bonaparte, with a force of 40,000 men, were faced by 23,000 Spanish hopelessly extended over a front of 150 miles (240 km).

Córdoba fell without a fight on 24 January. The Junta which had been ruling the country from Seville decamped for Cádiz on the 23rd, followed by the military commander, the Duke of Albuquerque, with his troops. The city fell into the hands of an excited mob; nothing was done to destroy the arsenals, the largest in Spain; and vast quantities of munitions, as well as tobacco to the value of £1 million were lost to the invaders when they took over on 29 January.

Soult lost no time in despatching General Victor to take Cádiz, but he arrived too late to intercept Albuquerque's 12,000 troops, Stewart landed to reinforce the garrison.

The city remained the only enclave in Spain unoccupied by the French and was the home of the Cortes (parliament) which promulgated the famous liberal constitution of 1812, with its declaration that the Spanish nation is free and independent with the right to establish fundamental laws belonging exclusively to the nation. This constitution was held up as a model throughout Europe— only to be swept aside by Ferdinand VII on the restoration of the monarchy in 1814.

Meanwhile, all the rest of Andalucía lay open to the ravages of Marshal Soult, a connoisseur of other people's paintings along the lines of Field Marshal Goering,

LAS MINAS DE RIO-TINTO.

RIO-TINTO (HUELVA).—PERSPECTIVA DE LA CORTA Ó TRABAJOS Á CIELO ABIERTO EN EL CRIADERO DEL SUR.

HUELVA.—MUELLE-EMBARCADERO DE LA COMPAÑÍA MINERA DE RIO-TINTO, EN EL PUERTO.—(De fotografías de Laurent.)

who had entered the city two days before, blowing up the only bridge over the wide salt-water channel between the mainland and the Isla de León on which Cádiz is built.

Despite a French blockade lasting for years, Cádiz was under no serious threat thanks to the presence of gunboats in its harbour and larger units of the Spanish and British navies further out. In the hour of their peril the Spanish forgot earlier fears about the landing of British troops, and in February 1810, 3,500 men under General William

Left and **above**, early industry: olive-pressing rollers and the Rio Tinto mines.

who accumulated his extensive collection simply by theft, and of General Sebastiani, the plunderer of churches.

French occupation: Sweeping as the French victory had been, their hold on Andalucía was tenuous and confined to the larger towns and cities. The French were never safe from the activities of the guerrillas, which tied down huge numbers of troops. In the words of an officer in the French hussars, M. de Rocca: "Their most popular pastime was to sit in the rocks amongst the olive groves at the end of the suburb, and tranquilly smoke their segars while they fired at our videttes... The mountaineers hung their French prisoners or burned them alive… The women, the old men, and even children were against us. I saw a young boy of eight years playing among our horses' feet; he offered himself as a guide, and led a small party of hussars straight to an ambuscade. When he reached it he suddenly ran off towards the rocks, throwing up his bonnet into the air, and crying with all his might, 'Long live our King Ferdinand VII' and the firing instantly began…"

Ferdinand VII's repudiation of the liberal constitution of Cádiz was far from being the end of the matter. A first fruit of his autocratic policies was the revolt and loss of the American colonies between 1810 and 1824;

and the struggles between liberals and absolutists rumbled on through the 19th century with the outbreak of the two Carlist wars. By the time of World War I, two very powerful trade unions had emerged, dominated by the anarchists and Marxists.

Century of strife: The Spanish Civil War of 1936–39 found Andalucía, like the rest of Spain, deeply divided. With its great and often neglected estates, absentee landlords and landless labourers—the *jornaleros*—it had long been a stronghold of the anarchists (CNT). As long ago as 1883 the Civil Guard, claiming that the whole upper class of Andalucía was threatened, had put down the so-

called conspiracy of *La Mano Negra* (The Black Hand), and 14 militants were garrotted in the main square of Cádiz.

In 1892 there was another alarm when 4,000 rioting peasants marched into Jerez and looted shops. In fact, the *jornaleros* had, and have, very real grievances. For four or five months from spring to autumn they were hired on a day-to-day basis and were unemployed for the rest of the year. Hugh Thomas, quoting from Ramos Oliveira, writes in *The Spanish Civil War*: "The *braceros* (labourers) would assemble at dawn in the village square, as in a slave market, 'dressed in a loose cotton jacket with sandals of hemp or esparto grass', and those who had nothing, political or industrial, against them would be chosen for work. Those who refused the wage offered were not missed, since the agent would bring in labour from a neighbouring village."

The agrarian problem has beset Andalucía throughout its history, and the traditional surplus of labour, which in the 16th century caused mass emigration to the Americas, was later to result in Andalucíans leaving in their thousands to find employment in the industrial cities of northern Spain and, recently, in Western Europe generally.

One regime after another has tried to find a solution. In 1836 Juan Alvarez Mendizábal expropriated the Church from its properties and succeeded only in substituting one fairly benevolent landlord for others more grasping. The Franquists extended irrigation schemes and built model villages for the workers in the cotton fields. Since General Franco's death the pace has quickened and *polígonos industriales* (industrial zones) have been created around Algeciras and Huelva, with unfortunate repercussions on the environment and traditional ways of life.

A switch from the labour-intensive production of olive oil to crops such as sunflower, which can be harvested with the aid of machines, has led to riots and the destruction of machinery reminiscent of the Luddites in 19th-century England. Andalucía has won a measure of autonomy, but behind the facade of the holiday playgrounds of the Costa del Sol it is problems such as these which challenge the region's parliament.

<u>Left</u>, troops in the Sierra Nevada in the Civil War. <u>Right</u>, Italian planes bomb the Republicans.

Almost overnight, it seems, Andalucía has become *de mode*. For a long time this was the poor relation among Spain's regions, crushed by the burden of poverty and feudal legacies, drained of its manhood and its brightest minds. Some Spaniards viewed it as part of the Third World, inhabited by a decadent aristocracy and illiterate rustics with laughable accents.

There was some truth in the stereotype. Until the 1960s Andalucía still seemed "a land bottled for antiquarians", as the English traveller Richard Ford described it early in the 19th century. Many of its ways and values had changed little since medieval times. It was a pleasantly picturesque world, provided you were comfortably off or only passing through: a land of whitewashed villages, vast estates and daunting sierras with bull-breeders and sherry barons, flamenco dancers and gypsies lurking around every corner. The injustices and the misery were masked by the beauty of the region and the graciousness of its people.

Andalucía remains unique. The ritualised life-style of the oldest of Western civilisations continues. The flamboyance, the anguish and the passion are still there. But now the region is rushing into the 20th century. Mass tourism has turned rigid *mores* upside down along the Mediterranean coast, television has reached the remotest hamlets, and four-lane highways have brought the region within a day's drive of the Europe that is north of the Pyrenees. Poverty still exists, particularly among the landless farm labourers, but these days the car parks are packed outside those temples of consumerism known as *hipermercados*.

Age of change: Nobody laughs at the Andalucían accent these days. After all, the country's prime minister and his deputy are both from Seville. High society, which once spurned Andalucía's lack of culture, has flocked to classes nationwide to learn the *sevillana*, a high-spirited flamenco dance. European Community funds are reinvigo-

Preceding pages: sitting out the midday heat; preparing for a fiesta in Ubeda. Left and right, beauty and portrait lookalike in Córdoba.

rating agriculture and the colossal investment and international contacts created through Expo'92, celebrating the 500th anniversary of Columbus's voyage to the New World, are stimulating new awareness and activity.

Youngsters whose parents can barely read tinker with their computers and dance to the same deafening disco music as counterparts in other European countries. Uniformity spreads as fast as the video craze. "Andalucía is Europe's California," claims the

propaganda. Well, not quite. We are talking about a society moulded by layer upon layer of ethnic, religious, social and cultural influences. Andalucía's history has roots in Africa and Asia as well as Europe.

Mattress tactic: Time and again it has demonstrated its ability to absorb and adapt new invaders, whether they be Phoenicians, Moors or Castilians. In his perceptive essay *Theory of Andalucía*, José Ortega y Gasset, one of the most eminent 20th-century Spanish intellectuals, drew comparisons with China in the region's capacity to accommodate conquerors through the "mattress tactic". Andalucía's tactic before violent attack was "to give way and be soft. In this way it always ended up intoxicating the harsh impetus of the invader with its delightfulness."

The microchips may be down now that Andalucía is officially a part of Europe, but it is difficult—horrendous—to imagine the *sevillano* or the *malagueño* giving up his three-hour lunch, his addiction to the bulls or even turning into a clock-conscious Anglo-Saxon.

Other Spaniards may have the same tastes, but the Andalucíans raise this healthy respect for priorities, for living life to the full, to an art form. They inhabit an area which is naturally bountiful and their culture has

for Andalucíans to remain consistent in their customs and faithful to their culture.

Virgin virtues: Everything is personal to an *andaluz*, including his religion. He rarely attends church—that is for the womenfolk—but will fiercely proclaim the virtues of his Virgin as opposed to that of another community. Isidoro Moreno, a leading anthropologist, feels that the intensity of personal relations explains a good deal about Andalucían society and its segmentation. "It appears very open," he comments. "But people fool themselves. The personalised relations encourage many groups of a few persons and it is difficult to penetrate them."

Socialising is a vital ritual to the Anda-

always been an agrarian one, unlike that of the bleak steppes of Castile, a region of dour warriors where man has frequently battled for the upper hand with his own land.

What particularly sets the Andalucían apart is his taste for making a show of himself for strangers. Anybody visiting Seville can be forgiven for thinking he has strayed on to a grand opera stage. Ortega y Gasset suggested that this collective narcissism, this propensity to contemplate himself and delight in himself, while it could produce affectations, resulted in the Andalucían reaching a better and clearer self-knowledge than that attained in other societies. Thus it was easier

lucían. The old custom of the *tertulia*, whereby friends meet regularly to discuss everything under the sun, still endures. In bar and club a man keeps his personal relationships well-tuned. This is carried to extremes at the Seville Fair, where Andalucíans uninhibitedly put themselves on show to all, but an outsider soon finds that he is attending a week of personal reunions.

Julian Pitt-Rivers, whose study of the mountain village of Grazalema (Cádiz) is regarded as a landmark in anthropological research, points out: "In a *pueblo* community, personal relationships have a higher priority than legal considerations."

When English researcher Ronald Fraser arrived in Mijas (Málaga province) in 1957, he immediately noticed that "the *pueblo* was the focus of life; it had the 'urban' quality dear to the Andalucían of human concourse and discourse. The strength of family life, immediately apparent, was its cement. Exaggeratedly, it appeared that everyone was related, that the village was one extended family."

Foreigners: Thirty years later, after the tourist boom had transformed the Costa del Sol, Mijas treasurer Francisco Jurdao found that some things had hardly changed. When queried whom they trusted more, 76 percent of the villagers favoured *mijeños* over for-

obtaining satisfaction from government. Democracy, a novelty, has still to prove itself in a land where taking to the mountains as an outlaw was a frequent recourse under oppressive regimes.

Despite the drift to the cities, the family still rules supreme, revolving around the mother, a venerated figure and willing slave. She reigns over the home and raising the children is generally left to her. More independent-minded young fathers may be seen pushing the baby pram on Sundays, but not many would let it be known that they occasionally did the washing-up. That would be inviting gibes about their masculinity.

Spanish television has daringly run adver-

eigners (only three percent). Asked what action they would take if the town hall proposed something against their interests, 77 percent said they would voice any protest through a relation or an influential person.

This reflects a cynicism ingrained by centuries of oppression and misrule. Andalucíans are not surprised when their politicians indulge in cronyism and line their own pockets; experience has taught them to distrust authority and that using *enchufes* (connections) is the most effective way of

<u>Left</u>, playing cards in a bar in Priego de Córdoba. <u>Above</u>, a fan shop in Ecija.

tisements attempting to persuade men to help wives with the kitchen chores. But the idea appears laughable in a land where the *machismo* cult still rules and women are only beginning to challenge their accepted role. Exaggerated pride is one of the negative aspects of this all-important manliness; bigheartedness and grand gestures are two of the more appealing characteristics.

Local rivalry: Poor communications and illiteracy have contributed to the Andalucían's suspicion of everything beyond his own group and community. Isolation has led to intense rivalry or even enmity between towns and villages. Denigrating other towns

WAR AND PEACE

Buried in the files of Spain's town halls are tales of many a forgotten conflict and Quixotic confrontation. Nevertheless, the revelation in the early 1980s that two humble Andalucían municipalities were at war with powerful European nations did provoke a certain amount of local astonishment.

Inspired by local pride, fearless in defence of Spanish honour, Lijar and Huescar had been engaged in hostilities with Denmark and France since the 19th century, a challenge of which unaccountably neither Copenhagen nor Paris seemed aware. A flurry of diplomatic activity was necessary before peace was finally declared in two of the region's remotest and most tranquil areas.

Small and poor, the village of Lijar lies in the heart of the harsh Sierra de Filabres in Almeria province. The 650 inhabitants scrape a living from the arid soil and from their work in the nearby marble quarries. But their spirit is indomitable. How else could they have carried on a 100-year war against the might of France?

Don Miguel García Saéz, fervent monarchist, lawyer, journalist and crusader, was the instigator. As Lijar's mayor, he was indignant when he heard that King Alfonso XII had been insulted and stoned by the mob while passing through Paris. At a meeting of the seven village councillors on 14 October 1883, he formally declared war on France, contemptuously reckoning that each Lijar inhabitant was equivalent to 10,000 Frenchmen. Don Miguel (a fiery individual known popularly as The Terror of the Sierras) noted that Spain had more than enough valour to "wipe the cowardly French nation off the map".

Although the war lasted a century, there was no bloodshed. Few tourists, let alone soldiers, manage to negotiate the winding roads that lead to the hamlet amid the sierras.

Yet, when news of the war leaked out, many of Lijar's inhabitants were reluctant to drop the matter. They felt France's recent stance towards Spain, not least the attacks by French farmers on

Spanish agricultural products, hardly justified a change. Finally, however, after intense diplomatic negotiations, France despatched its consul from Málaga and a peace treaty was signed with the required pomp on 30 October 1983. The main square, the Plaza del Generalísimo, was renamed the Plaza de la Paz.

Huescar, a town of 10,000 people in the northeast of Granada province, had forgotten all about its war with Denmark until a diligent local historian unearthed town hall records dating back to 1809, when a good part of Spain was occupied by Napoleon's forces. The Spanish government, which was lodged at that time in Seville, issued a royal order declaring war on Denmark as an ally of Napoleon.

When news of this reached Huescar, the local council hastened to issue its own declaration, on 11 November 1809, expressing for good measure its "eternal contempt for the enemies of Spain". Somehow Huescar forgot to revoke that declaration.

For 172 years hostilities dragged on without casualties. Indeed, Denmark appeared unaware even of Huescar's existence until news of the find in the archives was broadcast by a Danish radio correspondent.

This prompted swift action by the Danish ambassador in Madrid who wrote to say: "It is surprising that this bellicose matter has not been resolved. But I believe it is never too late and I hope to have the opportunity to put matters right."

For reasons of political expediency, some of Huescar's councillors favoured maintaining a symbolic state of war. But even they agreed that Huescar's armed forces, consisting of eight municipal policemen, might not be sufficient to combat Danish tanks. Peace talks finally went ahead on the condition that "they preserve the honour of our city and promote understanding with the Danish people".

Before a treaty could be signed, Huescar did manage to take two prisoners of war. They were reporters from a Danish newspaper who were lightheartedly handcuffed when they arrived at the town hall. When it was decided to remove the handcuffs, however, the key had been mislaid and they had to be escorted to a blacksmith to be freed.

is a widespread custom. Rhyming slander is popular, on the lines of "*Loja, la que no es puta es coja*" (In Loja, the women are either whores or lame) and "*Buena es Granada, pero junto a Sevilla no vale nada*" (Granada is all right, but it is worth nothing compared to Seville).

In the mountain village of Frigiliana the people look down physically and figuratively on the neighbouring Costa del Sol town of Nerja, dirt-poor until recently, now a flourishing tourist resort. "Not too long ago they were penniless fishermen. They came here to beg. Now they act as though they're superior. The truth is that they are not *gente seria* literally, serious people. You can't rely on

and villages and only chance encounters could lead to marriage outside. Even courting a girl from within the same village was a laborious process, since the *novio* was required to spend countless evenings visiting his girlfriend's home but never, in theory at least, being alone with her.

One of the great opportunities to break out occurred on the Mediterranean coast with the cane-cutting season every spring. Hundreds of young men spent several weeks engaged in this gruelling task, chopping the sugar-cane with machetes, loading it for transport for the refineries. The workers lived in often abysmal conditions and the pay was low, but it was a rare moment of free-

them," say the *pueblo* people, mixing past history and recent envy.

The new rich of the tourist resort polish their late-model cars, pack their modernised houses with gleaming, veneered furniture and scoff: "Those sierra bumpkins! They don't even speak Spanish up there."

Courtship and canes: But attitudes are changing. The *moto* (motor-cycle) has helped. Until the 1970s, rural communities were often highly inbred because youngsters had no way of visiting neighbouring towns

Left, villagers in Lijar's Plaza de la Paz. **Above**, olive workers still have a low standard of living.

dom, a chance to earn extra cash and meet girls away from family pressures.

The sugar-cane business has slumped but today most youngsters can afford a motorcycle and many have a car. No longer confined to their own villages, their choice of *novias* is no longer restricted to second cousins and the girl next door. Girls too have unheard-of liberty, until early marriage chains them effectively to the home.

Easier communications and a more relaxed moral code are contributing to marriages between communities which in the past turned their backs on one another. In the Alpujarras region, a teenager said: "It wasn't so long ago that they tossed in the fountain a lad from the next village who dared to come here at fiesta time to court one of our girls."

Links with the past are most strongly in evidence in the fiestas. Some customs are believed to date from neolithic times, such as the cult of the dead (on the night before All Souls' Day relatives hold a vigil in cemeteries and light candles before the tombs of the departed). Archaeological finds, such as the life-size statue of the Dama de Baza and the nude figure known as the Diosa de Sevilla, appear related to fertility rites and testify to the worship of a mother-god hundreds of years before Christ.

Virgin worship: As in all agrarian societies, ety and non-stop singing, dancing and drinking coalesce in a spectacular release of emotion. As Josephs points out, "the ecstatic wine-dance of antiquity is still practised as religious ritual, incorporated now into the worship of the Virgin, but unchanged as dramatic ritual and devotion-diversion." Andalucíans' capacity to launch themselves into another dimension on such occasions sets them apart from more "developed" urban man who has become so removed from his primordial roots that he has to rationalise existence on a psychiatric couch.

The *andaluz* remains a creature of nature, childlike in his enthusiasms, his emotions close to the surface, with an urge to live each

the earth has an almost mystical importance and explains the astonishing emotions aroused by the Virgin, an image of enormous importance in this region, who—as American Hispanist Allen Josephs convincingly argues in his book *White Wall of Spain*—is a Christian incarnation of the pagan earth-mother and goddess of fertility.

One of the Virgins which excites most fervour is La Blanca Paloma (The White Dove), Queen of the Marshes, and it is easy to see pagan connections with the pilgrimage which attracts a million or so people to her sanctuary at El Rocío, in the marshes near the mouth of the Guadalquivir. Fanaticism, pi-

moment vividly. He may never read a newspaper but poetry excites his deepest sentiments; he may not be baptised García Lorca, Antonio Machado, Vicente Aleixandre or Rafael Alberti, but he is a poet at heart.

Gypsy flavour: Perhaps it is this poetic licence within Andalucíans which leads them to create their own myths. Once a personality has been elevated to this mythological status, he or she is untouchable. This is particularly so in the bullfight and flamenco worlds where gypsies, who have contributed a particular colour and vivaciousness to Andalucían culture, are among the leading performers. Matador Curro Romero is capable of magic when the conditions are right. More often, shaking with fear at the sight of the bull, he simply refuses to fight and disappointed fans hurl their seat-cushions at him.

"The amazing thing is that inside the *plaza de toros*, people may scream abuse," mused Antonio Ordoñez, the retired matador. "But with every step Curro takes away from the *plaza* the public's memory becomes shorter. By the time he has covered 100 metres people are clapping him on the back and telling him what a great job he has done."

Another adored gypsy matador, Rafael de Paula, was arrested for conspiring to kill his wife's lover. Far from ruining his career, this made him more popular. Released from jail,

ears would be cut off and they would be permanently expelled.

Harsh treatment has always been the gypsies' lot. Although today there is no longer legal discrimination and they account for less than 1 percent of the region's population, they often face hostility. In January 1984, a thousand inhabitants of Torredonjimeno (Jaén) tried to lynch a gypsy family and five people were badly burned when their house was put to the torch. In July 1986, 30 houses at Martos (Jaén) occupied by gypsies were set on fire. In both cases, the *gitanos* were blamed for outbreaks of crime.

Payos (non-gypsies) are ambivalent in their feelings towards these nomadic non-

his entrance into the bull-ring in Seville was the occasion for a hero's welcome.

Flamenco would not exist in its present form had not the gypsies wandered in from Egypt around the 15th century, bringing a flavour of the Orient with them. True to form, the Catholic monarchs issued an edict in 1499 ordering the "Egyptians" to settle down and get regular jobs within 60 days instead of wandering about the kingdom. Otherwise, they would receive 100 lashes and exile the first time; the second time, their

Left, bullfighting plays a key role in local culture.
Above, chef and his team on the Costa del Sol.

conformists whose only escape from poverty is usually through music or the *toros*. García Lorca, however, was lyrical: "The *gitano* is the highest, the deepest, the most aristocratic, the blood and the alphabet of Andalucían and universal truth."

Gitano fire has played its part in creating the Andalucían character. It is a complex, contradictory character, one which fits about as easily into the computer age as does La Virgen del Rocío and the fiesta associated with her. Building "Europe's California" in the land where the Kings of Tartessus and the Caliphs of Córdoba once held sway is going to be a fascinating exercise.

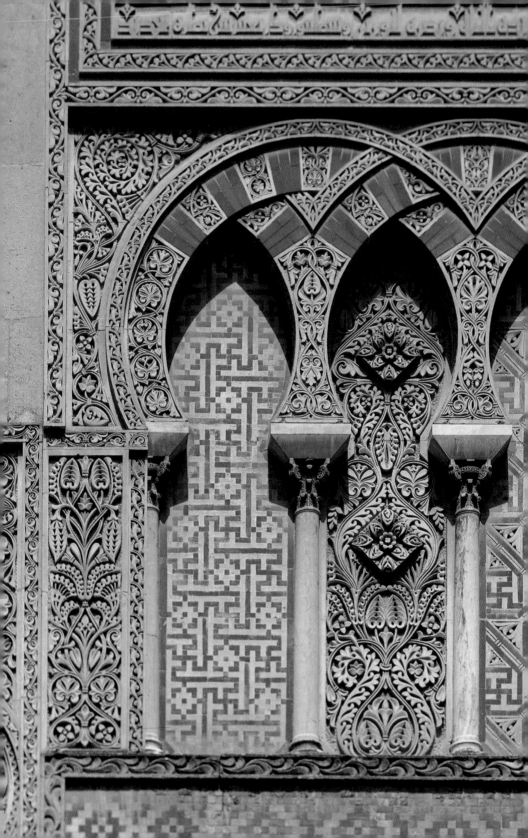

When King Hassan of Morocco made his first official visit to Spain in 1989, he was presented with the freedom of Madrid. Holding the symbolic key to the gates of the city, he declared that he intended to lose it so that the doors of friendship between the two countries could never be locked.

The remark struck a chord among both Moroccans and the people of Andalucía. Residents of Morocco's ancient city of Fez dream even now of returning to al-Andalus, the land of milk and honey they were forced to flee 500 years ago. They listen to groups playing "Andalucían music", a style reflecting the origins of flamenco, and some of them are said still to preserve the keys of their old homes in Granada.

Andalucía has absorbed, changed and been changed by successive waves of settlers. The Moors (derived from the Roman *mauri* or *maurusci*, a name applied to the Berbers of the Atlas Mountains) left perhaps the deepest imprint during their stay of 700 years on Spanish soil. In the end they suffered pain and persecution, but retained their attachment to the region.

The same may be said of the Jews, who contributed profoundly to Andalucían commercial and intellectual life before being brutally and foolishly expelled.

Artistic influence: One meets with the Moorish inheritance at every turn in Andalucía, although at times the influence is so subliminated into local culture that its origin is almost invisible. The most striking aspects to a visitor are obviously the architectural gems, such as the Alhambra palace of Granada with its delicate stucco designs and light-as-air pillars and patios, the Great Mosque of Córdoba with its red-and-white arches marching into the shadows, the Giralda tower soaring over Old Seville. Almost every community—many bearing clearly Arab names such as Almachar, Benamahoma, and Zahara—is dominated by the crumbling (or recently restored) walls of an *alcázar* (fort).

Many of the region's churches are built on

Preceding pages: ornate facade of the Córdoba mosque. **Left** and **right**, Moorish-style craftwork.

the site of mosques and traces of Moorish-style structures are common in the brickwork, archways and roof tiles.

Indeed, features of Mudéjar art—strictly, work executed by Moslems living under the Christians—continued to be used in buildings throughout Spain and beyond long after the Moors had been ousted. Even today, potters from Granada to Seville carry on the tradition, turning out products little different from those used in medieval times, employing similar techniques and designs to those

used by the Moors.

In the Alpujarras region of Granada province, which was the last stronghold of the Moriscos (Moslems converted to Christianity), the flat-roofed houses strongly resemble Berber dwellings.

Work and speech: Irrigation techniques owe much to the Moors, who worked hard and ingeniously to turn Andalucía into a garden. Many of today's channels carrying water from mountains to fields follow routes they first traced. The Moors are credited, too, with introducing sugar-cane, peaches and apricots to the peninsula.

Poetry and silk-weaving, leatherwork and

literature flowered. Caliph al-Hakam II collected 400,000 books in his library and Abenabbás, vizier to the ruler of Almería, had a similar number of volumes in his own collection.

The Spanish vocabulary is crammed with words adapted from the Arab tongue. A *fonda* (inn) was a *funduq* to the Moors. *Jaque mate* (checkmate) comes from *al-sah mat* (the king has died). *Alfaque* (bank or shoal), *alcornoque* (cork tree), *aljibe* (cistern) and *aljama* (Moorish or Jewish quarter) are just a part of the linguistic legacy.

And as for the cries of *"Olé!"* that greet a matador's fine pass in the bull-ring or the emergence of the Virgin from her temple, comparisons, as academics often point out.

Ironically, after centuries in which the term *moro* has been used as a pejorative, in recent years the Andalucíans themselves have joined the search for Arab roots.

Serafín Fanjul, professor of Arab Literature at Madrid Autonomous University, feels this has led to false, romanticised conclusions. He is scathing about this nostalgic trend, "more emotional than well-founded, more fantasy than fact", which he sees as an attempt to make up for Andalucía's lack of regionalist spirit and a language of its own. He laughs at such contradictions with Islam as the Andalucían taste for ham and wine ironically enough, a favourite pork snack is

linguistic researchers claim these are the echo of the Moslem exclamation "Allah! Allah!"

It is possible to see signs of the Moorish inheritance in the way Andalucíans look and act: those smouldering dark eyes, hawk-like noses, and jetblack hair; the flaring of temperament and flare for show; the Oriental flavour of the anguish distilled in *cante jondo,* a variation of flamenco; a taste for haggling; the love of fine language and indifference to niceties of time. Too much, however, can be made of characteristics which are shared by many Mediterranean peoples, and it is easy to draw many more called *pincho moruno*—Moorish kebab). He points out that many of the indications trotted out to demonstrate Andalucía's Moorish connections can just as easily be found in other parts of Spain.

The expulsion of thousands of Moors and Moriscos from the region to be replaced by settlers from the north certainly diluted the Arabness of Andalucía. The fanaticism that inspired those purges also plunged Spain into dark centuries of religious persecution and intellectual stagnation.

Initially, the *Reyes Católicos* (Queen Isabella and King Ferdinand), flush with their 1492 victory over the Moorish Kingdom of

Granada, were generous with the Moslems, guaranteeing them the right to conserve their customs, but this attitude soon changed.

End of an elite: The Spanish Inquisition had been set up in 1478 (the Inquisition already existed, most strongly in France and Italy). Eventually it was to investigate the Moors who feigned conversion but were found to be still following Islam. At first, however, it was intended to deal with the "evil influence" of the Jews.

Persecution had not been unknown to the Jews living in al-Andalus, but during the Golden Age of the Caliphs around the 10th century, they, the Christians and the Moors, had managed to live peacefully alongside

one another, and intermarrying.

This was an era when art, trade and agriculture flourished in a climate of tolerance. Recognised as valuable members of the community, the Jews were skilled artisans, weavers, financiers and merchants with connections in Baghdad and Damascus.

Some were influential in government. Hadai Ben Shaprut, diplomat and doctor, was a powerful adviser to the Caliph of Córdoba, Abderraman III, and a promoter of Talmudic studies. An 11th-century philo-

Left, stucco detail from the Córdoba synagogue. **Above**, modern mosque in Marbella.

sopher, Bahya Ben Paquda, exercised profound influence on Jewish mysticism with his writings, first composed in Arabic. Among those who attended Córdoba's Talmudic school was Moses Maimonides, later to distinguish himself as physician to the Sultan Saladin and as a great thinker.

Lucena, a Jewish stronghold in the Córdoba caliphate, was virtually independent. According to one contemporary writer, "The Jews who dwelt within its massive walls were richer than in any other region subject to Islam and were much on guard against their rivals."

When the crusading armies of Castile conquered Andalucía, Arab and Hebrew books were consigned to the flames. Soon heretics were joining them on the bonfires; 2,000 men and women were burned in Seville in the year 1481. The Jews were suspect both because of their religion and their wealth, which provoked jealousy.

In 1492 the first Inquisitor General, Tomás de Torquemada—himself a *converso* (converted Jew)—persuaded Isabella and Ferdinand to issue an edict giving the Jews three months to be baptised or leave the country. It was forgotten that the conquest of Granada would not have been possible without Jewish finance.

More than 170,000 Jews refused to renounce their faith and were driven out of Sepharad (the Hebrew name for Spain) where their ancestors had lived for 2,000 years. Scattered about the world, half a million Sephardic Jews today still use the Judaeo-Spanish tongue known as Ladino. Some, like the ousted Moors, claim still to possess the keys of their Spanish homes.

At a stroke Spain lost an educated elite. To complete the impoverishment of Andalucía, the monarchy soon made life impossible for the Moors, closing their mosques, torturing them and denying them basic rights.

In 1567, King Philip II decreed: "You must abandon your language, your religion, your traditions, your customs, clothing and finery and, above all, that mania of yours, so little Christian, of bathing yourselves daily. You must forget your ancestors, and baptise yourselves and give yourselves names like ours." The bloody War of Granada resulted, and in 1609 all Moriscos were ordered out of Spain.

This was a time when merely refusing to

eat pork was enough for somebody to be suspected as a heretic and dragged to the torture chambers. Although the Inquisition claimed thousands of victims, the numbers are often exaggerated. It should be remembered that it was a brutal era; according to some estimates, more than 300,000 "witches" were burned in Europe, two-thirds of them in Germany and an estimated 70,000 in England.

After the purge: The Arabs had been too long in Spain for their influence to be wiped out. Moriscos remained in Spain, adopting Christian names while hiding their true beliefs or embracing Catholicism. Their blood, and that of the Jews, had mingled with that of

the conquerors and not all the statutes of *limpieza de Sangre* (literally cleanliness of blood) could change that. Semitic features are not hard to find in modern Spains.

Descendants of the *conversos* played prominent roles in Spain. They included Santa Teresa of Avila and great writers of the Golden Century of Spanish culture. Greater religious freedom, beginning last century, allowed Jews to return to Sepharad and they are once more in evidence in the arts, business and government.

Seville's labyrinthine Jewish quarter, known as Santa Cruz, and Córdoba's Judería, complete with synagogue, attract many visitors. Names like Platero (silversmith) indicate a connection with the Jewish artisans of the past and it cannot be coincidence that Córdoba has an unusually large number of silver-workers and jewellers. A church in Lucena is built on the synagogue's foundations and a local potter pointed out to me several words used in his craft which derive from Hebrew.

With the approval of a democratic Constitution in 1978, Spain once more allowed religions other than Catholicism to establish themselves in the country and this was the signal for a revival of Islam and for mosques to spring up in many locations.

Spanish Islam: Possibly 200,000 persons now follow the Moslem creed in Spain. Most are of Moroccan origin, while some are from the Middle East oil states. Members of the Saudi Arabian royal family are among those who have bought property on the Costa del Sol and established their own mosque at Marbella. Along that increasingly cosmopolitan section of coast, signs in Arabic compete for attention with those in English. At Pedro Abad, near Córdoba, the Ahmadiya sect from Pakistan has built a mosque in an effort to widen its influence.

Spanish converts to Islam have created their own communities in the main Andalucían cities, sometimes demonstrating the special zeal to be found among all converts. One fundamentalist group plans to erect a mosque in the Albaicin, Granada's old Arab quarter where a number of converts live by making such handicrafts as hand-painted ceramics and embossed leatherware, largely for sale to tourists.

If this creates the sensation that the clock has been turned back, the Islamic association Al Andalus wants Spain to go further by fulfilling the surrender conditions promised to the Moors in 1492. "Arab should be the language of Andalucía, every citizen should have the right to bear arms and the Andalucíans who were expelled should have the right to return," are among its claims. Not too many Andalucíans appear to go along with this, however. In the 1986 regional elections, the association's Andalucían Freedom party gained 6,000 votes.

Left and **right**: scenes from the annual modern-day invasion of Moors, who cross to Morocco from Algeciras after driving across Europe.

MOROCCAN MIGRATION

Another stifling day dawns in Algeciras, a grimy seaport on the southern tip of Spain. As the sun's first rays etch in the harbour, a convoy of battered vehicles chugs aboard an ancient, Morocco-bound ferry.

The boat's exhausted passengers are Moroccan migrant workers who have spent two days waiting on the quay. Their waterside vigil was preceded by a sleepless, thousand-mile dash across France and Spain. The discomforts and dangers of this epic trek, the last of Europe's mass human migrations, do not, however, deter these industrial nomads. For these Moroccans, a fortnight's rest in the desert kingdom justifies the annual purgatory that begins when the farms and factories of France, Germany and the Low Countries shut for the summer holiday.

For four weeks at the end of July and beginning of August, over 750,000 Moroccans scurry across Spain like hordes of iron-clad lemmings. Sickness, hunger, fatigue, even road signs are ignored by the thousands of Arab drivers who coax their venerable estate cars and vans towards Algeciras.

This motorised migration began in the late 1960s after the initial flood of impoverished Moroccans to labour-hungry Europe. Prosperity soon swelled the trickle of returning migrants to a torrent.

Throughout the long haul, their ageing automobiles serve as refuge, removal van and strong box. As many as a dozen family members may be shoe-horned into one vehicle for the five-day trip, sitting atop blankets, clothes, sacks of green tea, and the year's savings.

For the entire trip, 90 percent of the vehicles have just one driver, whose major experience behind the wheel comes during the journey home. Coupled to the unfamiliarity of driving are the compounded fears of breakdowns, losing the way, or being attacked. These accumulated worries persuade the Moroccans to travel in perilous convoys.

Unfortunately, these convoys can be fatal. The drivers imitate the reactions of the rest of the straggling column: when the lead car overtakes, the others will swerve blindly into the traffic like kamikaze dodgems. Each year, suicidal manoeuvres kill an average of 20 Moroccans and injure a further 250 during Operation Transit. One year 11 members of a family of 13 were killed when their van collided head-on with a lorry near Córdoba.

Most of the accidents and robberies occur on the final stretch to Algeciras. Negotiating Seville is perhaps the biggest hazard. Trapped in the city's chaotic traffic, they fall victim to young highwaymen riding mopeds. In the treeless, open country around the Andalucían capital, migrants who stop to rest, pray or brew mint tea are regularly bushwhacked.

On the last leg to Algeciras, the Atlantic glistening through the pine trees reassures squinting eyes reddened by barbiturates swallowed to keep awake at the wheel. The arrival of many vehicles at the port is reminiscent of stricken bombers returning to base. Cars limp in trailing exhausts or with tyres torn to ribbons. Others are towed or shepherded in, lopsided by shifted loads or broken suspensions.

Cooped up in the filth of the quayside, the Moroccans represent a captive market. The stalls that ring the harbour charge exorbitant prices for basic necessities like bread and water. Petty thieves and bogus ticket sellers prowl the vicinity for unguarded vehicles or gullible migrants desperate to queue-jump. Yet, the Moroccans are remarkably philosophical about their predicament. Few complain, and those who have been to Mecca point out that conditions are worse on the pilgrimage.

One hour's steaming across the Straits of Gibraltar lies Ceuta, a sliver of Spain in North Africa. When the migrants reach this Spanish enclave, they are just 2 miles (3 km) from home. However, this five-minute drive can seem an eternity if there are hold-ups at the border dividing Spain from Morocco. The migrants blame this on Moroccan policemen demanding bribes.

After customary delays at the flyblown frontier, the ramshackle cavalcades lurch forward and disappear into the tawny haze of Morocco. The odyssey is over—until next year.

Hardly a day goes by in Andalucía without a fiesta somewhere. Usually it has religious significance, sometimes it is to celebrate a historic event, often its roots lie in pagan rites, virtually always it is the signal for drinking, dancing and singing. It can be a simple village affair with a procession to a local shrine followed by a dance in the plaza or a full-blown, week-long extravaganza such as the Seville Feria (or Fair). A few of the most interesting and colourful fiestas are listed here, but there are hundreds of others. Dates of fiestas can vary from year to year so check beforehand with local tourist offices and town halls.

January: *Día de la Toma,* Granada, 2 January: The city celebrates the victory of the Catholic Monarchs in 1492 over the Moorish Kingdom of Granada with a solemn procession in which Queen Isabella's crown and King Ferinand's sword are carried from the Cathedral and through the streets of the city. *Cabalgata de Reyes,* 5 January: Spanish children do not receive their presents at Christmas. Instead, they are brought them by the Three Kings who arrive on this night. To mark the occasion, towns hold colourful processions, featuring music, floats and clowns. In major cities, the Kings arrive, magnificently robed, on camels.

February: *Carnival:* Banned during the Franco regime because it was considered subversive, Carnival (*Carnaval* in Spanish) is celebrated colourfully and exuberantly. Ayamonte and Isla Cristina (Huelva) are noted for letting their hair down, but Cádiz is most renowned for the scope and liveliness of its celebrations. Groups compete to poke irreverent fun at authority and well-known personalities. Fancy dress dances, fireworks and a grand parade on the Sunday after Ash Wednesday are part of the entertainment. *Semana Santa:* Andalucía celebrates Holy Week (March or April) with a colourful mixture of solemn piety, medieval pomp and

pagan revelry. Every community has its processions, the biggest and most lavish taking place in Seville and Málaga. They begin on Palm Sunday and reach a climax on Good Friday.

Some highlights: in Seville, the early hours of Good Friday when six processions are in the streets, including that of the much-venerated Virgin, La Macarena; in Málaga, Wednesday when a prisoner freed from the city jail walks in the Jesús Nazareno el Rico procession, and Thursday when the Spanish

Legion struts through the streets, parading the image of the Cristo de la Buena Muerte; Baena (Córdoba), processions distinguished by thundering drums; Arcos de la Frontera (Cádiz), where the floats are edged through steep, narrow twisting streets with inches to spare; Rio Gordo (Málaga), Good Friday and Easter Saturday, Passion Play enacted by the villagers. The singing of *saetas,* emotional flamenco laments, along the route, is a feature of the Easter processions.

April: *Seville Fair* or *Feria* (end of April or start of May): More than 300,000 bulbs light the fairgrounds until dawn and thousands of *sevillanos* dance, drink and sing a whole

Preceding pages: bouquet for a knight on horseback; carnival band; Seville Fair procession. Left, party spirit at Torremolinos. Right, oiled celebrant at Baza's El Cascamorras.

week away. Daily, from around midday, elegant horse riders in traditional Andalucían dress and carriages bearing mantilla-crowned ladies parade haughtily through the fairgrounds. Leading matadors take part in the afternoon bullfights, after which hundreds of *casetas* (entertainment booths set up by clubs, groups of friends, trade unions) throb to music and conversation. Dancing of the light-hearted *sevillana* never seems to stop during the *feria*. Accommodation is difficult to find.

Romería: Santuario de la Virgen de la Cabeza, near Andújar, Jaén, last weekend in April: As many as 250,000 people make the annual pilgrimage to a lonely hilltop in the

ing, but on a smaller and more intimate scale than the Seville extravaganza.

Day of the Cross, celebrated on or around 3 May: One of the most light-hearted fiestas, a celebration of spring with pagan roots. Crosses are set up by neighbourhood groups and decorated with flowers and greenery and passers-by are treated to food, drink and music. This fiesta is being revived in many towns, but flourishes particularly in the cities of Granada and Córdoba and communities in Córdoba province such as Añora, La Rambla and Montilla.

Córdoba Patios Festival: The first fortnight in May is almost one long fiesta in Córdoba. For this one, the old quarter opens

Sierra Morena. The *romería* begins on Saturday 20 miles (32 km) south, in Andújar. Some make the journey on foot, waggon or horseback. Thousands of others arrive by car and coach. They camp out around the shrine, the scene of a famous siege during the Spanish Civil War. The Virgin, also known as The Little Dark One and the Queen of the Sierra Morena, emerges for a triumphal procession on the Sunday.

May: *Jerez (Cádiz) horse fair*: Sherry flows like water during this fiesta in the first week of May, which features some of the finest horses and flamenco, equestrian competitions, bullfights and general merrymak-

its doors and shows off its flower-garlanded patios, balconies and secluded squares. Events include a *romería*, concerts and flamenco. Shortly after the Patios Festival, the Córdoba Fair begins.

El Rocío (Huelva), Pentecost (sometimes in early June): This is Andalucía's most popular fiesta, a bewildering mixture of religious devotion and uninhibited carousing. It attracts up to a million pilgrims, some riding or walking but most now arriving by motor vehicle. Religious brotherhoods do it the hard way, spending several days trekking over dunes and marshland from all points of the compass to the sanctuary of La Virgen del Rocío, known as La Blanca Paloma. After paying respects to the Virgin in this lonely spot amid the marshes near the mouth of the Guadalquivir, the visitors hold a huge party. Wealthier pilgrims own or rent houses, the rest sleep where they can. The climax comes in the early hours of Monday morning when youths from the Almonte brotherhood storm the altar and carry the Virgin off, to return her several hours later.

June: *Corpus Christi* (sometimes in May): Granada celebrates this in individual style with a procession featuring La Tarasca, a figure mounted on a dragon's back, *cabezudos* (big heads) and effigies of Moorish and Christian kings. Many towns deco-

where a flamenco mass is then celebrated.

July: *Virgen del Carmen*, 15 and 16 July: Fishermen pay homage to the Virgin, placing her in a fishing boat for a sea trip as rockets soar overhead. Celebrated in many coastal towns, including San Fernando and Barbate (Cádiz), Málaga, Estepona, Fuengirola, and Nerja (Málaga province), Salobreña (Granada) and Garrucha (Almería).

Lunes del Toro, Grazalema (Cádiz), Monday following the Virgen del Carmen fiesta: This remote mountain village stages its own Pamplona-style fiesta, releasing bulls to run through the streets.

August: *Summer fiesta,* Málaga, first two weeks: Horses and carriages parading

rate the streets for the solemn Corpus Christi procession, one of the most notable displays being in Zahara de la Sierra in the sierras of Cádiz. In Seville, 10 young boys known as the Seises, in medieval dress, dance before the Cathedral altar before a procession through the streets.

Gypsy romería, Cabra (Córdoba), third Sunday in June: This offers an explosion of emotion as thousands of gypsies escort the Virgen de la Sierra to her hilltop sanctuary

Left, Málaga's Verdiales fiesta in full flow.
Above left, figures from Seville's Semana Santa.
Above right, the Virgen del Rocío procession.

through city streets, concerts, bullfights, a funfair, all-night dancing and singing at the fairground, and a colossal fireworks climax are featured during this fiesta as the *malagueños* strive to outdo the Seville Fair.

Noche del Vino, Cómpeta (Málaga), 15 August: The sierra village of Cómpeta, noted for its strong, sweet wine, serves it free and stages popular entertainment in the church square.

Virgin of the Sea fiesta, Almería, end August: Almería pays homage to the Virgen del Mar with more than a week of sports, bullfights and merrymaking.

Exaltation of the River Guadalquivir,

Sanlúcar de Barrameda (Cádiz), third or fourth week of August: It includes an unusual sports event when horse races are run on the beach of the Guadalquivir estuary.

September: *El Cascamorras,* Baza (Granada), 6 September: The town starts its annual fair with a bizarre event, the arrival of the Cascamorras, a man sent from the neighbouring town of Guadix to recover a disputed Virgin. Oil-daubed youths paint him black and chase him through the town. Two days later he is given a place of honour in the Virgin's procession.

Corrida Goyesca, Ronda (Málaga), first fortnight: During the Pedro Romero fiesta in the town, which is regarded as the cradle of modern bullfighting, participants in the fights in the 200-year-old Plaza de Toros wear dress typical of Goya's time. Cattle trading, equestrian competitions, dancing and pop musicians are other attractions.

Moors v Christians, Valor (Granada), 15 September: This remote village in the Alpujarras region, the last stronghold of the Moors, enthusiastically re-enacts a battle between the Moors and Christians, complete with a castle siege and deafening gunfire.

Encierros (bull-runs), Jaén province: Young men show their courage by running before the horns of bulls released to run through the streets in a series of fiestas in such Sierra de Segura villages as Iznatoraf (first week of September), Chiclana (second week) and Villacarrillo (second week).

October: *Cristo del Paño romería,* Moclín (Granada), 5 October: All manner of miracles are credited to a standard once carried by a Castilian soldier during the wars against the Moors. Depicting Christ, it is carried in procession and attracts thousands of pilgrims eager to seek a cure from everything. This unusual fiesta is said to have inspired some scenes in García Lorca's play *Yerma*.

December: *Verdiales fiesta*, Málaga, 28 December: City and countryfolk travel to the Venta del Túnel, just outside town, to enjoy the Verdiales, a primitive, driving music dating at least from Moorish times. *Pandas* (gangs), wearing dazzling headgear, descend from the Málaga mountains to engage in frenzied competition, employing guitars, fiddles, cymbals and tambourines.

Right, the Rocío fiesta is an occasion for spontaneous and prolonged celebration.

Alfonso the Wise, King of Castile and León, could hardly have imagined, when he declared the profession of bullfighter to be disreputable in his Code of Laws, that one day whole families would take up and sustain this dangerous profession. Today's bullfighters are often members of dynasties similar to the lineage of royal sovereigns.

The dynasties of *toreros*, and bullfighting itself, for that matter, all began 300 years ago in the beautiful setting of the Andalucían city of Ronda where the country's oldest bullring still stands. The oldest known dynasty, the Romeros, came from Ronda; the newest, bourgeoning hope of bullfighting today, Francisco Rivera Ordóñez, is the heir to three truly legendary families in the history of bullfighting—Dominguín, Ordóñez and Rivera—and also boasts indirect ties with that Andalucían town.

First fighters: Francisco Romero was born in Ronda at the very beginning of the 18th century. He started the tradition of bullfighting on foot, with sword and muleta (small cloth). But his greatest merit really lies in having fathered a whole dynasty.

Juan Romero, son of Francisco, had no less than four bullfighter sons—José, Pedro, Gaspar and Antonio—a circumstance not at all unusual at that time, considering that it was common for children to adopt their father's trade. Antonio had the misfortune of being killed by a bull in 1802, but Juan's second son, Pedro, was eventually proclaimed the "Father of Modern Tauromachy" (bullfighting).

Born in Ronda in 1754, Pedro Romero is credited with having killed over 5,600 bulls in his career without ever suffering a major injury. From a family noted for its longevity—his father lived to 102—Pedro Romero killed his last bull in the Madrid bull-ring at the incredible age of 79. He also founded the very first bullfighting school in Seville, under the auspices of Ferinand VII, a forerunner of the dozen schools which exist in Spain today.

Another significant dynasty was that of

the Cándidos, who stood out during what is referred to as the heroic age of bullfighting—called thus because of the fierceness of the animals and the great risks taken by the *toreros*, who had not yet developed the fully refined techniques of today.

José Cándido was noted for killing a bull with a dagger in one hand, and his hat, used as a lure, in the other. Cándido was killed by a bull in Puerto de Santa Maria, but not while he was performing the aforementioned death-defying feat; when rushing to the aid

of a *banderillero* in danger, he slipped in a pool of blood on the sand and was fatally gored.

Jerónimo José Cándido was only nine years old when his father died, but in the end he, too, chose to follow in his father's footsteps by first joining the *cuadrilla* of Pedro Romero. This was the custom at the time, and a rather sensible one at that. A bullfighter learned his trade as a *banderillero*, or assistant, in the *cuadrilla* or squad of an experienced matador and only when he was sufficiently practised did he finally break out on his own.

Nowadays, things work backwards. *Ban-*

Left, matador waiting for his moment. **Right**, cuadrilla painted by Daniel Vazquez Diaz.

derilleros are customarily unsuccessful *novilleros* (novice bullfighters) or has-been matadors, who join the *cuadrillas* of the younger, up-and-coming bullfighters.

The next major family of bullfighters, the Costillares, began with brothers Juan and Joaquín Rodriguez, the latter of whom was the first to adopt the rather unusual nickname of "Rib Cage".

Joaquín Jr, born in Seville in 1748, was the recognised creator of the *volapié* sword manoeuvre, the manner in which most bulls are killed today. The *volapié* involves positioning the bull, encouraging it to charge, and moving in simultaneously to a potentially deadly, mutual encounter between man and beast. Until then all bulls had been killed by the difficult *recibiendo* method, in which the matador adopted a firm, immobile stance, incited the bull to charge, and then plunged in the sword as best he could. This method requires a brave, strong, prompt-charging animal.

Francisco Arjona Cuchares was the most famous of the Arjona dynasty. His father was Manuel Arjona Costuras, his brother was also a bullfighter and his maternal grandfather, Curro Guillén, was killed by a bull in the Ronda ring in 1820. Cúchares was a capable and versatile *torero*, who went to Cuba at the age of 50 to perform in a special bullfight, only to die of yellow fever soon after his arrival.

Golden Age: During the height of bullfighting's popularity the most passionate rivalry ever encountered in the art existed between two *sevillanos*, Joselito el Gallo and the "revolutionary" Juan Belmonte.

The Gallos were of pure, gypsy lineage. An inspired, unpredictable, superstitious bullfighter, when in the ring Rafael el Gallo could simultaneously perform some of the most memorable and unparalleled artistic work imaginable, then flee scandalously from the bull, by jumping headfirst, most undecorously into the *callejón* (protected area of the ring). It was Rafael el Gallo, the gypsy *torero* personified, who defined bullfighting as "having a mystery to tell… and then trying to tell it".

His father José was the classic, cerebral, masterful *torero*, the prototype of what every bullfighter should be: dominating, superior, arrogant, brave and elegant. He made his debut at 13 and dominated the ring

until Juan Belmonte came along. Belmonte, another singular, gifted and revolutionary *torero*, was responsible for redefining the very ground rules of bullfighting, converting the popular spectacle into the refined art of today and not a mere display of athletic skill and ability.

Short and without the physical prowess of his rival, Belmonte was obliged to create a new technique, in which the bull was the one to move about and not the bullfighter. In order to dominate the animal, he obliged it to charge.

Never were passions so high as during this Golden Age, when everyone from the butcher and the baker to figures from the

literary and art world ardently defended their favourites. Belmonte lived on to become one of the most important bullfighters of all times, but one thing was lacking to convert him into a legend to match his rival, according to writer Ramón de Valle Inclán, in a historic exchange. "All you are missing, Juan, is to die in the ring," said the writer, to which Belmonte stuttered in reply: "I will do my best." An ailing Belmonte committed suicide on his Seville ranch in 1962, just six days short of his 70th birthday.

Tragic family: One of the longest dynasties in bullfighting history was nicknamed "Bienvenida", because its founder was born in the small town of Bienvenida in the province of Badajoz in the middle of the 19th century. Manuel Mejias Rapela adopted his father's bullring pseudonym and became a truly popular matador until a bull from the Trespalacios ranch abruptly terminated his career with a near-fatal goring during a fight. Mejias earned a sobriquet in his own right, that of "Papa Negro", the Black Pope of Bullfighting.

Papa Negro had six bullfighting sons, each of whom stood out for his art, courage, elegance and refinement, both in and out of the ring, although unfortunately luck did not smile on them. The oldest of the boys, the "almost perfect" *torero* Manolo, died at the

intelligent handling of the bulls. He died of spinal injuries resulting from a tossing while fighting a calf "for fun" on a country outing. The dynasty is represented today by the long-since retired and respected Angel Luis and Juan, who had less glittering—and safer—professional lives.

Role model: The great Antonio Ordoñez, his father Cayetano (nicknamed "Niño de la Palma") and his four brothers, Cayetano, Juan, Pepe and Alfonso, were natives of Ronda. Cayetano Sr was Ernest Hemingway's bullfighter model in *The Sun Also Rises* (called *Fiesta* in the United Kingdom), although Hemingway later became Antonio's most ardent fan.

age of 25 from what might have been cancer. The solid, classic, scientific Pepe, who had never suffered a serious injury in his entire career, died aged 54 of a heart attack while bullfighting in Lima, Peru. Rafael passed away under mysterious circumstances at the age of 16.

Antonio was the best loved of them all and a favourite son of the demanding Madrid public; he was the epitome of elegance, both as a bullfighter and as a gentleman and will always be remembered for his artistic and

<u>Left</u>, Rafi Camino, latest in a long dynasty.
<u>Above</u>, effigy of a hero in the Córdoba museum.

Antonio Ordoñez, certainly considered one of the greatest *toreros* of all times, interpreted the art of bullfighting with the maximum purity, classicism and bravery. He appeared on the scene at the beginning of the 1950s to challenge his future brother-in-law Luis Miguel Gonzalez Dominguín, the capable, technical and powerful rival of Manolete in the 1940s.

This exciting period in bullfighting inspired Hemingway to write a series of essays for *Life* magazine, which were recently published in book form as *The Dangerous Summer*.

The Vázquez lineage, one of the most

popular to emerge from Seville and the most representative of the *sevillano* style of fighting, is continued in the ring today by Pepe Luis Vázquez, Jr. Characterised by a colourful, vivacious and spontaneous technique, enhanced with graceful adornments, the *sevillano* school is in striking contrast to the purer, classical, more profound and spare *rondeño* style, of which Antonio Ordoñez is the best exponent.

Like his father, Pepe Luis is long on art though short on daring, as is the case for most *artistas*, and a very serious goring in 1989 during the Seville Fair represented a serious setback in his career. The professional aspirations of his younger brother Ignacio were

tury. He was followed by Miguel Litri II whose son Manuel was killed by a bull in Málaga in 1926. Manuel's half-brother, Miguel III, became the top matador of the 1950s, noted for his unmatched bravery, forming a striking duo with Madrid-born Julio Aparicio, whose son has been enjoying great *novillero* triumphs in the rings.

Rafael Camino's classic, artistic style is in fine counterpoint to Litri's daring control of the bulls and he has inherited his father's pure, cerebral concept of fighting. An outstanding swimmer and soccer player, Rafi wanted to become a pilot before he suddenly realised that "he was born to be a bullfighter".

brought to an abrupt end when he lost his right eye while trying to kill a young bull.

Today's heroes: Two of the most promising newcomers on the present scene, Miguel Baez Litri and Rafael Camino, are the sons of immensely popular *toreros* in their own right. Miki (Miguel's pet name), and Rafi grew up together and took the *alternativa* together on the very same day in the Nîmes bull-ring. The *alternativa* ceremony, granted by a senior bullfighter, converts a novice into a fully-fledged professional.

The saga of the Litris began in their native Huelva, where the first Miguel Baez Litri was born at the beginning of the 19th cen-

Among today's bullfighters, at least 40 matadors and just as many *novilleros* have some direct or indirect relationship with previous *toreros*: Roberto Dominguez, Juan Antonio Ruiz Espartaco, Jose Mari Manzanares, Emilio Oliva, Luis Francisco and Juan Antonio Esplá, El Boni, Rafi de la Viña, Juan Mora, Antonio Posada, all are the sons of bullfighters of varying fortune.

It is understandable that the children of not overly successful *toreros* are encouraged or freely choose to follow in their footsteps in an attempt to achieve the glory denied their fathers, but it is more difficult to understand why the son of a *torero* who has attained the coveted top status of *figura de toreo* would risk life and limb in the rings. There are only eight or 10 top fighters and the price they must pay for the honour is steep.

High pressure: Top *toreros* perform in 60 to 80 *corridas* a year, for wages varying according to the size and category of the ring, from 1.5 million pesetas in a small town to 5 million pesetas for the major San Isidro Fair in Madrid. These apparently impressive fees are reduced considerably after the salaries of a minimum of eight employees are deducted, along with all their hotel, food and travel expenses, manager's commissions, publicity, taxes, sequined suits, capes, swords and other paraphernalia.

In summer, the schedule is overly pressing and bullfighters criss-cross the country with barely enough time to rest before the *corrida*. A *torero* hardly ever sees any more of a city in which he appears than the hotel and the bull-ring. And only rarely do plane schedules and airport locations coincide with bullfight commitments, so most journeys must be made by car overnight.

Amongst the true fraternity drinking, smoking and partying are frowned on, but young, ambitious *novilleros* make these

Left, Roberto Dominguez and supporters. **Above**, a moment of prayer before the ring.

sacrifices willingly, seduced by the overwhelming desire to reach the zenith of their profession, only later to experience remorse about adolescent years spent with no friends, no teenage diversions, and under the burden of an eternal sense of fear and responsibility. Often, their seniors did all they could to discourage them from pursuing this very difficult, unpredictable and self-sacrificing profession.

Litri Sr left all the worst calves on his ranch for his son to fight in the hope that the spectacular bumps and bruises Miguel received would discourage him from continuing in the trade; but they didn't. Then, on the day of his son's *alternativa*, he gave him this advice: "Don't let anyone get the better of you, not even me. You're a Litri and that means you have to give the public all your art, courage and skill, and, if necessary, your life." Litri said he knew he would be a bullfighter from the very first moment he stood before a brave, fighting calf, when "the strangest sensation came over me". He was eight years old at the time.

There is something in the blood of the best-known dynasties that keeps them returning to the ring. In Francisco Rivera Ordoñez Jr are the fruits of three important bullfighting dynasties, the Ordoñez family through his mother, the Dominguíns, through his maternal grandmother, the late Carmen Gonzalez, and the Rivera blood, inherited from his father. Francisco Riva Paquirri was killed by a bull in 1984 when at the height of his career—an event that shocked the bullfighting world but which hasn't discouraged his son, who has been fighting calves on his father's and grandfather's ranches ever since he can remember. Francisco Jr's financial prospects were already secure no matter which road he chose to follow in life and yet Francisco was very clear about his future. He told his mother the day of his father's funeral: "Now, I am more convinced than ever, mama, that I want to become a bullfighter." He was then nine years old.

Most towns in southern Spain have bullfighting during the appropriate season. Unfortunately the displays on the Costa del Sol are often not of good quality, and do not make a fitting introduction to the art. Try to see your first fight at one of the best-known rings, with a well-known matador.

The earliest origins of flamenco, a synthesis of music and dance which has come to be identified with the essence of Spain, are unclear. Flamenco crystallised in the gypsy communities of southern Andalucía in the mid-18th century, and much speculation as to its ancestry has focused on the Middle Ages, when gypsy tribes from Rajasthan in India migrated through Egypt and North Africa into Spain.

Today's flamenco certainly shares common features with Indian and Arab song, and other linguistic evidence supports the Arab connection—the word flamenco may have come from the Arabic *felag mengu*, meaning "fugitive peasant". Gypsies have always adopted and adapted the musical styles of their host communities, however, and flamenco also contains strong traces of Jewish and Byzantine Christian religious music, as well as regional Spanish folk styles.

Gypsy cult: The historic heartland of flamenco is the triangle of flat delta between Seville, Jerez and Cádiz, but the music spread with the movements of the gypsies. Catalonia, home of the great dancer Carmen Amaya, and Asturias spawned powerful local styles. The songs known as *farrucas*, for example, originated in the non-flamenco north and arrived in Cádiz with Galacian and Asturian sailors. *Payo*, or non-gypsy artists, gradually acquired the flamenco arts, at first by marriage into gypsy families, and later, as the genre became a professionally dispensed commodity rather than a closed private entertainment, by choice and study.

The rise of flamenco to an art appreciated by the educated and moneyed fits the familiar pattern of similar musical forms such as the Blues, which started as rough but vital lower-class entertainment. The word "flamenco", both an adjective and a noun, denotes a way of life, and a person who is unsettled, uncommitted, emotional, unpredictable, quite possibly criminal, in every sense anti-bourgeois. In this sense, the new young flamenco-rockers, of whom more

Preceding pages: flamenco in Granada's Sacromonte. Left, that unmistakable pose. Right, Paco de Lucía, top flamenco guitarist.

later, are truer to the origins of the music than some of the established concert performers who have built professional careers.

Types and styles: The flamenco repertoire is based on songs with specific uses or contexts—songs about work or religion, dance tunes, or semi-spontaneous musical expressions of the joys and sorrows of everyday life. The oldest and most typically gypsy songs, such as the *tonás*, are sung unaccompanied, except for some basic percussion. The *martinetes*, originally created in the

blacksmiths' forges of the old gypsy district of Triana, in Seville, are still sometimes recorded with the clang of a simulated hammer and anvil.

The numerous styles of flamenco are sometimes—but not by all and not without disagreement—divided into the categories of *cante grande* (great song), *cante intermedio* (intermediate) and *cante chico* (little). The *cantes chicos* are brighter, lighter, and often accompanied by dance. Examples are the very common *bulerías*, *alegrías* and *tangos*. Many are named after their place of origin: *malagueñas, rondeñas, sevillanas*, etc. A small number, the *can-*

ciones de ida y vuelta, are re-adaptations of hybrid rhythms created in the Hispanic-American colonies. These styles, which include the *guajira*, the *rumba*, the *colombiana* and the *milonga*, are much in evidence in new flamenco.

The pinnacle of the true flamenco singer's art, however, is the body of great songs, often referred to as *cante jondo* (deep song), the *soleares* and *seguiriyas*, which are expressive of the deepest, most heartfelt emotion—frequently tragic—and are therefore most difficult to perform and most prized.

Deep song: It is in the *cante jondo* that the quality known as *duende*, literally spirit or demon, is most crucial. *Duende* is consid-

the upper class would hire groups of flamencos to animate parties at their houses late into the night. Even as late as the 1950s, it was still possible to find musicians and singers in the bars of flamenco districts such as Cádiz's La Viña who would improvise for little more recompense than a few rounds of *fino* sherry. These days the gypsy inhabitants of the caves of Granada's Sacromonte, who do considerable business "improvising" for tourists, will require more than a few drinks.

The major development of flamenco into a public entertainment started in the 1850s, with the growth of café *cantates* featuring established gypsy artistes, among them the first flamenco stars such as El Planeta and El

ered to be a form of involuntary inspiration which takes over a performer and exalts his singing to a high art, provoking a murmur—or roar—of "*olés!*" from the audience as a particularly gut-wrenching *copla*, or verse, spirals to its fierce climax.

Just as *duende* is not programmable, so the art of flamenco is at odds with the concept of rehearsal. Flamenco was, and at its best still should be, an impromptu communal activity that grows with the feeling of the moment (plentiful supplies of alcohol helping matters considerably). Its earliest manifestation as a commercial entertainment was still very much in this spirit; wealthy *aficionados* from

Fillo. From this period dates the *cuadro flamenco*—the group of four to a dozen singers, guitarists and dancers, taking turns at solos.

Gaudy kitsch: By the 1920s, the so-called Golden Age of flamenco had degenerated into a tinsel age, with the popularity of the art leading to increasingly cheap, gaudy and inauthentic spectacle. This period of decadence continued through the Franco dictatorship, though by the late 1950s a process of regeneration had started, with artistes such as the great singer Antonio Mairena leading a return to the original purity of the form.

The Franco years saw a broadening of

Andalucían-based music into a flamenco-tinged range of popular song styles, a process which the government encouraged as the music was politically uncontentious, easy to identify for tourists, and colourful. The light but dramatic song form known as the *tonadilla* became popular, interpreted by Spanish Piaf-equivalents such as Conchita Piquer, Juanita Reina and, later, Rocio Jurado. The *folclóricas*—Lola Flores, Isabel Pantoja and others—purveyed a similar, glossy flamenco cabaret music.

Flamenco's associations with Franco, of course, alienated large numbers of youthful, progressive Spaniards and the general image of the music of the south, including pure

and Los Chichos, mixed electric and acoustic guitars with bass and drums to create a fast, catchy pop sound based on the gypsy rumba rhythm. (The southern French group, the Gypsy Kings, were to score world success with a very similar sound 15 years later.)

In pure flamenco, two young performers who were to assume huge stature consolidated their careers. The brilliant *payo* guitarist, Paco de Lucía, began his work of combining an impeccable technique with an explorative approach which included the incorporation of a range of Latin-American melodies and rhythms, as well as a number of jazz and rock collaborations with international musicians such as guitarists John

flamenco, in the 1960s and 1970s was old-fashioned and lacking in vitality. But by the time Franco died in 1975, a number of developments in flamenco and flamenco-linked music were under way, which were to herald the return to form of Andalucían music.

Rock stars: On the pop/rock front, the Cano Roto sound, named after a rough gypsy suburb of Madrid, was born around 1973. Young gypsy-dominated groups, such as Los Chorbos, Los Grecas, Los Chunguitos

McLaughlin and Al di Meola.

Most importantly of all, a young gypsy *cante jondo* singer from near Cádiz began to build a major reputation, as much for his wild rock-and-roll lifestyle as for his searing, *duende*-inhabited voice and charismatic presence. El Camaron de la Isla (his stage name, *camaron*, means shrimp and refers to his skinny frame) combined more than anyone else the qualities of rock and flamenco.

Through the immediate post-Franco years a new cult of the south simmered. A key influence in the incorporation of flamenco traits into the world of rock and fashion was Kiko Veneno, a Seville-raised rock guitarist

Left, art in action. Above left, Martirio brought a surreal touch to sung flamenco. **Above right,** Raimundo Amador of the group Pata Negra.

whose 1977 punk-influenced album, *Veneno*, featured the guitar-playing of the brothers Rafael and Raimundo Amador, descendants of an old Triana flamenco dynasty. It was Veneno who discovered and groomed the girl singer Martirio, who achieved minor fame as much for her clothes—fantastic, semi-surreal, semi-kitsch versions of comb-and-mantilla costumes—as for her quirky music.

Fashion boom: The most widespread and dramatic popular manifestation of a boom in Andalucían music was undoubtedly the vogue for *sevillanas* dancing which swept the nation in the late 1980s. With the election of a Socialist government (dominated by Andalucíans such as Prime Minister Felipe Gonzalez) in 1984, the last vestiges of the Franquist stigma were removed. By the end of the decade, every major city in Spain had its complement of *sevillanas* academies and discotheques where everyone attempted to simulate the elegant arched posture and swirling steps of the dance.

While flamenco-rock experiments have continued—led by the groups Pata Negra, fronted by Rafael and Raimundo Amador, and Ketama, comprised of young members of the Jerez Carmona family—traditional flamenco has flourished too.

The dozens of local government-funded summer festivals throughout the south have continued to provide abundant audiences for the old custodians of the authentic *cante*, singers such as Pepe de la Matrona, Bernada de Utrera and Rafael Romero, guitarists such as Melchor de Marchena and Diego del Gastor, as well as younger stars like the Habichuela family, Tomatito, Enrique Morente, el Lebrijano, Vicente Soto and el Cabrero.

Today, the inventiveness of Andalucían music seems undiminished. El Camaron's 1989 album *Soy Gitano*, recorded with London's Royal Philharmonic Orchestra, reaffirmed him as a major innovator as well as an established traditional star. Experiments combining flamenco singers with Moroccan groups—El Lebrijano with the Orchestra of Tangier, José Heredia Maya with the Orchestra of Tetuan—look set to be repeated with increasing popularity.

Right, an English flamenco couple on the Costa display the style which has won them prizes.

On a September morning, deep in Andalucía, a deafening clanging of bells ring out from high in an ancient stone tower, and a thousand pigeons wheel through the blue sky over the plaza. Unfazed by what is going on around them, three men in blue shorts and white shirts, their arms around each other's shoulders, are rhythmically trampling piles of pale green grapes in a flower-decked square wooden trough.

A wave of applause sweeps through the grandstands in front of the cathedral and spreads through the crowd in the big square below, so loud that you can hardly hear the municipal band as it trumpets, toots and bangs away beside the bell tower. It is the annual celebration of the birth of the new wine, the lifeblood of the city of Jerez de la Frontera. In the grandstands there are quite a few onlookers whose ancestors have been celebrating the same event for centuries, perhaps with another ceremony and another type of sherry. They have such un-Spanish surnames as Domecq, Ferguson, Terry, Osborne, Williams and Gordon.

Early wines: Jerez, founded—or perhaps just found—by the Greeks under the name of Xera, was shipping highly prized wine to distant Rome in clay amphoras two millennia ago. It not only survived 500 years of domination by theoretically teetotal Arabs without having the vines ripped up, but actually prospered under their rule. The Moslems introduced distillation—for medicinal purposes, of course.

There is a record of wine shipped from the sherry district to "Plemma (*Plymouth?*), which is in the kingdom of England" as early as 1482, and British wine merchants were established in the Jerez area as long ago as the early 16th century. Columbus and Magellan both loaded wine from the sherry district aboard their ships; Shakespeare wrote enthusiastically about the glow it gives, and Sir Francis Drake sank the Spanish fleet near Cádiz and made off with 2,900 barrels of

Preceding pages: the Jerez horse fair. **Left**, Don José Ignacio Domecq, "The Nose". **Right**, barrels marked with the signatures of celebrity owners.

"sack" in 1587. It was not until the 18th century, however, that merchants, most of them from the British Isles, made sherry the world's most widely distributed wine.

Foreign interest: Well over 200 years ago the Gordons, a Catholic family from Scotland, arrived in Cádiz, near Jerez, and set themselves up in the wine trade. Not long afterwards, several Frenchmen established wine businesses in the area. Their names are still synonymous with sherry: Domecq, Pemartín, Lustau, Lacave and Delage.

In 1765, Juan Vicente Vergara y Dickinson, the son of a Basque father and an English or Irish mother, arrived in Puerto de Santa María and entered the wine trade. A great-great-grandson, Javier Vergara, still markets sherry under the label of Juan Vicente Vergara. Although the name Dickinson does not appear on the rosters of sherry producers, the Spanish custom of using the last names of both father and mother has preserved most of the foreign names for posterity. Some have undergone phonetic changes, however, such as Osborne, pronounced *Os-bor-nay*, or Garvey, pronounced *Gar-vay*.

Despite the foreign origins of a great many of the sherry families, they developed over the decades into a very Spanish aristocracy, integrating perfectly. They remained, or became, staunch Roman Catholics, at the same time absorbing tradition and folklore, like the impassioned gypsy music of Jerez, "the cradle of Flamenco". Scions became scholars, military officers, cattle ranchers, gentleman farmers, priests, poets, painters, politicians, even bullfighters. The women became mothers of huge families.

The Domecq dynasty: A bronze bust on a column graces a tiny garden on the Alameda Cristina in Jerez, and behind the bust is the 19th-century Domecq Palace, now used only

Haurie. Pedro Domecq managed to put it, and the sherry business in general, back on its feet, becoming a rich man into the bargain. He was also a pioneer, among sherry producers, in the profitable brandy trade; the most popular Domecq brandy is still labelled "Fundador".

Pedro Domecq ushered in an era of prosperity for Jerez, and Pedro Domecq SA is today a large corporation. Family members do not own the whole business, but a number of Pedro Domecq's numerous descendants still work for the company, including Fernando López de Carrizosa y Domecq, the president; José Ignacio Domecq González, a member of the board, with one of the most

as a VIP residence for official visitors. The bust is dedicated to *El Fundador* (The Founder), Pedro Domecq. He must have been quite a procreator too, for the Domecqs seem to outnumber all the other old sherry families.

Curiously, however, he did not actually found the great winery which bears his name. In the early 19th century a young man named Pedro Domecq, whose family was already living in Jerez, took over a large but failing *bodega* (wine cellar or winery) which had been established by an Irishman, Charles Murphy, in 1730, and had been subsequently inherited by a Frenchman, Juan

expert (and biggest) noses for wine in Jerez; Beltrán Domecq Williams, director of quality control; Manuel Domecq Zurita, the hardworking director-general of public relations, and José Ignacio Domecq Fernández de Bobadilla (son of "The Nose"), deputy technical director.

Alvaro Domecq Romero, a famous *rejoneador* (horseback bullfighter) and bull and horse-breeder, dedicates most of his attention to the Royal Andalucían School of Equestrian Art, of which he is the principal founder and technical director, and to the globe-trotting spectacle which he organised, *The Dancing Horses of Andalucía*. His son,

Alvaro Domecq Díez, and his grandson, Luis Domecq, are also *rejoneadores*. Once, in the ancient bull-ring at the cliff-hanging Andalucían mountain town of Ronda, all three of them took part in the same bullfight.

Not all of the clan form one big happy family. Painter Vicente Cervera, who calls himself Iván Domecq, using the surname of his maternal grandmother, María Domecq Rivero, took a family row to the news media, claiming he was cheated out of a houseful of valuable paintings.

Although of French origin, the Domecq clan, like many of the old sherry families, has always placed considerable emphasis on the ability to speak perfect English. It makes

the highly efficient director-general for Spain of John Harvey & Sons SA, speaks little English in spite of his surname. His children speak it well, however. Beltrán Domecq González, formerly of the big Bodegas Internacionales (where the best bottles are labelled "Duke of Wellington"), speaks the Queen's English impeccably; his charming wife, Anne Williams, does not, contrary to what her name suggests.

Some sherry producers were relative latecomers, like the Terrys, from Cork in Ireland, who got into the business in Puerto de Santa Maria not much more than a century ago. For a long time, their family business prospered, allowing them to establish an

sense, since Great Britain has traditionally been their best customer. Native English-speaking visitors to major *bodegas* are often surprised to find that their hosts, educated at Oxford or some other respected British university, actually speak better English than they do. The Domecq family's conviction of the importance of good English even extends to English schooling for the Madrid-based grandchildren of José Ignacio Domecq González.

All in a name: By contrast, Diego Ferguson,

Left, the Domecq family at home. **Above**, the grape harvest in full swing.

incomparable stable of Carthusian horses. Things went so well that in 1955 the family built an impressive monument to the Sacred Heart in a large porticoed patio surrounded by *bodegas*. The Terrys sold the winery and the horses in 1981. Today, Terry forms part of John Harvey & Sons, and the horses are the property of the state.

The tales of high-living and overprivileged "sherry barons" date mostly from the 19th century, reflecting the wealth which many families in the wine business accumulated from about 1830. Fine mansions were built and life was a whirl of extravagant parties. Before the advent of aeroplanes, good roads and even adequate railways, the "sherry barons" had their suits made by tailors on London's Savile Row, and their wives wore the latest Paris fashions. Landlords with great estates acted like feudal lords when dealing with their employees.

Horse play: A magnificent turn-of-the-century palace designed by the French architect Garnier for sherry-shipper Julian Pemartín (who had to sell it as soon as it was finished because a bank robbery left him penniless) stands, restored, in its original private park, now the grounds of the Royal Andalucían School of Equestrian Art in Jerez. Typical of the flamboyance of another age, it is no longer privately owned. The Andalucían regional government bought it in 1975 from its most recent owners, the family of the Duke of Abrantes.

Feudal though it may have been, the social structure did not go so far as to condone the *droit du seigneur*, with the barons lording it over local ladies; yet there are tales of more than one local girl who found it hard to resist the advances of the influential *señoritos*, who held the key to economic survival for the girls and their families.

In perennially depressed Andalucía, where there has always been a large population of landless farm labourers, dependent for their livelihood the year round on the earnings which they could only make during a few months of the year, the sherry families took to breeding fine horses, playing polo and riding in fancy carriages. Ostentation was one of their capital sins.

Even in relatively recent times, rumours of the extravagances and injustices of wealthy "sherry barons" have persisted. Eccentric behaviour, like that of the late José Domecq de la Riva, who was known as *Pantera* because he reportedly kept a live panther for a pet at his country home, was regarded as sinister by the locals. He also had a life-sized stuffed lion in his vestibule.

The elegant Villamarta Theatre, designed to bring the best performers and the latest shows to the cosmopolitan sherry aristocracy, was built too late. Its doors opened in the budding years of our century, just after the devastating phylloxera scourge arrived, destroying all the vines.

It took more than a decade even to begin to recover, grafting cuttings from the Palomino and Pedro Ximenez varieties on to phyllox-era-resistant root stocks from California.

Tough times: The 20th century was to prove a sobering one for the sherry dynasties. Their almost total dependence on a single market, Britain, led to the virtual collapse of business every time a war or other major disturbance interfered with shipping. Two world wars and the Spanish Civil War of 1936–39 whittled away the remaining riches of the dynasties. Then came the euphoric over-expansion of the 1970s, when most of the smaller *bodegas* were absorbed by larger ones and taken over by multinationals.

Barons or not, the sherry aristocracy did and does sport titles of nobility. *El Fundador* was the first Marquis of Domecq. The present one is Pedro Domecq Hidalgo.

Mauricio González-Gordon y Díez, Vice President of González Byass, is the Marquis of Bonanza. His family's winery, one of only two big ones to remain entirely in Spanish hands, was founded in 1835 by his great-grandfather, Manuel María González Angel, who shortly afterwards established a partnership with a British merchant, Robert Blake Byass. Apart from helping run the *bodega* which markets the biggest-selling *fino* (light dry) sherry in the world, Tio Pepe, Mauricio González-Gordon is an accomplished yachtsman.

One of the most memorable of the sherry aristocrats was the previous Marquis of Bonanza, Manuel María González-Gordon, known affectionately to all Jerez as *El tio Manolo* (Uncle Manolo). Gordon, who died in 1980 at the age of 93, wrote what is still regarded as the most definitive book on the wines of Jerez, entitled simply *Sherry*. His love of his product was epitomised on a small slip of paper under the glass top of his desk in the *bodega*, which said:
I must have a drink at 11.
It's a duty that must be done,
For if I don't have one at 11,
I must have 11 at one!

Tomás Osborne Vázquez, President of Osborne y Cía., is the Count of Osborne. His winery, founded in 1772 by Tomás Osborne Mann, with one *bodega* building which pre-dates the foundation of the company by four years (it was acquired later from Duff-Gordon), is the other big sherry company which is still entirely in Spanish hands, and furthermore entirely in the hands of members of the Osborne family.

José Mariá Ruíz-Mateos y Jiménez de Tejada, a tough businessman who used his family's old and reputable *bodega* in Jerez as the cornerstone on which to build Spain's largest private holding company, was amongst those *jerezanos* who bought a title. Highlights in the zig-zag career of this self-made Marquis of Olivara and Marquis of Montemayor (an Italian title) were the confiscation of his business empire by Spain's Socialist government in 1982 and his election to the European Parliament in 1989.

Business in style: Today's aristocrats are a more subdued breed than their haughty predecessors. With big multinational companies controlling most of the *bodegas*, the carriages, some dating from as early as 1730, together with a priceless collection of saddles and other riding gear from as far back as the 12th century, became the property of the School of Equestrian Art in 1986.

Other perfectly kept carriages are tucked away in buildings in corners of the gardens of the various *bodegas*, and the coach-drivers and footmen remain on the payrolls, practising regularly, ready to put on their fancy working clothes and demonstrate their dying art at the drop of a *mantilla*. But the elegant carriages and teams are no longer the proud possessions of sherry dynasties; they are living relics of a more opulent past.

Typical of leading figures in sherry today

men in charge are all business. The polo grounds at the Chapín Club, where José Ignacio Domecq, now in his seventies, used to play in Jerez, have not seen a match in years, although he and his son, José Ignacio "Junior", still engage in friendly matches at nearby Sotogrande or with Britain's Royal Family and other friends on their visits to the UK. José Ignacio "Senior" rides to the office every day—on a noisy little Guzzi motorbike, not a horse.

Pedro Domecq de la Riva's 35 magnificent thoroughbred Spanish horses and 19

Above, traditional barrel maker at work.

is Manuel Zarraluqui Arana, managing director of Croft Jerez SA, an economist whose association with sherry was on the marketing side in far-off Bristol, in the UK, until International Distillers and Vintners (IDV) sent him to Jerez to create a new *bodega* complex in 1970. He is skilled in international marketing and finance, and one of a new breed.

In these days when *bodega* owners are often multinational companies rather than living, breathing, wine-sipping human beings, the "barons" are as interested in cash flow as in flowing wine, preferring to leave the colour and flavour to their products.

Andalucía covers a lot of Spain, from the peninsula's highest mountains to the golden beaches of the Mediterranean, from dry, scrubby hillsides to lush river valleys. The cooking reflects this diversity. It can be as subtle and refined as a cool sherry sipped in the dappled shade of a grape arbour, as brash as a noisy *tapas* bar, as simple as the aroma of bread baking in wood-fired ovens.

Array of nibbles: The best introduction to authentic Andalucían food in all its diversity is the *tapas* bar, a very special way of life in southern Spain. In a *tapas* bar, wine, sometimes from the barrel, is dispensed along with a huge variety of foods, both hot and cold, which are usually consumed standing at the bar in the company of friends.

Tapas themselves may be as simple as plates of fat, herb-scented olives; toasted almonds; hard-boiled quails' eggs; paper-thin slices of salt-cured, raw *serrano* ham; sliced sausages such as paprika-red *chorizo*, peppery *salchichon*, smoky *longaniza*; aged cheese; prawns in their shells.

Then come *tapas de cocina*, those that are cooked. These include croquettes; batter-dipped prawns; ham rolls stuffed with cheese (*flamenquines*); bite-sized pieces of crisp-fried fish; vegetable fritters. And salads: *pipirrana*, a tomato-onion-pepper relish; *campera*, sliced potatoes, onions and olives in a lemony dressing; *remojón*, an exotic combination of oranges, onions and cod; *pulpo*, diced octopus with tomatoes, garlic and parsley; roasted peppers.

Seafood selections might include *gambas al pil pil*, prawns sizzled with garlic; clams or mussels *a la marinera*; *cazon en adobo*, tangy marinated, fried fish; *boquerones al natural*, fresh anchovies dressed with garlic and vinegar. Other dishes encompass meatballs, rabbit in almond sauce, chicken with garlic, tiny pork cutlets, stewed tripe with *garbanzos*, kidneys in sherry sauce, spicy Moroccan-style kebabs, lamb stew, sautéd mushrooms, and, of course, *tortilla*, a thick

potato omelette. Some *tapas* bars specialise in just a few selections, others may have as many as 40 different dishes, sometimes listed on a blackboard. A *tapa* really is just a nibble—in some bars, served free with a *copa* of wine. Those wanting a larger serving should ask for a *ración*.

The drink of choice is dry *fino*, either sherry or Montilla, both made in Andalucía. These are fortified wines, so the small portions of food serve to temper the effects of the alcohol.

Meal times are late in Andalucía: 2–3 p.m. for the *comida*, or midday meal, which for Spaniards is the main meal of the day, and 9–10 p.m. for the *cena*, evening meal. So *tapas* bars are places to pass a pleasant few hours before dinner.

Other popular eating places are *ventas*, country restaurants serving rustic country food, and *chiringuitos*, shanty restaurants right on the beach. Here you should try *espetones*, fresh sardines speared on sticks and grilled on a fire.

Simple fare: Perhaps it's because Andalucíans like to do their eating standing up that other Spaniards claim Andalucía has no

Preceding pages: fish display at a restaurant on the Costa del Sol. **Left,** sherry, one of the best-known products of Andalucía. **Right,** *tapas*, ready accompaniment to a pre-meal drink.

THE AL-ANDALUS EXPRESS

One doesn't have to be a train enthusiast to enjoy a ride on the Al-Andalus Express, a vintage train which runs between Seville and Málaga. The train itself takes up to 80 passengers at a gentle pace on a circuit of the region, via the cities of Córdoba and Granada; the décor, service, food and wine rival those offered by the Orient Express, but the bonus here must be the stunning landscapes of Andalucía.

The Al-Andalus Express, always heavily booked though by no means cheap, aims to re-create the great and stylish days of rail travel before World War I. It is rather like a modern, which come complete with showers, have also been added.

While passengers sleep on the train itself, they do so when the train is stationary; very little travelling is done after dark.

The décor is matched by the food and the service. Liveried porters handle the luggage on and off, and the restaurant at the rear of the train serves fine Spanish food and wine, with plenty of Andalucían specialities. There is a luxurious bar and a lounge compartment, where huge windows offer splendid views of the passing green and gold countryside.

Two itineraries are available. The first, a two-day return trip from Seville to Málaga, runs up the wide valley of the Guadalquivir and then through the mountains of the Sierra Nevada. Passengers

luxury hotel on wheels, but one built on traditional, even classic lines, using vintage rolling stock.

The restaurant car *Alhambra* and the lounge car *Gibalfera*, for example, were originally built in 1929 and have been carefully restored to their original glory, and most of the other coaches date from between the wars. The bar-coach, *Giralda*, was built in France in 1928 and came to Spain as long ago as 1941. One of the dining cars was built in Britain.

All have been totally renovated since 1985, and marquetry panels, beautiful lamps and seats all re-create the sense and style of the *belle époque*, true to every detail. Modern comforts and beautifully fitted single and double sleeping compartments,

join the train at Seville early in the morning, in time to breakfast on board and enjoy the scenery before arriving at the first stop, Córdoba. Here, professional guides meet the train and take the passengers on a tour of the old Jewish quarter and the Mosque, with breaks for lunch and shopping.

Dinner is taken on the way to Granada, where the train stops for the night, allowing everyone an undisturbed sleep before continuing next day down to the Mediterranean at Málaga, where there is yet more sightseeing before the return journey.

The second route rotates around Seville, particularly focusing on the sherry country of Jerez, with frequent stops to see the sights and (for larger organised groups) to visit the best *bodegas*.

cuisine of merit. In fact, this region arguably has the finest fruits and vegetables, seafood, hams, cheeses, nuts, oil and wine in the country. It is, certainly, simple fare without pretentions, but the subtlety of flavourings, the combinations and the freshness of the raw materials make it special.

Once upon a time Andalucían cuisine was the most extraordinarily refined in all of Europe. The opulent use of spices, herbs, almonds, rose water, orange blossoms and other exotic flavourings is its Oriental heritage, brought by the Moors.

The Arabs brought the first orange trees to Spain. These were bitter oranges, sour as lemons, but wonderful in marmalade. These

or a caliph. Andalucía has also been a land of intense poverty. People learned to exist on the barest essentials and yet still make them palatable. Thus, something as simple as *gazpacho*, the region's well-known cold soup, is both nutritious and delicious, yet is little more than bread, oil, garlic and a few vegetables. Wild rabbit and partridge, free for the taking, were once more common than chicken. Country people foraged for wild asparagus, mushrooms and wild herbs and greens, all of which still play a part in the cuisine.

The basics of Andalucían cooking are olive oil, tomatoes and peppers (both from the New World), garlic and onions together

trees are still used ornamentally everywhere in southern Spain, where their blossoms perfume courtyards and their juice is used in cooking, but the fruit is left to rot. These invaders from the East also contributed rice, saffron, cinnamon, nutmeg, aubergines and many other fruits and vegetables, which thrive in this temperate zone. While northerners were existing on coarse grains and simple gruels, the people of Andalucía were developing cooking into a high art.

Of course, not everybody lived like a king

Left, dining car on the Al-Andalus express. **Above**, universally available *paella*.

with fish on the coast and pork products inland. Potatoes are a staple, either fried as a side dish, or cooked in casserole with other ingredients to make a sturdy main dish. Though Valencia, land of *paella*, is famous for rice, Andalucía actually grows more rice than the Levante. *Garbanzos*, dried beans and lentils, usually cooked with locally made sausages and vegetables, are daily fare.

Andalucía is also known for the quality of its bread, baked fresh daily. In the old days a country family living far from town would bake bread in outdoor clay ovens, little changed since Roman days. Enough bread would be made to last a week. Nothing was ever wasted, explaining why many soups and sauces in Andalucían cookery are thickened not with flour but with stale bread.

Specials: The *cocido*, also called *puchero* or *olla*, is another basic all over Andalucía. Chicken, ham bone, meat, sausages, *garbanzos*, vegetables and potatoes are all cooked together. The broth is served with rice or noodles as a first course, followed by the meat and vegetables. These are home-cooked meals, however, not often found in restaurants.

Andalucían hams are famous. These are called *serrano* or mountain hams, because they're usually made in cool, dry mountain regions. Salt-cured and aged from seven months to several years, they are served raw as an aperitif.

The most appreciated hams are those with surnames, such as *de Jabugo* (Huelva), *de Pedroches* (Córdoba) and *de Trevelez* (Granada), and, in particular, those made of *pata negra*, black-footed, brown Iberian pigs, which roam semi-wild and feed on acorns. Their flesh is incredibly sweet. *Serrano* hams are very expensive.

The sweets of Andalucía, flavoured with aniseed, cinnamon, sesame and bathed in honey, especially show the Moorish influence. Each area has its specialities, some of which are made in convents by nuns who have kept the recipes secret for centuries. One such is *yemas*, sweets rich in egg yolk. In the wine-making regions of Jerez and Montilla, vast quantities of egg whites were once used for the clarification of the new wine. The remaining yolks were donated to the convents, where the nuns devised ways of turning them into sweets.

Tortas are round, flat cakes, studded with aniseed, often eaten for breakfast; *soplillos* are almond macaroons; *huesos de santo* or saint's bones, typical of All Souls' Day, are shaped to look like bones; *borrachuelos*, *pestiños*, and *empanadillas* are fried pastries, dipped in honey or sugar syrup; *polovorones*, *mantecados* and *perrunas* are crumbly biscuits, especially loved at Christmas time, as are *roscos*, ring-shaped biscuits, either fried or baked.

Some specialities, such as *gazpacho*, belong to all of Andalucía. But each province has its own culinary character and part of the fun of travelling is to enjoy the food as well

as the sights. Here's a culinary tour of Andalucía's provinces.

The cook's tour: Seville, cosmopolitan heart of Andalucía, is famous for its olives, served with sherry, but also cooked with meat, chicken and duck. Try, also, the home-cured olives, cracked open and cured in brine with garlic, thyme and fennel. Good Seville dishes are *menudo*, veal tripe; *rabo de toro*, braised ox-tail; *ternera mechada*, beef pot-roast; *huevos a la flamenca*, a flouncy version of eggs baked with ham, peas, asparagus, tomato sauce and *chorizo* sausage; *soldaditos de Pavia*, frittered bits of salt-cod.

This is the city where *tapas* originated, and you'll probably eat better in *tapas* bars than

in most restaurants. Authentic *yemas de San Leandro*, egg yolk sweets, are available only at the monastery of the same name (Plaza San Ildefonso 1). Several other convents also make typical sweets and pastries.

Following the great River Guadalquivir towards the sea, you come to the two Atlantic ocean provinces, Cádiz and Huelva, prodigiously endowed with fabulous seafood. In Huelva try *chocos*, tiny squid stewed with beans; swordfish in saffron sauce; fresh tuna in tomato sauce; skate in paprika sauce. *Mojama*, called the "ham of the sea", is salt-cured dried tuna, served in slivers as an aperitif.

Not everything in Huelva comes from the sea. The province boasts strawberry fields forever, the sweet fruit being exported to Europe. Especially delicious is *lomo de cerdo*, fresh pork loin from Huelva's Iberian pigs. The province also has excellent game and lamb, wild mushrooms and white truffles. The famous *pata negra* hams can be purchased straight from the manufacturers in Jabugo, Cortegana and Cumbres Mayores. Huelva has its own wine region, Condado, producing light white table wines.

Shellfish lovers will discover paradise in Cádiz, both in the city and coastal environs. Here are prawns, lobsters, crabs, oysters, clams, mussels at their freshest. For a real

casserole; *abajá de pescado*, fish stew; *lisa en amarillo*, saffron-tinted mullet. Cádiz has both a "dog" soup, *caldillo de perro*, a fish soup flavoured with sour oranges, and a "cat" soup, laced with garlic.

Not far from Cádiz is Jerez. Sherry, which varies from pale, dry aperitif wines to velvety-smooth dessert wines, is made here by a very special process, the *solera* system of blending. New wines are added to the top barrels and, after a proper rest, are introduced into casks of slightly older wine. Fully matured wine, after several such blendings, is drawn off from the end of the line.

Sherries have a higher alcoholic content than table wines, between 15 and 20 percent.

seafood treat, take a ferry across the bay from Cádiz to Puerto Santa Maria. Here on the promenade facing the port are various *cocederos* and *freiduras*, where you can buy 20 or more kinds of fresh cooked shellfish and fried fish, wrapped in paper cones.

The prawns from nearby Sanlúcar de Barrameda are incomparably sweet; the fried sole tastes as if it had jumped from the sea into the frying pan. Restaurants and *tapas* bars here and in Cádiz proffer myriad fish dishes: *urta a la roteña*, a tasty fish

The dry ones, *fino*, *manzanilla* and *amontillado*, vary from the colour of pale straw to topaz; their flavour is nutty without a trace of sweetness. Richer on the palate are the *olorosos* and *palos cortados*, old gold in colour and velvety in texture. These are also appreciated as aperitif wines. The sweet and cream sherries range from amber to mahogany and are good with biscuits for afternoon tea or with coffee and pastries after a meal.

Sherry is much used in cooking throughout Andalucía. Try *riñones al jerez*, kidneys braised in sherry; mushrooms stewed in sherry, sweetbreads with *oloroso*, chicken sautéd with sherry. Sherry vinegar, available

Left, Jabugo hams, expensive and excellent. **Above**, Jabugitos hanging to dry.

in Jerez and in select supermarkets, has been around for a long time, but is very trendy.

The dessert to try in Cádiz is *tocino del cielo*, tiny squares of dense, rich custard.

Along the Costa: With more than 85 miles (137 km) of coastline, the province of Málaga, too, is famed for its seafood. Try *fritura malagueña*, a mixed fish fry of fresh anchovies, so crisp you can eat them bones and all; try also fried rings of tender squid, prawns, and a piece of a larger fish such as hake. The genius of this cooking is in having the oil at the right temperature, so the fish emerges crisp and golden and still moist.

Other fish dishes are *pescado al horno*, sea bream baked with layers of potatoes, toma-

spaghetti. On the cosmopolitan Costa del Sol, however, you can eat French, Italian, Danish, Thai, Moroccan, Chinese, Indian and more. In fact, you might have to do some determined searching to find authentic Spanish food.

East of Málaga the coastline extends through a stretch of Granada and on to the province of Almería, Andalucía's most eastern region. This is Europe's winter vegetable garden, with miles of plastic-covered fields. Besides seafood and rice dishes, there are stews of vegetables with wheat berries and a paprika-flavoured soup, *pimentón*.

Inland: Granada province varies from the snow-covered peaks of the Sierra Nevada to

toes, onions and peppers; *rape a la marinera* or anglerfish (not in fact rape), sailor's style; and *lubina a la sal*, a whole sea bass baked in a case of coarse salt, which seals in all the juices. Here are superb fish soups, such as *sopa viña AB*, a creamy, sherry-spiked brew, and *cachoreñas*, flavoured with orange.

Besides the standard version of the cold tomato-based soup, *gazpacho*, Málaga has another delightful summer soup, *ajo blanco con uvas*, a tangy white soup made of crushed almonds, garlic and grapes. *Paella* can be ordered at many restaurants and beach bars. A variation is *cazuela de fideos*, seafood, peas and peppers cooked with saffron

the fertile plain to the subtropics of the coast where bananas, custard apples, avocados, mangos and sugar-cane are grown. Almond groves cover the inland hillsides; ground almonds are used as seasoning with rabbit, chicken and fish dishes and in a Granada speciality, *sopa de almendras*, almond soup.

From the Alpujarras, the mountain region, come *serrano* hams, much used in cooking. Try broad beans fried with chunks of ham or fresh trout sautéed with ham. Trout comes from Riofrio, a good place to stop for lunch between Málaga and Granada. The *tortilla sacromonte* is an omelette with bits of ham, sweetbreads, kidneys and peas; *choto al ajillo* is baby kid or lamb cooked with garlic.

A good place to savour typical foods, past and present, is at El Molino in Durcal, halfway between Motril and Granada. Located in a rambling old mill on the banks of a river, the establishment is part restaurant, part Andalucían gastronomic research centre. The menu includes Granada dishes dating from Moorish days as well as peasant dishes of today, such as a soup with wild fennel.

North of Granada are Andalucía's two inland provinces, Jaén and Córdoba. Wheat fields and olive groves dominate the landscape, except where it rises steeply in the north in the Sierra Morena. Here, venison, wild boar, partridge, hare and other game are like a very thick *gazpacho*, served with pieces of ham, and white *gazpacho*, made with almonds and spiked with apples or melon. A *revuelto* is creamy scrambled eggs with wild mushrooms and other vegetables.

The Restaurant Caballo Rojo in Córdoba is another which features the cooking of the Moorish and Sephardic cultures, with dishes such as anglerfish *mozarabe*, with raisins; lamb braised with honey and a touch of vinegar, and Sephardic-style broad beans with herbs. *Pastel cordobes* is a dessert of flaky pastry filled with sweet "angel's hair", candied threads of a melon-like fruit. The town of Puente Genil in the province of Córdoba is a centre for the production of

found. Lamb is excellent in both provinces, usually braised.

In Jaén, *ajoharina* is a delicious way of doing potatoes; *andrajos,* literally "rags", is a game dish with squares of pasta; *perdiz en escabeche* is marinated partridge.

Córdoba is known for its vegetable dishes, especially artichokes, which might be braised with, clams, in a Montilla wine sauce; cardoons, another thistle similar to the artichoke; wild asparagus; and aubergine. Summer specialities are *salmorejo*,

Left, avocados in Europe's winter vegetable garden. **Above**, eating out in Marbella.

dulce de membrillo, quince jelly.

Córdoba province also makes world-class wines, those of Montilla and Moriles, which are made by the same *solera* process as sherry. After visiting one of the *bodegas*, have lunch at Las Camachas in Montilla, a rambling, rustic restaurant on the main highway where the local landed gentry used to dine. You can still get a good *revuelto de trigueros*, eggs scrambled with wild asparagus and mushrooms, or a plate of good ham to accompany your *fino*.

A final word of warning: *menu* in Spanish refers to a fixed price meal; if you want a menu, you must ask for *la carta*.

THE GOOD-TIME COSTA

At the base of the jagged piece of Spain that reaches out towards Africa is the Costa del Sol. Devoid of most of the attributes that normally constitute paradise, this stretch of coast has, nevertheless, managed to persuade the world that this once neglected slice of the Mediterranean is a land of heavenly delights.

The metamorphosis of the section of Andalucían seashore once described by English author Laurie Lee as "beautiful but exhausted… seemingly forgotten by the world" has been such that writer and critic Kenneth Tynan more recently described it as an "inbred and amoral" land of Sodom and Gomorrah. Individuals as diverse as a Germanic prince of minor importance and Britain's longest-serving woman Prime Minister have played their part in its recent development.

Name changes: Back in the 1950s, before the tourist boom exploded along the Spanish Mediterranean, the Costa del Sol was a diffuse title applied to the coastline between Almería province and Gibraltar. Local jealousies and a surge of self-confidence have since persuaded large chunks of this coastline to throw off the blanket term.

To the east of what is now recognised as the Costa del Sol lies the Costa de Almería and the Costa Tropicalia of Granada. To the west is the most recent satellite: Costa Gaditana, the sweep of coast that takes in the desirable development of Sotogrande. Today, the Costa del Sol has shrunk to a 68-mile (110-km) rump of coast pertaining to the province of Málaga.

The precise date of birth of this rough diamond of Spain's monolithic tourist industry has never been recorded. The first signs of life flickered back in the 1920s when Marbella, a dirt-poor fishing village, was popular with British army officers and their families on leave from Gibraltar. During this period, the iron ore mine in the hills behind Marbella was run with British expertise; this handful of mining engineers represented the

Costa del Sol's first resident expatriate community.

Prehistory: The year 1932 is regarded as the turning point in the making of the Costa del Sol. So legend has it, a lady called Carlota Alessandri purchased a piece of barren hillside at Montemar, west of Torremolinos. Asked what she intended to plant there, she replied haughtily: "Plant? I shall plant tourists! This could be the beginning of the Spanish Riviera."

This budding Spanish Riviera died sud-

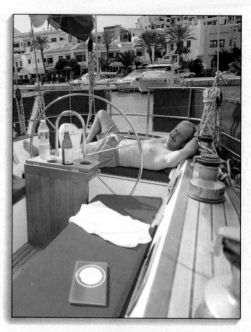

denly in the summer of 1936 when the Spanish Civil War erupted. Those foreign residents unable to flee the conflict under their own steam were scooped up by a Royal Navy destroyer and deposited in the British colony of Gibraltar.

After World War II, the Marquis of Najera, a Spanish nobleman, took up residence in Torremolinos. In his wake came well-to-do Spanish families, and an unusual collection of European diplomats and colonial officials unable or unwilling to adjust to a retirement devoid of constant sunshine. They often considered the regime in their home countries too liberal and soft.

Preceding pages: a nice little boat in Puerto Banus. Left, a wet welcome to the Costa. Right, yachting in the sun is a leisurely pursuit.

The dash of blue blood and large measure of eccentricity brought to the new-born Costa del Sol by these disaffected noblemen and exotic bureaucrats provided an excellent cocktail in which artists, writers, film stars, and their acolytes could flourish. Torremolinos and its environs gained a much-needed niche on the "place-to-be" circuit. These halcyon days probably saw the coining of what has become the Costa del Sol's unofficial motto: "It's not who you are, it's who you say you are that counts."

Centre of the fringe: In the 1960s Torremolinos became the pivot for bohemians who were drawn like moths to the bright lights of the Costa del Sol. The basic requisites of

ance as a mining centre. Spanish nobleman Ricardo Soriano, the Marquis of Ivanrey, introduced his wealthy friends to the village, which he promoted to them as an up-market destination.

The Marquis's nephew, Prince Alfonso von Hohenlohe of Liechtenstein, was so impressed that, on his father's instructions, he bought a decaying farm house and a 24-acre (9.6-hectare) fig tree plantation on the outskirts of the primitive fishing village for £2,000. In 1953 the pudgy prince turned the farmhouse into a hotel, and put up some small bungalows on the land. His rich and titled friends came to stay in droves at the seafront accommodation that Prince Al-

hedonists—wine, drugs and a dive with a sea view—were cheap in T-town, the patronising name this strange fauna gave to a hamlet which had once been proud of its water mills. Among this colourful and cosmopolitan flotsam-and-jetsam swam literary giants like Ernest Hemingway and James Michener, the American novelist who based his book *The Drifters* on characters plucked from amongst the Costa del Sol's lotus-eaters.

While Torremolinos throbbed with life on the lunatic fringe, further down "The Coast" (as the Costa became known in trendy circles), Marbella began to lose its import-

fonso named the Marbella Club.

It was the opening of the Marbella Club that attracted the "café society" to the now snobbish Costa del Sol. This exclusive tag was secured by a stream of famous visitors that included King Leopold of the Belgians, the Duke and Duchess of Windsor, Gina Lollobrigida, Sophia Loren and the crooner Frank Sinatra.

Not all the beautiful people were just passing through. A curious selection took up residence, living off the Coast's flamboyant image. Still the finest specimens of the Costa del Sol's jet-set contingent are maverick Spanish nobleman and ageing rake Don

Jaime de Mora y Aragon, and Gunilla von Bismarck, a descendant of the Iron Chancellor. The monocled, immaculately dressed Don Jaime, who once eked out a living playing the piano at the Marbella Club, and the imposing, flaxen-haired Gunilla, who has made self-promotion an art form, have been the essential guests at Costa del Sol "happenings" for the past two decades.

Bucket stops: Inevitably, the rest of the world refused to be left out of the fun and frivolity that engulfed the "Sun Coast", and so between Torremolinos and Marbella a string of bucket-and-spade resorts sprang up to cater for the deluge of package tourists who had to come to the Costa del Sol to see

tates, discovered they had neighbours who sat around their swimming pools and talked wistfully of the East End, Eindhoven or Essen.

In the 1970s two events occurred which completed the Costa del Sol's evolution from up-market tourist destination and occasional retreat for the weird or wealthy to international playground that is monotonously dubbed the California of Europe: the 1973 oil crisis and Middle East turmoil persuaded many rich Arabs to seek safer havens for their sudden riches; and in 1979, Margaret Thatcher swept to power in Britain.

Arabs and Brits: The Arab invasion of the Costa del Sol was led by King Fahd of Saudi

for themselves if the place was for real.

Increasing numbers of these holidaymakers decided that the Costa del Sol was to be their playground too. To cater for the demand in sunshine homes for sun-starved northern Europeans, concrete wedding cakes that blocked out the sky sprang up on the seashore, and instant Andalucían villages spread like measles across the hinterland. The fortunate few who had sat around their swimming pools and talked wistfully of lost thrones, fading empires or forfeited es-

Arabia. Accompanied by an entourage of 60 relatives and minions, he set up home just down the road from the Marbella Club in a multi-million dollar palace which was built to resemble the White House in Washington. The complex comes complete with mosque and heliport.

Among the Arab multimillionaires to encamp on the Costa del Sol was Adnan Khashoggi, a Saudi Arabian arms merchant whose obscene banquets and outrageous fiestas actually managed to offend the jaundiced tastes of the Costa del Sol's home-grown debauchees. His sumptuous yacht moored in Puerto Banus did, however, draw

<u>Left</u>, **Prince Hohenlohe, founder of the Marbella Club.** <u>Above</u>, **Danish bar on the Costa.**

droves of tourists to the kitsch marina, and his need of a public relations officer kept Don Jaime de Mora y Aragon in the manner to which he had become accustomed. Caddishly, Khashoggi's fair-weather friends and apologists on the Coast remained silent when Khashoggi was indicted in the United States on charges of embezzlement.

The Costa del Sol had always been popular with the British even before Mrs Thatcher was first elected prime minister in 1979. But it was her removal of exchange controls that allowed thousands of Britons to invest their golden handshake, black money or red-hot cash in a little place in the sun. These prosperous sentinels of the Thatcher revolution

laid claim to large swathes of the Costa del Sol. They helped shove the Spaniards into the minority in Costa townships like Mijas, where Spanish is spoken only by the maid or the gardener on sprawling developments such as Miraflores and Calahonda.

Crooks on the Costa: If it was Arab and British money that cemented the Costa del Sol into its present position as an international investment centre, it was the Costa del Sol's proximity to the cannabis plantations in Morocco's Rif Mountains, and the absence of an extradition treaty between Spain and Britain that helped the coast gain the dubious title of the Costa del Crime.

Nobody asks where you made your money on the Costa. The British police estimate that there are 300–400 fugitives from British justice on the coast, plus a further 600 from the rest of Europe.

The fortunes generated by drug trafficking have seen the growth of a sophisticated extension of the European underworld. A booming local economy and the ease with which a foreign face goes undetected aid the crooks that haunt the Costa; in addition, the hostility of nearby Gibraltar to the local Spanish authorities proves a stumbling block to solving many crimes and gathering valuable evidence.

The snatch in the late 1980s by French gangsters of Melodie Nackachian, a fragile creature of Lebanese-Korean parentage, as she was being chauffeured to her posh English school in Marbella, demonstrated how deeply foreign mafias had infiltrated the community. For an entire week, hundreds of Spanish police combed the "Costa del Kidnap" while the world's press highlighted this unhappy episode in the chronicles of earthly paradise. The huge police drag net that eventually rescued the child from her tormentors also flushed out other international delinquents like a Yugoslav gunman wanted for various murders in four European countries. The Spanish government's response was to reinforce the Coast's over-stretched police with detectives trained to hunt down foreign criminals.

Even so, in early 1990 a man on a bicycle was able to ride up to the Marbella villa of ex-train robber Charlie Wilson, calmly ring the bell, wander in and shoot Wilson beside his swimming pool. The assassin then disappeared without trace in the bent town of Marbella.

Despite constant tales of bank robbers and drug barons living it up in their sunny hideaways, of property sharks defrauding pensioners, of drug-crazed muggers preying on paraplegic tourists, the Costa del Sol's reputation as a good-time girl who is kind to everyone remains intact. It is perhaps the fusion of fact and fantasy that makes the Costa del Sol so alluring. The Costa del Sol is, after all, whatever you want her to be.

Left, Gunilla von Bismarck, a veteran socialite and party hostess. Right, Torremolinos water chute, for when the beach palls.

PLACES

The autonomous region of Andalucía is Spain's most populous, with 6.5 million inhabitants in its eight southernmost provinces. The area it covers is huge, totalling 34,700 sq. miles (89,800 sq. kms), an area the size of Portugal and twice the size of the Netherlands.

Within these confines the variety of landscape is tremendous. To the north is the long ridge of the Sierra Morena, a mountain range that effectively seals the region off from the rest of Spain, where the rich *sevillanos* go hunting; to the south is the Costa del Sol, playground of foreigners, where Europe's worst mix with Europe's best. In the centre lies the flat agricultural plain of the Guadalquivir. To the east are the arid desert lands of Almería and the mountains of Granada, and to the west the marshlands of the Coto Doñana nature reserve. On the horizon from almost anywhere is North Africa, whose influence is felt in the history and the towns of this southernmost region of Spain and of Europe.

Each of Andalucía's old cities, Seville, Córdoba and Granada, has a major Moorish monument of world significance: in Seville it is the Giralda, in Córdoba the Mezquita and in Granada the Alhambra. But others have their claims to fame: Cádiz, the home of the Armada and the signing of the first Spanish constitution: Ronda, the birthplace of bullfighting; Huelva, Columbus's stepping-off point for the New World. In the province of Almería the landscape is so jagged and surreal that film directors have fallen over each other to shoot their westerns there; nearby Jaén is the undulating, soft heartland of the olive growing industry, and has been for centuries.

Here too are mile upon mile of urbanisation, ranging from the most select villas of Marbella to the worst excesses of Torremolinos tower blocks, where Spanish is a minority language. And tacked to the bottom of Andalucía, like a plug on the bottom of Europe, is Gibraltar, for long the source of much dispute between Spain and Great Britain, and no doubt long to remain so.

Distances between provinces and cities are not enormous, but travel times may well be longer than expected, either because of the poverty of the roads, which can deteriorate quickly, or because of the weight of traffic, particularly in the coastal areas. But this is not the place for being in a hurry; it's too hot, and, besides, you might miss something if you go too fast. Take it gently—at the pace of the pages of this book.

Preceding pages: fiesta girl in Seville's Plaza España; tile panel from Seville encouraging early tourism; tourist retreat on the Costa del Sol. **Left,** looking down on the city of Jaén.

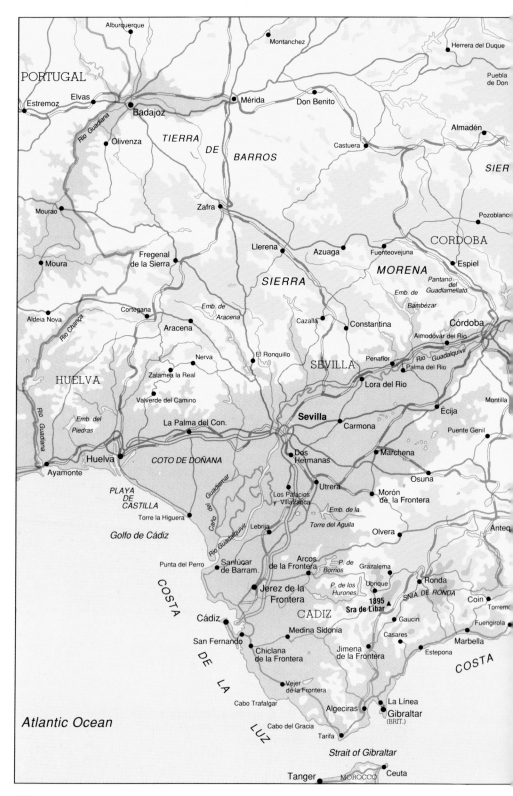

Alburquerque

Montanchez

Herrera del Duque

PORTUGAL

Estremoz   Elvas   Mérida   Don Benito

Badajoz

Puebla
de Don

Almadén

Rio Guadiana   Olivenza   Castuera

TIERRA   DE

SIER

Mourão   BARROS

Pozoblanc

Zafra

Moura   Fregenal   Llerena   Azuaga   Fuenteovejuna   CORDOBA
de la Sierra

Espiel

MORENA

SIERRA   Pantano
del
Aldeia Nova   Cortegana   Emb. de   Guadlamellato

Rio Chanza   Emb. de   Cazallá   Bambézar
Aracena
Aracena   Constantina   Córdoba

Nerva   El Ronquillo   Almodóvar del Rio

Zalamea la Real   SEVILLA   Penaflor   Rio   Guadalquivir

HUELVA   Palma del Rio
Valverde del Camino   Lora del Rio
Montilla
Emb. del   La Palma del Con.   Sevilla   Écija
Piedras   Carmona
Rio   Puente Genil
Guadiana   Huelva   COTO DE DOÑANA   Dos   Marchena
Hermanas
Ayamonte   Osuna

PLAYA   Utrera   Morón
DE   de la Frontera   Anteq
CASTILLA   Torre la Higuera   Los Palacios
y Villafranca   Emb. de la   Olvera
Golfo de Cádiz   Lebrija   Torre del Aguila

Punta del Perro   Sanlúcar   Arcos   P. de   Ronda
de Barram.   de la Frontera   Bornos   Grazalema
COSTA   P. de los   Ubrique   Coin
Jerez de la   Hurones   SNIA. DE RONDA
Frontera   1895   Torreno
Cádiz   CADIZ   Sra de Libar   Gaucin
Fuengirola
Medina Sidonia   Casares
DE   San Fernando   Marbella
Chiclana   Jimena   Estepona
de la Frontera   de la Frontera
LA   Vejer   COSTA
Cabo Trafalgar   de la Frontera
Atlantic Ocean   LUZ   Cabo del Gracia   Algeciras   La Línea
Gibraltar
Tarifa   (BRIT.)

Strait of Gibraltar

Tanger   MOROCCO   Ceuta

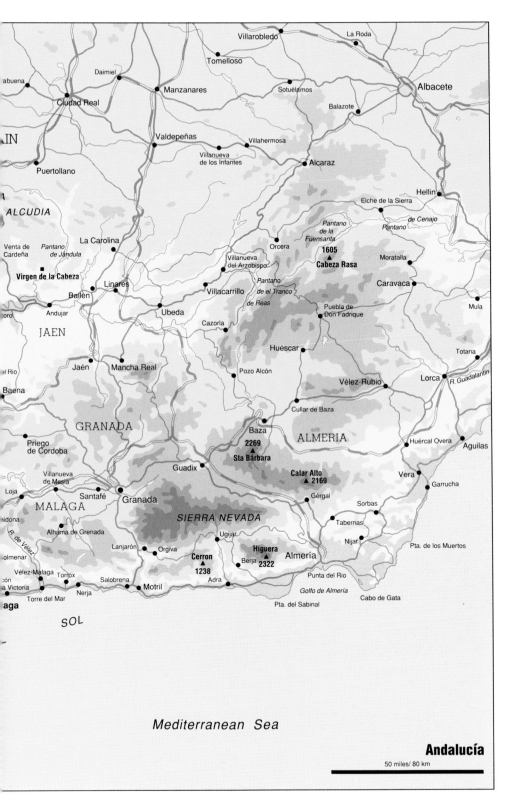

Villarobledo
La Roda
Tomelloso
Daimiel
Manzanares
Sotuélamos
Albacete
abuena
Ciudad Real
Balazote
IN
Valdepeñas
Villahermosa
Villanueva
de los Infantes
Alcaraz
Puertollano
Hellin
Elche de la Sierra
ALCUDIA
de Cenajo
Pantano
de la
Fuensanta
Pantano
Venta de
Cardeña
Pantano
de Jándula
La Carolina
Orcera
1605
Cabeza Rasa
Moratalla
Villanueva
del Arzobispo
Virgen de la Cabeza
Linares
Villacarrillo
Pantano
de el Tranco
de Reas
Caravaca
Bailén
Andujar
Ubeda
Puebla de
Don Fadrique
Mula
oro
Cazorla
JAEN
el Rio
Jaén
Mancha Real
Pozo Alcón
Huéscar
Totana
Baena
Vélez-Rubio
Lorca
R. Guadalantin
Cullar de Baza
GRANADA
Baza
ALMERIA
Huércal Overa
Priego
de Cordoba
2269
Sta Bárbara
Aguilas
Villanueva
de Mesia
Guadix
Calar Alto
2169
Vera
Loja
Santafé
Gérgal
Garrucha
MALAGA
Granada
Sorbas
hidona
Tabernas
Alhama de Grenada
SIERRA NEVADA
Nijar
Pta. de los Muertos
R. de Vélez
Ugijar
Lanjarón
Orgiva
Higuera
Almería
olmenar
Cerron
2322
Vélez-Malaga
Torrox
Berja
1238
Adra
Punta del Rio
cón
Salobrena
a Victoria
Nerja
Motril
Golfo de Almería
Cabo de Gata
aga
Torre del Mar
Pta. del Sabinal
SOL

Mediterranean Sea

Andalucía

50 miles/ 80 km

139

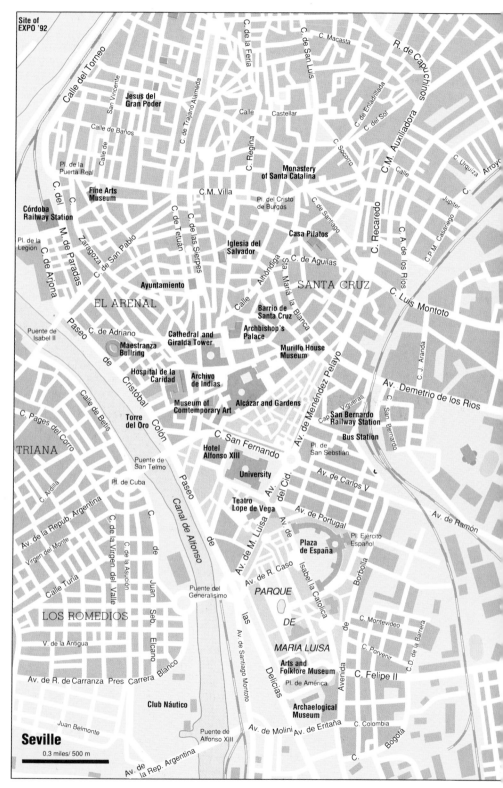

Site of EXPO '92

Calle del Torneo

San Vincente

Jesus del Gran Poder

Calle de Baños

Calle de

C. de Trajano Alameda

C. de la Feria

C. de San Luis

C. Macasta

R. de Capuchinos

Calle

Castellar

C. de Enladrillada

C. del Sol

C.M. Auxiliadora

C. Urquiza

Arroyo

Pl. de la Puerta Real

C. del

C

M. de Paradas

Zaragoza

C. de San Pablo

C. de las Sierpes

C. de Tetuan

Fine Arts Museum

Córdoba Railway Station

Pl. de la Legión

C. de Arjona

C.M. Villa

Pl. del Cristo de Burgos

C. Regina

C. Socorro

Monastery of Santa Catalina

Calle

C. del Sol

C.P.M. Casariego

C.

Jupiter

Casa Pilatos

C. de Santiago

C. Recaredo

C. A. de los Rios

Iglesia del Salvador

Almóndiga

Sta. María la Blanca

C. de Aguilas

SANTA CRUZ

C. Luis Montoto

Ayuntamiento

EL ARENAL

Calle

Barrio de Santa Cruz

Archbishop's Palace

Puente de Isabel II

Paseo

C. de Adriano

Cathedral and Giralda Tower

Maestranza Bullring

Hospital de la Caridad

Archivo de Indias

Murillo House Museum

C.J. Aranda

de

Cristóbal

Museum of Contemporary Art

Alcázar and Gardens

Av. Demetrio de los Rios

TRIANA

C. Pages del Corro

Calle de Belis

Torre del Oro

Colón

C. de Menéndez Pelayo

Cap

Vigueras

San Bernardo Railway Station

Bus Station

San Bernardo

C. Ardilla

Puente de San Telmo

Pl. de Cuba

Hotel Alfonso XIII

C. San Fernando

Pl. de San Sebstián

Av. de la Repub. Argentina

Virgen del Monte

C. de la Virgen del Valle

C. de la Asución

C.

de

Juan

Seb.

Elcano

University

Teatro Lope de Vega

Av. del Cid.

Av. de M. Luisa

Av. de Carlos V

Av. de Portugal

Pl. Ejército Español

Av. de Ramón

Calle Turia

Canal de Alfonso

de

Puente del Generalisimo

Plaza de España

Isabel la Catolica

Borbolla

LOS ROMEDIOS

V. de la Antigua

PARQUE

DE

de

C. Montevideo

C. Porvenir

C. D. de la Barrera

Av. de R. de Carranza

Pres

Carrera

Blanco

Av. de Santiago Montoto

MARIA LUISA

Arts and Folklore Museum

Pl. de América

Deliċias

Avenida

C. Felipe II

Club Náutico

Archaelogical Museum

C. Colombia

Juan Belmonte

Puente de Alfonso XIII

Av. de Molini

Av. de Eritaña

Bogotá

C.

Seville

0.3 miles/ 500 m

Av. de la Rep. Argentina

SEVILLE AND ITS PROVINCE

If Andalucía is the embodiment of the Spanish clichés of flamenco, gypsies, fiestas and bullfights, then Seville, its capital city, is logically its heart; after all, this was the home of Carmen, the lover Don Juan and Figaro, the Barber of Seville. But this city is not extrovert outside its principal fiestas, despite a notice in a Seville bar which forbids patrons from bursting into song or breaking into dance.

Seville was once known as the Great Babylon of Spain; today its plazas are dripping with orange trees, its *bodegas* stacked high with barrels of *fino* and its bars hung with Jabugo hams looking like fleshy bats. But outside the tourist season modern Seville seems to have got tired of the clichés: it is comparatively quiet, thoughtful, and under-visited. There is no super-abundance of places to sit and watch the world go by, the food is nothing remarkable and the flamenco performances are not as magnificent as perhaps they ought to be. Nevertheless this is as rewarding a city as any, anywhere in the world.

Glory and decay: Although it had long existed as a settlement, the Romans first put the city they called Hispalis on the map. In their wake came the Moors, whose various rival factions tried to outdo each other by embellishing their city with palaces.

Seville reached its richest and busiest in the 15th and 16th centuries when it functioned as the major gateway to the New World discovered by Columbus. The treasure ships landed their cargoes on wharves on the side of the Guadalquivir, and the plunder passed through the royal counting house and into the treasury coffers.

At the time Seville, with a population of 85,000, of whom 7,000 were slaves, was probably the fourth largest city in the world, after Naples, Paris and Venice. The ships departed and returned in convoys (in 1608 there were 283 sailings from Seville to the New World), thus creating periods of great activity and great inactivity. It was during the inactivity that chaos ruled.

Seville had an underworld whose gangs were always at each other's throats. Such was the wealth passing through—and being filtered off by—the city that corruption was common, and the justice system was the cause of endless complaints to the king in Madrid. In the jails the condemned included clerics penalised for forgery and sodomy; city records keep details of the executions. A man convicted of bestiality was burned and his donkey (his partner in the act) hanged; a condemned Moor on the gallows complained bitterly that a tavern still owed him half a flagon of wine, and he didn't want to leave this world before he'd collected the debt.

The streets were full of people with no particular employment but plenty of work—if they were prepared to do it. *Regatones* (street-hawkers) and *progerones* (vendors) were at every corner. The *progerones* were licensed to sell on the behalf of individual members of the

irl in the
ty of
armen.

public and thus functioned as the city's pawnbrokers; the *regatones* sold parts of cargoes that hadn't necessarily followed their legitimate path. It is these street scenes in particular that are recorded by one of Seville's best-known artists, Bartolomé Murillo, whose work is on show at many locations in the modern city.

The river brought good and bad. With the gold on the ships came disease, and in bad epidemics up to 600 people died every day. But the trade couldn't go on for ever and eventually a combination of increasing ship size, increased river silt, improvement of facilities at Cádiz at the river mouth and a decreasing flow of desirable goods from America dragged the business down. Seville lapsed into a quiet, almost provincial, country town.

Not a lot has happened since. For a city of 645,000, Spain's fourth largest, it is a surprisingly quiet place, perhaps best known for its annual fiestas of the Spring Feria (fair) and Semana Santa (Holy Week).

Landmarks: A visitor to Seville intent on seeing most of its attractions needs a keen sense of direction. This narrow-streeted city is confusingly built, and it is easy to stumble upon a landmark without any prior warning. Moreover, in the ultimate gesture of romanticism, many of the maps show the Guadalquivir as a river flowing through the city. This is not so: after centuries of flooding, the river was finally diverted earlier this century and its original course blocked with a causeway near the Córdoba railway station; the stretch of water in the city is actually the Canal de Alfonso XIII and does not flow. The diversion of the river not only saved the city from floods but has also enabled Seville to continue to function as a surprisingly large sea-port (wharves just beyond the Parque de Maria Luisa).

However, by 1992 those maps which are currently romantic but wrong will be right, and those which are boringly correct will be wrong. As part of their preparations for Expo'92, which is hosted by Seville, the city authorities are digging up the causeway and the river will be restored to its old route.

Visitors to Seville prior to 1992 will find many parts wrapped up. Underneath the tarpaulins restoration is under way to ensure that everything looks its resplendent best when the world and its media arrive *en masse*.

Fertile ground: The biggest and best of the monuments are located in a small band of the city stretching from the Cathedral southwards down to the Parque de Maria Luisa and the Plaza de America. This band of history is one of the most rich, densely packed and varied of city centres in the world.

The **Cathedral** (Santa Maria de la Sede) is in the *Guinness Book of Records* simply for being big, but the close-packed streets that surround it make it hard to appreciate the building as a whole from the outside. Perhaps it is appropriate thus, for the building is composed of different structures from different eras, and its immensity is best appreciated from within.

A faded photocopy of the *Guinness Book of Records* certificate sits in the glass information case alongside the Cathedral's floor plan: 413 ft (126 metres) long by 272 ft (83 metres) wide by 100 ft (30.5 metres) high, Sta Maria has the largest interior in the world, and is the third largest cathedral overall in Christendom, after St Peter's in Rome and St Paul's in London. The immensity of this inner area may not instantly be apparent, however, both because of the gloom and because the centre of the building is occupied by the choir (*coro*) and Capilla Mayor, which reduce the open space and prevent any real impression of the building's shape.

It is worth visiting the Cathedral at least twice: once in the morning at around 9 a.m. when the Capilla Mayor is illuminated and in use, the cathedral roof echoing with the dim voices of the red-robed clerics. At this time most of the gleaming nuggets around the walls will be in darkness, but the huge golden altarpiece or *retablo* (begun in 1482 by Flemish sculptor Pieter Dancart) at the back of the Capilla Mayor is at its best. The altarpiece, which is of gilded hardwood, contains 36 tableaux of the life of

The Giralda, Seville's Moorish minaret.

Christ and measures 66 ft (20 metres) in height, almost to the roof.

Best of the parts: You will have to revisit, however, to see the Cathedral's other qualities, and the whole is not as beautiful as the sum of its parts. On the northern side of the building, the **Patio de Los Naranjos** (viewed from an entrance from the street) is still, as its name suggests, filled with orange trees. This, with the Giralda tower, is the most accessible evidence of the original Moorish mosque (built in 1172) that preceded the Cathedral on this site. The bulk of the present Cathedral was built between 1401 and 1507; thus the principal structure is Gothic, with additions in the shape of the *coro*, altar and Sacristia de los Calices, which are late Gothic (1496–1537); the Capilla Real (1530–69) at the eastern end is plateresque and further additions to the southern end are baroque.

Various exhibits are open to the public; these include a wealth of silverware within the treasury (**Sacristia Mayor**), a rather grand and gloomy chapel with display areas on either side. The **Sacristia de los Calices** (with a very pretty arched roof) contains an exhibition of paintings including works by Goya, Valdés Leal and Zurbarán, although these are not labelled.

Beyond exhibitions of illustrated manuscripts and clerical vestments from the 18th century is the **Sala Capitular**, recently restored but still sadly neglected. This is the most glorious and unusual of rooms, built in elliptical shape with leather seats and marble floor specifically for the purpose of hosting the meetings of the Cathedral Council. But the stucco from its ceiling is falling off and the lighting is less than flattering.

At the eastern end is the **Capilla Real** (Royal Chapel), the most used and most ornate of the side chapels, with the tombs of Alfonso X and Ferdinand III.

Next to the southern entrance is the grand but rather comic monument to Christopher Columbus, the great man's tomb carried by four papier mâché figures who represent the four kingdoms

The Barrio de Santa Cruz.

that made up the Spanish crown at the time of his voyage—Castile, Navarre, Aragón and León. Columbus is not buried here, but his body was moved here briefly after returning from Cuba.

Literally and figuratively, the highspot of the Cathedral has to be the tower, that much-photographed, much-imitated 308-ft (94-metre) minaret which is and has been locally admired ever since its inception at the orders of Moorish ruler Abu Yacub Yusuf in 1184. The Giralda is said to be the best relic of the Maghreb dynasty anywhere in the world and was held in such esteem by the Moors that they wanted to destroy it rather than let it fall into the hands of the Christians. Every museum or gallery in Andalucía seems to have a painting of the Giralda, every souvenir shop has a model, every town an imitation: it is Seville's Eiffel Tower, and it probably deserves the affection it gets if just for its history and its view.

Two different hands are clearly at work in its construction: the lower part is the original Moorish tower, most of which was destroyed in an earthquake in 1356. The Giralda was then rebuilt by Hernan Ruiz in 1558, and topped by the figure of Faith with her shield standing on a globe which rotates with the wind (a duplicate is currently in the northwestern corner of the Cathedral, and very bizarre it looks at ground level). Whatever you make of the Giralda from below, you have to walk up the ramps within it (designed so that horsemen could ascend) to look out over the city, particularly as this affords a rare opportunity of relating one Seville landmark to another. This was once the site of the first public clock in Spain (*c*.1400), and today's bells make a dreadful row. From here you can see the full immensity of the Cathedral, which is more visually interesting from above than it is from the side.

Granada's rival: The second architectural triumph of the Moors in Seville is within striking distance of the Giralda, hidden behind imposing battlemented ochre walls. Much of the older part of the **Alcázar** was built by Pedro the

Town houses and tower by the Cathedral.

LEGENDS OF THE GUADALQUIVIR

In the misty past a king named Gargoris ruled a land near the edge of the world. Ashamed when one of his daughters gave birth as a result of incest, he ordered the baby boy abandoned in the wilderness. But the wild animals tended and fed the helpless creature. Later, when the boy was tossed in the sea, he floated safely ashore where he was adopted by a deer and grew up fleet of foot. Finally, the king accepted the boy as his son and heir and named him Habis. Habis proved a good and civilising king, and his successors ruled in Tartessus for many centuries.

So goes the legend, one of the many centred around Andalucía's long history. Habis may never have existed, but Tartessus certainly did. The name has been attached to a river, a city and a kingdom famed for its wealth.

Although historians, archaeologists and other researchers have argued interminably about its exact whereabouts, it seems clear that 3,000 years ago Tartessus flourished somewhere on the coast between the Straits of Gibraltar and modern Huelva. The most likely location for the city was near the mouth of the Guadalquivir river. This possibility was strengthened in 1958 by the unearthing at El Carambolo, near Seville, of a treasure hoard, consisting of 21 large pieces of gold jew-

ellery. Experts claim that this dates from the era of Arganthonios, a king of Tartessus who, according to the historian Herodotus, lived 120 years and died in about 550 BC.

References are frequent in the Bible to Tarshish, the Hebrew name for Tartessus. Chapter Nine, Second Chronicles, relates: "For the king's ships went to Tarshish with the servants of Hiram: every three years once came the ships of Tarshish bringing gold, and silver, ivory, and apes, and peacocks." Copper, gold and silver undoubtedly came from the sierra of Huelva, where the Rio Tinto mines are still worked. The Tartessians sought tin to forge bronze, sailing north as far as the southwestern corner of Britain. According to Greek mythology, the legendary hero Hercules travelled to Tartessus. One of his Twelve Labours

was to steal the cattle of Gerion, the three-bodied giant, from an island in "the far west", said to be in the Tartessus river. A Temple of Hercules once existed on a small island just off the coast at Sancti Petri, south of Cádiz, and Hannibal is believed to have consulted the priests there before his elephant march over the Alps.

Ancient myth and history interweave in Andalucía and particularly along the 400 miles (660 km) of the Guadalquivir.

One of the first bridges the river passes under is said to have been built in one night, while Queen Isabella slept, so that she would not wet her feet on the march to conquer Granada. Lower in their course the waters idle under the Puente del Obispo on the Baeza–Jaén highway, where an inscription notes that the Bishop of Mondoñedo paid for it in 1518 and promises "to those who pass over it and say an Ave María in honour of the Virgin he concedes 40 days' remission of their sins".

In Córdoba province, the Guadalquivir curves around the well-preserved Almodovar castle. The bats that flutter at twilight around the battlements are said to be the spirits of those who suffered there, crying unheard pleas for mercy.

Legend says that the Torre del Oro (tower of gold), which commands the river in the centre of Seville, acquired its name through King Pedro the Cruel's obsession for a beautiful woman with magnificent golden tresses. The king seized her from the convent where her husband had left her while he was away at war, and locked her in the tower. She tried to destroy her beauty by cutting off her hair and seeking to ruin her face with acid. The enraged monarch forced his attentions on her, then sent her back to the convent to die. Her husband, seeking revenge, joined Pedro's brother in bloody rebellion.

The Coto Doñana, a marshland at the mouth of the river that became a royal hunting ground, is associated with one of Goya's most famous paintings. While staying in the old Coto palace, the artist allegedly painted *The Naked Maja,* using as a model his lover, the Duchess of Alba. The evidence is slender, however; moreover, the naked Duchess would have found it difficult to remain still for long with so many mosquitoes around.

Cruel in 1366 (who, among other things, murdered some of his guests), in Mudéjar style. It architecture echoes the Alhambra in Granada, although additions have been made since (including kitchens built specially for General Franco's visits). The *azulejos* or wall tiles are at their best here; opinions vary on the source of the name *azulejo*, which some say derives from the over-riding use of blue (azul) in the tiles, but others claim derivation from the arabic *al zulaich*, meaning small stone. Whatever their origin, their impact is un-doubted and many a visitor is silenced by the delicacy of the work here.

The palace fronts the inner courtyard (Patio de la Monteria). On the right-hand side is an **audience hall** and chapel founded by Queen Isabella in 1503; the audience hall has various 18th-century paintings depicting the overthrow of the Moors. In the **chapel** (fine artesonado ceiling) the altar paint-ing has a nautical theme appropriate to the rooms, which were specifically built for the planning of naval expeditions. A

figure hidden in the Virgin's skirts is supposedly Columbus.

The main entrance to the Moorish palace is surmounted by an inscription to Pedro the Cruel. Inside (turn left) it is the *azulejos* that dominate the eye, and make every room, although bare, look different and richly furnished. The en-tranceway leads into the **Patio de las Doncellas** (maids of honour), the cen-tral courtyard which gives access to the other rooms. Tiled and pillared in simi-lar fashion to the main patio at Granada, this courtyard has a more compact grace and quieter beauty.

Notable in the apartments are the **Ambassador's Hall**, the biggest of the side rooms, which has a domed roof (unfortunately dimly lit) and superb geometric and floral carvings on the walls. The hall has often been featured by the Moroccan film industry. Beyond is the small **Patio de las Muñecas** (dolls), which was the private gathering place of the family and is named after two tiny faces at the foot of one of the arches; the faces have been eroded by

time and are now rather more sinister than pretty.

The Catholic kings also made their mark on the Alcázar in a style which is more familiar, notably in the Charles V apartments, built at Charles's behest. These are located down the covered walkway that leads off to the left of the Patio de la Monteria and across the inner garden. Underneath the walkway are the baths of Maria Padilla, mistress of Pedro the Cruel, who herself is said to have had several lovers. Men of the court lined up for the strangely erotic act of drinking her bathwater—all except one who excused himself on the grounds that "having tasted the sauce, he might covet the partridge".

The decor of the **Charles V apartments** seems clumsy in comparison with the Moorish craftsmanship elsewhere. The tapestries (which depict Charles's expedition to Tunisia) are much faded; they were completed in 1554 by the Dutch artist Vermayen, who included a self-portrait in his upside-down map of the Mediterranean.

Return to the walkway for access to the Alcázar's **gardens**, which display characteristic features of Moorish design, including fountains, fish ponds, box hedges and small orange groves. These gardens are a welcome oasis in a city which is sadly under-supplied with places to sit and watch the world go by.

Pretty cliché: The northeastern wall of the Alcázar borders on the **Barrio de Santa Cruz** or former Judería (Jewish quarter), entered by a forbidding little archway in one corner of the Patio Banderas. This corner of Seville maintains some of the expected cliché: the Seville *patio* is here in superabundance, with courtyards decorated with *azulejos* visible through wrought-iron gates; here young men play and sing flamenco in the small squares. In the summer the narrow, white-washed streets are cool and as quiet as on a Sunday morning until the bars and restaurants fill up in late afternoon.

Complainants will say that Santa Cruz, with its carefully tended squares and hanging baskets, is overly prettified, but it remains the best place to be on a summer evening. Look out for the **Bazaar Isbilia** (Calle Ximenez de Enciso) with its odd mix of Moroccan, Spanish, Thai and other cheap but interesting gifts; the **Murillo House Museum** is a reconstruction of the sort of house the artist would have lived in, but is not very captivating.

The Plaza de Santa Cruz is the site of the best known of the three traditional flamenco venues in town, **Los Gallos.** Out of the host of shops for tourists in this quarter, perhaps the most atmospheric is Antonio Linares's souvenir shop on Plaza Allianza, which contains a bizarre and extensive collection of junk and quality antiques.

Monuments: Between the Alcázar and the Cathedral is a square, rather unappealing, sober building, once the **Lonja** or stock exchange, which now houses the **Archivo General de Indias**. This collection comprises some 38,000 folders of documents relating to the discovery of the New World and the establishment and rule of Spanish colonies. Although it is not instantly obvious from

Tile in the Seville Alcázar.

the outside (go up the marbled staircase and fill in the visitors' book), a small exhibition is maintained in one of the long galleries, while elsewhere academics study the bulk of the documents. The exhibition usually includes a page or two from Columbus's diary or letters.

Alongside the Lonja in Calle Santo Tomás (barely noticeable entranceway) is the **Museum of Contemporary Art**, which features work principally by artists from Andalucía. The last room at the top contains the best of a patchy collection, particularly some fine Sevillian ceramics by Francisco Cortijo.

On the other side of the Puerta Jerez roundabout at the southern end of the Avenida de la Constitución is the **Hotel Alfonso XIII**, a pompous, luxurious, old-fashioned hotel with uniformed, autocratic staff. The hotel was built in imitation of the Seville *patio* style specifically for the 1929 Ibero-American exhibition, and is worth having a cup of tea in.

Alongside the hotel is one of the biggest buildings in the western world, erected in 1750 to house the tobacco factory in which the mythical Carmen supposedly worked with 10,000 other *cigarerras*. Now this rather grim building echoes with the cries of students, for this is the **University**'s faculty of science and law.

Park properties: Beyond the university are the beginnings of Maria Luisa park and the site of Seville's Ibero-American exhibition of 1929, of which some buildings remain. These include the biological research station for the Coto Doñana nature reserve (Avenida de Chile), which is not open to the public but has a striking courtyard in pink marble littered with animal carvings.

Most notable of the remains of the exhibition is the **Plaza España**, surrounded by a semi-circular building which took 15 years to build and functioned as the Spanish pavilion at the time. It now houses government offices and, apart from the tile pictures featuring Spain's every province on the outside, is rather a disappointment and far too young to be considered of any archi-

Plaza España.

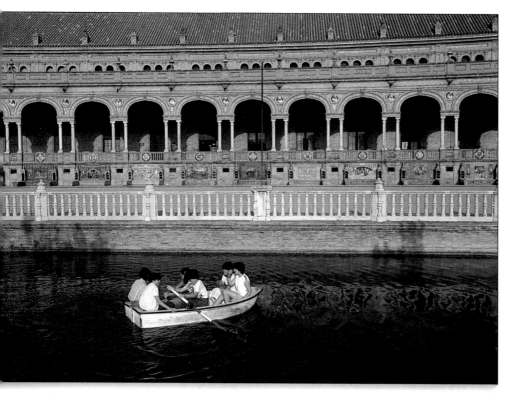

tectural merit. Still, the Plaza itself, with its shaded waterway and bridges, is pleasant.

Better still is the jungle that is the **Parque de Maria Luisa** itself. A judicious mixture of careful manicuring and rank outgrowth, of delicate landscaping and unharnessed riot, of familiar European plants and flowers and more exotic species from Africa and the Americas, the park is an essential picnic space in a city that at times becomes stiflingly hot. It is full of small sources of amusement: the *azulejo* benches buried deep under foliage; sweating joggers; ceramic frogs spouting water; duck sanctuaries full of doves.

The **Plaza de America** marks the end of the park. Surrounded on three sides by museums or government offices, the Plaza is packed with very greedy doves which can readily produce an experience worthy of Hitchcock.

The **Archaeological Museum** on one side of the square has an extensive collection from local excavation sites, with representative material from the earliest recorded history (neolithic and Tartessian) through to Roman and Moorish times. Pottery and silver and goldwork reflect the trading connections of Andalucía, with fine Phoenician painted ceramics. The Roman collection, in particular, is impressive, symptomatic of the extensive and significant Roman cities that once surrounded Seville, of which there is a long list and a map (Latin and Spanish names) on one wall.

Opposite, the rather sleepy **Arts and Folklore Museum** (with excellent background classical music) promotes the expected aspects of Andalucía— bullfighters, the Seville Fair, gypsies and costume. More surprising is a massive and illogical ploughing exhibition and a display of Christian paraphernalia; some of the mocked-up house interiors are worth lingering over.

Waterside attractions: Back towards the centre of town, the 13th-century **Torre del Oro** (once covered with gold, thus the name) stands like a chess piece on the bank of the river. The tower once

Torre del Oro, housing the Maritime Museum.

served a defensive purpose by anchoring a chain that stretched across to the other bank, but now is repeatedly captured on postcards. It houses a **Maritime Museum,** which, although it contains nothing of any significance, is stuffed with fascinating odds and ends, from shark's jaws to paintings of the famous navigators. Murals here show how Seville in the 1700s was surrounded by a girdle of boats.

A street back from the river is the **Hospital de la Caridad**. Founded in 1674 as a charity hospital for the homeless and the sick by Don Miguel de Mañara, this building still serves that purpose. It is best known to visitors, however, not for the rather picturesque old gentlemen who hobble about the courtyard, but for the quality of the chapel. The latter, one of the most complete in Seville, has paintings by Murillo and Valdés Leal; Leal's two works above and opposite the entrance are particularly pungent, showing the transitory nature of life which passes *in ictu oculi*, in the blink of an eye.

A little upstream to the north is the **Maestranza**, the bull-ring, which seats 14,000 spectators and is the second oldest in the country after that at Ronda. If you don't want to see a fight, go on a guided tour. The ring was started in 1758, but in all its history only one matador has been killed within its premises. In the museum the head of the mother of the bull that did the deed is mounted on the wall; what happened to the bull itself no one knows; it was rather hard luck on the mother to have had a courageous son. To make the spectacle complete, the bull-ring has its own mini-hospital for the quick treatment of injured fighters, including a viewing window through which the public can watch the blood flow.

A bridge to the north crosses the river to the **Triana** district, once known as the gypsy quarter but now principally visited during the day for the ceramic factories which still work here and at night for its restaurants and bars (expensive along the riverside **Calle Betis**; cheaper along **Calle Castilla** and nearby side streets). A favourite for local specialities is **Casa Cuesta**, officially called the Cerveceria Ruiz, on the corner of Castilla and San Jorge. Opposite, a dark, dank and dangerous-seeming alleyway, appropriately named the **Callejón de la Inquisición** (Seville witnessed some of the Spanish Inquisition's greatest purges), leads down to the river.

Livelier nightlife is focused on the **Arenal** area back near the bull-ring; in the Calle Garcia de Vinuesa (also the home of the **Hotel Simon**, a stylish small hotel based around a typical Sevillian patio) is a line of old-fashioned *bodegas*, stacked high with sherry barrels, walls plastered with old bullfight posters. A visit to Seville is not complete without sampling a *fino* or *amontillado* in one or other or several of these establishments.

Shops and markets: From the top of García de Vinuesa the Avenida de la Constitución leads up to the Plaza Nueva, which has the **Ayuntamiento** or town hall (built 1572) on one side. Behind it is the Plaza San Francisco,

once used for tournaments. To the north is the **Calle Sierpes**, which runs through the heart of the shopping area.

Narrow streets from the top right of the Plaza San Francisco lead to the church of **El Salvador**, surrounded by shops selling wedding dresses. This church, which is rather ramshackle from the outside and filled with gold *retablos* on the inside, was built on the site of a mosque and has Arabic inscriptions above the side door. From its northeastern corner narrow streets lead up to the **Plaza Alfalfa**, a busy little square with an excellent patisserie, which hosts the pet market (particularly birds) on Sunday mornings, well worth visiting.

A little further east is the **Casa Pilatos** (built 1480), property of the Duke of Medinaceli, so-called supposedly because it imitated Pilate's house in Jerusalem. The ground floor is in Mudéjar style complete with pillared *patio*, but does not match up to the Alcázar. The life-styles of the owner and his predecessors, as mirrored in the rooms upstairs, are more interesting.

The other Sunday market is further north still on the **Alameda de Hercules**, a broad avenue marked at one end by two pillars topped by statues of Julius Caesar and Hercules. The market is largely junk, but the people are interesting, many noticeably of gypsy or Moorish origin. This is the red-light area of Seville; the houses are often deserted and decaying, and much of the city hereabouts is empty. One or two churches are worth visiting in this quarter, however: notably the **Monastery of Santa Clara**, with the ancient **Torre de Don Fadrique** (1252, and still very solid). The church of **Jesus del Gran Poder** (the powerful Jesus) has an unusual feature in its image of Christ carrying the cross on the altar; worshippers file behind the altar to kiss or touch the image's heel to help speed their beseeching prayers.

Standing by itself in the western side of the city is the **Fine Arts Museum** (Plaza del Museo), recently closed for restoration. The museum has a fine

Courtyard of the Casa Pilatos.

collection of Seville ceramics and works by Andalucían artists as well as El Greco and Goya.

Celebrations: In the early part of the year, before the heat becomes intolerable, Seville hosts two very important and exhilarating fiestas in swift succession, Semana Santa and the Feria. The **Feria** (mid-April) started as a market for agricultural produce and machinery but has developed into an exuberant celebration of the arrival of spring, with dancing, drinking, displays of horsemanship, fireworks, bullfighting competitions and more, over the course of a week. **Semana Santa** (Easter) has a more religious origin and features processions of 57 floats carried by 57 hooded brotherhoods who each have their own image of Christ or of the Virgin; from the crowd come passionate songs of devotion (often sung by professionals employed by the city specifically for that purpose).

Both celebrations attract large numbers of people to the city, pushing up prices and making accommodation almost impossible to find. If you can be in Seville for either or both, it is likely to be an experience you won't forget.

The province: The industrial and residential influence of Seville extends some way out into the countryside, but there are no further towns of any real size in the province. To the north lies the Sierra Morena, a vast belt of hills covered with rough woodland; to the south lie agricultural flatlands dominated by the river; to the west is the province of Huelva; and to the east the soft rolling agricultural land, the Campina, extends down a chain of ancient settlements.

A traveller heading due south in the winter may find the minor roads frustrating; a combination of heavy rain and high tides (as in the disastrous winter of 1989–90) can mean that many a route is cut by swollen streams. The central town to these flatlands is **Los Palacios**, a quiet, rural place and the site of an agricultural research station.

Further south, **Lebrija** sits atop a hill in more rolling countryside towards the wine region of Jerez. A new *mirador* in the centre of this cobble-streeted town has an excellent view, but perhaps better is that from the old Roman remains at the top of the hill past the ancient church. Lebrija is a pretty place with a particularly houseproud *ayuntamiento* and its own radio station.

Utrera, to the east of Los Palacios, shows the influence of nearby Seville in its commercialisation and faster pace. The Arab castle has been partially restored. Opposite the church of Nuestra Señora de los Angeles (well maintained with an excellent vaulted ceiling) is a convent; as with many Spanish convents, the chapel is divided by a wooden screen, from behind which the nuns direct their worship at the distant altar.

Roads west out of Seville, once across the Guadalquivir, swiftly leave the city behind. One of the future purposes of the Expo'92 site is to extend the city further in this direction. Up the far bank of the river to the north are the Roman sites of **Santiponce** and **Italica**. Santiponce boasts a Roman theatre which looks out over the main road. Italica, about a mile further on, was the

esus del
ran Poder
the church
the same
ame.

principal Roman city of the region, and the birthplace of three emperors, Trajan, Hadrian and Theodosius. Excavations have revealed the amphitheatre and numerous streets with a couple of mosaics. There is also a small museum, but much of the more interesting material unearthed in Italica is in the Archaeological Museum in Seville.

Hills and towers: Roads north from Seville cross the flat river valley and ascend into the **Sierra Morena**, a thinly populated belt of hills which provides the plain with its water. The Sierra's main attraction is its coolness after the heat of the lowlands; in the winter it is a hunting centre, and the small towns of **Cazalla** and **Constantina** (the latter surprisingly prosperous, with a dramatic figure of Christ on the hillside above) are filled with well-dressed young men from Seville swapping stories in the bars. The quality of the roads can be unpredictable. In the winter it may be safer to take the train; four a day service the combined Cazalla/Constantina station, and although the sta-

tion is not close to either town it makes a reasonable starting and finishing point for walking.

Three important historical towns lie east of Seville. **Carmona**, the closest, most interesting and most atmospheric, was an important Roman centre. A Roman amphitheatre and **necropolis** and museum lie on the Seville side of town; the necropolis is well laid out, complete with a crematorium whose walls are still discoloured by the heat of the fire, large numbers of small paupers' tombs and a couple of much grander burial grounds.

The town itself (ignore anything outside the old walls) commands an excellent view over the plain, particularly from inside the **Parador**, which is a conversion of the Alcázar del Rey de Pedro (town map available from the hotel reception) and one of the more magnificent of Spain's government-run hotels. Nearby is the ancient **Córdoba Gate**, well corroded but remarkably intact considering its age (originally 2nd century AD, with Moorish and ba-

Flooded road near Los Palacios.

roque additions). The gate still serves its ancient purpose, because Carmona has not grown at all in this direction.

The other gate, the **Puerta de Sevilla** (on the Seville side of town), is gigantic and features a double entranceway which could turn the town into a fortress. The building incorporates another Alcázar and a museum (open erratically). In front, in the newer town, the church of San Pedro has one of many imitation Giraldas in the province.

Ecija, some 34 miles (56 km) east, has many such towers. Unlike most Andalucían towns, this is built in a valley bowl rather than on a hill and consequently has no summer breeze to relieve the heat. The town hall promotes Ecija as "the city of sun and towers"; however, it is better known as "the frying pan of Spain" because of its relentless summer heat. Catch it on a cool day.

The church of **Sta Maria** (southwest of Plaza Major) has a Mudéjar *patio* filled with archaeological bits and pieces. The covered market is colourful, and Calle Caballeros (north of the main square) has several rambling and ornate merchants' houses, including the **Palacio de Peñaflor**, with a very unusual curved balcony. The town is littered with (crumbling) church towers, all of which echo the Seville Giralda in some shape or form.

South of Ecija, down unpredictable roads, is **Osuna**, again with a large collection of merchants' houses. Here the Giralda imitation is built into a grand facade on the **Calle San Pedro** (next door is the cream-cake (Palacio Gomera). The Arab tower on the way up the hill has a small private museum whose proprietress will proudly point out the principal attractions (mainly Roman sculpture). On the hill is the rather bleak, turreted **Old University**, and the **Collegiate Church of Sta Maria,** big and bare inside (entrance fee). Below is the **Convent of La Encarnación,** now a museum of religious art.

From Osuna the road, much improved thanks to Expo'92, makes for the Sierra Nevada and the city of Granada.

Shoe repair in Ecija.

EXPO'92: THE WORLD TAKES THE STAGE

It cannot escape the notice of visitors to Seville that something is going on in the city. If you are reading this in 1992, then that something will probably be part of the reason for your visit; if not, then the chances are you will be aware of Expo because half the city is wrapped up and undergoing renovation, in preparation for the eyes of the world.

Expo'92, a world fair on a scale that hasn't been seen in Europe since the Expo in Brussels in 1958, will open its doors in Seville on 20 April 1992 and run for six months. It will be sited on the Isla Cartuja, an island on the western side of the city around which flow the two courses (one natural, one artificial) of the Guadalquivir river. In the past the island was so prone to flooding that the only building on it was a monastery turned pigment factory, which is to be the central monument of the exhibition.

The fair will cover a ground area of 538 acres (215 hectares), contain more than 100 pavilions, 13 entertainment areas, 105 restaurants, 105 shops, a monorail, TV studios, and more. An estimated 250,000 visitors are expected to pass through its gates every day. The grand total will probably not exceed the 60 million visitors to the Expo in Japan in 1970, but a far greater proportion of the Seville crowds will be of all nationalities than at the Japanese event.

The cause for this celebration is the 500th anniversary of Columbus's discovery of the Americas. Columbus himself stayed at the monastery on the Isla Cartuja while planning his expeditions. Accordingly, the theme of the fair will be discovery in its geographical sense, but the Expo authorities have widened the term to include discovery in any realm of human endeavour, past, present and future, giving *carte blanche* for any national or corporate drum-beating.

The main exhibitions or pavilions are the work of individual countries (100 are participating) or international corporations. The landscaping and the infrastructure is the work of the Expo authorities, who are working hard to combat the worst of the summer heat with wind-channels and greenery.

The city of Seville has had a love/hate relationship with the exhibition from the start. The local newspaper has allotted four daily pages to Expo news and has often filled them with rumour and gossip, for the want of anything more substantial. Many a *sevillano*

will maintain that the Expo authorities are bureaucrats from Madrid who do nothing for big salaries.

However, Expo'92 is playing a major role in the regeneration of the city of Seville. For several centuries the city has been a sleepy place dominated by aristocrats and labourers but without any substantial number of professionals and middle class. Expo has brought the middle class from places like Barcelona or Madrid to Seville, bumped up the prices and gentrified inner city areas.

Creating the site hasn't just meant clearing the ground for the exhibitors to start work; it has involved new motorways, airport and communication facilities, bodily moving two railway stations in Seville, and even creating a new town (over the river to the west) for the 20,000 people working in Expo during its run. The whole of Andalucía will be affected by the show and many local towns are spending heavily in order to attract the overspill of visitors, who will be able to move more freely on new roads and new trains.

The Spanish government is investing $7 billion in these infrastructural developments; it expects to invest $583 million in preparation of the exhibition site but to break even on this investment through ticket sales and on sponsorships and concession and licence fees. The US is investing $45 million in its pavilion and IBM $30 million, but the biggest pavilion will be that housing the Latin American countries.

The Spanish have had to overcome some intellectual hurdles and some old antagonisms in pulling together the Latin American representation. Most of these countries were former colonies of Spain and their history is full of the misdeeds of what is now acknowledged as "clumsy" government. Accordingly, Spain is financially supporting the Latin American countries at the fair, and the whole episode of the plundering of the New World (Seville handled much of the treasure) is being glossed over. For the purposes of Expo, the discovery of America is only important inasmuch as it heralded the dawn of modernity.

Like the Ibero-American exhibition of 1929, which left Seville with a legacy of parkland, museums and several buildings of architectural significance, Expo'92 will leave its mark on the city. Business and educational institutions are already committed to move on to the site when the party is over; the Isla Cartuja will become a commercial and business information centre and an academic and technological complex.

CORDOBA AND ITS PROVINCE

Córdoba, seen in the last rays of the setting sun, glows with an inner light. Huge flocks of birds wheel over the quiet waters of the River Guadalquivir, which shimmers with the city's reflection. At this hour, in this light, it seems as if it were only yesterday that Córdoba was a city of a million inhabitants, the most important city in Europe.

The Moors, who swarmed across the Straits of Gibraltar in AD 711, chose Córdoba as the capital of al-Andalus, Islamic Spain. For a while their armies dominated most of the peninsula and even penetrated as far as southern France, before being repelled. Moorish Spain still answered to the Damascus caliphate until AD 756, when Abd-al-Rahman I threw off the Damascene rule, becoming Córdoba's first caliph and beginning a long process of consolidating many small kingdoms.

The heyday of the Córdoba caliphate came in the 10th century, under Ab- al-Rahman III. While parts of Europe languished in the Dark Ages, Córdoba became a centre of advanced learning in sciences, medicine, philosophy and poetry. Together with Baghdad and Constantinople, it was one of the three greatest cities in the world. Today it has a population of 300,000.

Monument to the Moors: Powerfully evoking this fabulous epoch is Córdoba's most important monument, the **Mosque**, the third largest in the world. Though it hasn't been used for Islamic rites since the city was conquered by King Ferdinand in 1236, today's tourists include many Muslims. The Mosque was begun in AD 785 by Ab- al-Rahman I on the site of an earlier Visigothic (Christian) church, which itself probably replaced a Roman temple. Its builders recycled a hodge-podge of building materials, taking Roman and Visigothic columns, bases and capitals of many materials, sizes and styles, and topping them with double horseshoe arches, candy-striped in pink and white.

The Mosque was enlarged by Abd-al-Rahman II in AD 833; again in 926 under al-Haken II, and finally by al-Manzor, chief minister of Hisham II, in 978. Covering 251,000 sq. ft (23,400 sq. metres), it has 856 columns; according to two youths armed with a ladder and a bucket of soapy water, it takes about three months to scrub them all.

The architectural style evolved with each addition, reaching the greatest splendour and technical mastery in what came to be known as the califal style of architecture during the caliphate of al-Haken. Features to note are great sky-lighted domes for extra interior light and an ingenious engineering system which consists of clustered pillars bearing intersecting lobed arches to support the domes.

The most dazzling part of the Mosque is undoubtedly the **Mihrab**, the holy sanctuary where the Koran scriptures were kept, which, incidentally, does not quite face Mecca. A scallop-shell dome covers this sanctum, which is richly decorated with mosaics of coloured and

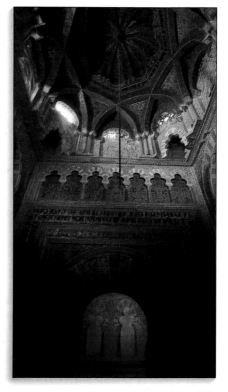

gilded tiles glittering in the magical light. Koranic scriptures border the Mihrab and carved stucco adorns the upper walls.

After Córdoba fell to the Christian King Ferdinand in 1236, the Mosque was reconsecrated as a Christian church and, in 1523, construction began on a **Cathedral** within its walls, requiring the removal of some 60 of the original columns and some of the most beautiful stucco work.

Visitors often react with shock at the desecration. Even Charles V, who granted permission for it to be built, is said to have declared later when he visited the work: "Had I known what this was, you would not have done it, for what you are building here can be found anywhere; but what you have destroyed exists nowhere."

On Sundays and feast days the Cathedral is busy with worshippers quite oblivious to the tourists gazing at the fabled cupolas of the Mosque. Here are two different worlds under one roof, a fitting image for Córdoba which over centuries has sheltered many cultures.

The Cathedral is of Gothic design with later additions in plateresque and baroque styles. Within, it is surprisingly light and intimate. Especially noteworthy are the choir stalls, carved by Andalucían sculptor Pedro Duque Cornejo; these depict, on either side of the Ascension, the lives of Jesus and the Virgin Mary in life-like detail. The Cathedral treasury (located in the sacristy next to the Mihrab) displays especially good examples of Córdoban silver and gold artistry.

The town: Across from the Mosque (on Calle Torrijos) in a 16th-century hospice is the **Palacio de Congresos**, a convention hall housing the tourism office. From here it is just a few steps to the river, crossed by the **Roman Bridge**, the best place to be at sunset. On the bridge is one of many images of Córdoba's patron, the Archangel Raphael, candles guttering at his feet. In the river bottom, overgrown with rushes where ducks paddle, are the remains of three Arabic mills.

Across the bridge is the **Torre de Calahorra**, a 14th-century military watchtower, which houses a museum depicting the glories of al-Andalus, Moorish Spain, with wax figures and a 50-minute diorama, with headphones in several languages.

A few blocks downriver from the Mosque is the **Alcázar**, a palace built by the Christian kings in 1327. This is supposedly where Queen Isabella told Columbus she would back his hare-brained scheme to sail off the edge of the known universe. The views from the tower of gardens and city are worth the climb—for the nimble. Ancient steps are not in the best repair.

The area around the Mosque, Córdoba's old quarter, is best visited on foot or by horse carriage. Many of the streets are hardly more than narrow alleyways where cars can't enter. Whitewashed houses present a blank facade to the street, broken only by an entryway closed by a *cancela*, a wrought-iron gate. Through this gate is glimpsed a *patio*, shaded by a palm, furnished with ferns, perfumed with jasmine, air-

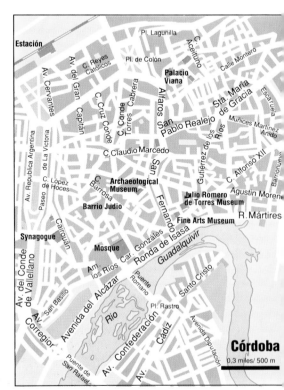

conditioned by a bubbling fountain.

Whether intimate heart of private homes or elegant courtyards of great buildings, the *patio* was developed as a survival technique, a cool oasis in the long hot summers. Calle Albucasis and Calle Manriquez are two streets with especially beautiful *patios*. Córdoba celebrates its courtyards during the annual fair, between 14 and 21 May, when many private *patios* are opened to the public.

Within the old quarter are several handsome mansions which belonged to noble families. Especially beautiful is the **Casa del Indiano** (Plaza de Angel Torres), another golden building, with lobed arches in 15th-century Mudéjar (post reconquest Arabic) style.

Within an easy stroll of the Mosque is the medieval Jewish quarter, the **Barrio Judio**, also entered through the **Puerto de Almodóvar**, one of the city's ancient gates (having the same name as Pedro Almodóvar, Spain's pre-eminent modern film director, who made *Women on the Verge of Nervous Breakdown*).

Monumental Córdoba is golden, but its *barrios* or neighbourhoods are usually pristine white, kept lime-washed by house-proud owners.

Jewish influence: If Córdoba is known for the splendour of its 10th-century achievements in art, architecture and science, a part of its glory is attributed to the Sephardim community, the Spanish Jews who settled here during the time of the Roman emperors, when they were allowed the same rights as other inhabitants of Baetica, Roman Spain.

After the fall of the Roman Empire, under the Visigoths, Jews were persecuted so severely that they were ready to aid and abet the Moslem invaders. In exchange, they enjoyed long periods of peaceful co-existence and a flowering of Sephardim culture during which many achieved rare heights in diplomacy, medicine, commerce and crafts.

Sepharad simply means Spain in Hebrew. Five hundred years after King Ferdinand and Queen Isabella decreed their expulsion in 1492, Spanish Jews, dispersed throughout the world, still

Plaza de José Antonio.

speak an archaic Spanish dialect. Were Columbus to come back to life today, he would find it easier to converse with the Sephardic Jews in, for instance, Istanbul than with modern *madrileños*. (The expulsion order on the Jews was officially rescinded only in 1968; the Spanish Constitution of 1978 further guarantees religious freedom.)

The Jewish **Synagogue** in Córdoba is one of only two remaining in all of Spain, where once there were hundreds (the other is in Toledo). Córdoba itself had 26 synagogues between the 10th and 15th centuries. This survivor, built in 1315, is entered from the narrow Calle Judios, through a small *patio*. Segments of Hebraic inscriptions and family history remain on the walls. The upper gallery, where women were seated, and the niche where the Torah was kept are still intact. Where the Mosque is awesome, the Synagogue is poignant.

Many Córdoban Sephardim achieved high status, either at the Moslem court or within the Jewish community. One was Maimonides, one of the greatest philosophers of Jewish history. A rabbi and Talmudic scholar with an Aristotelian bent, Maimonides was born in Córdoba more than 850 years ago, in 1135. By this time, fanatic Berber sects, the Almohads, had changed the political landscape, initiating a period of unrest and repression. Maimonides's family fled to Morocco. He eventually settled in Egypt, but Córdoba still claims him as a native son.

Near the Synagogue, in the **Plaza Tiberias**, under the bower of an enormous jasmine vine, is a statue of Maimonides, dedicated in 1965. He presides over the tiny square with kindly dignity, his slipper rubbed shiny by thousands of passers-by, possibly hoping some of his wisdom might rub off on them.

In the plaza named for Maimonides is a different sort of monument. Opening off a beautiful *patio*, in the house said to have belonged to Maimonides's family, is the municipal **Bullfight Museum** displaying posters, swords, capes and

Córdoba from the Mosque.

164

trajes de luz, the "suit of lights" worn by matadors. Córdoba is a famous town for bullfighters, home of two all-time greats, Lagartijo and Manolete.

Craft quarter: Behind the museum, again on Calle Judios, is the **Zoco**, a group of craft workshops around a central courtyard. Here artisans work in both traditional and modern styles, in silver filigree (for which Córdoba is famous), leather, wood carving and ceramics. Nearby, on Calle Tomás Conde 3, the street leading into Plaza Maimonides, is **Artesania Andaluza**, in a 16th-century house, featuring an excellent selection of Córdoban crafts, particularly ceramics. One of the exhibition rooms off the central *patio* has an ancient well.

The **Meryan** exposition rooms contain a pretty *patio* and leather workshops, run by two brothers whose family has carried on the leather crafting tradition for generations, on Calleja de las Flores, the much photographed "Street of Flowers" with its view of the Mosque tower. The shop shows hand-tooled leather handbags, briefcases, mirror frames, and studded coffers and polychromed leather work, called *guadameciles*, especially attractive as wall hangings.

Near the Alcázar, at Calle Enmedio 13, **Joyeria La Milagrosa** carries on the traditional Córdoban crafts of silver and goldsmithing. Before the holiday of Los Reyes, 6 January, when, instead of Father Christmas, the Three Kings come from Bethlehem bearing gifts, clients throng this elegant shop where salesmen unwrap velvet rolls to reveal gleaming gold trinkets.

Eating out: Many of Córdoba's best restaurants are located within the old city, almost in the shadow of the Mosque. The **Caballo Rojo**, Calle Cardenal Herrero 28, with a tavern on the main floor, handsome dining rooms upstairs, emphasises the typical, with a few specialities, such as lamb with honey, from Moorish times.

Restaurante El Churrasco, Calle Romero 16, specializes in grilled meats and big fish. The dining areas are tiny,

The Roman Bridge, best place to be at sunset.

around a *patio* where, in winter, the waiters place glowing hot braziers beneath the tables. Nearby, the Churrasco premises include an ancient *bodega* or winery (visits only by appointment).

Almudaina, at Campo Santo de los Martires 1, features fine Spanish and international dishes. Less posh, but full of local flavour, is the **Confederación de Peñas**, Calle Luque, just off the Plaza Benavente, where simple food is served at good prices in an attractive house with *patio*.

Córdoba's old quarter is full of corners and plazas to stop awhile, over a coffee or a *fino* Montilla, a dry wine from Córdoba's wine district, and just contemplate the city and its people.

An easy walk from the Mosque, along Ronda de Isasa (the avenue bordering the river), is the **Plaza del Potro**, which Cervantes mentions in *Don Quixote*. It is named after a small statue of a colt on top of a 16th-century fountain where two ducks paddle. The inn on one side of the plaza, where Cervantes once stayed, houses a municipal arts and crafts centre. Modern paintings hang where horses and mules were stabled. The plaza opens towards the river and the far bank is open countryside.

Art collection: On one side of the Plaza del Potro a 16th-century hospice with leaded glass windows houses the **Fine Arts Museum**, entered through a courtyard, elegantly tiled on one side. The collection is small but wide-ranging: a haunting head of Christ, dating from 1389; several paintings by Antonio del Castillo Saavedra (1616–68), including one of the Holy Family, showing Mamá dressing a rosy-cheeked Babe; Pedro Duque Cornejo's clay sketches for his carving of the Ascension in Córdoba Cathedral; a wonderful painting by Joachim Sorolla of a woman with downcast eyes and a red hat, and a whole section devoted to Córdoban sculptor Mateo Inurria, including a life-size sculpture of the Roman philosopher Seneca, another Córdoban, looking wise and wizened.

Sharing the same courtyard is the **Julio Romero de Torres Museum**,

Moorish sweetmeats, sold from the convent of Santa Isabel.

dedicated to the work of this Córdoban painter who depicted popular scenes and "poster girls" early in this century. Closed for restoration, the gallery was due to reopen by the end of 1990. As is the **Provincial Archeological Museum**, Plaza Jeronimo Páez, with impressive displays of artefacts from the Bronze Age through Roman and Moorish times.

Córdoba is restoring and spiffing up quite a few of its buildings, getting ready for 1992, when this city will share some of the limelight with nearby Seville. Also getting a facelift (and an underground car park) is the **Plaza de la Corredera**, a 17th-century arcaded plaza with brick facades and wrought-iron balconies. Once the site of bullfights and other public spectacles, the plaza now encloses a lively morning street market, with stalls selling everything from live rabbits, pigeons and chicks to cheap shoes and clothing, used tyres, dubious antiques and junk jewellery. The clock-tower building houses a remodelled municipal market.

A few blocks up from this plaza, on Calle Capitulares, is a curious architectural landmark, Córdoba's **Ayuntamiento** or town hall, built six years ago in very modern style, incorporating the ruins of a Roman amphitheatre in its foundations. Beside it rise the columns of a Roman temple.

Córdoba's municipal government, incidentally, is the only one of Spain's provincial capitals to be headed by a Communist mayor, Herminio Trigo Aguilar. His administration is encouraging the development of facilities for meetings and conventions to lure travellers beyond the day-trippers, who disembark from their air-conditioned buses, troop through the Mosque, and are gone again. Projects for two or three new four-star hotels were in the planning stages at the time of writing.

Across from the town hall is the **Church of San Pablo**, also being restored, a beautiful Romanesque building fronted with spiral columns.

From here, Avda Alfonso XIII leads into Córdoba's great central plaza, **Las**

eft, in
udería.
ight, the
est
estaurants
re in the old
ity.

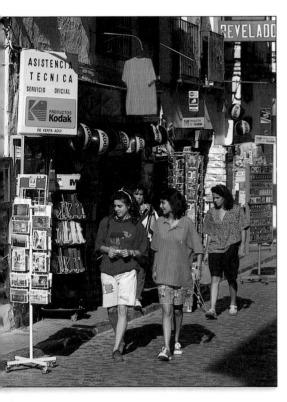

Tendillas. Street sweepers wield huge brooms made of wild grasses.

At opposite sides of the plaza, two important shopping streets lead outwards. Jesus Maria has lots of tiny shops, such as **Hortigon**, at No. 4, selling handmade lace and embroidery. Calle Jose Cruz Conde, Córdoba's principal shopping street, has boutiques, shoe shops, leather and fur stores (leather and fur at **Peletería Internaciónal**). The street ends at a broad avenue, Ronda de los Tejares. In the Plaza San Nicolas is **Antiquedades Enrique**, which is a good place to search for antiques.

Bulls and convents: Another special *barrio*, or neighbourhood, of Córdoba is **La Marina**, named for the beautiful Gothic church of **Santa Marina**, This is the *barrio* of bullfighters and here is an extravagant homage to Manolete. Around the corner from the church, in the **Convent of Santa Isabel**, the Clarisa nuns keep up an old Andalucían tradition, confecting pastries to sell to the public. Ask for a *surtido*, an assortment,

to sample the best of Córdoban sweets.

Very near the Marina church (along Calle Morales) is the **Palacio Viana**, a 15th-century palace which belonged to the Marquis of Viana. Finding it difficult to maintain such a large establishment, the family advertised the palace for sale in a French newspaper. A Córdoba bank rescued the landmark and opened it to the public in 1981.

The palace presents an austere white facade to the street. Inside, it is a dreamworld, enclosing 13 courtyards, each with different plantings, and interior halls, salons, bedrooms and bathrooms, which still have a lived-in look. Furnishings are a mixed bag and great art shares wall space with the fairly ordinary. There are exceptional displays of ceramic tiles dating from the 13th century; old sabres and muskets; Córdoban polychrome leather wall hangings; china and porcelain; Baccarat crystal chandeliers; fabulous carpets.

Córdoba has a lively custom of the *tapeo*, stopping at one or several *tabernas*, neighbourhood bars, for a *copa* of **Country *finca*.**

dry Montilla wine, a *fino*, and a selection of *tapas*, small plates of appetizers, both hot and cold.

Two good tabernas in the old quarter are **Guzman** and **Santos**, both in the Judería; **La Alegria**, on Menendez y Pelayo, and **La Canoa**, just off Ronda de los Tejares in the new city.

Córdoba is known as a flamenco town. The best dancing and singing take place at popular fairs and special flamenco festivals. El Cardenal, on Calle Cardenal Herrero, facing the Mosque, has a good *tablao*, or flamenco show (closed Sundays and Mondays; tel: 48 03 46). The town also hosts international guitar festivals and has orchestral, theatrical and operatic seasons.

In the hills: A few miles to the west of Córdoba, on gentle hills above the river plain, is **Medina Azahara**, the city that, when it was begun in AD 936 under the rule of Abd-al-Rahman III, was intended to become the new capital of al-Andalus. Intensive building went on for 25 years, creating a sublime city, with a golden-domed great hall, exquisite mosque, gardens and pools filled with quicksilver. The caliphal court moved here in AD 945. However, hardly had it been built, when, in 1010, swarms of invading Berbers began to destroy it again.

Excavation and restoration of the city began in 1911, with a slow sifting through the sands of time. Master craftsmen still carry on the work, restoring traditional plasterwork, mosaics and columns, and the whole site is open to the public.

Continuing west, the Córdoba to Seville river road (C-431) passes through a rich agricultural region of fruit and citrus orchards, wheat, sugar beets and cotton. After the autumn cotton harvest, fluffs of cotton border the road like snow drifts.

At **Almodóvar del Rio**, on a hill dominating the river valley, is a picture-book castle, built by the Moors and later embellished. Halfway between Córdoba and Seville, on the Guadalquivir river, is **Palma del Rio**, famed for its citrus groves and as the birthplace

riego de
Córdoba.

of the popular bullfighter, El Córdobes. The 15th-century convent of San Francisco in Palma was the jumping-off point for missionaries to the New World, such as Fray Junipero Serra, who established California's missions. The monastery has been converted into a small hotel and restaurant where, in season, the menu features venison and boar taken in the nearby **Sierra Morena**.

This mountainous region, happy hunting ground of the aristocracy, has become very popular for its *monterias*, formalised hunts, where on a single good day some hundred deer are shot. (Information and reservations from CATUR, Calle Vallellano 19, Córdoba; tel: 29 44 44.)

Wine and oil: South of the capital (main road to Málaga, N-331) is Córdoba's wine region, centred around the towns of **Montilla** and **Moriles**, where wine has been made since the 8th century BC. Comparisons with sherry are inevitable, for Montilla wines are produced by the *solera* system of blending in the same way as the more widely marketed Jerez wines.

One winery open for visits is **Bodegas Alvear** in Montilla. (Tel: 65 01 00 to verify hours for tours.) Others are open by appointment only. The region celebrates its wine harvest festival the last week of August, with some honest grape stomping.

Other towns in the region worth a visit are **La Rambla**, with more than 50 ceramic workshops; **Cabra**, with the 13th-century sanctuary of the Virgin of the Sierra; and **Lucena**, which was a totally Jewish town in the califal epoch, specialising in trade and crafts. Lucena is still a centre for copper, brass and bronze workshops (a good display at Metal-luce, Avda. José Solis 10). Outside the town are many furniture factories where newlyweds from all over Andalucía come to furnish their homes at factory prices.

Adjoining the vineyards is Córdoba's important olive oil region, centred around **Baena** (main road to Granada, N-432), dominated by its Moorish for-

Goats are highly prized throughout Andalucía.

tress and surrounded by undulating hills tufted with olive trees. Beyond Baena the terrain becomes more craggy, with villages such as **Luque**, built against a grey rock, and **Zuheros**, with a church on the edge of an escarpment.

Prime site: The jewel of the province is surely the town of **Priego de Córdoba**, on a bluff above the Rio Salado, a salt-water river. Known as the capital of 18th-century Andalucían baroque architecture, Priego has several beautiful churches in this style, notably La Asunción, with a white-and-gold dome in the Sagrario chapel, and La Aurora, where the altar is garlanded with tiny fragrant jasmine flowers strung on threads. The Fuente del Rey is a monumental baroque fountain with natural springs. Locals say when the water level is high enough to cover the private parts of Neptune, whose image presides over the spring, there will be sufficient water for the crops.

In the 18th century Priego had a thriving silk industry, which brought wealth to the town. The fine buildings, including a number of noble mansions with handsome wrought-iron balconies and window grilles, date from that time. The old quarter of town, where passageways hung with flowerpots are no more than an arm's breadth, dates from Moorish times. Here, the neighbours keep up the curious custom of carrying an image of a favourite saint, complete with tiny altar in a carry-case, from house to house. A complex schedule allows each family to keep it one day.

South from Priego, almost to the Málaga and Granada borders, is Córdoba's lake region, from **Iznájar** and all along the tributaries of the Rio Genil, which shelters numerous species of wildlife, including Europe's last 100 Malvasian ducks.

In spring and autumn Córdoba and its environs fairly sparkle. Winters are moderate; summers are wretched. Even the Córdobans leave their city for the coasts. At sunset, streets come alive and, as in most Andalucían cities and villages, people—including children—stay up late, enjoying the cool of night.

Left, the Montilla wine is like sherry. Right, bodegas welcome visitors.

GRANADA AND ITS PROVINCE

Legend has it that, when the Arabs were finally ousted from the Kingdom of Granada in 1492, their defeated king, Boabdil, could not contain a sigh as he looked back at the magnificent city his ancestors had forged over nearly seven centuries and which he was now obliged to surrender to the Spanish. The site of this legendary sigh is 8 miles (13 km) south of Granada, a pass in the hills which is called *El Suspiro del Moro*, the Arab's Sigh.

The modern visitor to Granada will have cause to sigh, too—with wonder at the Moorish conquerors' good taste: the sheer aesthetics of Granada, the beauty of its setting between the everlasting snows of the **Sierra Nevada** and the tranquillity of the extensive fertile **Vega** or plain, seem to belong to the world of Japanese art.

For the first-time visitor to **Granada**, a warning and a few words of advice. The centre of the city is polluted and noisy, the narrow streets being simply incapable of coping with the volume of traffic which churns through at all hours of the day and night. The visitor who arrives by car may well find himself swept through and out the other side without either having recognised the centre of the town or seen a trace of its much-vaunted monuments. Unlike some other famous Spanish towns, Granada does not keep all its historic jewels neatly in one place, nor does it have a clearly recognisable centre.

So, the advice: use a map to get familiar with Granada's layout before you hit the streets. Locate the places you plan to visit and decide in advance that the city's traffic is not your problem. Then, giving the local driver the respect due to a pedestrian-hostile, anarchic beast, go about your explorations.

Historians still argue over the origins of the name Granada. Some go back to Noah's daughter, Grana, others citing Hercules' daughter Granata. For the visitor's purposes, this debate is sterile since Granada began to be interesting

with the Arab conquest of Spain in AD 711 and the progressive evolution of the Kingdom of Granada in architectural and cultural terms. As for the origin of the name itself, the happiest theory is the most poetic: that looking down from the hills on the red houses, tiny squares and twisting streets of the town, the Arab conquerors found it looked like an open pomegranate (*una granada* in Spanish) and affectionately called it by that name.

Granada's hilly situation offers many excellent vantage points from which to get a first overall view. The most obvious is the **Alhambra** itself, from whose ramparts and towers one can look down on the Albaicin, across to Sacromonte and southwestwards over the town to the Vega.

From the terrace of the **Hotel Alhambra Palace**, built in 1910 when Granada was enjoying a prosperous period thanks to its booming sugar industry, one can contemplate Granada old and new and see how the Vega, "a blooming wilderness of grove and garden and

teeming orchard", as Washington Irving described it in 1829, is being relentlessly eaten into by the advancing army of high-rise buildings. Kitsch enthusiasts should not miss a visit to this hotel for its sumptuous Moorish-inspired decoration.

The **Mirador San Cristobal**, on the road which winds up and out of Granada in the direction of Murcia (number 7 bus from the city centre), provides the best view of all and an excellent starting place for the newcomer to Granada. Across the valley of the Darro river the fortress and palace of the Alhambra seem to grow out of the burnt sienna rock and the dark green vegetation, asymmetrically in harmony with the natural landscape. Behind the fortress, the snow-capped peaks of Sierra Nevada; at one's feet the Albaicin.

Hub of the old city: When Granada became an independent Arab kingdom at the beginning of the 11th century the royal court was in the **Albaicin**, only to be transferred to the Alhambra on the opposite hill 250 years later. Today it is still easy to imagine what the Albaicin must have been like when it was the hub of Moorish Granada (whose population in the 14th century reached 400,000, twice that of today) with its 30 mosques, its potters and weavers, veiled women fetching water from the *aljibes* or public water tanks (still used as recently as the 1960s), and then disappearing into the privacy of their walled garden or *carmen*.

To enter the Albaicin, which one should first do without any formal list of places to see, is to leave civilisation as we know it behind. Or, rather, to enter a civilised world where the smells of jasmin, of damp, of heat or of cooking take over from car fumes, where the dominant sound is burbling water and where mules are still used to carry bricks and bags of cement, not by courtesy of the tourist board but simply because they are the only means of transport suitable for the narrow, steep streets.

Sadly, little trace of Arabic architecture remains in the Albaicin, where churches and convents—of which there

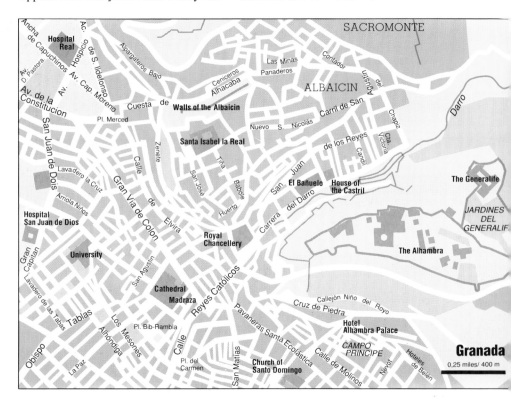

are 22 enclosed orders, many famous for the delicious sweets and pastries they produce—rapidly supplanted the mosques after the reconquest of Granada by the Catholic Monarchs, Ferdinand and Isabella.

The 11th-century Arab baths, **El Bañuelo**, on the Carrera del Darro, on the left shortly after the bridge where the Darro River disappears underground, is an exception. Entering through a leafy *patio*, full of peace and birdsong, the baths are perfectly restored with sunlight playing through the stars and octagon shapes of its roof. The palace of Dar al-Horra or **Queen's House** (Callejon del Gallo), built for King Boabdil's mother in the mid-15th century, is another survivor of reconquest. It is behind the convent of **Santa Isabel la Real**, also formerly an important Moorish palace.

Despite a recent influx of foreign residents, who are buying up houses as young local families move away to modernity and comfort, the inhabitants of the Albaicin are still remarkable for their friendliness and good sense of neighbourliness. Stopping for *tapas* on a summer's evening on one of the district's infinite plazas is a pleasurable experience.

Holy hill: Up the hill north of the Albaicin is **Sacromonte**, literally, "the holy hill". Until recently the best-known part of Granada along with the Alhambra, the Sacromonte of caves and gypsies has practically disappeared today. Severe floods in 1962 made many of the gypsies' caves uninhabitable and the occupants were rehoused in a high-rise complex west of Granada, bringing about not only the death of Sacromonte but the break-up of the strong gypsy community there, with the consequent weakening of traditions.

Only three caves still offer *zambras*, gypsy fiestas of flamenco music and dance. Enrique el Canastero, owner of one of these and son of the late and famous gypsy dancer Maria la Canastera, laments that, whereas he absorbed the rhythm of flamenco from the day he was born, parked in a wickerwork

playpen (*canastero* means basket-maker) at the mouth of his mother's cave when neighbours came in to dance and sing or play the guitar, his own children show little interest in the art. They have been brought up amongst cars, colour television and a fragmented community.

Further up the road, past the caves, is the **Abadía de Sacromonte**, recently reopened to the public following the restoration of five fascinating subterranean chapels. Founded at the end of the 16th century on the very site where the remains of four Christian martyrs were discovered, including the patron saint of Granada, San Cecilio, the Abadía is at present struggling for survival. Here, on the last Sunday of every month, the gypsy community comes to hold a special mass around their own Christ, *El Cristo del Consuelo*, a statue by José Risueño, the 18th-century Granada sculptor.

Across the valley from the car park of the Abadía, horizontal streaks are visible on the hill opposite, traces of the elaborate irrigation system devised by the Moorish monarchs to bring water from the mountains to the Alhambra and Generalife gardens.

Packed centre: Trapped in the hubbub of modern Granada are the **Cathedral**, built wilfully on the site of the main mosque of Granada and considered the most important example of Renaissance architecture in Spain, and the **Royal Chapel** (Capilla Real), built to house the tombs of the engineers of the unification of Spain in the 15th century, the Catholic Monarchs.

The warmth of the colour of the stone used for the exterior of these buildings contrasts with the bleak austerity of the interiors, especially the Cathedral. Here it is well worth putting a 25-peseta coin in the slot provided to the right of the altar in order to light up the altarpiece, thus momentarily infusing life into the colossal building. Don't miss the collection of Dutch paintings in the sacristy of the Royal Chapel.

Across the way from the Cathedral is what remains of the **Madraza**, the Arab

San Juan de Dios, hospital for the poor.

university founded in the 14th century by Yussuf I. This used to be one of Granada's most impressive buildings but today only the oratory remains (across the *patio* on the left); its intricate Arabic decoration was covered over for centuries, only to be rediscovered under a layer of plaster in 1893.

It is well worth nosing around and behind the Cathedral: not just in the *souk*-like streets, but also the **Plaza Bibrambla** with its flower stalls and old ladies selling plants and the **Plaza Pescadería**, where you can buy cottage cheese from the Sierra Nevada or freshly picked Boletus mushrooms from the Sierra Cazorla.

The **University of Granada**, founded by Charles V in 1526, opens on to the Plaza Universidad at the end of the Calle Jeronimo. Today the building houses the busy law faculty.

The **Hospital San Juan de Dios** (Calle San Juan de Dios), founded by Saint John of God in 1536, still functions today as a hospital for the poor, run by the Sisters of St Vincent de Paul. The number of patients has dropped from 500 to 50 but, far from being on the verge of closure, this unique mixture of modernity and medievalism will soon expand again as the hospital is brought under the social security scheme. It comprises two *patios*, the first planted with stunted palm trees, the second with orange trees, and around the walls of the old building, paintings depicting the life of St John of God are surrounded by frescoes and ceramic tiles. Here, patients in striped pyjamas and felt slippers wander in the midst of dilapidated history.

Bibliophiles should not miss the university library housed in the imposing building of the **Hospital Real**, situated above the **Triunfo** garden with its fountains and magnolia trees. Built at the beginning of the 16th century, this hospital, which over the centuries passed from hospital for the poor to hospital for venereal diseases to old people's home and then to lunatic asylum, is now the administrative headquarters of Granada University.

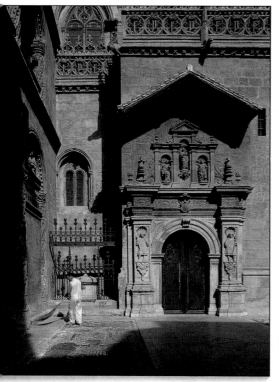

Not far from the Hospital Real lies the **Monasterio de la Cartuja**, yet another product of the Catholic construction boom following the expulsion of the Moors in 1492, this time a brilliant example of Spanish baroque in all its wedding-cake splendour.

Famous men: Three Granada locations are inextricably connected with the life and death of the poet **Federico García Lorca**, shot dead by General Franco's nationalist forces on 19 August 1936. The first is his birthplace in **Fuentevaqueros**, a village 10 miles (16 km) to the west of the city, today a museum.

The second, **Huerto de San Vicente**, was bought by Lorca's father as a summer house where the poet spent many summers from 1925 onwards, and which he remembered with fondness when absent from Granada. This house, 50 years ago a cool country home with a splendid view of the Alhambra, is rapidly being swallowed by the city. It is open to visitors and will soon be made into a museum, too; the surrounding fields will be saved from the grasp of speculators and transformed into a park.

The third place tragically connected with Lorca is **Viznar**, a village 5 miles (8 km) north of Granada, where the poet was taken and shot in the course of the Spanish Civil War.

Manuel de Falla, the composer of *El Amor Brujo* and *El Sombrero de Tres Picos*, was *granadino* by adoption only, but his name has become firmly linked with the city where he lived from 1919 until the horror of the Civil War precipitated his departure in 1939 to Argentina, where he died in 1946. The house he lived in is now a museum, situated in the district of **Antequeruela**, under the shadow of the Alhambra.

The Province: The **Sierra Nevada** provides excellent skiing from December to March or April. In addition, this 55-mile (88-km) range, with peaks reaching 10,000 ft (3,000 metres), has been called "the botanist's paradise".

Las Alpujarras, one of Spain's most fascinating corners, deserves a visit all to itself. The villages are so remote, yet each with its own story to tell, and the

Neighbourhoo **meeting.**

roads so slow that it is difficult to combine a visit to this mountainous region, tucked between the Sierra Nevada and the coast, with that of any other part.

It was to these hills that the Moors, fleeing the closing circle of the Catholic Monarchs at the end of the 15th century, took refuge. It was here that droves of families from Galicia and Castile arrived to take over the land left by the same Moors, many now Moriscos or converts to Christianity, when they were finally driven from Spain by Philip II a century later. There is a tradition of foreigners living in the Alpujarras, which was started by the Moors and continued by writers and artists (including Gerald Brenan) in the early part of the 20th century.

To the north: The N-342 leaves Granada down what in pre-Roman times was a vitally strategic route linking Antequera with Cartagena and Málaga with Murcia and where the Romans laid the Via Herculea. The road is high, rarely falling below 3,000 ft (1,000 metres) and winds through astonishing landscapes where barren hillocks and escarpments are interrupted from time to time by pockets of green, with mountain peaks always somewhere on the horizon.

The town of **Guadix** has many excellent historical monuments. Like so many other Andalucían towns, the splendour of the Christian development here after the Reconquest seems to have been in direct ratio to the former importance of the town as an Arab stronghold. But the real fascination of Guadix and the surrounding region is its caves. The troglodyte population of Guadix has been put as high as 40 percent of the town's inhabitants, representing some 2,000 inhabited caves, not to mention a further 4,000 or so in outlying villages such as Purullena. The whitewashed chimneys of the cave-dwellings, sitting for no apparent reason on the rock or barren scrubland that looks like a science fiction film-set, often with TV aerial not far away, are sometimes the only exterior sign that a home has been gouged out of the malleable clay.

hicken feed
the
pujarras.

THE ALHAMBRA

Probably no other monument in Europe has exerted such fascination over travellers and historians over the centuries as the Alhambra of Granada. Nor any other palace inspired so many poets, composers, painters and writers. The German historiographer Jeronimo Münzer, who visited the Alhambra in 1494, wrote: "There is nothing like it in Europe: it is all so magnificent, so majestic, so exquisitely fashioned that, looking at it, one cannot be sure that one is not in paradise."

It is a miracle that the palace, its gardens and the summer residence, the Generalife, can still be termed "the best-preserved medieval Arab palace in the world". In 1526 the Emperor Charles V decided to build his palace within the confines of the Alhambra and 50 years later the Arab mosque was knocked down to make way for the Church of Santa Maria.

Other events joined with the general abandonment of the royal city to threaten its survival: an earthquake in 1522; the rebellion of the Moriscos (Moslem converts to Christianity) in 1570; an explosion of gunpowder in 1590; the partial destruction of the ramparts by Napoleonic troops, who used the Alhambra as their garrison, in 1812.

It is largely thanks to the "discovery" of the Alhambra by writers and artists in the 19th century that the monument was at last recognised as unique. Chateaubriand, Merimée, Victor Hugo and Gustave Doré were all profoundly influenced by their stay in Granada, while Washington Irving, Théophile Gautier and Richard Ford enjoyed the extraordinary privilege of lodging within the Alhambra itself in the quarters where Charles V spent his honeymoon. Irving's *Tales of the Alhambra* are essential reading.

Visitors arrive at the foot of the fortified hill, on the **Plaza Nueva**. If your legs and lungs are up to it, it is well worth walking up the Cuesta de Gom-

erez and through the **Puerta de las Granadas** (Gate of the Pomegranates), built on Charles V's orders in 1536 to mark the entrance to his palace, in order to feel the incomparable freshness of the elm woods which cover the hill.

The visitor who arrives on foot will enter the fortified royal city through the **Gate of Justice** (Puerta de la Justicia or Bib Xari'a). Like most of the Alhambra, this gate was built in the 14th century by Yussuf I. The reign of this Nazarite king, and that of his son Mohamed V, which together stretched from 1333 to 1391, saw the construction of practically all the most important elements of the royal palace as we know them today.

Visitors arriving by bus or car will find themselves looking down on the imposing structure of Charles V's Italianate palace. Walking along the side of this, to the left, they can join their fitter fellows outside the ticket office on the **Plaza de los Aljibes**. This square commands the first of many magnificent views, this time over the Albaicin and the abandoned caves of Sacromonte.

The Alhambra (from the Arabic *ga' lat al-Hamra*, the red castle) is made up of three parts: the Royal Palace, the Alcazaba or fortress and the Medina or Alhambra Alta where up to 2,000 members of the royal household lived. Of the latter, little remains, and gardens cover the foundations of the houses.

The **Royal Palace**, begun by Yussuf I and finished during the reign of his son, Mohamed V, is also composed of three distinct parts, which lead from the most public to the most private of quarters, ending up with a visit to the baths or *hammam*. Inside the entrance to the palace is the *mexuar* where citizens of Granada were received and justice meted out; from here, one enters the *serail* where official, diplomatic life took place; and, finally, the *harem*, the monarch's private quarters.

The *mexuar* is the least well preserved part of the Royal Palace, having been converted into a chapel shortly after the expulsion of the Arab court and also damaged by the 1590 explosion. At the end of the main room is an oratory with a glimpse of the intricate geometrical motifs so prolific elsewhere.

From here a small courtyard (Patio del Cuarto Dorado) leads to a room which served as a waiting room for those to be received by the king; this is the **Cuarto Dorado**, or Golden Room.

The entrance to the *serail*, through the left-hand door at the end of the *patio*, follows a zig-zag route, thus protecting its access. Within this part of the palace diplomatic life was intense, especially in the latter half of the 14th century when the power of the Arabs in Spain was being so relentlessly sapped.

Central to this part of the Alhambra is the Patio de Comares, or **Patio de los Mirtos** (Courtyard of the Myrtles), which, with the reflection of the buildings in the water of the pond, constitutes an amazing example of the symmetry of pure Arab art. Critics refer to it as "the Parthenon of Arab art in Spain".

Off this *patio* is the majestic **Ambassadors' Room**, probably the room which leaves the most lasting impression on the visitor. The domed ceiling, **Palace of Charles V.**

reaching a height of over 50 ft (15 metres), is made of inlaid cedar wood and represents the firmament. The monarch used to sit with his back to the light, facing the entering visitors, thus keeping a clear advantage over them.

From the Courtyard of the Myrtles one passes into the *harem*, built around the **Patio de los Leones**, the Lions' Courtyard. Here the Sultan and his wives lived, as did the Queen Mother, a key figure in Moorish court life.

When visiting the rooms leading off the central courtyard (the King's Room; the Abencerrages' Room; the Room of the Two Sisters; the Room of the Sultana), bear in mind that the occupants of the rooms—servants excepted—spent their time in a reclining position; the design reflects this perspective.

Amid the overwhelming richness of the *harem* as a whole, several architectural and decorative features are distinctive. First there is the anti-earthquake device, a lead plate inserted at the top of the 124 white marble pillars. Next, the lions themselves: the 12 lions corrobo-

rates the theory that the lions represent the Twelve Tribes of Israel and the two marked with an equilateral triangle on the forehead, the Chosen Tribes.

The paintings on leather in the King's Room, where human figures appear, were probably done by Castilian artists who found refuge in the Moorish kingdom from the reign of terror of Pedro the Cruel. Look out for the traces of "blood" in the fountain in the Abencerrages' Room, "proof" of the veracity of the legend which tells of how 36 members of the Abencerrages family were beheaded one by one as they entered, a king's revenge for his wife's infidelity.

No visitor should leave without climbing up into the Alcazaba, a military bastion whose origins go back to pre-Roman times, for the 360-degree view. Or up the Hill of the Sun, behind the Alhambra to the Generalife palace, the summer residence. The gardens here are perhaps the most magnificent in Spain and the sound of running water is particularly soothing for anyone who has had enough of heat and monuments.

Gardens of the Alhambra.

ON FOOT AND SKI
IN THE SIERRA

Many parts of inland Andalucía are excellent for walking but no part is better than the Sierra Nevada, Europe's second highest mountain range after the Alps. Here some people rock-climb or mountain-walk, but for amateurs who do not want to use more equipment than just good boots, the **Alpujarras** are ideal. This sensationally beautiful group of mountain valleys runs east and west some 19 miles (30 km) southeast of Granada, between the small towns of **Orgiva** and **Ugíjar**.

It was in the Alpujarras that some 60,000 Moriscos (Moslems nominally converted to Christianity) continued to live when the Kingdom of Granada fell to the Christians in 1492. But after their revolt of 1570 they were forcibly re-settled throughout Spain. As a result, the Alpujarras is now only the home of about a tenth as many people as it once was. They live in little white villages dotted about the valley sides, not unlike the White Towns near Ronda.

Two twisting mountain roads connect Orgiva and Ugíjar, dipping and rising to call at most of these villages. Fortunately for walkers, the villages are also still the centres of networks of mule and donkey tracks, often centuries old and paved with stone though little more than a metre wide.

The climate, too, is delightful. Although the whole area is high, it is possible for the hardy walker to bed down in a sleeping bag on an open hillside as late as mid-October. But not, be warned, in a river bed: during a storm these can become terrifying torrents. The owner of an abandoned farm near Los Tablones remembers one storm a few years ago when it was impossible to make conversation because of the continuous crashing together of boulders in the Rio Guadalfeo, though the river was 200 yards away. There is anyway no need to sleep rough. The villages have simple but clean *fondas* (inns).

How to prepare: A map of not less than 1:50,000 is essential, but some of the mule tracks are hard to follow. Starting boldly from a village, they tend to disappear after one or two miles, and there will be a gap before the fringe of the next village's network becomes clear. Asking the way is easy with only a little Spanish (you won't find much else spoken) but the lazy Andalucían dialect is even lazier in the Alpujarras, and understanding the answers is difficult.

A good plan is to start at Orgiva and move eastwards, ultimately reaching Ugíjar, but weave north and south to stop at particular villages. One not to miss is **Yegen**, both for its charm and because it was here that Gerald Brenan, British author of many books on Spain, lived between the two world wars. Today his house carries a plaque commemorating him. "Fifty years ago," one old villager remembered, "there was much singing and dancing in this house—and I was the singer."

The Alpujarras was so utterly remote in Brenan's time that his housekeeper was astonished when she first visited the sea to find it so large. And irritated:

eft, Europe's outhernmost ki resort. Right, in the streets of ubión.

what was the use of it all, she thought. You couldn't wash clothes in it or irrigate land with it.

Also not to be missed is **Trevélez**, which stands some way up the subsidiary valley of the Rio Trevélez and claims to be the highest village in Spain. From Trevélez, the energetic can climb north to the Puerto de Trevélez, though the route is none too easy to find. It crosses many of the irrigation channels constructed by the Moriscos which are still such a feature of the Alpujarras and will sometimes be found so high up a valley side that it seems the water must flow uphill to reach them. The view from the pass, of another 13 little white villages dotted about the vast landscape, then more and more ranges of mountain, is reward for the effort of getting there.

The first half of October is an ideal time for exploring the Alpujarras on foot. The weather is cooler and this is the time of fiestas, which move eastwards up the valley. Free wine flows from the Fuente de Vino at Cádiar, and at Ugíjar two Spanish passions—for religious processions and for explosive fireworks—reach a fine climax.

Sun and snow: From the top of the Veleta ski lift at the resort of Solynieve you can usually see the Mediterranean. On a good day, or so they say, you can even see the distant coast of North Africa. But most people come up to this delightful resort of the Sierra Nevada not for the views but for the skiing.

Solynieve (sun and snow) is the southernmost ski resort in Europe. Set on the south-facing slopes of the Sierra Nevada, about 20 miles (32 km) north of the Moorish city of Granada, it was the site of the World Championships in 1977, and its facilities have since improved. There is reliable snow cover from early December until the end of March or early April, which attracts keen skiers from all over Europe and Spain, as well as swarms of local enthusiasts from the surrounding cities of Andalucía. Although the resort centre itself is concrete, modern-garish, and far from pretty, the skiing is first class.

Mule market in the Alpujarras.

190

Solynieve boasts 30 miles (48 km) of groomed downhill piste and a reasonable amount of off-piste, and services this with 18 assorted lifts and tows. The runs are largely easy "blues" or moderately difficult "reds", but some of the shorter pitches off the Veleta II drag lift are quite steep enough for even a committed intermediate skier. There are five hard "blacks", and most winters allow ski-touring across the mountains of the Sierra Nevada. As with most modern resorts, Solynieve also has snow cannon to fill in the bare patches.

All this makes Solynieve a first-class resort, and the *sol* is usually well in evidence throughout the winter. Facilities include a mountain nursery for toddlers, and a children's ski-school for those aged between six and 12. Prices are at a sub-alpine level and the food is good. It all helps.

The *après-ski* in Solynieve is based on a large number of bars—28 at the last count—piano bars, restaurants, and one large disco, the Nevada 53. There are good restaurants in the main hotels, the Melia Sierra and the Kerria Nevada, and especially at the *parador*, set high on the Veleta. Cuisine on the Sierra ranges from French at the popular Pourquoi-Pas through to Castilian and Andalucían specialities at the Ruta de Veleta, a restaurant popular with King Juan Carlos and the Royal Family of Spain when they come skiing hereabouts. That apart, there are *tapas* bars and small restaurants.

Finally, to add a touch of difference to this ski resort, it has access to the other charms of Andalucía, none of which are rendered unattractive by the winter. One excursion is just down the mountain for a day in Granada, to see the gardens of the Generalife and the Alhambra Palace, as well as the old city. Moreover, the sea is so close that hardy souls can ski, sail or even swim all within a day, and the transfer time from the airport at Málaga is two hours—a great drive through superb mountain scenery, unlikely to be disrupted by the massive traffic queues which spoil many a European skiing week.

erald
renan's
egen.

JAEN AND ITS PROVINCE

A massive, undulating sea of 150 million olive trees, Jaén province, 5,212 sq. miles (13,498 sq. km), has always suffered from being labelled as a place of transit.

Named Giyen (caravan route) by the Arabs and the gateway of Andalucía by the armies of the Christian Reconquest, trudged through by armies and saints and traders over the centuries, it still tends to be thought of as somewhere to drive through rather than somewhere in which to stop.

In this sense, Jaén's character has been moulded around the natural crossroads carved through the centre by the tributaries of the Guadalquivir. Now only freight trains and chains of lorries criss-cross the plains and slowly roll up the motorway loop to Despeñaperros, the precipitous pass leading to the central sierras.

But under the surface and in cultural terms Jaén remains a border province: Castile and Andalucía meet in the architecture, regional dishes and local temperament, said to be both more receptive and more self-contained than that of the deep south.

From the main roads, the geometry of the silvery olive trees imposed on the blotchy cream and rust hills gives the countryside a deceptive rural uniformity. But after a day or two of slower exploration, when the mesmerising effect of the *olivares* has worn off, you begin to notice the changes of landscape in the sierras framing the province and the surprising richness of the historic towns built along the crossroads of power.

The north–south artery (N-323) which brings you into the province encapsulates the province's embattled frontier history. Here, on flat plains spiked by the old lead mining chimneys, three key battles, turning points in Spanish history, were fought within a few miles of each other: Beacula, at Castulo (now Linares) where the Romans defeated the Carthaginians; Na-

vas de Tolosa, the first great victory of the Andalucían *reconquista*; and finally, the battle of Bailén, where the tide turned against Napoleon in 1808.

There is little to see at either Bailén or Linares—an industrial town now known largely for its bars, bull-ring and most famous son, composer Andrés Segovia—but the trophies taken at Navas are kept in the church at nearby Vilches. Also, splendid ruined castles have survived from the century of the Reconquest: Baños de la Encina, won and lost again six times by the Christians; Alcaudete, a dusty olive town above a sea of olive trees still owned by only five families, and, in the far south, Alcalá la Real, where the later church dropped into the fortress has a strangely post-modern effect.

Bases of beauty: The real architectural gems, however, are the small towns of Baeza and Ubeda, which lie a stone's throw apart on the old road running east to Levante. Both were key military bases of the *reconquista*, which grew from hotbeds of aristocratic squabbling

into cultured cities stuffed with Gothic, Renaissance and baroque architecture.

Their astounding richness gives the lie to guidebooks which suggest that there is little of architectural interest in Andalucía outside the great Moorish cities. *"Borrachera espléndida de romanticismo!"* (What a glut of romanticism) exclaimed Andalucían poet García Lorca, overcome by the melancholy air of **Baeza's** past grandeur at dusk. These days its honey-coloured palaces, churches and civic buildings, dating largely from the peaceful, wealthy 15th to 17th centuries, have a cherished air.

Star features include the studded **Palacio de Jabalquinto** (currently housing one of the best restoration schools in Spain), the **Convento de San Francisco** (ruined and controversially restored), the austere seminary with its faded antique graffiti on the walls—graduating students' names written in bull's blood—and the **Plaza de los Leones**. But there is so much to see here that you need at least a half-day to explore properly.

Less historic, but compulsory for many Spaniards, is a quick look at the house where poet Antonio Machado wrote some of his best work, and a longer visit to **Casa Juanito**, the roadhouse restaurant on the outskirts of town which serves excellent regional cooking.

Ubeda cannot match up to its smaller sister town for general mood since its past has been absorbed into the fabric of a larger place. But it does have the unmissable **Plaza de Vázquez de Molino**, an architectural set-piece in a class of its own. The rectangular plaza, widening at one end, runs down from the stunningly rich domed chapel of **El Salvador** (built as a family pantheon and still privately owned by the Duques de Medina Celi) past a balanced, beautifully proportioned sequence of austere palaces unbroken by modern additions, considered by many to be the purest architectural expression of the Renaissance in Spain.

At the far end, the Palacio de las Cadenas faces the church of **Sta María**

Alcazar de los Reales, a church built on the site of the old mosque. The overall effect of monumental calm—kept from being museum-like by the *parador* and *Hogar de pensionistas* where old dears chat and play cards—deserves hours of long and slow contemplation.

The 50 or so other sights spread around the rest of Ubeda—palaces, churches, seigneurial and modernist houses—are best attacked with the help of the tourist office's walking itinerary; even if your energy flags, don't miss **San Pablo**, the facades in the **Calle del Horno Contador** and **Calle Real**, or Vandelvira's **Hospital de Santiago**, sometimes compared to the Escorial for its severity (its modern conversion into a cultural centre is also a good example of the Spanish knack for putting new wine in old bottles).

On the edge of town, the long-established craft workshops making ceramics and *ubedies* (ornamental straw mats) are not cheap, but for once they offer genuine craftsmanship.

To the east of Ubeda stretch the best of the province's olive groves. Despite terrible inequalities of wealth, they have kept the worst of southern poverty at bay, giving the stone towns and villages a solid, contented feel. As a local proverb puts it: "*A quien Dios quiso bien, casa le dio en Jaén.*" (Whoever God wished well, he gave a house in Jaén.) Lovely mansion houses, castles and churches, often given a good sacking in the Civil War, are scattered here in the smaller villages such as Sabiote, Ibros, Rus and Torrepergil.

Provincial centre: After such concentrated architectural beauty, **Jaén** city, perched above the western plain with its back to the sierras, seems surprisingly thin on monuments. But what it lacks in quantity—it was repeatedly stripped by war-time sackings and is now largely a modern business and services capital—it makes up for in scale.

The cathedral is a massive pile built over three centuries, with a wonderful mish-mash of Gothic to baroque styles; the Arab baths, superbly excavated and restored over 14 years, are among the

Preceding page: fiesta celebrant in Ubeda. Below, Plaza de los Leones, Baeza.

largest and best preserved in Spain; within its walls the museum has one of the best collections of prehistoric Iberian material in the world.

Equally, the streets, both the wide avenues of the commercial zone and the alleys of the old town stacked against the curving hillside on a series of *cantones*, or terrace walls, have the zip and energy you find only in such self-possessed Spanish provincial cities. The animated bars and taverns in San Juan and the 19th-century balconied streets around the Cathedral make for a good evening's drinking and conversation.

Higher up the hill in **La Magdalena**, the old up-and-down Moorish quarter with the castle of Santa Catalina looming above it, family life spills out on to the steep pebbled alleys, and the soaring Gothic vaulting of its church, the oldest in town, is like a refreshing drink of water after all the rich visual decoration elsewhere.

In the hills: Each of the three main sierras framing the province has a dis-

tinct personality. The western **Sierra Morena**, where Castilian severity meets Andalucían light, is the emptiest, left largely to cows and deer, except in late April when 500,000 pilgrims flood through on foot, horseback and by car to pay homage to the diminutive Virgin in the sanctuary of **Nuestra Señora de la Cabeza**.

Outside the church stands one of the most moving elegies of modern war, capturing both the idealism and futile sacrifice; a simple stone tablet tells in detail how Capitán Cortes, leading 250 Nationalist troops and a handful of local villagers, defended the sanctuary against eight months of Republican onslaught until he was finally killed and the enemy burst in to find only 30 starving men.

On the plain below, **Andújar**, once a great walled city and evangelical centre with 48 towers and 12 gates, is now dominated by a sunflower oil refinery. A fine El Greco is kept in the church of Santa María la Mayor.

It also makes a livelier base for ex-

ploring the northwest than Marmolejo, the small spa-town, or La Carolina, laid out as a grid by Charles III, the enlightened despot who drew up grandiose plans for settling the sierras in the 18th century.

Park land: To the east, the more obviously beautiful alpine scenery of **Cazorla** and **Segura** has changed dramatically in the past 20 years. The once isolated mountains and remote valleys, famous for their shepherds and the province's best olive oil, are now part of a national park visited by 750,000 people a year.

The transition has not been easy: the flood of visitors makes fire a real hazard in summer, restrictions on industry have aggravated unemployment and traditional occupations—logging, shepherding, seasonal work in the olive groves—continue to decline while a stronger tourist economy would clash with the ecological balance. A subsidised switch to organic farming looks likely to provide a happier compromise.

The olive oil industry has also seen many changes. The thrust now is to replace ancient trees with new, high-yield plantings, to extend mechanisation as far as possible and to emphasise quality. But until someone invents an effective olive-picking machine the fruit is still hand-picked, mainly by day labourers working on the vast estates.

Increasingly small growers and olive mill owners are forming cooperatives, to pool resources and cut production costs. Only in this way can they hope to win a place in the important international market—with the government's promotional help.

Meanwhile, the villages remain quietly beautiful, especially hilltop **Segura de la Sierra** (the massive keys to the Arab castle and baths are kept at the Casino café) and **Hornos**, where the panoramic view from the village square trumps any Hollywood special effect.

To the south, the main town of **Cazorla**, recently swollen by people moving down from the sierras to take town work, is still pleasantly higgledy-piggledy and rural despite its grand ruined cathedral and castle; there is an interesting market with produce brought down from the sierras on Mondays and Saturdays, and a clutch of restaurants which serve the sturdy local dishes such as game sausages or, for those who will brave the unromantic realities of peasant cooking, roast lamb's head and feet.

The southern sierras, **Magina** and **Pandera**, gentler around the great central massif, are also soon to be put on the tourist map as a national park. Attractions here may sound a curious mixed bag: two churches like small cathedrals at **Huelma** and **Cabra** (ask for the keys at the priests' houses), the picturesque village of **Cambil** squeezed into its narrow gorge like a plump woman into a corset, neolithic cave drawings above **Jimena**, a tumbledown spa at **Jabalcuz** and ghostly pictures on a stone floor in **Bélmez** (a natural phenomenon which has been baffling scientists for nearly 20 years). But, as in so much of Jaén, they are made immensely pleasurable by the lack of any commercialisation or crowds.

Left, hillside town of Cazorla. **Right**, Cazorla's best method of transport.

OLIVE OIL

These days a mechanical vibrator is used to shake the trees and plastic crates are used instead of baskets to collect the fallen olives; a tractor rather than a mule hauls the olives to the mill, and great stainless steel vats have replaced the clay amphoras of the Romans. But these are only superficial changes; very little has altered in the production of olive oil since Roman times.

Not for want of trying. It's just that nobody yet has figured out how to mechanise the cultivation and milling of olives. Which is why good olive oil costs so much.

The Romans planted olive trees across what is now Jaén, Córdoba and Seville above the River Quadalquivir. After milling the oil was transported down river to the sea, to be shipped to Rome.

The Moors extended the cultivation of the olive across much of the peninsula. They called it *az-zait*, meaning "juice of the olive". From this derives the Spanish *aceite*, the generic word for oil. The tree in Spanish is *olivo*, from the Latin, but the fruit, *aceituna*, is from the Arabic.

Olive cultivation reached its zenith in Spain in the early 16th century. Today, the country is the world's largest producer of olive oil, with 11 percent of all cultivated lands planted in olives, supporting more than 600,000 families. Andalucía alone produces about 20 percent of the world's total. Jaén province produces the most oil—and some of the best.

Olive oil is extracted by purely mechanical means and, unlike other vegetable oils, can be consumed without further refining and purification. At the mill, the *almazara*, olives are first thoroughly washed, then crushed by stones or steel wheels to release the oil. The pulp is spread on to mats woven from esparto grass or nylon synthetics. These are stacked on an hydraulic press, which squeezes the pulp tighter and tighter, allowing the oil to flow out through channels.

The oil is filtered into a series of settling tanks. The oil rises to the top and is drawn off, while the sediment and water content settle to the bottom. The resulting product is pure virgin olive oil, first pressing.

The quality of that oil depends on several factors, such as variety of olive, soil and climate, but, most importantly, how the olives were picked, transported, stored and

milled. The best oil, labelled "extra virgin" or "fine virgin", comes from olives which are picked ripe and milled immediately. Its colour can vary from pale gold to amber to greenish-yellow, depending on the type of olive. It is usually completely clear after filtration. New oil has a slight bitterness, appreciated by many people, which disappears with a few months' maturation. Two and even three pressings might be made from the same olive pulp.

The product is used extensively in Andalucía. In a typical village home the housewife serves her family the midday meal. The fish, croquettes, pork and potatoes are all fried in olive oil. The salad is dressed with olive oil. For breakfast, toasted slabs of bread are dipped in a bowl of olive oil placed in the centre of the table. When mother makes the typical Christmas sweets, studded with aniseed, filled with sweet fruit jam, they are deep-fried in olive oil.

Everything from glowing complexions (before commercial moisturisers, Spanish women used olive oil and water whipped together) to strong hearts and good digestion has been attributed to olive oil. Modern nutritional science is verifying the folklore.

Countries such as Spain, Italy and Greece have a markedly lower incidence of death from coronary disease than such widely differing peoples as Americans, Finns and the whites of South Africa. The Mediterranean peoples show higher total intake of fats, predominantly from olive oil. The other groups consume mainly animal fats, such as butter, lard and cream. The difference is that olive oil contains no cholesterol.

Olive oil doesn't break down at frying temperatures, giving off toxic material, as do other oils. Tests also show that olive oil makes crisper fried potatoes with a thinner coating than either sunflower or soya oils. Potatoes fried in olive oil absorb 12 percent less oil than those fried in sunflower and 47 percent less than in soya oil, resulting in a lower calorie intake.

As a result of the new emphasis on healthy eating, the industry is benefiting from a small boom. Virgin oil's designer-label status is giving it a competitive edge, in spite of its price. To encourage production of the highest quality oil, a control board authorises a few select *denominación de origen* labels, or "guarantee of origin", for virgin oils. So far, there are four in all of Spain, two of which are in Andalucía: Sierra de Segura (Jaén), where olives mix with pines on steep hillsides, and Baena (Córdoba), where olive groves meet vineyards.

ALMERIA AND ITS PROVINCE

For much of this century, Almería's harsh landscape of sun-scorched sierras and rocky plains, savagely beautiful in some areas but bleakly featureless and dusty in others, was jokingly dismissed by Spaniards as a forgotten corner. Even Gerald Brenan, sentimentally protective as he felt about his own province, found it hard to disagree when somebody called it *el culo d'España*, the backside of Spain.

Not that Almería (3,386 sq. miles, 8,774 sq. km) lacks a history of wealth and glory. Under Arab rule, the city of the same name grew from an important port and arsenal to become the seat of one of the most powerful 11th-century *taifas*, or splinter kingdoms, ruling much of Murcia and Andalucía. An industrial city with a population of 200,000, it was famed for its silks and trade with the East, said by chroniclers to be outshone in splendour only by Córdoba, Baghdad and Alexandria.

Today the ruined castles strategically scattered around the province are all that remain of that power; piracy, the Reconquest, invasion by the Turks and earthquakes exacerbated the struggle with the heat and aridity to pitch Almería into centuries of rural poverty.

But in the past 30 years the *almerenses*, tenaciously hardworking and independent, have turned all that around by finding gold in their liabilities. Now the desert-like climate powers a massive hothouse agriculture business spreading over more than 49,400 acres (20,000 hectares) of the coastal plain and is the main prop of a buoyant year-round tourist industry.

Together, these new areas of economic growth have hauled the average per capita income up from the lowest in the country to one of the highest, bringing with them new social and environmental problems: a steadily falling water table, high suicide rates, a major shift from the interior to the coast and tensions over immigration. According to locals it has also eradicated a fatalis-

tic streak in the *almerense* character.

Nonetheless, nearly half the province's population still lives in villages of under 2,000 people in the quiet, little known interior. Here the old extremes remain, the landscape either magnificently raw in the sierras which slice from east to west across the province, or painstakingly tamed around the strings and pockets of *cortijos* and villages following the contours of the valleys. The mountain roads, said to have as many turns as a local *bolero* or *fandango*, make for spectacular driving, snaking up to passes where the sierras seem to drop away into rumpled folds, then swooping back down to the *ramblas*, or dusty dried-up river beds, which are the most characteristic feature of the countryside

The coast: Tourism, which has developed largely since the early 1980s, has left much of Almería's coastline untouched. To the west, the **Campo del Dalís**, now locally better known as the **Costa del Plástico**, is temporarily preserved by the vast plastic greenhouses,

or *invernaderos*, closely packed between the foot of the mountains and the beach; at good moments, with the sun glinting on the opaque green plastic roofs, the sea seems to have flooded the plain, but on the whole they make an unromantic, semi-industrial backdrop for sunbathing.

In the centre sits **El Ejido**, a boom town that was unmarked on most maps until recently, but now, with a population of over 40,000, ranks second in size in the province. Sprawling along the dead straight highway and clogged with fruit lorries emblazoned with images of the Virgin Mary, it is an Andalucían variation on an American truckers' town.

Just down the road are the province's two high-rise resorts, **Roquetas del Mar** and **Aguadulce**, both pleasantly spacious and sedate by comparison with the hard-core Costa del Sol. Nonetheless, there are more attractive bases within reach of both the beaches and the inland valleys: **Enix**, a flowery hillside splash of white with a 17th-century church plus a good hotel outside the walled village, or **Berja**, a larger market town with shady squares and seigneurial houses.

The coast to the east of Almería could hardly be a greater contrast. Marshland and working salt-beds with a colony of flamingoes run south to the dramatic, volcanic headland of the **Cabo de Gata**, protected as natural parkland since 1980 for its flora, fauna and underwater life, said to be some of the best in the Mediterranean.

Abandoned squat windmills, watchtowers and the atmospheric redrock ghost town at **Rodalquilir**, once Spain's only gold mine, give a quiet, mournful beauty to the scrubby headlands, while the coast itself swings north through wonderfully unspoiled bays like the **Playa de Morrón de los Genoveses**, once the crater of a volcano, and the shingly, black-beached fishing hamlet at **Las Negras**.

Either San José or Isleta de Arraez provide quiet villa accommodation or, a short drive inland, there is **Níjar**, fa-

Almería's coast is Europe's winter garden.

208

mous in Spain as the setting for the real-life tale of passion and revenge which inspired Lorca to write *Blood Wedding*. Sloping down the foot of a sierra from the cramped old town, it has more life of its own than the coastal hamlets and good shops for buying pottery and cotton rugs.

Further north, beyond **Carboneras**, where smoke belches out from a large cement works, there is more spectacular scenery and the long, fine beach of Algarrobico before a ribbon of low-level development runs towards **Mojácar**.

Until the 1960s, this was a quiet white village with labyrinthine alleys inherited from the Arabs and everyday traces of the ancient Indalo culture, most famously in the women's custom of half-covering their faces with *cobijas*, triangular shawls. Now, like so many small places which are discovered and colonised, it has become a chintzy resort where it is hard to pick out the interesting architecture and history amongst the boutiques and bars, many of them British-owned. Neighbouring **Garruchas** is plainer but less precious by far, with some excellent fish restaurants down by the port and, to the north, long golden beaches with Spain's first official naturist (nudist) hotel.

City centre: At the centre of the southern coast sits Almería city, the Moorish "mirror of the sea", still dominated by the massive walls of its 11th-century **Alcázaba** looming protectively over the old town and broad double bay.

In the past 50 years the city has grown from "a bucket of whitewash thrown down at the foot of a bare, greyish mountain", as Brenan described it in 1939, to a modern provincial capital with characterless commercial and industrial zones which have gobbled up the green *huertas* (gardens). But the new is neatly sectioned off from the palmy, peeling old town by the **Rambla del Obispo**, which runs down to the port, and the *almerenses'* easy-going warmth keeps the friendly atmosphere of quieter, slower times; they like to say that here, "*nadie se siente extraño*". (Nobody feels like a stranger.)

From the Alcázaba—by far the most impressive monument of the province, with its magnificently severe Moorish fortress architecture overlaid by the more grandiose Catholic upper courtyard—you can first breathe in the atmosphere and scale of the city. Open to the sea and fenced in at the back by the mountains, the old town, or *barrio monumental*, runs east from the fishing port and hillside gypsy **Chanca** quarter—often described by the guidebooks as "colourful" but more realistically also as desperately poor—gradually smartening towards the broad, shady 19th-century **Paseo de Almería**. At the back, you look out over the remaining stretch of the ramparted city walls, rebuilt by Charles V, which once ran down to the sea.

Down below, the 16th-century **Cathedral** is another reminder that long after the Reconquest Almería remained a vulnerable defensive outpost; its bulky golden exterior, built as much against piracy as for worship, belies the graceful vaulting and superb woodcarv-

actus used be almost e only crop.

ing on the *coro* inside. Elsewhere in the network of narrow one-way streets, there are large and small tree-shaded squares, a handful of small churches and all kinds of small shops. At night the bars and cafés take over, turning the alleys between the Cathedral and the Paseo into a fashionable crush.

Inland attractions: As the province's main road junction, Almería is also the best access point to the sierras and valleys of the interior. On the main roads to Murcia and Granada there is little of interest except for the oriental moonscape west of **Tabernas**, uninhabited but curiously familiar as the film-set of classic spaghetti westerns and epics like *Lawrence of Arabia* and *Indiana Jones*, and worth a detour to visit the gloriously tacky old film-sets with piped music and dust eddying across from the Indian reservation to the gallows.

Back in the real world, a few miles further on, **Sorbas** has galleried houses hanging out over the kitchen gardens in the river valley and is one of the few places where the rough local pottery is still made and sold. Apart from this, the smaller roads that wind along the two main valleys, named after their rivers, the Andarax and Almanzora, are more satisfying.

The **Andarax** valley, abruptly lush below the harsh sierras, prospers on orange trees and vines producing the famed sweet white Ohanes grapes that have been exported round the world since the middle of the 19th century. It is easy to see why the Moors, drawn by the watery greenness, came here to retreat from the coastal heat. They named the village of **Alhama** after its thermal waters and Boabdil chose **Laujar**, on the fringes of the Alpujarras, as his last home in Spain after he was run out of Granada; today Alhama has a splendid old-fashioned spa hotel and Laujar remains a favourite *almerense* destination for Sunday outings.

Initially, the **Almanzora** valley seems less appealing. Filmed with dust around the ugly marble quarries of Macael and elsewhere sleepily impoverished by the closure of iron mines and **Observatory at Calar Alta**

the railway, it is less obviously picturesque. But at the top of the valley there are two lovely villages: **Purchena**, sometimes fancifully compared to a miniature Granada for its dramatic setting slapped up against a rock face (ask for the key to the fine 17th-century church), and **Serón**, attractively clumped below a ruined castle on a dome-shaped hill—from where you explore the dramatically beautiful, little-explored **Sierra de los Filabres** with the help of the provincial map of the Instituto Geográfico Nacional (the best large-scale reference map).

The best of the winding roads leads from **Cantoria** to the villages around **Cóbdar**, a world of their own at the bottom of a precipitous valley. As if to make the point, **Lijar**, a village with more bars than shops, proudly displays the plaque commemorating peace with France after a private hundred years' war declared by the mayor in 1883. Another good route is the track from Serón which leads up past a picturesque abandoned mining village—now being

reconstructed—to the highest point of the province, **Calar Alta**, 6,937 ft (2,168 metres), where there is an astronomical observatory with the most powerful telescope in Europe and a stunningly empty panorama.

To the north of the Almanzora, there are only scattered *cortijos* and the Santuario de la Saliente (which has a good bar and restaurant) in the "burnt, cactus-sharp, breathless sprawl" of hills, as Rose Macaulay described them. In the valley beyond, soon to be sliced through by the Autovía del Mediterraneo, are the "two Vélezes"—named after the marquises who owned huge tracts of the surrounding countryside—which have been emptied by emigration.

Nobody is quite sure how these *pueblos* got their second names. **Rubio**, the larger of the two, carries their aristocratic imprint in a series of churches, convents and mansions; but the restored ruins of the 16th-century castle at **Blanco**, the small sister village, are more impressive for their scale and setting, with a splendid view over Murcia.

Mini
Hollywood,
film-set
town.

CAVES AND
CAVE LIVING

Twenty thousand years ago, man dipped his finger in ochre and traced the outlines of fish and deer on cave walls in southern Spain. Today, evidence of these early cave-dwellers is still coming to light. Meanwhile, to the astonishment of many travellers, more than 30,000 people still live underground in Andalucía.

This is not so much due to backwardness as to convenience. Many of the caves are comfortably fitted out with all modern conveniences and their inhabitants prefer them to concrete apartment blocks. Attempts to persuade the latter-day troglodytes to move have failed.

Living quarters: In 1985 the Junta de Andalucía, the regional government, recognised this fact and began a programme to improve the caves. Of 9,500 caves in the region, 8,600 were found to be inhabited permanently.

Most of these are in the provinces of Almería and Granada. The rehabilitation programme began with 31 caves in **La Chanca,** in the shadow of Almería's Arab fortress. This zone, notorious for its poverty, is mainly inhabited by gypsies, as the **Sacromonte** cave area of Granada used to be. However, after a storm caused caves to collapse, many of Sacromonte's gypsies moved to apartment blocks. By night a number return to offer flamenco entertainment to visiting tourists, but they don't necessarily live there anymore.

Most cave-dwellers are not gypsies and there is no stigma attached to living as they do. Indeed, they have a special pride in their homes and showing visitors they are as good as any. Some work in offices and factories.

Many are small farmers or landless labourers who keep their mules or goats—and sometimes their cars—in adjacent caves. As one asked: "Where would I put the donkey if I moved to one of those newfangled apartments? Would he fit in the lift?"

Troglodytes are to be found in the valleys of the **Andarax** and **Alman-**

zora rivers of Almería province, but the greatest number are in communities in and around **Guadix**, in Granada province. In the latter region, they inhabit an area of harsh eroded hills where the compact, impermeable clay is ideal for excavating waterproof caves. Bars, a *discoteca*, a church and shops can all be found wholly or partly underground.

Walking through a troglodyte suburb, it is possible to find oneself tramping over somebody's roof without realising it until one notes a whitewashed chimney—these days usually with a television aerial attached to it. Red peppers hanging out to dry and pots of geraniums add vivid colour to the entrances of cave-homes.

In-cave conveniences: Far from being dank and inhospitable, man-made caves are often as comfortable as any conventional dwelling and are usually immaculately whitewashed. They have several rooms. The outer wall, pierced by one or two windows, may be of rock or of bricks. For ventilation, a chimney thrusts up to the surface. Washing

Left, cave houses at Purullena. Right, cave-dwellers.

machines, refrigerators and other modern appliances are also common. Proper drainage and sewage is being installed. Some caves even have telephones.

The inhabitants like the tranquillity of their homes compared to modern apartments, which act as echo chambers to noise. They also point out that the temperature rarely varies from 16° to 18° C (62° to 68° F), summer or winter. Caves have title deeds like normal dwellings, but they are cheaper. A reasonable one may cost only a million pesetas. And if you want extra space, you can always chip out a new room.

It is believed that the Moriscos (Moslems converted to Christianity), fleeing from persecution in the 16th century, took refuge underground, but people have probably inhabited caves continuously in the Guadix–Baza region since early times.

Older caves: Traces of prehistoric man's campfires, paintings and ceramics have been found in many parts of Andalucía. Priceless relics of early man and of the invaders who swept through the province are still to be discovered beneath its surface. Indeed, archaeologists have a difficult time keeping up with the past. Almost daily, a plough or a bulldozer uncovers traces of early human endeavour.

Often by the time anybody in authority arrives, Bronze Age tools, Phoenician pots or Roman scarabs have disappeared, buried in concrete or sold for a few pesetas to the first comer. Many a home holds an artefact that would be coveted by museums.

New finds throw light on prehistoric man and his customs along the Mediterranean. One discovery occurred in the cave of the **Boquete de Zafarraya,** on the border of Málaga and Granada provinces, where investigators' torches revealed the large bones and lower jawbone of a Neanderthal man, possibly dating back 85,000 years. Other traces of Neanderthal occupation have turned up in caves at Piñar (Granada), Vera (Almería) and in the Gibraltar area.

There are abundant indications that, as the last Ice Age receded (around 40,000 years ago), Cro-Magnon man

took up residence in Andalucían caves. Regarded as our direct ancestor, he was an artist, used tools and was skilled in hunting. Arrow and spear heads and other evidence of his presence have been found in such Almería caves as that of **Zájara** at Vera, and **Ambrosio** at Vélez-Blanco. In the **Doña Trinidad** cave, near Ardales, in the mountains behind Málaga, a drawing of a horse is believed to date from the Upper Palaeolithic period.

Evidence of fertility cults and primitive religious rites are common in the caves that have been explored. Near Vélez-Blanco in Almería province, the **Cueva de los Letreros** shelters prehistoric inscriptions which include the *Indalo,* depicting a man holding an arc over his head. This symbol was long believed to ward off the "evil eye" and more recently it was chosen by Almería's artists to represent their movement.

Biggest and best: One of the most significant discoveries occurred on 12 January 1959, when five boys playing on a hillside near the hamlet of Maro, in Málaga province, came across the entrance to an immense grotto. Investigators found evidence that it was inhabited at least 15,000 years ago and that it had also been used as a burial chamber.

Remains of shellfish and the bones of goats and rabbits have been found in these caves, as well as wall paintings depicting deer, horses and fishes. Drawings representing a female deity and red-painted pebbles indicated that religious rites had taken place.

Known as the **Cueva de Nerja**, the series of chambers with their impressive stalactites and stalagmites were first opened to the public in June 1960, when a French ballet company presented *Swan Lake* there. For several years a summer festival has been held in the cave. Since then, Nerja has become a tourist attraction and music and special lighting has been added.

In contrast, visitors to **La Pileta** cave in the mountains near Ronda find their way along miles of limestone galleries by the light of oil lamps. Scoured out millennia ago by an underground river, the caverns of La Pileta provided shelter for man as long ago as the Upper Palaeolithic period when he daubed the image of a stag's head on a wall. Numerous mysterious symbols adorn the walls and there are suggestions of a fertility cult, particularly in the painting of a pregnant mare.

La Pileta was discovered in 1905 when José Bullón Lobato, whose family still owns the cave, was searching for *guano* (bird droppings) to fertilise his land. Seeing a large hole, he let himself down 100 ft (30 metres) by rope into a chamber. Its walls were sooty from fires and ceramic shards were scattered about. Penetrating further, he noted human remains and a series of vivid wall paintings. Later exploration turned up human skeletons, silex, bones, polished stone tools and ceramics from the Neolithic period.

Buried treasure: Caves honeycomb many areas of Andalucía and undoubtedly numerous treasures have still to be discovered. The existence of some caves has been known to residents for centuries, but for one reason or another they have not been fully explored.

This was the case with the **Aracena** cave in the sierras of Huelva province. It was flooded until early this century. Then the water was pumped out, to reveal a dazzling array of stalactite and stalagmite formations. Now known as the **Gruta de las Maravillas** (Cave of the Marvels), it attracts large numbers of visitors.

Somewhere in the Alpujarras region another cave awaits discovery. In this mountainous terrain, Aben Humeya, the last king of the Moriscos, defied the Christian armies. However, he reigned for only 10 months. His own followers schemed against him and strangled him. According to legend, he possessed a great treasure, which he had hidden in a cave near the village of Trevélez.

Four hundred years have passed. Many have sought Aben Humeya's treasure in vain. Perhaps, one day, another group of boys playing hide-and-seek on an Andalucían mountainside will stumble across an opening.

Cueva de Menga at Antequera.

MALAGA AND ITS PROVINCE

Of the millions of visitors who flock annually to Málaga province, very few stray more than a couple of miles from the beach. But the province has a lot more to offer than its famous coast.

Any exploration of Málaga province should start—though it probably won't—with **Málaga** itself. Originally Phoenician, it sided briefly with Carthage before becoming a Roman *municipium (*a town governed by its own laws). In 711 it fell to the Moors within a year of their invasion of Spain and was the port of the Kingdom of Granada until 1487, when it was taken by the Christians after a four-month siege followed by brutal burnings.

Since then, too often for its own good, it has been a place of revolution. It was on Málaga's San Andrés beach that the rebel General Torrijos and his 52 companions were shot in 1831. In revolt against the repressive government of Ferdinand VII, this young Spanish general landed on today's Costa del Sol, encouraged by an invented story that the Málaga garrison would join him. Instead it surrounded and captured him.

In 1931, and again at the start of the Civil War, left-wing citizens burned Málaga's churches and convents, and it held out against General Franco's Nationalists until 1937. When it finally fell, its refugees were murderously bombed and shelled as they escaped up the coast road towards Almería.

Málaga's historical ruins can be found mainly on the high ground at the eastern end of the city. First comes the Moorish palace or **Alcázaba,** a maze of pretty little gardens and courts, now the city's **Archaeological Museum.** Connecting this with the **Gibralfaro Castle,** formidable double walls and great square turrets ascend the hill, while a rocky path climbs beside them. At one point a *mirador* gives a view over the harbour and down on to Málaga's **bullring**—where Gautier, son of Alexander Dumas, enthusiast for romantic Spain, saw 24 bulls killed in three days and 96 horses left dead on the sand—and he thoroughly approved of the carnage.

At the top of the climb you will discover that you could have driven up from behind the hill after all, but you won't resent the drink stall there. Restoration of Gibralfaro Castle started in 1989—let's hope it is not quite so thorough as in the Alcazaba.

Rivers and roads: The great dry river bed which cuts the city in two is also part of Málaga's history. Until 1927, when the Rio Guadalmedina was dammed in the hills above, this would regularly flood; in the disastrous flood of 23 September 1628 well over 400 people were drowned before the *corregidor* and 200 helpers managed to open the flood gates and let the water out to sea.

Today Málaga has become a city of careering traffic, in which only brave foreigners drive on weekdays and only the suicidal on a Saturday night. The *malagueños* are happy-go-lucky and it won't be long before you see one of them slam his car into another's.

For a peaceful place away from this frenetic speeding, go to the **Protestant Cemetery**, which lies beyond the bullring, approached along avenues of orange trees. Founded in 1830, it was Spain's first Protestant cemetery, and Captain Robert Boyd, the Englishman who financed Torrijos's revolt and died with him, was one of its first customers. Before then Málaga's Protestants were buried on the beach below high-water mark, where not only did the sea wash their bones out of the sand but the fishermen were afraid that the bodies of these heretics might infect their fish. In a little walled enclosure near the cemetery's summit are the tiny shell-covered graves of a dozen children. Málaga was not a healthy place for northerners in the mid-19th century.

White Towns: Málaga province, all of it that lies inland, has more to offer today that is genuinely Spanish or historically interesting than its coast. Typical are the so-called White Towns of the west of the province near Estepona, and a simple circuit includes two of the best known, **Casares** and **Gaucín**. Double your guess at the time it will take and be prepared to drive boldly past *cortedo* (road closed) notices, which usually mean only that it is rugged.

Taking the MA-539 through Manilva, Casares will first appear dramatically below the road where it passes the leather factory and restaurant. Its two or three hundred white-walled, red-roofed houses, rising up the far side of a deep rocky gorge, seem so closely packed together that if one was taken away the rest would tumble. At the top, in earthy red brick, stand the shell of its ruined church and the remains of its Moorish fort.

Casares has been discovered, but not spoiled: menus have English translations but the food is still Spanish. On any summer evening the central plaza and narrow surrounding streets will echo with that special Spanish roar, created by most of the town's male population talking to each other at the tops of their voices. From Casares's summit there are splendid views to the

Casares, like spilt paint in the hills.

peaks of the Sierra Bermeja and, in the opposite direction, towards the valley of the Rio Genal.

Gaucín lies in the sierra beyond, and a first view is equally dramatic though, unlike Casares, it sits high up, spread across a saddle between rocky peaks. Gaucín, with its long narrow streets, remains even more Spanish in character—loaded mules and donkeys are common and piles of fodder stand at street corners—but it was discovered long before Casares.

Its **Fonda Nacional**, barely advertised, hiding behind a roller blind like most houses in Gaucín, has been catering for British visitors since about 1800, and was once known as El Hotel Inglés. Today's owner will show two ancient visitors' books with entries, mainly in English, from the 1870s onwards. Most entries are enthusiastic about the stabling, food, cheap prices and absence of bed bugs, though a few complain about the temper of Don Pedro Reales, the host of the time, who was always quarrelling with his wife. "What I like most is the squeak he uses when happy", wrote Arthur J Benntich in October 1896. The British stopped at the *fonda* when riding between Gibraltar and Ronda, frequently along "detestable" roads on saddles which seemed to have been "made by the Inquisition".

Gaucín also has a **Moorish castle**, perched high above the town, recently well restored. From here you can see Gibraltar and the coast on a clear day, but the gates will be chained unless you find the ancient custodian before you climb. Up here died that great hero of Spanish history, Guzmán the Good, who, when besieged by Moors at Tarifa and told his son would be killed, preferred to make that sacrifice than to surrender. The Spanish can behave just as brutally to each other; during the Civil War, at the famous siege of Toledo's Alcazar, the defending commander was offered the same choice and he too let his son be killed rather than surrender—though it is less fashionable to admire him because he was fighting for Franco.

Into the hills: For a more adventurous circuit take the little-used but perfectly serviceable MA-557 due north from Estepona and climb by some 50 hairpin bends to **Puerto de Peñas Blancas**. This is a beautiful route, through terraced hillsides of red earth and rock, newly planted with bright green pines, past occasional cork oaks, looking, with their bare chocolate trunks and bushy tops, like clipped poodles. Piles of harvested cork lie by the roadside. The pass itself, at 3,266 ft (980 metres), has a magnificent view of the coast lying far below in blue haze.

To the north the view includes four White Towns, dotted here and there on the wooded mountain sides. Each has its charm, and **Jubrique**, the first the road descends to (by another 50 hairpin bends), is one of the most delightful. It climbs almost vertically up the side of a gorge with steps in its main streets. Chain curtains hide a few tiny bars, one of them optimistically called a discotheque, skinny cats slink round corners, bougainvillaea cascades from balconies, and everywhere there are the

Artistic licence with San Pedro de Alcantar.

smells of fresh white paint or—in season—jasmine. Where are the men of the village, for you see mainly women? Most have gone to work at the coast; profitably, judging by the new houses being built at Jubrique's fringes.

Any circuit north from here will include 10 or more similar White Towns and villages. They can be enjoyed for what they are, since few have exceptional architectural features, though there is a fine castle at **Benadalid**, also kept locked, now housing the cemetery.

North again, on the steep western side of the valley of the Rio Guadiaro, is the remarkable **Cueva de la Pileta**, discovered in 1905 by a local farmer who was looking for *guano* (bird droppings) to manure his fields. "CALL" says a notice where the steps to the cave mouth begin. Sometimes the present owner, grandson of the discoverer, will emerge with his previous handful of visitors; sometimes he will come trudging up the hill from his farm below.

Inside there are no coloured lights. Indeed, there are no lights at all apart from paraffin pressure lamps, which visitors are asked to help carry. Bats flutter above, while the guide shows prehistoric wall paintings and magic symbols (the most impressive a huge fish which seems to have swallowed a small seal) or drums a tune on one of the remarkable stalagtites. "My grandfather came looking for bird shit", says the guide, "and found a golden egg".

Frontier land: The cave lies in the **Sierra de Grazalema**, a national park of more than 116,135 acres (47,000 hectares). The formidable bare grey mountains of this park make one of the most impressive landscapes of southern Spain and conserve much wildlife— 136 bird and 40 mammal species, the brochure claims. It is a splendid area to explore on foot, and can be sampled near **Cortes de la Frontera**.

Names like this which include the word "Frontera", of which there are several, date from the two and a half centuries before 1492 when the area was indeed the frontier between Christian Spain and the surviving Kingdom **Tolox.**

of Granada. Descend 3 miles (5 km) from Cortes to the River Guadiaro, ignore local discouragement and drive south down a dirt lane till the valley narrows and the track ends at a small reservoir. From here it is possible to walk and scramble among pines and oleanders down the fine **Angosturo de la Guadiaro** (Guadiaro Gorge). The railway shares the gorge with the river, but often retreats tactfully into tunnels.

Another circuit of the hills starts from Marbella, up the C-337. After 7½ miles (12 km) a side road leads high into the Sierra Bermeja to the **Refugio de Jua-nar**, orginally a *parador* until the Spanish government sold it. A pleasantly simple place, decorated with animal horns, it used to be patronised by hunters who came to shoot the famous Spanish wild goat. These are now protected but can be seen at dawn or dusk. A couple of miles further up a dirt road is the new **Mirador de Puerto Rico**. Its view is restricted but dramatic since it looks down directly on to Marbella. Up here pine forests give the sierra an al-

pine feeling, and it is the more surprising to find an extensive olive orchard, with the ruins of a farm where its cultivator must once have lived.

Water therapy: The C 337 leads on to Mondo, then by minor roads to the pretty town of **Tolox**, filling the end of its valley. At the valley's head, the 19th-century hydro was until the mid-1980s a ruin of rusting cisterns and broken windows. Today the cisterns are silver-bright and the hydro building a fresh yellow with green tiled roof. Here on any day in summer 50 or 60 patients, mainly Spanish, sit at little tables breathing the fumes of the water, to which they are connected by transparent plastic tubes with plastic mouth-pieces, as if whispering their problems to the spirit of the spring. White-coated nurses attend, sell glasses of the water to drink, or help other patients to bathe their eyes.

On the way back to Marbella, stop at the little restaurant at **Puerto de Ojén** for simple Spanish cooking and sample the speciality: domestic goat. The restaurant stands just west of the road behind iron gates and was founded by an Andalucían who, like many others, went abroad to make money (plastering houses in Switzerland) then returned to invest his savings in his home province.

Tolox is not the only revived hydro of Málaga province. North from Fuengirola, past the sprawling but prospering mountain town of Alhaurín el Grande—where the British writer Gerald Brenan made his third Spanish home up the fertile Guadalhorce valley—a mountain road of many bends and alarming precipices leads to **Carra-traca**. The first odd thing a stranger notes about this small village is a surprising smell of sulphur permeating its narrow back street. The smell comes from behind the tall stone walls of the *balneario,* where a spring of sulphurous water flows from the mountainside at a rate of 700 litres a minute.

It is said to have been discovered by Juan Camisón—so-called because he wore a long shirt to cover his sores—who saw a goatherd bathing his goats with the spring's water, and success-

Torta Española, well worth stopping for.

fully tried some on himself. An almost identical legend describes the discovery of the famous waters at Bath, England.

Fame came to Carratraca in the 19th century, when royalty arrived to take the waters and gamble at its three casinos. The village's best surviving hotel, **Hostel de Príncipe**, ordered by the Spanish king Ferdinand VII, is a social historian's dream; with its great acacia-shaded courtyard, caged birds, black-tiled passages as rocky as any mountain road and antique plumbing, it is pure fossilised late 19th century.

The baths themselves are Roman in their splendour. Two magnificent oval ones are surrounded by columns and a connecting architrave, their enclosing walls set with brilliant blue and yellow tiles. They are open to the sky and the scrubby mountainside rises directly behind. The coolish waters (67° Fahrenheit, 18° Centigrade as they emerge) are heated to body temperature for the comfort of bathers. Rows of modern (19th-century) bathrooms, a pump for drinking from and a doctor's surgery complete the complex.

Lakeland splendour: North from Carratraca lies what has been described as Andalucia's Lake District, though the phrase gives little idea of these opaque blue reservoirs with their sandy beaches, lying at the bottom of steep pine-clad valleys. They are slowly, fortunately very slowly, being discovered by the exhausted from the coast. Here the rich can dine well and the poor picnic, camp and fish.

The return to the coast leads down the **Garganta del Chorro**, an astonishing gorge with walls 600 ft (180 metres) high, where the earliest reservoir was built. When it was opened by King Alfonso XIII in 1921 the **King's Path (El Camino del Rey)** was built for him. It survives but is only for the reckless. For hundreds of feet this narrow pathway is attached to the vertical face of the gorge. No doubt it was in good condition when King Alfonso walked it but today its hand rail is missing from long sections and sometimes the path itself has gaps. When the father of the present Spanish king visited El Chorro in 1987

he sensibly declined the walk. Just the same, Spanish youths, obsessively flirting with death, venture out on the path.

Visitors are advised to walk through a couple of short railway tunnels to get a remarkable view of the *camino* on the opposite cliff face, and sometimes a ring-side view of rock climbers scaling the vertical rock above the path. Most astonishing is the thought of the Spanish workers who, 70 years ago, attached this circus-trick of a path to the mountain face.

Moors and vultures: High up to the west of the gorge, in a remote and once barely accessible area known as **Mesas de Villaverde**, there is now a new storage reservoir to which winter water is pumped for use in summer. Here, around the year AD 900, Umar Ibn Hafsun is said to have set up a kingdom in defiance of the Caliph of Córdoba, with a capital town by the name of Bobastro. Little can be seen today except the ruins of a mosque built into the hillside.

At the village of **El Chorro** (from which the Camino del Rey is reached) take a dirt road in the opposite direction to Valle de Abdalajis and, a couple of miles before reaching it, look up left to another rock face. Circling high above you may see some of Andalucía's surviving vultures. There are not so many as there used to be, because fewer herds of goats and sheep wander the mountains and fewer of these are left for dead, but the vultures have been saved by feeding them occasional unwanted carcasses. They are not pretty birds, well described as flying mattresses with escaping feathers. Prettier but less easily seen on this route are Alpino swifts.

Eccentric collector: From Valle de Abdalajis the road to the coast leads back down the Guadalhorce valley to Pizarra where, above Zalea—one of the new villages Franco built—Gino Hollander lives. A New York film maker, Hollander came to Spain about 30 years ago, living at first near Torremolinos where, more native than the natives, he would ride up to some local bar on a white horse, having arranged for his wife to be waiting there to hand him a

The King's Path crosses El Chorro Gorge.

glass of sherry. Now at Zalea he devotes himself to various good causes, the principal of which is collecting in his **Hollander museum** all kinds of artefacts from an older Spain before it finally disappears.

He also displays his own paintings—he claims that he sold 12,000 before he came to Zalea, and will complete four or five of these "abstract impressionist" works in a morning—and the artistic creations of his children. The anatomically inventive metal horse outside Málaga International Airport was sculpted by his daughter Siri. Another of Gino's causes is rescuing injured creatures, and a visitor should not be alarmed if a one-eyed owl swoops low over his head as it crosses his studio.

The ancient city of Antequera, third in importance of the province, is most easily approached by the N-35 up the Guadalmedina valley, but another approach, the MA-423, passes the most remarkable of the province's natural phenomena: **El Torcal**. Photographs show the towering shapes of some of its spectacular limestone pillars, sculpted by wind and rain to look like piled-up heaps of limestone sandwiches; but these images do not show their extent, or their situation, high up in the Sierra de Chimenea, where they will often be lapped in cloud blown up from the distant coast.

El Torcal has been saved from exploiters, who would have liked to quarry it, and is now a *Parque Natural* (nature park) though a regrettably intrusive restaurant/café has been allowed at its centre. Fortunately you can quickly lose sight of this and wander undisturbed in one of the weirdest of natural landscapes. Prehistoric man lived in this sierra some 6,000 years ago and his remains have been found in the **Cave of the Bull**.

Crossroads of history: The abrupt descent from El Torcal to **Antequera** leads down the **Boca del Asno** (Ass's Mouth Gorge), site of one of the many battles fought around here between Moors and Christians, this one a Christian victory, during the period when

Barbara and Gino Hollander in their museum.

226

Antequera was an almost isolated outpost of Moorish Granada. Its history is far older, and it too has its share of prehistoric caves, even if they date from about 2,000 years after the Cave of the Bull.

Two of the most remarkable, **Cuevas de Menga** and **Viera,** lie just outside the town on the Granada road; look for a filling station named Los Dolmenes. The caves are set in a once-elegant but now shabby public garden of cyprees trees and stone benches. Though nothing remains inside these huge caverns, their horizontal roof stones are quite sufficient to wonder at. One alone is estimated to weigh 180 tons, and they make the stones of such northern European burial chambers as the long barrows of England's Salisbury Plain look like pebbles.

A little further out of town (by the sugar factory), **El Romeral** dolmen is smaller but more interesting, its domed chambers supposedly influenced by the famous Treasury of Atreus at Mycenae. From here, indeed from almost any-

where in Antequera, there is a good view of the oddly shaped rock which sticks up from the plain to the east and is known as **La Peña de los Enamorados** (Lovers' Rock), because the imaginative can see it as two entangled lovers. One legend makes their story a Romeo and Juliet tragedy, the young man a Christian, his girl a Moor. The pair threw themselves into the valley below. To the more prosaic admirer, the rock looks like a large misshapen nose.

The Romans came to Antequera before the Moors, both to the city itself and to a newly discovered settlement at Singilia Barba to the west. There is a fine 1st-century AD bronze, the Antequera Ephebus, in the city museum. But religion, and above all Christianity, gives the city its character even today. Nowhere can there be so many churches (about 24) for such a small town, nor such an odd selection of belfries.

For a close impression of a few of them, stand in the **Plaza de Guerrero Muñoz,** which the city museum, an 18th-century palace, also faces. For an

ntequera.

aerial view, climb to the Moorish castle, a fine ruin, approached through the formidable **Giant's Arch** (1585), which inevitably also leads to the large church of Santa Maria. The castle finally fell to the Christians in 1410 after a five-month siege. Local legend says that, far below it, passages run underground to emerge at two places in today's city. Because the defenders needed water? No. Partly so that they could emerge and take the besiegers in the rear, but more importantly because they needed women.

Wine tour: Tasting the famous wine of Málaga can start in Málaga city at **Antigua Casa Guardia**, close to Paseo del Parque, where 21 big barrels line the back wall and every variety can be tried. Before the 1870s Málaga wine was known all over Europe, considered at least the equal of sherry. Though unfortified, it was strong, often 18° proof (typical table wine is 11° proof), because made from sweet raisins.

Then two things happened, one rapid, the other gradual. In just a few years the vines of Europe were destroyed by the phylloxera bug. In other countries they were regrown, grafted on to American rootstock which is immune, but for some reason this did not happen in Málaga. Perhaps the world was already losing its taste for sweet wines, and this was the more gradual but ultimately more disastrous blow to Málaga wine.

But some is still made, even a so-called *seco*, to cater for modern taste. However, it is better to accept that the real thing should be sweet and set out on a tasting tour in which every little *pueblo* will claim that its own is the best. Climb from the coast at **Torre de Mar** to **Vélez Málaga**, the market town for the eastern half of the province where herds of goats still wander the streets, and on Sundays in winter those so inclined can watch cock-fighting. Turn northeast and circle through **Arenas**, **Corumbela**, **Archez**, **Competa** and back to **Torrox**. The wine of Competa is considered the finest, but there are less raisin-flavoured varieties which taste like pure liquified muscatel grapes.

At **Archez** ask for the famous tower, a reminder of Moorish times, since this church bell tower was the minaret of the Moorish mosque, its square sides set with blue tiles and elaborately patterned in relief with brickwork. Though wine is made in these villages, here too raisins are an important industry. Below south-facing farms, they are set to dry in what look remarkably like outsize cucumber frames.

Bandit land: This whole area of arid hills and deep valleys between Málaga and the Sierra de Tejeda was once notorious for its bandits. One of the most infamous is remembered at **Venta de Alfarnate**, an inn claiming to be Spain's oldest. Certainly it was in business in the late 17th century. Here the much-feared El Tempranillo arrived one day in the mid-19th century and, being inhospitably made to use a crust of bread to spoon up his soup, forced the other guests to use their teeth to grind up (so the legend goes) their metal spoons.

The direct road, if you can call it that, from Alfarnate to **Periana** is still unmetalled. Worrying to a motorist as this is, because of its pot holes and total loneliness, it gives a better idea than any words of what travel in Spain was like until well into this century. Most Spanish roads were unmetalled until after World War II.

From Periana—where *anis* is made, the strong equivalent of Greek *ouzo*—there is an even less advisable track to **Ventas de Zafarraya**, the 3,000-ft (900-metre) pass where Málaga province ends and Granada province begins. Even driving on today's new road, the climb to the pass is dramatic, the great grey peaks of the Sierra de Tejeda growing ever more spectacular ahead as sweep after sweep of the road seems to bring them no closer.

Finally the pass comes, and here the road is crossed by an apparently inexplicable abandoned bridge. It once carried the track of a railway from Málaga, known as the *suburbano*. Anything less suburban it would be hard to imagine. Perhaps the promoters realised they had made a mistake in their planning, for the line never got any further and its track is now used only by herds of goats.

Bodegas Scholtz, specialists in Málaga wine

COSTA DEL SOL

It is impossible to write about the Costa del Sol without regret. What a lovely coast it must have been, with its small sandy bays and fishing villages, connected to each other by no more than dirt roads, backed from end to end by a dramatic line of sierras which, as well as being beautiful, made it almost frost-free at any season. Even in 1957, when the first two hotels had arrived at Castell de Ferro (between Málaga and Almería), the owner of the smaller, a cunning Catalan, was heard to offer to exchange it for "three Leyland lorries" so that he could return to his home province and make real money. How things change.

But if the Costa is scenically and ecologically a disaster it can still be fun. The climate remains delightful, the sea is warm and the sandy beaches are still there, even if it is difficult to see them for the sunbeds. Some of the new building is architecturally exciting; a place like Torremolinos is a curiosity, to say the least, and little-spoiled mountain villages are never far away.

West end: The least changed section lies closest to Gibraltar, where the horrendous N-340 runs a few miles inland. Here, belatedly, the Spanish authorities are trying to prevent building on the very edge of the waves. Beaches without high-rise blocks can still be found by walking north from the new hotel at **Santa Margarita** on the outskirts of **La Linea**.

Where the road returns to the coast, near the mouth of the Rio Guadiaro, the latest artificial harbour, **Puerto Sotogrande**, is nearly complete. The best known of these, **Puerto Banús**, close to Marbella, acquired a reputation in the 1970s as the playground of the rich and wicked. They are still there, judging by the huge yachts, so huge that they seem to overhang the jetty, but for most visitors Puerto Banús consists of arcades of alternating fish restaurants and boutiques. You can dine well here, if at a price. Architecturally, it is a bizarre but attractive recreation of the traditional Andalucían style, decorated with mock minarets and Moorish arches, its jetties fringed with palm trees.

The *puertos* which have been built since are similar, though smaller, and because they have failed to achieve Puerto Banús's notoriety, have more charm. **Puerto Duquesa**, 6 miles (10 km) northeast of Puerto Sotogrande, is a good example. At Puerto Benalmádena just outside Torremolinos architectural pastiche reaches a climax, its maze of cool white courtyards with Moorish decorations topped by roof-lines which have igloo curves, the whole suggesting that some inspired Arabian chef has been let loose with half a million tons of icing sugar.

Estepona, most westerly of the Costa's swollen fishing villages, now a largish town, has so far avoided too many high-rises and remains Spanish, with an old quarter of narrow streets and bars. Originally Phoenician, then Roman—the remains of Salduba aqueduct are nearby—Estepona also has one of

the little round towers built in Moorish times which line the Costa and were designed as look-out points rather than for defence. The long esplanade has a pre-World War I elegance.

The town also has no fewer than two 18-hole golf courses—Nairobi was once said to have more of these per head of (white) population than anywhere else in the world, but the Costa must now easily hold the record.

Costa Natura, 2 miles (3 km) to the east, maintains its Spanishness for another reason: it stands more than a mile from the sea. It was to **San Pedro** that the early British and American settlers escaped when Marbella swelled out of recognition, and they still meet at bars in the "English Arcade" to read English newspapers, borrow English books, talk of "home"—and experience the added excitement that some customer may be a notorious fugitive English criminal. Another artificial port is to be built at San Pedro, where until now there have been eucalyptus groves to which extended Spanish families come on Sundays to set up tables and eat vast spreads of pre-cooked *paellas* and *tortillas*. San Pedro was also Roman, and the Costa road itself was the Roman Via Augusta, leading eventually all the way to Rome itself.

Beyond the facade: Another 7 miles (11 km) east, **Marbella** may be swollen out of all recognition, its main street a jam of east–west traffic, but at its centre an old town survives, of narrow white traffic-free lanes. At the centre of this is its showpiece, the **Plaza de los Naranjos**, planted with orange trees and overlooked by the 16th-century **Casa del Corregidor**, one of the town's few old buildings. On a hot summer night this plaza, set from side to side with dining tables, lit by an orange glow, becomes one vast open-air restaurant, and can delight even hardened Costa-watchers.

The rest of Marbella, which a visitor normally sees, is modern and ugly. But it has extensive beaches as well as less easily found curiosities. Walk east from the port, past a terrace of single-storey fishermen's huts where they still live **Fuengirola.**

and mend their nets, past the derelict pillbox where a noseless syphilitic lives with his cats, past two broken gantries out to sea, and in a narrow grove of eucalyptus, pine and palm below the highway, a few of the beach huts of the original artists and beachcombers of the 1950s can still be found.

Just outside **Fuengirola**—17 miles (27 km) east of Marbella—**Sohail Castle** was intended for defence. Standing on a lumpy hill, with views up and down the coast, it was originally built in 956, some 250 years after the Moorish conquest of Spain, by Abd-al-Rahman III, the best known of the Umayyad Caliphs. Fuengirola grew up under its protection. Even after the Christian conquest of the Kingdom of Granada it survived for a few years and was not finally captured and levelled until 1497. The present castle was built in 1730, to prevent trade with Gibraltar which the British had occupied in 1704.

Eighty years later, in 1810, it was connected with one of the more shameful (from a British point of view) epi-sodes of the Peninsular War. A British expedition of 800 men under General Blayney landed here and advanced on Mijas, but found the country too difficult and retreated to the castle. Here Blayney disposed his troops "with the utmost contempt of military rules" and as a result was forced to surrender to 150 Polish troops who were fighting for the French. For more than five years there have been plans to turn Sohail Castle into an auditorium and arts centre, but little has been done except clear debris from the large central courtyard.

Tourist retreats: The mountain villages of **Mijas**, 5 miles (8 km) above Fuengirola, and **Benalmádena**, 5 miles (9 km) above Torremolinos, now have more connection with the Costa than with inland Spain. Everywhere are English pubs and shops selling sheepskin jackets, local pottery or more contemptible tourist junk. At Mijas you can take a ride in a four-wheeled carriage under a huge striped umbrella, pulled by a well-fed pony, or visit a mobile museum to see the 2,000 most curious

Glitzier urbanisations ignore the sea.

things in the world. Despite all this, there is fresher air up here and fine views from both villages down on to the coast. With their clean white houses and green shutters, they are good examples of the Spanish genius for giving even tourist traps a certain enchantment.

Benalmádena on the coast road is merely an extension of Torremolinos without the latter's element of fantasy. It is in **Torremolinos** that the Costa's excesses froth over into self-parody. The grotesquely overgrown village, with its hundreds of bars, lush vegetation and overhead walkways is like some Hollywood director's concept of what a Spanish resort should be—except that it is real. A TV screen in the main plaza repeats interminable bullfighting episodes and in the evening a gaunt gypsy lady brings her tape recorder and twirls to its flamenco music. At night there are discos, homosexual bars and just about every other sort of entertainment.

Small ironies are that the sun-hungry must climb up and down some hundreds of steps to reach its central beach, and that this beach faces more east than south, so losing its sun early in the evening. Never mind: there are other beaches east and west, set with similar phalanxes of sunbeds under their raffia umbrellas.

Málaga itself does not have a beach, though it once did. Here, according to the 18th-century British traveller, the Rev. Joseph Townsend, its youth would come in the evenings of the hot months of the year to bathe for hours at a time. The sexes were kept apart and the young ladies were guarded by sentinels with their muskets loaded. Whenever, therefore, a young man was determined to intrude, he went in disguised as the female attendant of "some easy fair one". For their bathing today the *málagueños* must go west, to the soiled sand dunes across the Rio Guadalhorce at **San Julian**, or, more fashionably, east to the beaches of **El Palo**, **Cala** and **Rincón de la Victoria**.

There is not much to choose between these places, with each offering a bewil-

Moorish-influenced architecture, Torremolinos.

dering choice of beach restaurants, the usual sunbeds and rather narrow (thanks to the highway) sandy beaches. At Rincón the main road has at least been built a few feet further inland, but tall blocks of flats line an otherwise more attractive shallow bay.

Inland: For a different world, turn inland at **Torre de Benalgabón** and climb past the freakishly emerald green fairways of yet another golf course, past one of the cliffs over which the smouldering rubbish of the Costa is tipped, to the tiny villages of Benaque and Macharaviaya. They first appear far below the road, delightfully set against the grey peaks of the Sierra de Tejeda: just a couple of straggles of white houses. More immediately below, on the steep valley sides, are their vineyards.

Macharaviaya is the smaller and more charming, with cobbled streets and a huge dilapidated church. How could such a tiny place need a church of this size, you may wonder, but in the 18th century it had a factory and an important industry: the making of play-

ing cards, with a monopoly for supplying them to the Americas. In the church's crypt are memorials to the Gálvez family, the local landowners who brought the village its prosperity. They were powerful Spanish colonialists, who extended Spanish influence up the west coast of America as far as San Francisco Bay. Alas for Macharaviaya, the Gálvez family died, its monopoly lapsed and the factory closed.

Benaque, slightly larger, is no more prosperous. At the end of a road to nowhere, you may still see the local housewives outside its one grocery shop, haggling about the prices of trousers with a peddler who has brought them on a bicycle. Peering into the dark doorways of its white houses, you will see the villagers sieving and packing raisins; raisin production is today its only industry.

Seaview: At **Nerja**, 32 miles (52 km) east of Málaga, the famous **Balcony of Europe** does not run parallel to the sea, as its name suggests, but is a marble-paved projection above a headland, set

with palms, decorated with a couple of cannon recovered from the sea. The Spanish king Alfonso XII gave it this appropriate name in 1885—there is nothing ahead but the Mediterranean, with Africa somewhere beyond the horizon. He was here to comfort the people after the devastating earthquake of the previous Christmas Day.

Tucked in below the balcony to the east is a small sandy cove with fishing boats, while, beyond, the coast curves away in a big crescent of cliffs backed by mountains. **Mona**, 2 miles (3 km) round this curving bay, has its own balcony, a palm walk above surrounding market gardening slopes, with fine views east. While Mona is still relatively unexploited, there is no pleasanter place than **Casa Mona** (facing west) to sit with a glass of wine as the evening sun sinks behind the mountains beyond Málaga.

Turn away from the coast for the other explanation for Nerja's explosive growth: here, in 1959, five young Spanish boys went on a bat-hunting expedition, felt warm air coming up from a crack in the rocks and discovered the now famous **Cuevas de Nerja** (Nerja caves).

Today, dozens of busloads of tourists come daily to see these astonishing underground caverns. Needless to say, one has been fitted out as an auditorium where ballets are performed, and all are paved with walks and are well-lit, while soft music, not the squeak of bats, echoes above among the stalactites.

The caves remain a staggering sight, if only for their immense size. Prehistoric man used them 20,000 years ago, and a typical skeleton is displayed in a glass case. It appears she died of mastoid infection.

Beyond Mona, where the Sierra de Tejeda come down to the sea, Málaga province's section of the Costa ends as it began, still more or less unexploited, though with an entirely different character. Steep, stony hillsides protect small rocky coves, and if you successfully climb down you can still bathe alone beside some local farmer's banana tree plantation.

RONDA

Encircled by mountains, riven by the deep fissure of the *Tajo*, Ronda was one of the first small Spanish cities (with 33,000 inhabitants today) to earn a place on the tourist map. Mentioned by geographers and travellers from Strabo and Pliny through Ibn Batuta to the Baron de Bourgoing, it received its most enthusiastic write-up from Richard Ford, in his famous *Murray's Hand-Book for Travellers in Spain* (first edition 1845): "There is but one Ronda in the world, and this *Tajo*, cleft as it were by the scimitar of Roldan, forms when the cascade is full... its heart and soul. The scene, its noise and movement, baffle pen and pencil, and, like Wilson at the Falls of Terni, we can only exclaim, 'Well done, rock and water, by Heavens!'"

Ford wrote the above in the heyday of the Romantic movement, which was to draw to Andalucía Scottish artists David Wilkie and David Roberts, French men of letters Théophile Gautier and Alexandre Dumas *fils*, the great lithographer Gustave Doré, and a succession of writers hardly less ecstatic about Ronda than was Ford.

In 1906 the Hotel Reina Victoria on the edge of the inland cliff was completed and immediately became popular as a hill station and retreat for the officers of the Gibraltar garrison. In 1913 the poet Rainer Maria Rilke stayed here for several weeks and wrote his *Spanish Trilogy*, including the eulogistic lines on observing a shepherd tending his flock on the hillside: "Even today a god might secretly enter that form and not be diminished."

Later came swashbuckling Americans Ernest Hemingway and Orson Welles to hobnob with leading matador Antonio Ordóñez, a son of Ronda, and painter David Bomberg, who brought his intensely Jewish determination to reveal the soul of the landscape.

The face of change: With such a legacy of international interest, Ronda has a lot to live up to and is probably the reposi-

tory of too many expectations. For the inevitable has happened. Urban sprawl, an industrial estate and bleak municipal housing have occupied the commanding heights; unfortunately there was nowhere else for these necessary developments to go.

It is wise to approach Ronda today with circumspection. The best routes in, yielding the best views of the old city, are from Algeciras and from San Pedro de Alcántara. If you enter from Seville or from Granada, take the new ring-road round the town, as if aiming for San Pedro, and then double back into Ronda on the unblemished flank.

From this side, you first encounter the **Barrio de San Francisco**, which is rather like a small mountain *pueblo* picked up and deposited under the city walls. Here there is a lively market every Sunday and an important animal fair early in October, held in the oblong square surrounded by village houses. The most striking building, reached through the Moorish Almocobar gate, is the fortress-like church of the Espíritu

Santo, the first one built after the recapture of Ronda from the Moors in 1485.

Winding up the hill into the old city, the first motorable turn on the left leads into the **Plaza de la Ciudad**, a charming square with cypresses and medlars and river-bred oleanders in the neat flowerbeds inside low box hedges. The square is flanked by an early 18th-century barracks, now the town hall; by a 19th-century boys' school on the site of the Moorish fortress (left ruinous after the Peninsular War); by the convents of the Poor Clares and of the Little Sisters of the Cross; by the main church of **Santa Maria la Mayor**, and by the law courts.

The church, under a great barnlike roof, has interesting features: a late Gothic nave, baroque choir stalls, High Renaissance east end and sanctuary, and a tower whose lower stages belonged to a minaret. Facing the square is an arcade supporting a gallery from which priests and notables would watch bullfights. The permanent bull-ring was built later.

Arab style: Not far from the Plaza de la Ciudad is the **Palacio de Mondragon**. This is a grand town house with a stone Renaissance facade, cobbled porch with mounting block, front patio of about 1570 and rear patio *arabe*, which is really *mudéjar* (post-Reconquest in the Arab style). There are few remaining examples of domestic building to show for nearly eight centuries of Moorish occupation, but the nearby Casa del Gigante has a patio with arabesque stucco work of the 14th century.

An alley leads from the Plaza de Mondragon into the **Plaza del Campillo**, which is open on one side to the mountains. Here stood one of the three Moorish gates into the city. Halfway down a steep slope are the remnants of an outer wall and gateway, through which winds a track down to the market gardens and abandoned water mills in the valley.

From the Plaza del Campillo, Calle Tenorio leads back to the main road which bisects the old city. The steep Cuesta de Santo Domingo then leads down past the Casa del Marqués de

Ronda's bull-ring, the oldest in Spain.

Santa Pola (with basements preserving some traces of Moorish wall-painting) to the so-called **Casa del Moro**. This is a 19th-century pastiche with dark hanging gardens, from which the Mina de Ronda, a staircase cut inside the rock, descends to the river bed. During times of siege, it was manned by a live chain of Christian captives passing up pitchers of water to supply their masters in the citadel, "whose fierce king"—according to a romantic travel book of 1923—"drank only from the skulls of enemies; cutting off their heads and making them into goblets inlaid with splendid jewels".

Next comes the **Palacio del Marqués de Salvatierra** with an interesting facade showing colonial influence. Just below this the **Roman Bridge**, rebuilt in 1616, crosses the gorge.

Lower down yet is the **Arab Bridge**, also completely rebuilt. It is adjacent to the crumbling **Arab Baths**, which form an outpost of the town thrusting out into the fields. From this point, a rough pebbled track leads up under the Salva-tierra palace to the third city gate of medieval times.

Beyond bridges: The old city is an agreeable architectural hotchpotch based on a Moorish groundplan, but not all of it in good repair: the whole is greater than the sum of the parts. The **Puente Nuevo** (New Bridge) crosses the gorge at its deepest and narrowest point and is a uniquely assertive feat of engineering, more like a solid causeway with apertures than an aerial span over the abyss. Begun in 1755, after a previous effort collapsed, it seems to have been first opened for transit in 1784; its architect José Martin de Aldehuela fell to his death inspecting the structure shortly before its completion. Once it was open, tightly corseted Ronda spilled out on to the tableland known as the **Mercadillo**, which was used until then mainly for markets and fairs.

The **Plaza de Toros** (the oldest bull-ring in the country) opened its doors on 11 May 1784 and played a leading role in the development of the modern bullfight under the determined guidance of

Barber with bullfight memorabilia.

Pedro Romero (1754–1839), the foremost matador of his age. An annual *corrida goyesca* in dress of the period is held every year in his memory during the September fair.

A little higher up than the bull-ring on the same side of the street is the **Alameda**, a shady public promenade dating from 1806, which ends in a balustrade on the brink of a sheer drop of several hundred feet. "The view," says Ford, "from this eminence over the depths below, and the mountain panorama, is one of the finest in the world." Few will accuse him of hyperbole.

It is not necessary to go beyond the Alameda (or the neighbouring church of La Merced, which once housed the arm of Santa Teresa of Avila) other than to reach the **Hotel Reina Victoria** on the highest point of the new town. With the coming of coach tours, this has entirely lost its Edwardian atmosphere. It is worth visiting to see the room where the poet Rilke stayed, preserved with some mementoes, and for a drink on the terrace at sunset. But for lodging, the comfortable **Hotel Polo**, near the Alameda, is just as good and you are more in touch with the life of the town.

***Paseo* places:** Despite its claim to an aristocratic and warlike past, and its delight in legends of brigands and smugglers, Ronda has for long been a lively commercial centre for almost 30 smaller towns and villages. This is borne out in the **Calle de la Bola**, a traffic-free shopping street running from the bull-ring due east for more than half a mile. Ronda's answer to Las Ramblas of Barcelona or Calle Sierpes in Seville, it is packed both before lunch and for the evening *paseo*. Modern times have brought tourists pink as prawns, buskers and trinket stalls recognisable from any international city.

But almost all the traditional elements are there, too: the agricultural brokers and livestock dealers with their caps and canes and muddied boots, gypsies tugging at the sleeve, blind lottery sellers crying out the winning number, rotund bourgeois couples perambulating on tiny well-shod feet, and

Watching time pass.

children dressed up as brides or sailors for their first communion. The old culture is not beaten yet.

Ronda, worth two or three days for itself, is also the best centre for excursions to the **White Towns**; to the **Cueva de la Pileta** with palaeolithic cave paintings that predate Altamira's; to Roman **Acinipo** (popularly Ronda la Vieja) with substantial remnants of its theatre and panoramic views, and to the various nature reserves.

Nearby nature: The **Reserva Nacional de la Serranía de Ronda**, covering most of the mountainous area from the Sierra de las Nieves, south of Ronda, almost to Marbella, has been in existence since 1919. It is famous for a rare species of prehistoric pine, the *pinsapo*, which grows only above the 3,200 ft (1,000 metre) line, and for the *capra pyrenaica* or ibex; some pairs of golden eagles also survive. Access by jeep trail via the *pueblos* of El Burgo, Yunquera or Tolox is relatively unrestricted, though shooting is fiercely limited.

Another Reserva, that of **Cortes de la Frontera**, in the direction of Algeciras, has recently been coupled with the new and much larger Parque Natural de Grazalema to form an area of nearly 120,000 acres (50,000 hectares), including 13 villages, mainly in the province of Cádiz. The flora and fauna on this side are more varied but access is more strictly controlled and some of the routes in the *pinsapares* (which also exist here) are closed during the summer months as a precaution against forest fires. The park office is in the small town of **El Bosque** en route from Grazalema to Jerez.

Many small Spanish cities have leapt from the 18th into the 20th century in the past two or three decades, some with disastrous results. Ronda has managed its modernisation not quite as romantics would desire but with a solid feeling for its role as Capital de la Serranía.

And nothing can detract from Ronda's incomparable setting: such experiences as the stroll in the Alameda at dusk and the "sundowner" on the terrace of the Victoria are unimpaired.

he Serranía
e Ronda.

EXPLORING THE WHITE TOWNS

The lowlands of Andalucía are characterised by large whitewashed agricultural villages from which hosts of landless labourers used to go out to till the big arable farms of the river plains. Though certainly "white", these villages are bleak and functional; not all members of the White Town species are charming or pretty. But the higher you climb into the sierras, with their more rugged terrain, the smaller and more picturesque the towns and villages (both can be called *pueblos*) become.

In the hills large monocultures give way to smallholdings, herding and forest crops such as chestnut and cork. Glimpsed from the road or railway, whether framed in forest green or tucked under some vertiginous fang of rock, the mountain *pueblos* fuel nostalgia and inspire the hope that they will be as unspoiled on closer acquaintance.

The various tourist organs have striven mightily to establish these White Towns as the great attraction of the Andalucían interior. Some *pueblos* bear the official sign *Ruta de los Pueblos Blancos*; others, no less attractive, do not. The major promotion is concentrated on the province of Cádiz and the western half of the province of Málaga. As some 50 or 60 *pueblos* are commended in a number of leaflets, a little inside knowledge may help.

Regional differences: Some of the *pueblos* netted in the official trawl belong to the Atlantic or "Spanish" coast (as opposed to the foreign-dominated Costa del Sol), which runs from the Bay of Cádiz to the Straits of Gibraltar. They are not dealt with here—impeccably white and faultlessly iron-grilled and flower-potted though most of them are—because tourism, albeit national rather than international, is a large part of their economy and they are not representative of the modes of survival in the hinterland.

A few miles inland all this changes, because the effect of tourism, though not absent, is much less direct. There is large-scale migration of labour to Madrid, Barcelona or the coasts; the remaining townsfolk or villagers pursue a traditional pattern of life and the odd stranger remains a rarity.

Though the mountain roads have improved vastly in the past few years, virtually all the other elements of tourist infrastructure are still absent. There are few beds. There is no government-sponsored scheme of village housing adapted for seasonal letting as in Italy. So the best way of exploring the *pueblos blancos* (other than for genuine campers who are well catered for) is to set up base camp in Ronda, Arcos de la Frontera or possibly Olvera.

Key routes: Running on a spine between the River Guadiaro and its tributary the Genal, the Ronda–Algeciras road whets the appetite of the White Town addict, though a minority of the 15 or so *pueblos* of the Genal valley fall within the official designation. All are small. **Gaucín**, on the main road with roughly 2,500 inhabitants, is the largest; most have in the region of 1,000; Alpan-

Preceding pages: Grazalema. **Left,** Setenil. **Right,** whitening a White Town.

deire has shrunk to 210. Perched on steep wooded slopes (the chestnut is the main crop), they have names—Atajate, Alpandeire, Benarrabá, Benalauría, Benadalid, Farajan, Jubrique, Genalguacil—that speak of their Berber past.

After the Reconquest of 1492 and their nominal Christianisation, these townspeople all joined the Morisco (converted Moslem) rebellion of 1570. Resentment smouldered on for centuries and bred a wary, sometimes violent race, whose villages were accessible only by steep mule track. The greatest revolution in their lives has been the recent construction of well-engineered roads. Now their populations increase markedly in the summer months with migrant workers returning to stay with elderly relatives for the holidays and fairs, and in some cases to rebuild and modernise their family homes.

A good example is **Genalguacil**, with a population of just over 1,000 in the heart of the area. Its charming name means "Vizier's Garden" and it exhibits a certain hill-station gaiety, exemplified by the fine municipal swimming pool, packed with young people. This local renaissance is essentially Spanish; there is no special provision for foreign tourists and no hotel. But there is a shady camp site down by the bridge over the River Genal between Algatocin and Jubrique, and there is a direct link from Jubrique to Estepona on the coast.

The River Guadiaro (joined lower down by the Genal) rises above Ronda to debouch in the Mediterranean a little north of Gibraltar. The railway hugs it closely much of the way; a minor road (MA-501) also follows it in a switchback fashion, rising to the White Towns of **Benaocaz** and **Montejaque**, renowned for their *embutidos* (tinned pork products) and mountain-cured hams; then plunging down to the station of Jimera de Líbar before rising again to **Cortes de la Frontera**.

Cortes is a pleasant, medium-sized *pueblo* (population just under 5,000) on a high shelf above the Guadiaro: it is clad in standard dazzling white, with the **White Town transport.**

exception of its distinguished stone town hall from the period of that enlightened despot Charles III (1759–88); it also boasts a proper bull-ring of masonry and a fine *alameda* or public promenade.

Cortes derives its relative wealth from the municipal cork forests which stretch for over 30 miles (48 km) to the west. With these advantages, it exudes a kind of confidence. In one of the noisy bars you may well be bought a drink and, on departure, urged: "Speak well of Cortes!"

From Cortes, the road winds westwards through the forest with only occasional clearings for a smallholding with witch-like cottage, to the remote crossroads of **Puerto de Galis**, whose *venta* (inn) is open 365 days a year from 6 a.m. to 9 p.m., the only hostelry for miles in any direction. Little black pigs roam freely among the tables on the terrace; inside, the pork is on the table.

Eminent places: From Galis, a bumpy road (CA-511) descends towards the undulating arable farms and bull-

breeding pastures of the province of Cádiz. The towns become larger. Alcalá de los Gazules, Medina Sidonia and Arcos de la Frontera (all on eminences above the plain) are approved White Towns. All three were strongholds of Moorish tribes until the Reconquest, when they passed into the hands of Spanish nobles who then abandoned them in favour of the larger cities.

Alcalá, with several wayside restaurants on the Cádiz road, is the seediest and its flat-topped houses climbing up to the church and fort are the most Moorish. **Medina Sidonia**, bearing the name of the Armada's admiral, excites some expectations: it is a windswept place on top of a conical mound and its monuments are mostly ruinous, although it has a fine main square.

Arcos, on its inland cliff above the Guadalete (giving it a certain family resemblance to Ronda) is the most spectacular and probably the best base camp for the area. But it has an ancient reputation for witchcraft, sorcery and incest, which has not been entirely deodorised

Lunes del Toro fiesta, Grazalema.

by the luxurious government *parador* and the tourist propaganda; the whiff of it lingers in the tortuous streets.

Yet perhaps the strangest atmosphere of all is to be found in low-lying **Bornos** on the shores of a reservoir squeezed out of the waters of the Guadalete. White-washed walls are the backdrop for a pullulating street life marked by gypsies, squatting or cross-legged, playing cards on the pavements which they share with a large population of evil-looking hounds. Above this picaresque scene rise the remnants of the palace-castle of the Riberas and other grand but gutted buildings. From the desiccated lakeside beach with its *chiringuitos* (shanty bars) there is a superb view of the Sierra de Grazalema. With its decayed grandeur and raffish character, Bornos makes a perfect foil for the purity of the mountains rising across the glassy water.

The cities of the plain, intriguing in their way, do not quite live up to the *beau idéal* of the White Town. For this we must return to the mountains where the whiteness of the walls is matched by a simpler, sturdier character in the people. In this category **Grazalema** (some 20 miles/32 km west of Ronda) must rank high. Grazalema was once more populous, as is testified by its three handsome parish churches, one gutted in the Civil War (1936–39) and still a shell today. When its wool trade collapsed in the 19th century, the town shrank and some houses on the rim crumbled back to nature or became byres for beasts.

But latterly its romantic setting, fine views and the cool shadow cast across it in the evening by the towering peak of San Cristobal, the popular hill station for the summer months. It boasts a municipal swimming pool, hotel and camp site, and is the gateway to the nature reserve that bears its name.

If there is any criticism, it is that Grazalema is just a little too sanitised. **Zahara de la Sierra** on the other side of the spectacular pass of Las Palomas (over 4,000 ft/1,200 metres) is equally picturesque and less self-conscious.

Church of Santa Maria, Arcos de la Frontera.

One of the most publicised sights in the region is **Setenil**, a small White Town set in the ravine of the River Guadalporcun, a dozen miles to the north of Ronda. It has two or three streets of semi-cave houses whose roofs are formed by overhanging rock, giving their neat white facades the appearance of mushroom stems under a spreading fungoid crown.

Passing under the walls of **Torre Alhaquime** (a little hilltop village which has dashingly endowed itself with a post-modern promenade) you come to **Olvera**, White Town *par excellence*.

King of them all: With around 12,000 inhabitants Olvera is a larger place than its immediate neighbours. Its silhouette is almost outrageously dramatic with Moorish keep and Christian basilica soaring above the tightly packed slopes of blindingly white houses under biscuit-coloured tiles, running down to a clear perimeter, where the countryside begins. Famous as the refuge of outlaws and murderers in the 19th century, Olvera today has a reputation for religiosity. A monument to the Sacred Heart of Jesus on a natural outcrop of rock dominates the lower town and people have been known to crawl miles on their hands and knees, in fulfilment of a vow, to the popular sanctuary of the Virgen de los Remedios.

Olvera's streets are neat and somewhat stern. The handsome facades make few concessions to the floral trimmings beloved of the brochures. Indeed, the householders have the curious habit of hanging their refuse bags and buckets from the window grilles, which must be anathema to the tourist office.

But the local fair, late in August, is among the most lavish in the region and one of the lengthiest: five nights until 5 a.m. or later of stalls, sideshows, bars, attractions, spectacles of song and dance and private club enclosures; while by day there are football matches, clay-pigeon contests and two or three novice bullfights in a portable ring.

Community centres: The survival kit of the mountain *pueblo* is made up of migrant labour, some jobs in agricul-

Olvera.

ture, some in building, social security for the old and a strong belief that the *pueblo* is the natural unit of society. Tourism plays no part except to provide work on the coast in catering or "construction", the building labourer's grand euphemism for his trade.

Although less closed than before, the White Town still remains a very self-contained unit. The cafés and bars are patronised almost exclusively by men; they are more like clubs, though the stranger will be served with perfect courtesy. The churches are closed except for services, so it is necessary to find the priest to get the keys to visit them. Corner shops and tiny supermarkets are the best sources of information.

Beds are not plentiful. Olvera, a large *pueblo* by mountain standards, has one *pension* in the town and a new *hostal* on the outskirts; most of the smaller *pueblos* have no lodgings.

There are two new institutions of great importance to contemporary *pueblo* life: the municipal swimming pool and the discotheque. Both are for

the young. It is the firm belief of local government that without them the young folk of the *pueblo* would vote with their feet for the cities, and in this they are probably right.

The pools are, of course, open to all and some make very agreeable oases on a hot day's sightseeing (as in Grazalema, Setenil, and Genalguacil). The discos may not seem exactly what you came for but there are some amazingly plush examples (Ronda, Cortes, El Burgo) which you may well be shown with pride.

At **El Burgo**, on the road from Ronda to Málaga via Coín, an unremarkable bar front is the gateway to a vast cork-lined cavern of a disco decorated with tropical love scenes in black silhouette on gold panels. According to the owner, all the youth of the *pueblo*, including young married couples, flock in on Saturday nights. All behave impeccably. "Drugs? No, everyone here respects the rules. If they transgress, they are banned for good and their social life is ruined." That sums up the White Town attitude to the law. The sanctions of the *pueblo* are stronger than those of the authorities.

The summer fairs might be thought of as a way into White Town life and it is true that people let their hair down and talk more freely in the bars at fairtime. But especially in the smaller *pueblos* (under 3,000 inhabitants) the annual fair is really no more than an extended family party lasting several nights. With the exception of brilliant fireworks against flawless night skies, the attractions are minimal and not particularly traditional.

The young dictate the choice of music: there is a brand of modernised flamenco, but genuine *cante jondo* is hard to find. As at all parties, they are little fun if you don't know anybody, but if you go with a Spanish family or a knowledgeable friend you can have a whale of a time.

The White Towns, then, do not conform to the quaint, folksy image of tourist propaganda. But that is their strength. They set out to delude no one, but are marvellously themselves.

Left, porch, Vejer de la Frontera. **Right**, Ulrique.

CADIZ AND ITS PROVINCE

"Cádiz, from a distance, was a city of sharp incandescence, a scribble of white on a sheet of blue glass… sparkling with African light. In fact it was a shut-in city, a kind of Levantine ghetto almost entirely surrounded by sea—a heap of squat cubist hovels enclosed by medieval ramparts and joined to the mainland by a dirty thread of sand."

Laurie Lee, who wrote this description in 1969 in *As I Walked Out One Midsummer Morning*, would notice changes in the substance of Cádiz, if not in its essence. The dirty thread of sand has been replaced by a thick, black hawser of tarmac and the town is now moored to its province by another asphalt cable arching across the bay to Puerto Real. Within the ramparts—not medieval but mainly 17th and 18th-century—Cádiz is still a Levantine ghetto, but made up of four and five-storey tenements packed tight behind the defences and the roadway that encircles the historic city.

Frontier town: Ghetto Cádiz is a walled enclave of humanity, a frontier town, founded as an outpost of the Phoenician trading empire on what was once an offshore island. Gadir, the defended place, they called it then.

The Phoenician patron of the city, the god Melkart, was Hercules to the Romans, and the twin bronze-clad columns of his temple became a man-made marker beyond which man did not dare travel. This was the frontier of land and ocean, of Europe and Africa, of Old World and New.

During the wars between Carthage and Rome, when dominion of the Classical World was at stake, Gadir was the Carthaginian gateway into Europe. Here, in the temple of Melkart, Hannibal swore his undying hatred of Rome and Hercules let him down.

When the Roman legionaries turned Gadir into Gades, they transformed the city into Europe's gateway to Carthaginian Africa, building a lighthouse on the present Punta de San Sebastián. The

290-ft (90-metre) tower with its gilt bronze statue survived, so they say, until the Moors came in the 8th century.

In 1263 Moorish Cádiz and western al-Andalus fell to the Christian king Alfonso the Wise. Cádiz, repopulated by Christian Spaniards, became part of the *Frontera*, which gives its name to so many towns and villages in the province of Cádiz. Nothing remains of Alfonso's castle except the arches of two postern gates across alleyways landward of the Cathedral: **Arco de los Blancos** and **Arco de la Rosa**.

Wayward heart: Cádiz meant much to Alfonso. It gave him a haven from which to launch his ill-fated attack on Salé, in the Moroccan heartland of the Infidel. He wanted to be buried in Cádiz, but his wishes were not carried out. His body now lies in Seville Cathedral; his heart was removed to the monastery of Santa Maria de las Huertas in Murcia.

The dismembered Alfonso no doubt turned in his several graves as his successors spent the next two centuries

Preceding pages: offshore on the Costa de la Luz. Left, city gate, Cádiz. Right, in Roman times the girls of Cádiz were famous for their dancing.

WRECKS AND
WRECKERS

At the entrance to the Bay of Cádiz, just beyond the fortified island of San Sebastián, lies the *Bucentaure*, flagship of the French fleet at the Battle of Trafalgar (1805).

The *Bucentaure* was seized by the British Admiral Nelson as a prize of war. Badly damaged, she was taken under tow towards Gibraltar, but the storm that wrecked so many of the Trafalgar warships broke her tow-rope and very nearly sent her to the bottom. The Frenchmen on board managed to turn her about and they made for Cádiz. There, near the La Olla rock, she went down. All those aboard were taken off by the *Indomptable*, but shortly after, overloaded with 500 sailors and marines, the *Indomptable* also went down in a storm between Rota and Puerto de Santa Maria.

The *Bucentaure* was not the first ship to go down in the Bay of Cádiz. Nor was the *Indomptable* the last. As the mud and silt of the Guadalquivir shifts slowly beneath the waters of Cádiz bay, evidence of shipwrecks is uncovered. A handful of shards of Phoenician or Greek pottery, a Roman amphora, a medieval stone anchor, a culverin or cannon of the Indies fleet, or just the rotting ribs of a fishing smack.

From documents kept in Seville's Archive of the Indies a total of 377 shipwrecks have been catalogued throughout the whole of the Gulf of Cádiz—the geographers' name for the Spanish tourist board's Costa de la Luz.

But the number of ships recorded is considerably more, for most of the sinkings involved more than just one vessel—and the vast majority of these occurred in the Bay of Cádiz itself.

The first ships known to have gone down on this coast foundered in November 1473. What type of vessels they were, their cargoes or the names of their masters or crews were of no interest to the medieval scribe who recorded the loss. All he tells us is that the three vessels belonged to one man, Anton Bernal, and that they were sunk by the Portuguese fleet as it chased the French pirate Coulom.

Other pirates roamed the coast in historic times. The great Barbary corsair, Barbarossa (Red-beard), raided all along the Gulf of Cádiz and east into the Mediterranean. Many of those crews which escaped his clutches and the slave markets of Algiers came to grief—like the *Bucentaure*—running for the safety of Cádiz bay.

For some, though, the Bay was not protection enough. In 1587, Francis Drake attacked the growing Spanish Armada as it lay peacefully at anchor in the bay.

Drake fired some 16 or 17 ships, seized six more packed with supplies and razed the town before standing off to spread terror up and down the coast. In less than three months during that summer, ranging from Cádiz to Lisbon, he captured or sent to the bottom some 60 fishing vessels and 40 coasters laden with materials for the Spanish fleet.

He successfully penned up that fleet in its various home ports and set back Spanish plans for the "Invincible Armada" for a full year.

The death of Drake—"English pirate" to Spaniards, national hero in England—was welcomed with relief and joy in Cádiz and the Spanish Court. Even today naughty children are threatened with a visit from the English pirate by their exasperated Andalucían parents.

After his death the English didn't leave Cádiz alone: within six months some of the finest exponents of Elizabethan state-sponsored terrorism had left Cádiz a smoking ruin again.

If Drake had "singed the King of Spain's beard", the new fleet under its leaders Essex and Howard was responsible for severe facial burns. They fell on the unsuspecting port with a force of some 80 English and Dutch men-o'-war. The Spanish were obliged to burn the galleons of the Indies fleet in the Bay to prevent their "sumless treasuries" falling into Anglo-Dutch hands.

Today little of this violent period of maritime history survives—just a few naval cannon built into house walls in Cádiz town. However a joint Spanish-Texan team of historians, archaeologists and divers are doing their best to discover and salvage a Spanish *Mary Rose*—hopefully in time for the 1992 world fair which is taking place in Seville.

reducing the rump of al-Andalus, the Kingdom of Granada. Cádiz remained the seaward end of Christian Spain's frontier until Granada fell and Columbus stumbled across America. With the opening up of the New World, Cádiz entered its own Golden Age.

But the promise of easy pickings attracted pirates—a roughish alley behind the Cathedral (the **Calle Piratas**) records their passing. And yet, despite the presence of Barbary corsairs like Barbarossa and Dragut off the Cádiz coast, the desperate pleas of the town's *Corregidores* (Governors) for new defences were ignored. The old castle crumbled while the Catholic Monarchs chatted with their fashionable Italian military engineers.

Eventually the massive Anglo-Dutch raid of 1596, under the command of the Earl of Essex, spurred the Spanish Crown to act. Coming soon after Drake's "singeing of the King of Spain's beard", when the old castle and the newly built **Muro de Tierra** failed to protect the town, Essex's sortie was

the last straw. The half-built circuit wall and the projecting gun platforms were quickly finished off, and the **Puerto de Tierra** replaced the already obsolete Muro.

Old gate: The Puerto de Tierra, which took on its present form in the mid-18th century, marks the entrance to the old town. Vandalised in the late 1940s, when two breaches were made in it for the benefit of motorists, the central gate tower is now all but cut off from its protective flanking bastions. The twin lions that defend the white stone escutcheon above the old gate stare out over pretty fountains set within an oval enclave of grass and flowers—all to be admired through the stream of traffic.

Inside the gate, Cádiz is a jewel of military architecture, defaced only by the railway to the north and by the conflicting Spanish passions either to glorify or to deride history. Right behind the gate itself are 18th-century barrack blocks and arsenals, some still in military hands and others taken over by the fire brigade. On the north side,

The promenade, Cádiz.

looking back over the shunting yards, the massive bulk of the Puerto de Tierra's north bastion looms above the toy trains. Beyond, the town wall is lost beneath tarmac and a not unattractive townscape until the **Murallas de San Carlos** and the **San Felipe Battery** are reached on the far side of the **Plaza de España**.

In the centre of the plaza stands the **Monument to the Cortes** (Parliament) of 1812. Built for the centenary of its short-lived liberal constitution, the monument commemorates the first, brief, democratic interlude in Spanish history, when most of the country was in fact occupied by Napoleon's troops. It was this Cádiz assembly and its resolutions that gave the word "liberalism" to the world.

From San Carlos the walls form a broad esplanade looking out to sea, though the bastions of Candelaria, Santa Barbara and San Carlos are off limits. Between Santa Catalina and the causeway reaching out to the fortified and still military islet of San Sebastián is the **Caleta**, a crescent-shaped beach dominated by the crumbling arms of the Balneario (bathing resort) de la Palma, built in 1925.

Among the rocks of the causeway, the poor of Cádiz still collect crabs as they did when Benito Pérez Galdós, Spain's Dickens, passed through the city in the 19th century—and as Gabriel, hero of his book *Trafalgar*, did in the century before him. In the narrow back streets by the Cathedral, they still sell the tiny, slime-green crabs to hardy *gaditanos* and to reckless visitors.

Churches and museums: From the Caleta the walls curve in towards the **Old** and the **New Cathedrals**—built in the early 17th and in the later 18th centuries. The New, to the Rev. George Borrow in 1842, "might be considered a fine monument of labour in some other countries, but in Spain, the land of noble and gigantic cathedrals, it can be styled nothing more than a decent place of worship". Though the building has been finished off since his day, there is no reason to dispute his verdict that its only

Declaration of Spain's first constitution (1812).

claim to fame is as the last resting place of one of Spain's best composers, Manuel de Falla.

Beyond the Cathedral is the former **Cárcel Real** (the Royal Jail), a late 18th-century neo-classical building, now undergoing restoration. Of similar date and by the same architect (Torcuato Benjumeda) is the impressive **Ayuntamiento** (town hall), and throughout the town are scattered neo-classical, and later, multi-storey *casas palacio*, town houses built for the gentry and wealthy merchants. Shortage of building land within the confines of the city forced even the well-to-do to build upwards and these *palacios* are unlike any elsewhere in Andalucía.

The **Museo Histórico Municipal** contains a remarkable model of Cádiz as it was in 1777, and the updated **Museo Provincial** in the Plaza de la Mina is well worth visiting for its archaeological collections from throughout the province.

Sherry country: North of Cádiz, over the swing bridge and past the mess of Puerto Real, is the motorway to Seville; there's a stiff toll. Better is the old road through **Puerto de Santa Maria** and **Jerez de la Frontera**, both ringed by the *bodegas* (wine warehouses) of Harvey, Terry, Tio Pepe and Domecq.

Santa Maria is a pleasant, if unremarkable, town with a castle half-hidden by houses and decorated with religious-patriotic slogans in Latin on its tiled towers. Around the town, tourist "attractions" are being built—the **Puerto Sherry** marina and apartment complex, planned with an eye to 1992 and to a fast buck, and the **Aguasherry** sun-and-fun *parque acuático*.

Jerez has grown rich on the wine trade. Nowadays it is a sort of posh Andalucían city suburb—genteel, well-heeled, self-satisfied and pricey—where the shops sell Burberrys, green wellies and sleeveless duvet jackets.

For most visitors, Jerez means sherry-tasting and watching the prancing Arab stallions at the **Real Escuela Andaluza del Arte Ecuestre** (the Royal Andalucían School of Equestrian

Art). For those with private jets this can be done by dropping in on the local airfield and taking in the Spanish Grand Prix as well, at the Jerez Circuit out on the Arcos de la Frontera road.

West of Jerez, across rolling brown and black claylands, is the fishing port of **Sanlúcar**, once the outport of Seville but now a sprawling, unkempt workaday place, a complete contrast to Jerez. The town looks out across the mouth of the Guadalquivir river to the marshlands of Doñana National Park. To the north, half buried in the dunes, is the castle of **Bonanza**.

Windy shore: The coast here is golden sand from Sanlúcar to Rota and, as it faces into the Atlantic winds, a paradise for windsurfers. An unexciting resort of second homes for the middle-class of Cádiz and Seville has grown up at **Chipiona**, once a fishing port and still a market gardening centre. Between Chipiona and Rota a few surviving stone and thatched cottages are crumbling into ruins, to be replaced by the ubiquitous flat-roofed cubes.

Rota is an American and Spanish naval base attached to a pleasant little fishing port with some surviving medieval defences. To get back to Santa Maria and Jerez, the road makes a long detour round the base and passes between civilian wasteland on the one side and military garbage on the other. From time to time the town is the scene of anti-US demonstrations.

A particularly Spanish institution can be found behind Rota, off the Jerez to Seville road. This is the out-of-town *casas de niñas*, providing an invaluable service to Spanish *machismo*. Accessible only to car owners, these clubs, painted lurid shades of pink and violet, are tactfully known as "meeting places" where paunchy *señoritos* can find a pick-up for the night. Here their little peccadillos pass unnoticed—and their married respectability remains intact and unsullied.

White Town territory: East of Jerez, beyond the race circuit, the countryside is more innocent and the wine is rougher. The roads rise gently towards the sierras that mark the boundary between the provinces of Cádiz and Málaga. The tourist board's *Ruta de los Pueblos Blancos* (White Towns route) and the *Ruta del Toro* (Bullfight route) open up.

Fifteen miles (24 km) out of Jerez de la Frontera along the N-342, is the first of the White Towns, **Arcos de la Frontera**. Like the better known and more spectacular town of Ronda, over the border in Málaga province, Arcos sits on a knife-edge of rock. The main street narrows to less than a car's width (or so it seems) as it rises towards the old town centre and the *parador* in the **Casa del Corregidor.** The plaza in front of the *parador* is a crowded visitors car park ringed with ancient buildings. From here there are views out over the broad valley of the Majaceite and along the cliff to the church of San Pedro.

The *parador* is an ideal stop for coffee in luxurious surroundings, but the local cafés down the hill offer the real atmosphere of Andalucía and, for breakfast, home-made orange marmalade on thick-cut toast.

The beach at Chipiona.

A road staggers down the north face of the Arcos rock to the Bornos reservoir and the Grazalema road, but there are more White Towns on and off the N-342. The small town of **Olvera** lies 42 miles (68 km) to the east. Its narrow streets of white houses are spread over the foot of a steep rock on which stands the Arab castle of Almedina. Further on is **Setenil**, a curious village hacked out of the living rock; the houses and bars are rock-roofed and in places the streets are shaded by threatening overhangs.

North of the Arcos to Grazalema road is **Prado del Rey** (the King's Field), a White Town with a difference. Founded by King Charles III in 1768 in an attempt to stimulate agricultural reform in Andalucía, this town is something of an early Spanish garden city with wide streets and leafy squares.

Sierra watching: In **El Bosque** a small information centre beside the river offers self-guided tours of the **Parque Natural de Sierra de Grazalema**. Set up in 1984 to protect the limestone scenery along the border between Cádiz and Málaga, the park extends from El Bosque to **Benaoján** in the east and **Cortes de la Frontera** to the south. Much of the ancient Mediterranean forest of holm oak and Montpelier maple still survives, but in places the activities of man have converted the forest to open ranges or brush. Here mountain goats can still be seen, with a superb range of birds of prey, including buzzards, griffon vultures and Bonelli's booted and short-toed eagles.

The towns and villages of the park and its adjacent hills record the area's frontier history. A string of *de la Frontera* towns runs from Morón to Arcos, Jimena and Castellar, with Cortes probing the Moorish heartland. Throughout the sierra itself the villages have still kept their Moorish names: Benmahoma, Grazalema (once Ben-Zalema), Benaocaz, Ubrique and Zahara, and the line of Ben villages on the Jimena to Ronda road.

Coming down from the sierra to the coast, there are glimpses of the **Rock of Gibraltar**, more impressive from the

Puerto Sta
Maria.

FROM SALT TO FISH

" *A Roma se va por bulas,*
por tabaco a Gibraltar,
por manzanilla a Sanlúcar,
y a Cádiz se va por sal."
(To Rome for bulls,
for tobacco to Gibraltar,
to Sanlúcar for sherry,
and for salt Cádiz.)
—Popular refrain

Without salt we would all die. Fortunately the amount we require can be obtained from just one boiled egg eaten for breakfast. And there is no need to sprinkle extra salt on it; the salt we see and taste in our 20th-century lives is purely a matter of culinary choice. Until recently, though, we ate much more than we do now—and in those days it was a luxury, not a health hazard as it is now regarded.

For much of human history, salt was one of the few means of preserving foodstuffs. True, drying was an alternative for some foods—fish and ham, the *jamón serrano* of inland Spain, for example—but salting was generally a less risky, tastier and more suitable method for a wider range of foods. Salt was also of great importance in certain industries, especially in curing leather and in some metal extraction processes.

Not so long ago, the marshes around Cádiz and west of Huelva were dotted with snow-white heaps of drying sea-salt, giving welcome relief to the grey-green flats. But over the past couple of decades the number of working *salinas* (salt-works) has dropped dramatically, leaving only the long rectangular pools, the *tajos*, where sea water was stored, to mark the passing of an industry that dates back to pre-Roman times.

Out of a total of 146 registered *salinas* in Cádiz province, only 46 are still in operation for their original purpose. And it is the smaller family businesses that have suffered most. More than 60 percent of the surviving salt-works are operated by just four companies. The big four hold over two-thirds of the salt marshes.

The "*Cádiz, salada claridad*" (salt-clear Cádiz) of Spanish poet Manuel Machado no longer exists. And all that the passing motorist can see of the Salinas de San Fernando is the *agua quieta en los esteros* (still water in the creeks) and a few diminutive salt heaps by the Chiclana to Puerto Real road.

Few Cádiz families still go down to the marshland creeks for the midwinter *despesque* (literally, the "de-fishing"), when fish and eels were caught in the tidal inlets. The summer and autumn salt-winning over, the fish were consumed with liberal quantities of wine and harrowing amounts of Andalucían singing at family celebrations throughout the townships around Cádiz bay.

Until the 1950s the marshes would have seemed little different from those of 2,000 years ago: the trapped sea water evaporating in the summer heat, the crystalline salts being scooped out to dry by weather-beaten peasants; the salt stored in white heaps before being shipped inland, or being used on the spot to cure hides and salt beef provided by the cattle brought down to the marshes for summer grazing, and in winter, fowling and fishing in the *esteros*.

Salted fish paste, known as *garum* to the Romans, was a valued item of trade. Roman amphoras, made in southern Spain for the transport of *garum*, preceded the legions to the Celtic city of Colchester in remote Britannia.

Beyond Rome's Rhine frontier the great, fat-bellied *garum* amphoras have also been found in the homesteads of Germanic tribal chiefs.

Nowadays the wild fowl and fish are reclaiming the marshlands as theirs, where modern industry and urban expansion allow. The abandoned saltings of the island of Saltés, where the Odiel and Tinto rivers meet the sea, are a recognised sanctuary to migrating water fowl.

And among the *tajos* of Cádiz and San Fernando new companies are setting up fish farms. The former salt-pans provide ready-made tanks in which to hatch and rear a range of different varieties for the nation that devours more fish per person than any other in Europe.

The process of change is remarkably undisruptive in the *salinas* of Cádiz.

hills than from the ugly industrial chaos around the Bay of Algeciras. **Algeciras** itself is best avoided but is almost unavoidable. It is the main Spanish ferry port for the North African destinations of Ceuta and Tangiers. Once a town "entirely free of malice" where "even the worst of its crooks were so untrained that no-one was expected to take them seriously", Algeciras has been changed, partly by pressure of constant traffic, partly from doing time under Franco.

Capital surf: On the road for Cádiz, Europe's southernmost town of **Tarifa** is a "bit of washed-up Africa" which is losing its African-ness to become the windsurfing capital of Spain's windsurfing coast. Atlantic winds constantly maltreat the whole length of this shoreline, but at Tarifa, trapped between Europe and Africa, they can be especially maniacal.

This "Most Noble, Most Loyal and Heroic City" takes its name from Tarif ibn Malluk, the first Moor to settle in Spain after the Moorish landings of 711. The earliest surviving part of Tarifa's

castle is 10th century, and its fall in 1292 to Christian Spain gave the place its nobility.

But it was Alonso de Guzmán's defence of the town two years later that earned it the other titles and the epithet "*el bueno*" (the good) for himself. Not that Alonso's son would have agreed, for his father's "goodness" was to sacrifice the boy to his Moorish captors.

Well into the 20th century, the women of Tarifa and nearby Véjer wore the severe, black *cobijada*—a full-length skirt with a burnous-type cloak which was attached to the waistband. Only the Spanish Civil War really caused the demise of this Moorish-style traditional costume, which was too useful for smuggling arms and supplies to Republican guerrillas behind Franco's lines and was accordingly outlawed.

Véjer de la Frontera is perhaps even more African than Tarifa. A white town of steep, narrow streets, it sits high on a hill with artificial Berber caves at its foot. Between Véjer and Tarifa is the Roman city of **Baelo Claudio** (now Bolonia or Bella), under restoration by the provincial government. Founded in 171 BC, the city's buildings have survived remarkably well. However, only cattle trample the grassy banks of the unexcavated area, munching steadily around signs forbidding humans to enter. For the time being, Baelo Claudio is not open to the public.

On the coast nearby is **Cape Trafalgar**, beyond which Nelson defeated the combined French and Spanish fleet in 1805. The region from here to **Barbate** has been the subject of a series of controversial land deals which involved the Spanish military and close relatives of members of the government.

Beyond Véjer, two more frontier settlements point the way to Cádiz: the fishing village of **Conil de la Frontera** and the former fishing and salting village of **Chiclana**. In the latter, Manuel de Falla composed his *Atlántica*; Chiclana is now an uninspiring dormitory town for Cádiz, and the frontier, whether Moorish or oceanic, is a long way away.

HUELVA AND
THE COTO DONANA

For most Spaniards Huelva is just another name to be learnt by rote in a *sociales* class. For most Andalucíans Huelva means the town of Lepe, locally famous for slow wits and strawberries. For the Portuguese, Huelva is on the way to somewhere else, and for the rest of the world it *is* somewhere else—but where?

Yet the province of Huelva was once the centre of the powerful Tartessos civilisation; its mines at Rio Tinto were, and are, internationally renowned, and it was from the mouth of the Rio Tinto that Columbus first set sail for the Indies. Perhaps it is the uninspiring, gentle landscape alongside the N-431 from Seville that puts people off exploring Huelva province.

The tedious A-49 *autopista* is even more discouraging, for it avoids the blood-red walls of **Niebla**. This town stands on the west bank of the Rio Tinto, the coloured river, which stumbles over its rocky bed, a natural kaleidoscope of yellow, orange and red. Once the centre of a wealthy Moorish kingdom, Niebla fell to the Christians in the early 13th century. It was during the siege of Niebla that gunpowder was reputedly first used in European warfare.

Beyond Moorish Niebla and its Roman bridge is the city of **Huelva**, the provincial capital. Founded over 3,000 years ago by Phoenician traders, the early port of trade spread over several *cabezos* (low hills) between the marshy estuaries of the Rio Tinto and the Odiel. Onuba, as the classical world knew Huelva, was an outlet for the Rio Tinto mines, and here Tartessans mingled with Phoenicians, Greeks, Carthaginians and finally Romans. The people of Huelva are now known as *onubenses*.

Huelva is a small town spoilt by industry which has been developed with a callous disregard for the place and its setting. Nevertheless, a refreshingly innocent small-town atmosphere has survived along Huelva's Gran Via.

Foreign influence: Huelva owes much to the last wave of foreign traders attracted by its mineral riches. The English-style "company village", the Reina Victoria *barrio*, built in the 1920s to house the Rio Tinto Company's employees, is one surviving vestige of British commercial colonialism. The local football club, now in the second division with the other "British" teams, was the first to be set up in Spain.

The golf club was another British introduction, and **Punta Umbría** beyond it was founded as the seaside resort of Rio Tinto's expat community, who made the trip from Huelva to the *Casas de los Ingleses* in a tiny paddle steamer. Now Punta Umbría is reached by road and the last "English Houses" were demolished in the 1960s. It remains a mercifully small holiday resort of discos, bars and night-clubs.

Behind Punta Umbría are the **Marismas del Odiel**, the marshlands at the mouth of the Odiel. The flats, from the Isle of Saltés to Gibraleón, have been declared a Paisaje de Interés Nacional (Landscape of National Interest) and

Preceding pages: Columbus monument on the Rio Odiel. Left, stork in Huelva's Coto Doñana. Right, Isla Cristina.

include two breeding reserves of special importance for herons and spoonbills.

On **Punta del Sebo**, the tip of land where the Tinto and the Odiel meet, stands a colossal statue to Christopher Columbus, the *Spirit of Exploration*, sculpted by American Gertrude Whitney, staring out to sea with blind determination and affected heroism.

Monkish enterprise: Over the Rio Tinto are the real monuments to the "Enterprise of the Indies". A complete contrast to the industry around it, **La Rábida monastery** is a haven of contemplative peace set in formal gardens. Dedicated in the 13th century soon after the fall of Moorish Huelva, this Franciscan monastery holds a special place in history. Here Columbus met the Friars Antonio de Marchena and Juan Pérez, who took his case to Queen Isabella and persuaded her to back the venture.

The monastery is centred round a Moorish courtyard, converted to a monkish cloister. The Friars provide a guided tour for a small contribution.

Just inside are the Columbus murals, painted by Vázquez Díaz in 1930 and giving a simplified picture history of the "Discovery" of America. Beyond is the church, built in the early 15th century, with traces of original wall paintings.

Upstairs, above the refectory, is the Sala Capitular (Chapter House) which, but for the modern paintings of Ferdinand and Isabella, is spartanly appointed with heavy Castilian furniture of the Columbus period. The ceiling is a fine piece of Spanish carpentry. Also on the upper floor is the Sala de Banderas, the Flag Room. Something of a place of pilgrimage for South American students attending the University summer schools at La Rábida, the room contains the flags of the South American nations and a casket of soil from each.

Inland from La Rábida is **Palos de la Frontera**. In the plaza, outside the church of San Jorge, the royal order giving the go-ahead to the "Enterprise of the Indies" was read out to the assembled seamen of the town in May 1492. In August that year Columbus's tiny fleet of three caravels set sail from

In the grounds of La Rábida monastery.

Palos, then an important sea port. The harbour Columbus used now lies beneath dark clayey fields between the present river and the Fontanilla (the Moorish well by San Jorge) from which Columbus provisioned his vessels.

From rhyme to wine: Further upstream again is the town of **Moguer**, the birthplace of poet and writer Juan Ramón Jiménez; his house in the Calle Nueva has been turned into a museum and library. Jiménez's is perhaps best known for his children's story, *Platero y Yo*, but his poetry eventually won him the 1956 Nobel Prize for Literature.

A poet of the 1927 generation, like García Lorca from the opposite end of Andalucía, Jiménez was able to escape Franco's bully boys—unlike Lorca—and became the Republican government's cultural attaché in the United States. Walking round the Jiménez's **Casa-Museo** (home-*cum*-museum) is uncomfortably like prying into the private grief of someone else's family. But it does give a remarkable insight into the man's creative genius.

Behind Moguer are the wine-growing lands of the *Condado* (county) de Niebla—the triangle of gently rolling farmland marked by Niebla itself, Palma del Condado and Almonte. The main *bodegas* are to be found in the three *del Condado* towns—**La Palma**, **Rociana** and **Bollullos**, the last being the centre of the largest wine producing cooperative in Andalucía.

Less commercially minded than their neighbours in Jerez, the *onubenses* insist that their wines are every bit as good as sherries, but different. The best time of year to test both arguments is September when Bollullos holds its *Feria Agrícola y Artesana* (Farm and Craft Fair) and its *Día del Vino* (Wine Day). At the same time La Palma celebrates its *Fiesta del la Vendimia* (Grape Harvest Fiesta), a harvest festival in honour of Nuestra Señora de la Guía which is accompanied by flower "fights".

But the area sees more visitors in May for the Romería del Rocío. For most of the year the village of **El Rocío** is a sleepy sprawl of low white houses set

RIO TINTO

"Beyond the lake rises Mount Argentario (Silver Mountain) as the ancients called it. The ore in its slopes glints and shines in the light when the sun's rays warm the earth's surface. The river Tartessos is ladened with nuggets of ore and washes the precious metal to the very doors of the city."

Thus wrote the chronicler Avienus in his *Ora Maritima* in the 4th century AD. Today the lake Avienus refers to is the nearly dry land of the Marismas and the sun glints on towering walls of freshly blasted mauve, purple and yellow-green rock. The Silver Mountain has been turned inside out and, at the bottom of the pit, huge trucks take away ore. Down there the lorries seem monstrous, their wheels twice the height of a man. From the lip of the crater they look like children's toys.

The Greeks and the Phoenicians trekked the length of the Mediterranean and braved the Pillars of Hercules to get that ore. The local Iberian tribes founded the Tartessos civilisation on the trade those sailors from the East brought—though the Greeks believed that the Tartessians sold their mineral wealth at give-away prices.

Early mining was little more than hacking ore out of surface rocks. Simple trench-like quarries still exist around the Tartessian city of Tejada la Vieja—the ancient town is being excavated and conserved as a Parque Arqueológico. It was left to the Roman engineers to develop the potential of Rio Tinto's resources.

The old river routes—down the Odiel and the Rio Tinto (which literally translates as the coloured river) to Onuba, modern Huelva, and from around Arroyo de la Plata (the silver stream) down the Guadiamar to Aznalcázar—were given up. The miners' prehistoric stone mallets were replaced by iron picks, and shafts were driven into the hillsides.

The Roman miners—first slaves, then free men—worked in galleries one metre in diameter, their only light coming from tiny oil lamps placed in wall niches at regular intervals. The miner's life was invariably short; Germanus, slave of Marinus, died aged 15. Sutrius was luckier; he made it to 30. Many of the known Roman shafts were blocked by rock falls. One prehistoric rockfall covered 14 Iberians, and the Roman miners of Rio Tinto had their own "burial club" to provide for those bodies that could be recovered.

The flooding of mine galleries is a perennial problem for the mining engineer, and the Romans generally solved it with systems of waterwheels (*norias*) to lift the water from one level to another. In a mine at Tharsis north of Huelva as many as 40 such wheels were discovered. Eight pairs of *norias* raised water 93 ft (29 metres) in a Rio Tinto mine. An example of one of these wheels is on display in the entrance hall of the Huelva museum. At the Sotiel-Coronada mine, the miners employed a belt-and-braces system of bronze buckets and winches, an Archimedes screw and even a pump.

The wealth of the mining area survived the fall of Rome, the attacks of the Visigoths and invasion by the Moors. The town of Niebla grew into a powerful Moorish enclave through its control of Rio Tinto.

But the easy pickings to be had in the Americas almost put an end to Rio Tinto. Why get your hands dirty grubbing out silver and copper when Aztecs and Incas gave it away? The new silver route, from Cádiz and Seville northward to Castile, by-passed the Rio Tinto mines.

Late and inadequate economic reforms and the loss of empire prompted a number of half-hearted attempts to get the mines going again in the late 18th and early 19th centuries. Lack of cash eventually forced the government to try to auction the mining rights, first in the 1850s and then in the 1870s.

The mines were finally bought in 1873 by a consortium of British and German bankers and businessmen headed by Hugh Matheson, a Scottish Presbyterian and a major figure in Victorian commerce. The consortium included two German businessmen then resident in Huelva, Heinrich Doetsch and Wilhelm Sundheim. Their names are recorded in the street names.

Now a major multinational, the Rio Tinto group of companies is, for good or ill, as famous, and as enigmatic, as Tartessos was to the Greeks.

around vast red-earth plazas as if it were auditioning for a part as a Mexican backwater in a western movie. Then at Whitsun El Rocío suddenly becomes the most popular spot in Andalucía—full of Spanish beauties dressed in brilliant flounced *sevillanas* and their menfolk in black velvet and frilled white shirts. By day, cries of "Viva la Virgén" and the creaking sway of flower-bedecked carts; by night *cante* and guitars, and the unsteady sway of wine-drenched *romeros*.

Wild terrain: El Rocío stands on the edge of the **Coto Doñana National Park**, Spain's biggest, and an absolute must for any visitor—no business schedule to western Andalucía is so tightly packed that a day cannot be set aside for Doñana.

Most of the park is a special reserve but guided trips in four-wheel-drive buses start from the visitors' centre at **El Acebuche**. The five-hour tours—which will last longer if there is a puncture—leave twice daily. It is prudent to book them in advance on tel: (955) 430432. They are pricey but worth it.

The convoys of three or four green *todoterrenos* (all-terrain vehicles) enter the park through **Matalascañas**, the only mini-Benidorm on Huelva's Costa de la Luz. Built in 1965, Matalascañas is on land that should have formed part of the park—but then the park is still not safe from those with money and *enchufe* (contacts) in high places.

In the park the route follows the beach, where oystercatchers, dunlins and sanderlings scurry officiously among the broken waves and sandwich terns and black-backed gulls swoop low across the cream sands. Once it has reached the Guadalquivir estuary the convoy then swings towards the centre of the park, through pine forest and Mediterranean brush, past the former hunting lodge of **Palacio de los Marismillas** and the neolithic *chozas*—reed and pine branch huts—of the charcoal burners.

In among the trees stands a wary red deer stag; a fallow deer flicks a contemptuous white rump at humanity, and

Left, the Rio Tinto or coloured river. **Below**, watching for wildlife in the Coto Doñana.

a black and bristly boar saunters across the sandy track. From time to time even a shy lynx shows itself.

Along the edge of the **Lucio del Membrillo**—almost solid land in summer, almost a lake in winter—the convoy stops at the deserted **Casa del Cerro del Trigo**. Here, in the right season, flock pink flamingos, greylags, spoonbills and all sorts of ducks, and at any time of the year the rare imperial eagle surveys his empire from the topmost branches of a pine.

The vehicles turn back toward the ocean again, through more pines, to the dunes; these moving mountains of sand are slowly but surely burying part of the pine wood. And over the crest of a dune, the sea appears again and the drivers swop the lead so their passengers always have a chance to be the first to spot a new species. Visitors to the National Park can only explore on foot around the El Acebuche centre and the smaller centre at El Rociana.

Outside the Doñana Park, the stretch of coast from Matalascañas to the out-skirts of Huelva is one long beach, backed by dunes and pines—a virtually unspoilt wind-surfers' paradise with exquisite Atlantic sunsets. The coast beyond Huelva is similar in many ways, though behind the dunes there are lagoons and wild or drained marshland. Around **Lepe** the fields are given over to strawberries, which are marketed as products of Valencia; **Isla Cristina** is destined to be developed as the resort centre of western Huelva.

The so-called coastal road, 3 miles (5 km) back from the shore, heads towards Portugal but only gets as far as **Ayamonte**, and its *parador*, on the banks of the Rio Guadiana, which forms the border between the two countries. European Community money is now being spent on a bridge here.

Backwoods: The **Sierra de Aracena** is, perhaps, the real jewel of Huelva province. The road out of Huelva city climbs steadily through the fields of Trigueros and Valverde until the mountains begin before Zalamea. A diversion to Rio Tinto and Nerva reveals the **Spot the Spanish lynx.**

purple and vermilion open-cast ore mines and then the wooded hills that lead to Aracena.

Aracena is a huddle of white walls and Spanish tiles around the hill-top Moorish castle. Tacked on to it is the massive, parapeted church built by the Knights Templar. From the castle there are views over the town and out over the surrounding hills. It pays not to look too closely, though, as the curtain walls were recently subjected to a programme of excavation and restoration that owes more to Belzoni and Drouetti's vandalism of Egypt than to modern archaeology—inside the curtain is an open trench where the castle's buried history used to be.

But Aracena's great attraction is below ground—the **Gruta de las Maravillas** (the Grotto of the Marvels)—a complex of caves over a mile in length and naturally furnished with curtains and pillars of petrified water. At the entrance to the Gruta is an excellent collection of minerals from throughout the world, and the cave's stalagmites and stalactites are particularly fine.

From Aracena towards Portugal the wooded sierra is dotted with little villages famous for their *jamón serrano* (cured ham). The best hams reputedly come from **Jabugo**, but villages like Fuenteheridos, Alájar, Castaño del Robledo and Cortegana are prettier and their hams just as good.

At **Almonaster la Real** another Moorish castle dominates a white-and-russet village. The castle church is a converted mosque with its internal brick pillars still intact after over a millennium; Almonaster is the common man's Córdoba. A bull-ring hangs suspended from the castle walls.

Halfway to Portugal is **Aroche,** with a Moorish castle, cobbled African streets and working medieval tile kilns. If Huelva is Andalucía's Cinderella, Aroche is Huelva's; nothing has happened in Aroche since a lost detachment of Christian knights stumbled across it in the 13th century and replaced the Moorish lord with a Castilian one. And even that did not change Aroche.

Ayamonte.

GIBRALTAR

Anyone who lands at Gibraltar airport—as over 120,000 visitors a year do today—confronts at once a significant fragment of Gibraltar's history. There, high up on the north face of the rock, which rises ahead like a great grey canine tooth, are the embrasures through which British cannon shot down on the Spanish during the Great Siege of Gibraltar, just one in a long history of wars which focused on this commanding lump of stone.

This particular siege lasted from 18 June 1779 to 30 January 1783 and was part of the American War of Independence, when Spain and France—to simplify a complex story—saw Britain losing her American colonies and ganged up to capture British possessions which they coveted. For Spain this meant Gibraltar above all.

General Eliot, in charge of the British defenders of the Rock, had other ideas. It was across the flat isthmus which separates Gibraltar from Spain and now supports the airport runway that Eliot's troops sallied out at 2.45 a.m. on 27 November 1781 in one of his most successful defensive actions. The British over-ran the three closest Spanish batteries, spiked their guns, set fire to their timber emplacements and blew up their powder magazines. Conveniently, the captured Spanish duty officer had the magazines' keys in his pocket and their replicas can be seen in Gibraltar's museum—the originals are in the British Army Museum, Chelsea, London.

The airfield's runway belongs to the history of a different struggle: World War II. It was built in the early 1940s, and, because the isthmus was narrow, had to be extended by the mining and dumping of a million tons of limestone into Gibraltar bay. It still seems none too long to air travellers who are liable to giggle with nervous relief when the roar of their plane's reversed engines halts it short of the Mediterranean.

Cold war: The siege of 1779–83 was the 14th the Rock had survived. Imme-

diately on the Spanish side of the airport's terminal building are the Spanish frontier gates, a reminder of what is now called the 15th siege, though this was a bloodless one. These gates were shut to Gibraltarians on 6 May 1968 on Franco's orders and a year later to Spaniards as well. Soon afterwards the ferry to Algeciras across Gibraltar bay was suspended and Gibraltar's telephone connections to Spain were cut. For 11 years the Rock was totally isolated.

The most dramatic effect was that Gibraltar, deprived of the 4,666 Spanish who used to cross from Spain every day, was forced to recruit some 3,000 Moroccans to do the more menial jobs. This partly explains the Arab costumes in Gibraltar's streets today.

Also prominent at the north end of the Rock are relics of Gibraltar's earlier sieges, in particular the solid and square Moorish castle and the Moorish wall zig-zagging up to it. Gibraltar, like the rest of Spain, formed part of the Roman Empire, and subsequently fell under Visigothic control when the empire col-

lapsed. But for 740 years from AD 711, apart from one brief interval, it was Moorish. Its name comes from the Moorish commander Tarik ibn Zyad (Gibel Tarik—Mountain of Tarik), who, historians now guess, landed on the Rock's east coast, perhaps as far north as Punta Mala.

British conquest: The Moors were finally driven from Gibraltar in 1462 as part of the Christian reconquest of Spain. For another 250 years the Rock was Spanish, and it was not till 1704 that the British first hoisted the Union Jack on the Moorish castle where it has flown ever since. In 1704 General Rooke was not actually claiming Gibraltar for Britain, but merely occupying it on behalf of one of several contenders for the Spanish throne. In 1714, however, by the Treaty of Utrecht, the Rock officially became British.

Between the Moorish castle and the shore stand the many defensive walls and gun batteries which the British then started to build. The old town which these were defending has gone, so badly damaged in 1727 during a Spanish attempt to recapture it (the 13th siege) that it was demolished and the area levelled to form **Casemates Square**. It is here that the ceremony of the keys is re-enacted twice a year, when at sunset the Governor of Gibraltar, in full dress uniform with white topee, is handed the keys by the Port Sergeant after he has locked various of Gibraltar's gates, just as General Eliot was handed them nightly during the Great Siege. The resident regiment plays *God Save the Queen* and the loyal Gibraltarians clap. Most of them are loyal: in 1967, 12,138 voted to remain British and a mere 44 for return to Spain.

Landmarks: From Casemates Square there are several ways to explore today's town, which extends southwards and can be pictured as a frill to the Rock's tall skirt. Still narrow, the town is today creeping up the Rock, as engineers manage to find footing for more houses on the steep slopes above. More land is also being created by filling in the old harbour.

The conventional route south leads

Preceding pages: Main Street bobby; the road into Gibraltar crosses the airport. Left, the Alcázar.

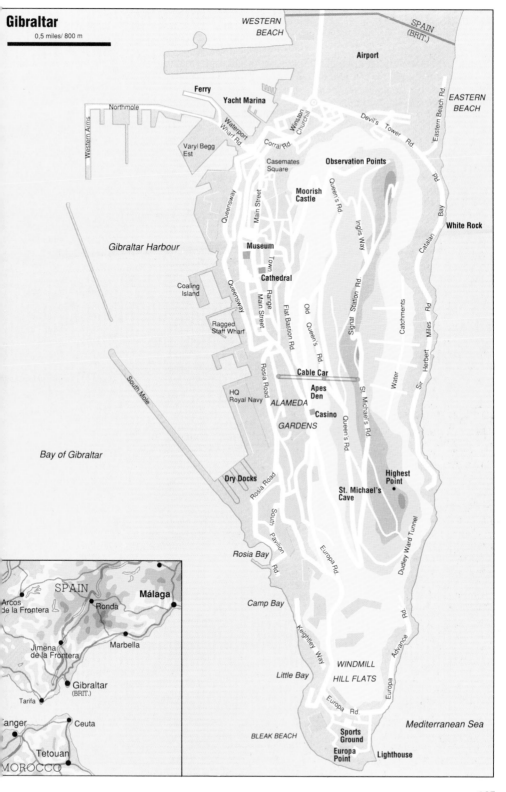

Gibraltar

0,5 miles/ 800 m

WESTERN BEACH

SPAIN (BRIT.)

Airport

EASTERN BEACH

Ferry

Yacht Marina

Northmole

Western Arms

Waterport Wharf Rd.

Winston Churchill

Devil's Tower Rd.

Eastern Beach Rd.

Varyl Begg Est

Corral Rd.

Queensway

Main Street

Casemates Square

Observation Points

Moorish Castle

Queen's Rd.

Inglis Way

Bay

White Rock

Gibraltar Harbour

Museum

Town

Catalan

Coaling Island

Queensway

Cathedral

Range

Main Street,

Flat Bastion Rd.

Old Queen's Rd.

Signal Station Rd.

Catchments

Sir Herbert Miles Rd.

Ragged Staff Wharf

South Mole

Rosia Road

Cable Car

Apes Den

Water

ALAMEDA

HQ Royal Navy

Casino

GARDENS

St. Michael's Rd.

Queen's Rd.

Bay of Gibraltar

Dry Docks

Rosia Road

South Pavilion Rd.

Highest Point

St. Michael's Cave

Dudley Ward Tunnel

Rosia Bay

Camp Bay

Europa Rd.

Keightley Way

Advance Rd.

Little Bay

WINDMILL HILL FLATS

Europa

Europa Rd.

Mediterranean Sea

BLEAK BEACH

Sports Ground

Europa Point

Lighthouse

SPAIN

Málaga

Arcos de la Frontera

Ronda

Jimena de la Frontera

Marbella

Gibraltar (BRIT.)

Tarifa

Tanger

Ceuta

Tetouan

MOROCCO

ROCK TALK

You have to admit that Gibraltar (Gib to its friends, and rather rude to its enemies) is a pretty rum kettle of fish, to mix a metaphor. Actually, mixed metaphors are rather appropriate to the peninsula that would rather have been born an island, just like dear old Blighty (the UK), two hours' flying time away.

Not that the people of the Rock would really like to be towed round to Britain and slotted into the coast, like a jigsaw piece of Empire returning to *alma mater*. Where on earth would it fit? Structurally it might match Cornwall or the west coast of Scotland, but an ideological fit would be an altogether more diffi-cult matter. Popular view is that old Blighty has gone soft, and is only really good for holidays.

The population of this 2½-mile (4-km) lump of stone called Gibraltar is a mixture of Spanish, Arab, Indian and English, but in many ways all are more English than the English. The street, hotel, restau-rant and pub names are furiously patriotic—such as Queen's, King's and Prince's—and the hotel receptionists all seem to be called Elizabeth.

The catering—only a matter of a few hundred yards from the excellent southern Spanish cuisine of just across the bor-der—features beans on toast, fish and chips, and steak in one or two unad-venturous ways.

The restaurants are called the Captain's Cabin or the Bombay Curry House; the pubs the Horse and Hounds, the George and Dragon or the Royal Oak (all in the same mock-Tudor style with red velvet upholstery). The craft shops, run by Indi-ans who speak Spanish, stock Moroccan and Chinese goods, and the lobby music is recognisa-bly James Bond signature tunes from the time when Sean Connery was young.

Main Street (which means what it says) is invariably crowded with shoppers, gossipers, tourists, joggers and parkers, all trying to do their thing on the same bit of space.

It is surprising that, during all the centuries of British rule (since 1704), Spain has not managed to shake the foreigners off this lump of rock; the colony is like a bit of sticking plaster on the toe of a giant, or like a football that just won't leave the foot, however much the latter kicks.

The Gibraltarians (20,000 out of a total popu-lation of 28,500, most of the remainder being members of the British armed forces and their wives) maintain a siege mentality and are furi-ously against the idea of assimilation into main-land Spain.

A referendum in 1967 produced only 44 voters in favour of returning to Spanish rule; so over-whelming was the vote that a skyscraper built at the time was named Referendum House in its honour. Presumably the guilty 44 have kept their heads well down ever since—or sensibly gone to live in Spain.

There could be no other island state which you enter by walking across the runway of its only airport, a strip of re-claimed land which is it-self highly contentious. Gibraltarians fiercely distrust mainland Spain, as evidenced by recent disputes over landing rights.

Spain argues that, as a member country of the European Community, it should have access to the airports of other EC countries, and Gibraltar airport would be particu-larly handy for visitors to the Costa del Sol. The British, who are rapidly liberalising their own air-space, have no argument with that, but the Gibral-tarians do.

"We must not let the Spanish land at our air-port," says the man on the street. "Next thing they'll want to own half of it, and then where will we be?" The net result is that, if a Gibraltarian wants to fly to Madrid, he has to travel via London.

The Spanish police on the nearby Costa del Sol are constantly frustrated by the presence of Gibraltar, which they claim is a haven for crimi-nals on the run, for drug-runners and for money laundering—all of which the Gibraltarians deny.

Once the novelty wears off and the history palls, then all that remains for the visitor to Gibraltar is the shopping, particularly for spirits and electronics. This is not the place for the latest in fashion or foodstuffs; brand names that left the shelves of Britain some years ago are still avail-able here. Gibraltar is not the market for the retailer's more adventurous lines.

along **Main Street**, among jostling tourists, past fish and chip shops, pubs claiming to have been serving fine ales since the 18th century and innumerable window displays of duty-free cameras and watches. Here, too, is the **Governor's Residence**, once a Franciscan convent, the back side of the **Cathedral** and a re-erected church archway, one of the few fragments saved from the old town.

At the southern end, beyond a defensive wall built in 1540 after the pirate Barbarossa had attacked Gibraltar and taken many of its people to sell as slaves, in a little dusty triangular depression is the so-called **Trafalgar Cemetery**. In fact, it was a cemetery from 1708 to 1835 and was used for the burial of English seamen who died from wounds received at three naval battles besides Trafalgar.

It was to Gibraltar that Nelson's ship the *Victory* was towed back, Nelson's body on board in a barrel of brandy. One tradition says that the body was brought ashore and placed in Vincent House, Rosia Bay, but others claim that the seamen of the *Victory* would never have parted with it. Certainly they insisted on sailing it home themselves in their temporarily repaired ship.

Cannon quarters: A route south with as much history and less tourism begins with the Wall Road and runs just within the great stone ramparts that protected the town from attack by sea. Here, in **Cathedral Square**, the most impressive of Gibraltar's cannon, a row of nine, faces out into the bay. Gibraltar must have more cannon per square foot than anywhere else in the world and these nine were no doubt among those which fired red-hot balls during the most famous of all engagements of the Great Siege. On 13 September 1782 D'Arcon's 10 bombarding vessels, specially constructed with double hulls in between which were sandwiched layers of cork, tow (hemp fibre) and sand, specially shaped so that the enemies' cannon balls would roll off into the sea, sailed into the bay. At first they seemed invincible, but gradually the

Gibraltar's Key ceremony.

red-hot balls imbedded in their timbers set them alight. By the end of the next day, nine had exploded or burned to the waterline and the tenth been abandoned and destroyed. Some 2,000 of their 5,000 crew members died and the planned landing was abandoned.

Close to Cathedral Square stands Gibraltar's admirable small **Museum.** As everywhere in Gibraltar, military history predominates, but the building incorporates the well-preserved 14th-century **Moorish Baths**.

Beyond the southern end of the town lie the **Alameda Gardens**, a pleasant spot though the effort of maintaining something so bosky in Gibraltar's climate is apparent, and **Eliot's Memorial**, his bust with its great hooked nose topping a column surrounded, inevitably, by four small cannon. A short climb leads to Gibraltar's best-known inn, the **Rock Hotel**, with its fine views across the bay to Algeciras.

Gibraltar's other curiosities are sited high up on the western face of the rock, a steep slope naturally coated with dense scrub and the home for a surprising amount of wildlife, from rabbits and partridges to the famous apes, but now laced with paths and small roads. The energetic will gain more by walking these (though a full circuit will fill most of a day) than by taking a rock tour in a minibus or taxi, or by being swept to the top in today's cable car, where a restaurant of the baked-beans-and-chips variety perches on the very edge of the Rock's vertical eastern face.

Here there was once a signal station, but it was eventually abandoned because its view was so often spoiled by the Levanter, the easterly wind which is forced up by the Rock to form a cloud over its summit. Beyond the lip, where wisps of cloud continually form, there is a view vertically down to the great concrete catchment area at the bottom. Water has always been one of Gibraltar's problems, and patches of the western face of the Rock have now also been concreted to collect more.

Apes and caves: Close by stands another of Gibraltar's defensive walls,

Bar girls in Irish Town.

this one built by Philip II, husband of Britain's Queen Mary. Steps lead down behind it directly to the **Apes' Den**. According to tradition, Britain will lose Gibraltar only when the apes go. During the last world war, Winston Churchill, hearing the numbers were getting low, signalled that they must be preserved. As a result, the army took charge and the Apes' Den was built.

They are friendly creatures, a lot smaller than postcards suggest, and will pose for the camera, obligingly rattle the branches of a dead olive tree and even sit on your shoulders—though if you make a sudden noise or movement they may run off with your handbag, wallet or spectacles. The apes of a less tame pack roam the Middle Rock area and are more rarely seen.

The apes were probably brought to Gibraltar by the Moors—there is a similar species in the Atlas Mountains—but according to another tradition they came across the Straits by underground tunnel. No doubt the supposedly bottomless **St Michael's Cave** are the origin of this story. In 1840 two British officers who descended into these caves never returned and no subsequent expedition has found their bones.

The entrance to the caves is further south on the same rock face, an easy walk from the Apes' Den. At once you step down into a vast cavern with such good acoustics that it is used today as a concert hall. More remarkable are the smaller caves beyond, where there are fewer coloured lights and the vast curtains of stalactites are left to make their own impression.

Vital tunnel: At the northern end of the Rock's western face is the entrance to the Upper Galleries, leading to those embrasures from which the British shot down on the Spanish during the Great Siege. When inspecting his troops one day Eliot was heard to say, "I will give 1,000 dollars to anyone who can suggest how I can get a flanking fire upon the enemy." One of his officers, Sergeant Major Ince, at once suggested tunnelling through the rock to make a

◂**Catalan Bay.**

way for cannon to be hauled up to the Notch, a projection high on the Rock's north face. After five weeks, using sledgehammers and blasting powder, the miners had made an 8 ft (2.4 metre) square tunnels 82 ft (25 metres) long.

At this point they decided to blow a side hole for ventilation. When the dust had cleared it was obvious that this hole already provided a perfect point from which to fire down on the isthmus. One of Lt Koelher's "depression guns", used to fire downhill, can be seen today in Casemates Square.

When the Great Siege ended and the commander of the French and Spanish forces, the Duc de Crillon, was shown the galleries he commented that the works were worthy of the Romans. Once the embrasures had been opened the miners were under fire from Spanish guns and, to protect themselves, employed two members of the Soldier Artificier Company with especially good eyesight to shout out when a shot was fired by the enemy and where the ball was coming from.

The galleries were continued for another couple of years after the siege was lifted and now lead to St George's Hall, a hollow under the Notch large enough to house a seven-gun battery, where a celebration dinner was held in 1979 to mark the 200th anniversary of Eliot's great sally. This was by no means the end of tunnelling on the Rock. During World War II the Royal Engineers built another 30 miles (48 km) of tunnel, which can be seen by arrangement. The Tunnelling Company of the last war could tunnel 181 ft (55 metres) in one week.

Older remains: Towards the northern end of the Rock stands the Moorish castle. Known as the **Tower of Homage**, the present castle is by no means the first to be built on or near the site, but dates from the middle of the 14th century. Massive and solid, it has little interior to see except four small upper rooms. In these the Spanish governor of Gibraltar held out for five weeks in 1467 against the Duke of Medina Sidonia who had already captured the rest of Gibraltar for his Queen, Isabella.

To indulge in seaside pleasures, leave Gibraltar town, go round the northern end of the Rock and reach the Mediterranean just south of the airport runway. Here there is a bleak sandy beach. Continue south along a rocky shore to the charming small settlement of **Catalan Bay**. Ignore the monstrous hotel on the point, which could as easily stand on any other beach from Bali to the Bahamas, and eat delicious fish at one of the little Anglo-Spanish pub-cafés down by the shore.

It was to Catalan Bay, in 1811, that the inhabitants of San Roque, then the first town across the Spanish border, fled when the French army approached in an attempt to stop the supplies which Wellington's army was receiving from Gibraltar.

Finally, for a view of Africa through a telescope, go to Gibraltar's southern tip, **Europa Point**, a barren area of old military foundations. From **Mediterranean Step** the shoreline of Morocco rests like a two-humped camel on the horizon.

Left, St Michael's Cave. **Right**, a Gibraltar ape who prefers Pepsi.

WILD ANDALUCÍA

Beyond the iron balconies and geraniums of the Andalucían *pueblos* are untamed places, where eagles ride the thermals, lynxes stalk the scrubland that fringes the salt marshes and otters play on the riverbanks. Travellers who seek out the wild side of Andalucía will find that they don't need to go far for untrammelled landscapes, with micro-climates which change dramatically around the next bend; snow, rain, drizzly hills, parched plain and endless sun all co-exist in this foot of Europe.

Facile comparisons come quickly: the high desert of Almería resembles Arizona so much that it became the backdrop for dozens of spaghetti Westerns in the early 1970s, while the weird karstic formations worn in the rocks of El Torcal recall Chinese landscape paintings.

Culture preserved: Yet, on closer examination, there is a thoroughly Spanish stamp on the land. Spain's southern mountains have retained their inaccessibility, and the traditional haunt of *bandoleros*, smugglers and fugitives is now a hideout for wildlife.

On the coast, isolated coves where shipwrecked sailors were washed ashore from the Spanish Main have been spared from high-rise hotels and swimming pools simply because drinking water was easier to come by elsewhere. Species of plants and birds which have been wiped out in more developed areas still flourish here, and belated legislation declares them ecological preserves. Splendid birds of prey—eagles, hawks, falcons and vultures—spread their great wings against the Andalucían sky.

Spain is more mountainous than any European country except Switzerland and there is abundant highland scenery in Andalucía. The **Sierra Nevada**, which inspired a namesake snowy range in California, rears up south of Granada like an immense whitewashed wall. From the highest summits of Veleta or Mulhacen, you may see the glint of the Mediterranean Sea and even over to North Africa. Despite a busy ski resort at **Solynieve**, reached by the GR-420, the highest road in Europe, there is plenty of solitude to be found on 14 peaks that reach over 9,600 ft (3,000 metres). Trails can be blocked with deep snow or landslides and sudden blizzards during the late autumn or early spring can be lethal for the unprepared daytripper.

Twenty mountain lakes relieve the starkness of the sierra above the treeline. Traditional belief is that these lakes are bottomless, haunted and linked to the sea. Alpine lichens, a rare wild pomegranate and edelweiss grow in these heights. Climbers can stay in remote refuges by prior arrangement with the regional mountaineering association, Federacion Andaluza de Montañismo (FAM), Calle Reyes Catolicos, 1. Planta 4, Granada.

In the northeast of Jaén province **Cazorla-Segura,** a natural park since 1986, is not exactly a wilderness, despite its mountain goats and stags, its dense forests and mountain peaks. Among the granite rock faces, evergreens and poplars there are village backwaters where descendants of muleteers and log-rollers eke out a living raising a few cattle or showing anglers the best trout streams. Arab fortresses and ancient church spires mark the horizon, and deserted *cortijos* are left to the elements. Some ruins date as far back as the Phoenician miners who settled near here.

The road from **Cazorla** to **Hornos** which runs through the park goes past a succession of simple roadside bars that fuels the hunters, present and past, including Generalissimo Franco, who took pot-shots at the game in this entire zone during pre-park days. A good portion of the reserve is still set aside for hunting. Huge antlered trophies and boars' heads stare down at the diners in the region's inns. If your Spanish is rusty, simply point to the appropriate creature mounted on the wall: venison, boar, rabbit or partridge is often the menu choice.

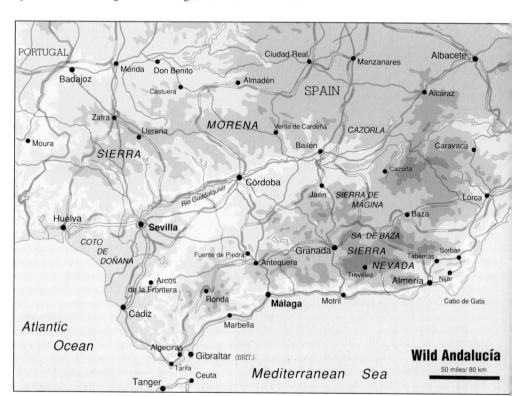

This remote mountain range has hawks, eagles, even the chance of a rare bearded vulture soaring overhead, and thousands of deer and boar. Iberian mountain goats (ibex) can be spotted here as well. Hikers can see primroses and the dwarf violets unique to Cazorla, and search out the little spring where the **Guadalquivir** (which means Great River in Arabic) is unceremoniously spat out from the depths of a mountain.

The **Alpujarras,** a squat range extending from the southern flanks of the Sierra Nevada into both Almería and Granada provinces, have drawn adventurous travellers ever since Englishman Gerald Brenan wrote of his life there in *South from Granada.*

Forty villages manage to survive in this beautiful if desolate zone, under threat of turning into desert ever since Arab irrigation techniques were replaced by the cultivation of cereals. Rooflines here are flat, like the North African Berber dwellings in the Rif Mountains, and the rough slate trim is an exception from the usual red-tiled *pueblos blancos* in most of Andalucía.

The Moors kept a secret stronghold here, along their former Silk Route, long after the Kingdom of Granada fell in 1492. The highest settlement in Spain, **Trevélez** is known also for mountain-cured ham, sorcery and folk medicine. **Bubión,** in the high Poqueira Valley, is home to an unexpected Spanish sect of Tibetan Buddhists.

Upland barricade: Stretching 200 miles (320 km) across the top of Huelva, Seville, Córdoba and Jaén provinces, the **Sierra Morena** (the Dark Range) hems in Andalucía from the plateaux of Extremadura and Castile. The sierra is so named because of the thick woods that shadow its slopes. It is not high; even the tallest peak barely tops 4,000 ft (1,200 metres). The scattered villages here are austere, and the local miners and shepherds are outnumbered by hunters. About a dozen pairs of wolves in the mountains are protected, but almost everything else is fair game and in season the forests ring with shotgun blasts. Lynx, wild boar, great stags,

Preceding pages: limestone formations at El Torcal; the Sierra Nevada near Lanjarón. Below, in the Sierra Cazorla.

STRANGERS IN ALPUJARRAS

The Alpujarras have always fascinated foreigners. This mountain fastness thrown down between the Mediterranean and Sierra Nevada has provided refuge and excitement for adventurers, recluses, the persecuted, the perverse and weirdos by the score. It must be something in the air. The towering bulk of Mulhacen, the rooftop of mainland Spain at 11,400 ft (3,500 metres) above sea level, forms the northern perimeter of the mountain range, which claims Europe's highest inhabited villages and navigable roads.

For the Moors, the first foreigners to move in, this wet, green wedge of Andalucía comes close to their version of para-dise: a garden flowing with streams. For nearly a century after the Catholic Monarchs snuffed out the flame of Islam in Granada, Moors forcibly converted to Christianity prospered in the Alpujarras. Hidden deep in the inaccessible valleys, the Moriscos—as these stubborn Arabs were known—finally rebelled against Spanish bigotry and intransigence in the year 1570.

Crushed by the omnipotent Catholic Church, the 48,000 Moriscos living in the mountains were banished to North Africa. Their rocky Spanish retreat was thoroughly looted before settlers from the impoverished regions of Galicia and Extremadura were allowed to take over Europe's last Arab domain.

Although the Alpujarras became a byword for poverty after the Moriscos' expulsion, the area never lost its allure for foreigners. They rarely stayed long, but came away with wondrous stories of a lost nirvana that only served to foment the legend of the Alpujarras as a forgotten land. The locals scathingly referred to these brave intruders as *los peludos*, the hairy ones.

In the 1920s, a young Englishman called Gerald Brenan took up residence in the Alpujarras in an attempt to educate himself in a corner of Europe untouched by the horrors of the Great War. Brenan rented a house in the Alpujarras village of Yegen for 120 pesetas a year, and set about reading the 2,000 books he had bought with him strapped to a mule. Brenan's self-imposed exile from Western civilisation produced some thoughtful books on Spain and its inhabitants, including one about his life in the Alpujarras, and a constant stream of visitors drawn from the artistic and intellectual fringes of Europe's flourishing bohemian communities of the time.

The writings of Brenan, together with boredom with Morocco's marijuana experience and closure of the hippy trail to Kabul due to war in Afghanistan, put the Alpujarras on the alternative tourists' holiday map.

By the 1970s, there were unmistakable signs of an invasion of modern-day *peludos*. Long-haired foreigners cruised this miniature Eden in camper vans, trying to locate a niche to hide them from the world. Abandoned farms and tumble down houses soon showed signs of vigour as exotically dressed communities from beyond the Alpujarras established their versions of paradise on the perpendicular scenery.

The mountains have been guaranteed a place in eccentric minds with the recent arrival of prophets of Oriental religions and their disciples. Five centuries after the Alpujarras echoed to the wail of Islam, the same hills and valleys now ring with the gongs of Buddhist and Shinto rituals. In 1982, the Dalai Lama inaugurated the O-Sel-Ling (the Place of Clear Light) meditation centre in the picturesque Poqueira Valley.

Five years after the divine presence of Buddhism's high priest in the Alpujarras, a chubby Spanish toddler called Osel, who lived with his parents at O-Sel-Ling, was acclaimed by international Buddhism as the reincarnation of a Tibetan spiritual teacher. Osel was carried off to Nepal to receive special tuition in a Lamasery. Unfortunately, the boy's grounding in Lamaism in the Himalayan kingdom was abruptly cut short when the Nepalese churlishly threw him out of the country on the grounds that he had been residing there illegally.

Osel has since returned to the safe confines of Poqueira Valley to contemplate his destiny. After all, in the makeshift philosophy of the "hairy ones", the Alpujarras must surely be an earthly paradise for those who wish to ponder life's imponderables.

roebuck and mule deer abound, with buzzards and royal eagles gliding high overhead to swoop down on the partridge, hare and rabbits in the brush.

In the **Sierra Aracena,** the far western section of this range, ancient oaks provide the acorns that feed the famous black-legged swine of Jabugo, which are transformed into the most prized hams in Spain, mountain cured and tender. In the town of Aracena, underneath the remains of a Knights Templar castle, are extensive caves with narrow multi-coloured caverns and stalactites of glistening white quartz crystal. Cork and chestnut forests are widespread.

Forests and fossils: In the **Serranía de Ronda,** along rose-streaked granite hills near the town of Grazalema in Málaga province, the woods shelter rare examples of the *pinsapo* pine. These evergreens are living fossils, relics of the forests that covered the earth during the Tertiary period. In the shade of these trees grows a delicate carpet of moss and tiny wild peonies. Rhododendrons also thrive in the damp of this peculiar micro-climate, one of Spain's wettest despite being so far south. In the caves of **La Pileta,** 16 miles (27 km) to the southwest of **Ronda** itself, Palaeolithic artists left their mark by painting bison, bulls, fish and horses on the walls.

Snowmelt rivers have rent deep ravines through this area. Gorges like Garganta Seca or Garganta Verde are nearly as impressive as the Tajo, a staggeringly deep gash made by the Guadalevín river which cleaves the town of Ronda in two. The *pueblos* nearby are known for leathercraft and weaving. The skies are patrolled by eagles, vultures and hawks, the land by Iberian mountain goats.

In the eastern uplands of Cádiz province the forest lands have been set aside as a reserve for vast stands of cork oaks. When the bark is stripped in sections along a branch and carted away eventually to become stoppers for bottles, a smooth russet-hued wood is exposed. This gives a limb the elegance of a slim arm clad in a long evening glove. The forests of cork oak in this reserve have

Cabo de Gata.

not been stunted by over-processing and harken back to primitive Iberian forests. The *canutos*, or river glens, support an unusual mixture of deciduous trees. Deer graze here, further south than anywhere else on the continent.

Shorelands and marshes: An extensive national park of 185,000 acres (75,000 hectares) in Huelva province, **Coto Doñana** is a birdwatchers' paradise, a bottleneck on the migration routes from Africa where 80 percent of all flocks stop over. Predators—lynx, badgers, foxes and snakes—ogle the birds almost as much as the ecologically oriented park visitors with their binoculars and checklists.

An English naturalist and hunter, Abel Chapman, brought this region to wide public attention at the beginning of the 20th century. It has extraordinary dunes, pushed by the wind into peaked sets that travel like ocean waves until they are finally anchored by dune grass and umbrella pine. Salt marshes, thickets of cork forest and scrubby Mediterranean highland are delicate and offi-cials permit only 56 visitors on the premises at any one time. Call the Huelva park authority on tel: (955) 43 04 32 to arrange permits.

Despite its protected status, the park suffers an annual invasion of about 1 million fervent celebrants who cut through on their way to the shrine of **El Rocío** (The Virgin of the Dew). On horseback, on foot, in jeeps or inside fringed wagons, girls in flounced dresses and men in the traditional *traje corto* make this famous *romería* the focal point of their year.

Political nesting: A slightly less raucous *flamenco*—which is also the Spanish word for flamingo—can be found feeding in the shallow lagoons of Doñana, although their sole Iberian nesting area is considerably to the northeast. The prime minister, Felipe González, regularly holidays at a cottage on the borders of the park and his deputy premier, Alfonso Guerra, heads the governing board of Coto Doñana. Not surprisingly, it has become fashionable and politically savvy for Spanish

Suffocated by sand in the Doñana desert.

socialists to spend the summer here.

The **Marismas del Odiel,** an estuary system at the mouth of the Tinto and Odiel rivers just outside Huelva, is the hatching ground for a third of the spoonbills in Europe. Even though high lead pollution levels along neighbouring Punto de Umbría have set off alarms for Spanish ecological activists, there is still a rich variety of wildlife here. It runs the gamut from miniature sandpipers to boar. At Saltes Island in the river mouth chameleons can still be found in some concentration.

Cabo de Gata in Almería province is the furthest southeastern corner of Spain, a parched scrubland spiked with century plants (a type of agave which was once thought to flower once a century) where a lighthouse scans its beam out into the Mediterranean. Numerous secluded coves and very clear water attract snorklers and scuba enthusiasts from all over Europe to this 64,000-acre (26,000-hectares) natural park.

Spared from tourist development because of a chronic water shortage, the bleak cape is still practically untouched, except for old salt works. Shallow tidepools at the base of sheer cliffs allow visitors to study sea life close up in a series of miniature open-air aquariums. Overhead, some 149 different species of birds stop over on their migratory routes up from Africa. Even pink flamingos can occasionally be glimpsed in the saline marshes. Palms grow wild on the inland heights of **Nijar**.

Arid zones: Almería's high desert and chaparral is protected within a trio of natural parks: **Campo de Tabernas**, **Karst de Sorbas** (both near the towns that bear their names) and the **Sierra Alhamilla**. Threatened by aluminium mining and off-road vehicles, the desert landscape is distinctive, with bleached outcroppings of calcite and strange round erosions perforating the sunburnt ground. Paths ramble past a few waterholes and thirsty animals. The only poisonous snakes are small vipers and tortoises are a protected species here.

Southwest of **Antequera** (Málaga province) is **El Torcal**, a surreal park of wind and rain-sculpted limestone formations, with two grades of hiking trails marked out. The most difficult demands about three hours. Shy green lizards and occasional scorpions hide here. Eastwards, close by the stunning gorge at **El Chorro**, these weird forms reappear with a somewhat diminished aspect, obscured by rows of pines in the government's attempts to fight erosion.

Wetlands: Northwest of Antequera, **Fuente de Piedra** is an isolated lagoon where flamingos nest each spring on muddy nests shaped like chimneypots. Up to 25,000 birds have been counted in a single season here. Their only other breeding ground in Europe is the Camargue, in southern France.

The shallow water and reeds in smaller neighbouring lagoons like **Campillos**, **Gosque** and **La Ratosa** are also fowl places, sought out by herons, storks and wild ducks.

A little further north, a series of shallow lagoons have been set aside as refuges for wild ducks, and numbers have increased almost tenfold after a strict ban on hunting anywhere in the reserve.

Valuable cork oak.

ON FOOT ACROSS ANDALUCIA

Intrepid walker Robin Neillands tramps through the region from top to bottom

I came into Andalucía from the north, out of the arid country of Extremadura. Parched by the sun, I was glad to get off the great plains and into the winding river valleys of this delightful southern region, with its orange trees and shady olive groves. After walking all the way across Spain, Andalucía seemed like paradise.

The northern frontier of Andalucía is guarded by the long mountain range of the **Sierra Morena**, the Dark Mountains, which are just high enough to be called mountains, rising to around 2,000 ft (700–800 metres). They offer good walking for well-equipped backpackers but rather less for those people who simply enjoy day-rambling. Up in the Sierra Morena there is a distinct shortage of accommodation and the distances between the small towns and villages tend to be rather long.

I crossed the Rio Zujar into Andalucía a little north of **Belalcazar**, which has the magnificent ruin of a Moorish castle, and, after scrounging some water from a friendly group of road-repairmen, walked on through the olive groves to **Hinojosa del Duque**, a very fine town with a grand church and a lively Plaza Mayor, where I spent a warm evening drinking Campocruz beer and chatting to the locals. They thought that anyone who walked across Spain must be crazy, and I felt inclined to agree.

Two features of Spain which will appeal to any walker are the *fonda* and the *plaza mayor*. A *fonda* is a small inn or boarding house, where you will find a clean bed and, with luck, dinner and breakfast, all at no great cost. Most *fondas* I encountered charged about 1,000 pesetas for the room, and perhaps as much again for dinner and breakfast. There is no luxury here, but at the end of a long day's walk, who cares?

Andalucía, being great horse-riding country, also has *posadas*, which are *fondas* with stables attached and fodder available. The *plaza mayor*, the main square, is the central feature of all Spanish towns and most villages. There you will find cafés, bars, restaurants, a fountain from which to fill the water-bottle. As I drifted south across Andalucía, out of the Sierra Morena and into the valley of the Rio Guadiato, I moved from *fonda* to *fonda*, passing my evenings in the *plaza mayor*, averaging 15 to 20 miles (24 to 32 km) a day, losing weight steadily but gaining an impressive tan.

Belmez, my first stop along the Guadiato, has a very fine *fonda*, serving local food. The magnificent castle overtopping the town stayed in view behind me all the next day as I walked down the river towards Córdoba, three days walk to the southeast. In **Espiel** the large café in the plaza looks rather grubby but conceals some glittering bedrooms, all with baths and marble floors and stripped-pine walls. In rural Spain it is always unwise to judge by outward appearances.

Left, Andalucían hunter. Right, long road across the plain.

After Espiel I struck a little south, right across the mountains and yet again through the forest; forests of oak trees grown to feed thriving herds of pigs, not the familiar big, white English pig, but the *cerdos iberica*, small, black and very agile, that can give you a fright when it comes surging out of the undergrowth.

I passed through Villaviciosa, another pleasant *pueblo*, then camped one night on the mountainside, dining on spring water and a *bocadillo* of ham and cheese. I arrived in **Córdoba** next day, more than ready for a little luxury at the *parador*. *Fondas* are fine but paradise is a good *parador*, with hot water and tablecloths.

Open land: Córdoba lies in the wide valley of the River Guadalquivir, the longest river in Spain. I left the city early in the morning, and it took two days to trudge south over the grain fields and olive groves, first to La Carlota and then to **Ecija**, a remarkable town crammed full of churches. Heading due south from here, walking hard for Osuna on a very rough track, I passed through vast cotton fields. Until then I had no idea that they even grew cotton in Spain, but there it was, white as snow and mile after mile of it.

This rolling land, east of Seville, is also horse-ranching country, full of famous herds. Some of the ranches date back to Moorish times, and some still supply horses to the Spanish army. I passed several herds, each with a fringe of foals, which were cropping the short grass; many came over to take a closer look at the man with the rucksack who was trudging steadily past in the heat of the day.

Walkers, especially the long-distance, backpacking variety, are not common in Spain. This meant that I attracted a lot of attention, but suffered from a lack of facilities. You need a compass and a stick to warn off dogs. The maps are not accurate, with the 1:50,000 scale maps dating from the early 1970s, and there are few footpaths which can compare with those way-marked networks to be found in other

Left, Robin Neillands. Right, Ronda, on the Alameda.

European countries. In Andalucía the waymarking is non-existent. But there are plenty of tracks, the locals do not mind if you wander across their land or through their farmyards, and you can camp anywhere except within the National Parks. One other word of warning: do carry plenty of water. Spain is a hot, dry, empty country and a well or a river can be rather hard to find or, even worse, dry when you get there.

My meetings along the way were all with country people: shepherds leading great jangling flocks of sheep, farmers who came trotting up on horseback for a chat, or with people gathering olives or mending the roads. It could be lonely, but it was rarely dull, and the scenery of Andalucía is never less than beautiful and often quite spectacular.

The road to Ronda: Osuna is a magnificent town, crowned by a great monastery and containing a very fine *fonda*, the Caballo Blanco. South of here the land started to ripple and rise again as I pushed on south for the best known of the White Towns, Ronda.

My first stop on the way was at a strange, half-empty little place, **El Saucejo**, a small town in the foothills of the sierra, after which I took off across the hills on a most splendid walk to the main Jerez-to-Antequera road, which lay somewhere across my path.

This walk took most of the day and required the assistance of a friendly farmer, but on the way, I caught my first glimpse of a real White Town, **Olvera**, far away to the west. Even at a distance, Olvera looked so beautiful that I decided I must go there. I crossed the main road and followed the track of a disused railway line.

Set in stunning countryside, crowned by a great church and yet another ruined Moorish castle, Olvera is quite large, a glittering place under the Andalucían sun. To the north lie range after range of hills, picked out with millions of olive trees ranged in line like guardsmen, while to the south more real mountains reappeared, rising up and up to the great sweeping arc of the Serranía de Ronda, my last major obstacle before the long

A welcome in every Plaza Mayor.

descent to the Mediterranean.

The country around **Ronda** offers superb walking. With plenty of farms and plenty of country people to point out the way, I made excellent time, at least until I came up to the steep escarpment of the Sierra de Salinas, a few miles northwest of Ronda, and could not find my way down.

Eventually, rather late in the day and at the cost of my compass, I forced my way down the mountainside, through the thorns and scrub oaks, crossed the valley for a mercifully long drink at a farmer's well, and plodded rather wearily into Ronda for another very welcome day off, staying in a small *fonda* just behind the bull-ring.

My favourite part of this town lies across the great El Tajo gorge from the bull-ring, a place where most tourists never seem to go, so with a stroll over there and a good lunch and dinner, my rest day in Ronda set me up for the last week of my walk, south to Gibraltar and then to Tarifa, on the very tip of Europe. I even washed the sweat and dust out of my clothes and by the following morning was fresh and once more ready for the road.

Recommended route: Ronda seems to be surrounded by mountains, which present a great wall for anyone walking south. But there is a way through, by first heading west towards Montejacque and then following the Rio Guadiaro and the railway line south to **La Jimera de Libar** along the river bank, over cuttings, even—once—through a tunnel. At Jimera I spent the night camped at a farm, where the farmer spent the evening showing me his pigs and bewailing the price of olives—about 30 pesetas a kilo for his current crop, which hardly makes picking them worthwhile.

From here I followed a footpath south to my next night stop at Algatocín, another White Town, followed by a gentle day to **Gaucín**, one of the better known White Towns of Andalucía, and very beautiful. By now, I was out of the real mountains and although the country was still hilly, this is the part of An-

Goatmilking above Ronda.

dalucía I would really recommend for a walking holiday. There are plenty of good paths, lots of accommodation at a range of prices, and the distances are not too great.

I left Gaucín about eight in the morning, a rather chilly morning as I remember it, and after crossing a col or pass at about 3,200 ft (1,000 metres) saw the land finally begin to fall away at last, in a long decline that must surely lead me to the still distant Mediterranean.

By three o'clock that afternoon, following clear tracks across country, I was in the town of **Jimena de la Frontera**, lunching at the Hostal Anon, which to my surprise soon began to fill up with English walkers out here on holiday. From them I learned that there was excellent day-walking in the countryside around the town.

Jimena is one of the fortified towns which once guarded the Frontera, the frontier between the Christians and Moors before the *Reconquista*. The sherry town of Jerez de la Frontera is another, and perhaps the most famous, of these frontier towns but Jimena is attractive and, like so many towns hereabouts, has a ruined castle on the hill above it.

Last leg: One of the walkers I met pointed out that the best way south from here lay along the valley below on an old *Camino Real,* a late medieval drovers' road, which ran beside the railway and the river and took me to Castellar de la Frontera, and then on for the night to Almoraima, where I found another good *fonda*.

The countryside in this area much resembled parts of Britain, particularly the Sussex South Downs, but there were great orange groves full of golden fruit in the valley, to remind me I was still in Andalucía, and more and more houses and people as I passed on to San Roque. From there, just across the bay, I could see my destination, the distinctive **Rock of Gibraltar** and the intended finish of my walk.

Gibraltar is one of those places to which distance lends enchantment, but which palls under closer inspection. I had a cup of almost English tea in the main square just to show willing, and then retreated back across the airport runway, through La Linea to **Los Barrios**, where I prepared for the last full day, a fairly long one across the steep and thickly wooded Sierra de Ojen to Tarifa. This day was fairly hard going, but there was always that glint of Mediterranean blue somewhere through the trees and, increasingly, a hint of a coastline ahead that could only be North Africa.

So on I went, over the hills, those relentless Andalucían hills, under the dwarf oaks and through the clutching thorns, and finally down and out on to the main road, to another narrow track, and then past the Puerta de Jerez, the main gate in the walls of the town into **Tarifa**, and down to the long sandy beach with the windsurfers.

Here the Mediterranean meets the Atlantic, here Europe ends and a few miles away across the Straits, Africa begins. I let the last effort of a wave wash the dust of Andalucía from my boots and began to think about home.

Bull taking a dust bath.

GOING TO MOROCCO

The legendary Pillars of Hercules—the Rock of Gibraltar paired with Ceuta's Monte Hacho on the African coast—formed a colossal entrance to the classical world. Modern travellers veer past this Mediterranean gateway and touch the face of Africa, only 10 miles (16 km) away from Spain at the narrowest point, so close that there has even been talk of a bridge. It is a short journey straight into the perplexities of Africa. Spain's North African enclaves, Ceuta and Melilla, may ease the transition into a thoroughly alien world, while entry direct into Morocco at Tangier or Tetouan will be abrupt, and bound to be either thrilling or frightening or both.

Getting there: The usual port of embarkation for Morocco is Algeciras. Ferries leave regularly for the 90-minute voyage to Ceuta (Sebta in Arabic) or 2½ hours to Tangier. Although often a glorious daytrip, with dolphins trailing in the ferry's wake, the crossing can be miserable. Sometimes it is fraught with delays and tedious passport formalities, and in July and August mobs of exhausted Moroccan migrant workers compete for seats and car spaces, sleeping rough at the quayside to keep their place in the queue.

In clear weather, the Transtour hydrofoils will speed travel considerably without increasing the price much; but they don't run on Sundays or when the Straits are choppy.

The trip to Tangier from Algeciras or Gibraltar takes an hour, but with only one departure a day. In summer three hydrofoils a day leave from Tarifa, the windsurfing mecca west of Algeciras, for a quick half-hour run to Tangier, but out of season, there are only three a week. In August, a ferry runs between Málaga and Tangier, a four-hour trip.

Gibraltar can be a quick escape-hatch, and is under-used by Moroccans, even though the frontier with Spain has long been reopened. In high season, there is a convenient hydrofoil link from Gibraltar to Mdiq, north of Tetouan, which takes over an hour. Book early for this, because Costa del Sol tour groups can easily fill all seats. In addition, GibAir has reasonable flights to Tangier and Casablanca.

To reach Melilla, Spain's eastern enclave, takes considerably longer. Trasmediterranea ferries travel by day from Málaga (an 8½-hour trip) or from Almería by night (also 8½ hours). Dreadful crowds mass up in August. If time is a priority, there are regular air connections from Málaga or Almería as well. For the most complete advice on crossing the Straits of Gibraltar, contact Turafrica, who are based in Fuengirola (tel: 952-471899 or 461452).

Cautionary words: Without your own set of wheels, you must expect some harassment at bus stations and taxi ranks on the Moroccan side. Speakers of French or Spanish will be able to negotiate reasonable fares for communal *Gran Taxis*. These are battered Mercedes which make routine trips between main Moroccan towns. Anyone who has visited Israel should apply

Preceding pages: crossing the Straits. **Left**, *parador* in Spanish Morocco. **Right**, a more fragrant but more stressful culture.

for a duplicate passport, as Arab League guidelines allow Moroccan border officials to bar a tourist with an Israeli visa.

Save exchange slips, for after 48 hours you may legally convert only half of your money back from dirhams. In Tangier and Tetouan many shops welcome pesetas or American dollars.

Today's Morocco is surprisingly dense with people, and there is virtually no solitude. Even if you think you are alone, you will be watched intently, so any sense of privacy vanishes. The meek might prefer to go herded in a tour group, but do remember that all those hustlers are only the most brazen face of Morocco. There is generous hospitality and frank curiosity here.

The usual advice is to travel south as quickly as possible to escape threatening border towns like Tangier or Tetouan. If you have time to delve deep, do press on to Fez and eventually to the Berber villages in the Atlas valleys. Even a fleeting encounter with the Moors will enhance your understanding of Andalucía.

Melilla: Spain's smaller and quieter enclave is a dreary duty-free port and centre of black market currency exchange. Spanish colonial buildings, few dating back as far as the first occupation in 1497, give its narrow hilly streets almost the look of a Latin American *pueblo*. Fittingly enough, the rebel forces that launched the Spanish Civil War started their campaign from this plaza on 17 July 1936.

Palms shade the Plaza Mayor where a zodiac is laid out in the stones. The *pueblo's* fortifications are almost over-restored, with drawbridges and the vestiges of moats. Moroccan merchants stride around in pointed slippers that match the bright yellow of the market melons. With a small community of Indian traders, the town is more cosmopolitan than comparable ones in more typical Spanish provinces.

Down the only road, which means that passing through town is unavoidable, **Nador** is truly the nadir of northern Morocco. The Spaniards deserted it in 1957 and now this bleak

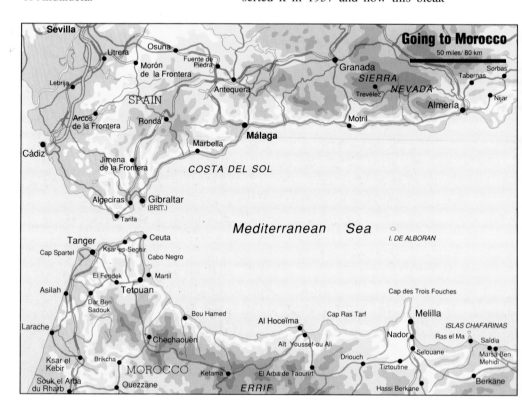

Going to Morocco

50 miles/ 80 km

place lacks most amenities you'd expect in a provincial capital. Riffian villagers work the cement factory, while the bored university students who helped initiate the 1984 food riots here keep to themselves. Move on quickly if you can. The surrounding countryside and beaches are a distinct improvement. Only when families descend in July and August does the lack of sanitation become apparent.

Kariet Arkmane, out past the airport, is an estuary favoured by flamingos. Further east, the road goes through the sheer Zegzel Gorge and up into the mountains. One cavern near Taforalt boasts an odd stalactite shaped like a camel. **Berkane** is the market town for the terraced orchards which the road climbs through, and the only semblance of a resort is over on the Algerian border. The sandy beach at **Saidia** extends for 9 miles (14 km), with a fringe of woods and a local town for a change of pace. There's a twin resort on the other side of the border.

Floating on the horizon are the **Islas Chafarinas**, a cluster of three small Spanish islands. The biggest one is **Congreso**, home to fishing eagles, cormorants, gulls and endangered monk seals which live nowhere else in Iberia. It is almost wilderness, aside from a tidy Spanish plaza and a lighthouse. Transport to the Chafarinas is by private launch, which may draw undue suspicion in this smuggling zone. Sporadic road checks for drugs and arms are common on all roads leading from Nador and Melilla.

Travelling west from **Nador**, the road passes a turn-off to a pretty valley cut through the foothills of the Rif Mountains by the Nekor river. Beyond lies **Al Hoceima**, a rather bland Euro-resort built around a wide bay, without much panache. It offers calm beaches and a good respite from the gruelling roads ahead in the Rif. On the landmark **Peñon de Alhucemas,** a fortress church has been converted to a mosque, the reverse of what has happened in most hilltop towns in Andalucía.

To continue west is to court danger.

Mixed bathing.

The hairpin bends and dizzying switch-backs that lead eventually into cedar forests are natural points for ambush, an art which has been perfected by generations of mountain tribes during intermittent bloodfeuds.

Kif in the Rif: The stony soil in the Rif region is poor, but can sustain terraced fields of cannabis. This crop was condoned by the Spanish Protectorate which figured that smoking kif would keep the tribes pacified. Puffing clay pipefuls of cannabis cut with harsh black tobacco was long tolerated as a harmless peasant custom, one that eased a hardscrabble existence.

Accordingly, in Jazz Age parlance, a cannabis cigarette became a "reefer". But when an enterprising American drug dealer introduced the Lebanese technique of pressing plant resin into blocks of hashish, underworld greed overwhelmed these isolated heights.

The heart of the Moroccan hashish business is **Ketama,** best avoided by anyone who wants tranquil travel. Bands of Riffian ruffians stop tourists and have been known to make deals at knife-point. Corruption is rife and the police not necessarily reliable. Once in custody, hapless tourists may find that their bribes are pocketed but not acted upon. Innocence is openly scoffed at. Just driving through this unsavoury area, beautiful though it is, may be grounds for suspicion in the eyes of officials.

Garrison town: Those who enter Africa at **Ceuta** (Sebta) won't need to contend with such stresses, for they haven't technically left Spain. Ceuta is a dusty garrison town with the dubious appeal of duty-free shops. Row after row of digital watches, portable radios, cigarettes, booze, batteries and bootleg cassettes are on sale.

Most tourists hurry through to the border at **Fnideq** where they can change their money and enter Morocco. However, it is worth dawdling in Ceuta to climb up to the **Hermitage of San Antonio** atop **Monte Hacho**, just to look across to Gibraltar. The mythological moment of standing atop a Pillar of Hercules is marred for some by a grandiose monument to General Franco, who in July 1936 crossed over from Ceuta with Nationalist troops at the beginning of the Spanish Civil War. The Spanish Foreign Legion museum is rather meagre, but the Cathedral of Our Lady of Africa is a proud assertion of Catholicism.

Ceuta was first snatched from the Moors in 1415 by the Portuguese and now bears few Arab traces. Strategic towers survey the Campo de Moros (Field of Moors), and the Spaniards hold on to this outpost with as much patriotic tenacity as the Britons show towards Gibraltar.

After the rather Frenchified resorts on the coast (Smir-Restinga, Cabo Negro and Martil), **Tetouan** itself may be overpowering. Clusters of insistent multilingual youths lie in wait for first-time tourists. Each promises protection against the other seedy types loitering nearby, with no motive other than friendship (plus, of course, an appropriate fee and a commission on any purchases). Their clamouring can become

Boys of Ceuta.

oppressive, along with the constant offers of hashish. Don't be tempted to shop until you've become more familiar with your surroundings. You needn't stick to the new town, even though the *medina* or city centre, with its main entrance off Place Hassan II, can be confusing at first.

The Berber name of Tetouan translates as "Open your Eyes", and a new arrival will be blinking in wonder after the first quick turn around the *souk*. This warren of vendors hawking pottery, brass, leather slippers and textiles is not as confusing as it seems, for each item is assigned its own area.

Tetouan's medina is not so immense that you need worry about never re-emerging. Since it backs up on a hill, you can climb up and survey the walls for an exit. The city ladies here are clad in tailored *djellabas,* sheer veils squared off below the chin, playing up their kohl-lined eyes. Men not wearing *djellabas* usually sport nylon track suits and woolly hats.

Turbulent history: More than almost any other place in Morocco, Tetouan is a true Andalucían town, built by Spanish Jews and Moslems fleeing persecution in the 15th century. Before that, it was a Barbary pirates' lair and a base for raiding Portuguese Ceuta. In contrast to imperial Moroccan cities where the architecture harkens back to the Almohad extravagance of 8th-century Spain, the tile trim and dainty wrought-iron balconies on Tetouan's white houses would fit into the popular quarters of Córdoba or Seville.

When Spaniards feared a menace to their stronghold at Ceuta in 1859, they seized the city for three years. Spanish soldiers came again in 1913, using Tetouan as a base for forays into the Rif. There is little sign of the prolonged aerial bombardment Tetouan suffered from the Republicans at the start of the Spanish Civil War.

Many who used to live in Tetouan's old Jewish quarter, the **Mellah el Bali**, have emigrated to Israel or moved to the "new" quarter along the Rue Msallah, which is a mere 300 years old. The name

Melilla.

mellah is derived from the Arabic for salt, and has come to be the generic term for an old Jewish neighbourhood. In the past, Jews were called on to salt the decapitated heads of criminals or enemies as a means of preservation for a grisly display on the ramparts.

A sizeable highland village south of Tetouan, **Chaouen** may draw its share of hippy backpackers and even the odd tour bus, but the Berber inhabitants stay unperturbed. Stone houses teeter over steep streets that are cobbled like mountain streambeds. Around many unscreened windows, some hand has brushed paint of an ethereal blue; this is believed to repel flies.

Until the Spanish marched on it in 1920, Chaouen had deliberately been kept isolated. Only four Europeans had laid eyes on the place, a sacrosanct pilgrimage site containing the *marabout* or shrine of Moulay Abdessalam ben Mchich.

As a hidden base founded to attack the Portuguese in Ceuta, the town attracted Marranos, refugees who were banished from Spain after the fall of Granada, and soon became rabidly hostile to all Europeans. Four centuries later, in 1921, the Spanish were driven out with a loss of 10,000 lives. The attitude towards foreign visitors has changed considerably since then, and there are a number of clean but basic *pensions* with rooms.

Chaouen is a gentle interlude in Morocco. It has an elaborate women's steambath (*hammam*) in the medina, and a separate one for men. Buses run daily to the border at Ceuta, just two hours away.

African perdition: The decadent, deviant image of **Tangier** is sometimes traced to its louche days as a neutral International Zone, from 1923–56, when a free-living cosmopolitan community was governed by a council of seven European nations plus a committee of Jews and Moslems. But American humourist Mark Twain had already dismissed "that African perdition called Tangier" years before. Successions of Phoenicians, Carthaginians, Romans,

Back streets, Melilla.

318

Moors, Portuguese and English who ruled this port city doubtlessly complained about the wily con-men and flagrant brothels they found.

Today, it's quite obvious that some of the locals are descended from Vandals and pirates. Nevertheless, if you keep your wits about you, pleasant adventures await in the wide boulevards of the Ville Nouvelle, the cafés of the Petit Socco or the Place de France, the broad beaches and the narrow alleys of the medina. The old bull-ring has been fashioned into flats, but local guides will prefer pointing out villas owned by millionaire celebrities.

The most impressive villa belonged once to the flamboyant Woolworth heiress Barbara Hutton. Malcolm Forbes, the American tycoon, kept a fanciful museum of tiny toy soldiers poised in grand battles open to the public and hosted his extravagant 70th birthday party near here in 1989, a few months before his death.

Since mosques are off-limits to Christians (or Nazarenes, as they are contemptibly labelled), sightseeing is a little restricted. But there is more to see than the shops and belly-dancing restaurants where gullible tourists are taken. Abandon the jostling medina crowds and try the Mendoubia gardens. Or to see what talented Moorish artisans can produce, visit the **Dar el Makhzen,** the former sultan's palace, for its displays of regional arts, especially the exquisite ceramics and some Delacroix sketches of 19th-century Tangier (also spelled Tangiers or Tanja).

The Café Detroit just below the palace is a relaxing spot for a glass of mint tea. This ubiquitous drink—more mint than tea and more sugar than either— was unknown until the British introduced tea here in the 18th century.

The British imperial presence is still felt at **St Andrew's**, an odd Anglican church which grafts a simple English graveyard on to an Arabesque fantasy, built in 1894. The old **American Legation**, the earliest US diplomatic residence, dates from 1777 when the Sultan Moulay ben Abdallah was the first sovereign to recognise American independence. The sultan's historic letter to George Washington is on display in the library.

Just outside Tangier are the highly touted **Caves of Hercules.** Although usually packed with sightseers, these seaside grottoes are worthwhile if you don't have time for the 18-mile (29-km) journey south to **Asilah**. A former Portuguese settlement and home to Raisuni, a cattle thief-turned-governor who specialised in extortion in the first decades of this century, Asilah is now a trendy artists' colony over on the Atlantic coast.

Bridge too far: After exposure to Tangier, you may want to flee in the opposite direction, back to the relative calm of Andalucía. An enormous bridge may someday link the continents, if discussions between the kings of Morocco and Spain are to be taken seriously. They even signed initial project papers in October 1989. Though the engineering is feasible, such a bridge is historically dubious. It would require a tremendous suspension of grudges on both sides.

The back page.

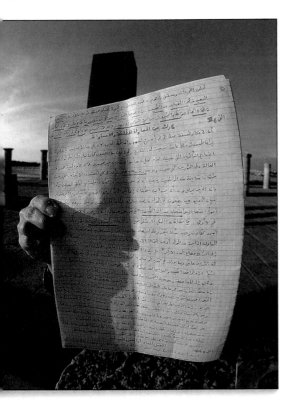

TRAVEL TIPS

GETTING THERE

BY AIR

Southern Spain has frequent air links with the rest of Europe and North Africa, as well as direct flights to North America. It is within two-and-a-half hours' flying time of London. Málaga and Seville airports have daily scheduled connections with international destinations, but in addition large numbers of visitors arrive by charter flights. Almería and Gibraltar are also important entry points.

The colossal growth of the Costa del Sol tourist industry has converted Málaga into Spain's sixth busiest airport, with five million passenger arrivals annually. Scheduled services are available from the major airlines, including Iberia, British Airways, KLM, Lufthansa, Sabena, SAS, and Royal Air Maroc. Málaga airport is undergoing a major expansion programme as is that of Seville. Air Europe flights to Gibraltar are popular with British independent travellers.

BY SEA

Few liners call at Southern Spain ports, apart from those on cruises. Trasmediterranea vessels, carrying passengers and vehicles, ply between Almería, Málaga, Algeciras, Cádiz and Seville and ports on the African coast and on the Canary Islands. There are frequent services across the Straits of Gibraltar, both by ferries and hydrofoils, from Algeciras to Ceuta and Tangier. In 1990 a daily Hovercraft service between Málaga and Ceuta was started by Real Marítima de Cruceros.

BY RAIL

By 1992, a new high-speed rail service is due to link Seville to Madrid, eventually connecting with similar services in France. The new trains are expected to halve travel time between these two cities, to just three hours. Up to now train services between Barcelona and Madrid and Southern Spain have often been slow, partly due to the inadequate tracks. RENFE, the state-owned railway, is updating its equipment. The most comfortable way to travel south is by Talgo trains, smooth-running expresses which run from Madrid to major Andalucían cities.

BY ROAD

Road access to Andalucía has improved dramatically in the past few years, as the network of four-lane routes has been extended. The *Autopista del Mediterráneo* (toll) runs all the way from the French border at La Junquera along the coast to Alicante. Major roadworks are improving connections between that city and Granada and Seville to create the so-called *Autovía de 92*. Completion of the *Autovía de Andalucía*, which follows the old N1V route to Córdoba and Seville, will slash driving time between Madrid and the region. The bottleneck created by the Despeñaperros Pass, the traditional barrier between Castile and Andalucía, has finally been removed and soon the whole route will have four lanes. Other auto-routes under construction will connect with the Costa del Sol and Huelva. An international bridge across the Guadíana river at Ayamonte is due for completion in 1991, allowing easy access to Andalucía from Portugal's Algarve coast.

Comfortable bus services offer economic travel from Northern Europe to major Spanish cities. Fares sometimes include meals and overnight hotel stops. There are daily bus services to the region from Barcelona and Madrid (one-way fares to Málaga are around 3,000 to 4,000 pesetas).

When driving through Spain, travellers should try to avoid peak holiday times, as the country has one of Europe's worst accident records. Easter and the first weekend of August are particularly black periods.

Travel Essentials

VISAS AND PASSPORTS

Thanks to official encouragement of tourism, entry checks have for long been little more than a formality for visitors from Europe, who do not even need a passport if they have a valid national identity card. Spain's entry into the European Community and the creation of a Single Market means that virtually all border restrictions on travelling into the country from EEC countries will be lifted.

At present EEC citizens can stay in Spain for three months as tourists while North Americans can stay six months. Extensions can be obtained on request. Visitors from Australia and New Zealand can stay for 30 days. Visas, which should be obtained in advance, are required for some other nationalities, including South Africans, and for certain nationalities holding diplomatic or official passports. Visitors from Latin America encounter few restrictions because of the close ties Spain has through blood and history with those countries.

MONEY MATTERS

All monetary transactions in Spain are carried out in pesetas. Coins are in circulation to the value of 1, 5, 10, 25, 100, 200 and 500. *Duros* (five-peseta pieces) are common but the 10 and 200-peseta coins are little seen. Check your change carefully as some of the coins are easy to confuse. Bills for 500, 1,000, 2,000, 5,000, and 10,000 pesetas are in circulation. Try to keep some small change about you, as it can be difficult to change large-denomination notes.

Visitors can bring in an unlimited amount of all currencies, but any sums over 100,000 pesetas in local currency and the equivalent of 500,000 pesetas in foreign currency should be declared. This will avoid problems on departure as sums in excess of these figures can only be exported up to the amount declared on entry.

Credit cards are widely used in Spain and even smaller towns have cashpoint facilities, where you should be able to use your bank card. Although most major cards are known, the most widely-used and accepted is Visa. Smaller establishments may be unwilling to take your Diner's or Amex card.

Travellers' cheques remain one of the safest ways of transporting your cash and Eurocheques are also widely accepted. Travel agencies and hotels will change currency as well as banks but it is worth checking rates—and commissions charged. You may often find that the savings banks (*cajas de ahorros*) offer a better deal than the big commercial banks.

Banks have varied hours. Normal opening times are: Monday to Friday, 9 a.m.–2 p.m., Saturdays 9 a.m.–1 p.m. During summer trading (June–September) banks do not open on Saturdays. Some banks now stay open until 4 p.m. on one or more days a week.

Important note: Unless you are importing very large sums of money, it is best to avoid transferring cash via banks. Many tourists have been left stranded for weeks, or even months, waiting for cash that inexplicably got lost in the pipeline. Even telexed cash can take days or weeks. With luck, this situation should improve as Spanish banks face competition from the foreign banks which are setting up shop as a result of Spain joining the European market.

HEALTH

Commonsense is the best preventive medicine. Don't over-expose yourself to the sun, which can be surprisingly fierce—remember that you are close to Africa. Don't drink too many iced drinks and don't over-indulge in alcohol The latter can produce devastating effects on your stomach, especially when eating unaccustomed food, which is often fried in olive oil and includes liberal doses of garlic and peppers. Take it easy until your body has become accustomed to changes in climate and diet. You are particularly warned to partake sparingly of cheap wine, as this is guaranteed to give you a headache or worse, and is foolish in a country where superb wines can be enjoyed for a few pesetas more.

Bottled water is safest for visitors. Tap water is generally safe to drink, although it may taste strongly of chlorine. Local stomachs are used to it, but those of newcomers may initially revolt. However, it is not necessary to clean your teeth in *vino blanco* as some visitors appear to believe. Drink only packaged, pasteurised milk and beware of home-made cheese as Maltese fever is common in rural areas. Do not go barefoot in gardens and fields as scorpions can give very painful bites.

WHAT TO WEAR

Light, easily washed clothing is all that you will need in the summer months. But remember that it can be chilly in other seasons, especially in the evenings in inland areas. Warm clothing and rainwear should be brought. During winter, snow has been known to fall on the streets of Granada and Seville.

Spain is much more easygoing and informal than it used to be under the puritanical Franco regime. For most occasions casual clothing is fine. However, if you are eating out at the best restaurants or attending important social functions, men are expected to wear suits and ties and women the latest fashions. Tourism resorts are very relaxed and topless bathing is the norm on most beaches. However, Spaniards respect those who act "correctly" and have little regard for visitors who parade through towns in swimsuits or scanty clothing. Nor are lightly-clad visitors welcome in churches. Rural areas are more conservative in dress styles than the anything-goes Mediterranean coast. Reserve your sexiest gear for the disco.

WHAT TO BRING

Bring a sun hat (especially if you are fair-complexioned), health insurance, first aid kit, needle and thread, sunglasses, spare spectacles, anti-diarrhoea tablets, insect repellent (particularly if camping), phrasebook and/or dictionary, essential contact numbers at home (bank, doctor, relatives), towel and soap.

Bring your own English-language books. Though available in tourist spots, books are expensive here. If you are driving your own vehicle, remember the car documents, international insurance and a bail bond in case of accident, an international driving licence (bring your national licence too), a red warning triangle, spare car light bulbs, fanbelt etc.

ANIMAL QUARANTINE

You can import your cat or dog into Spain on presentation of relevant health certificates, but check first whether you can take it freely back to your home country—Britain for example has stringent quarantine laws. Regulations require a health certificate and, depending on age of animal, proof of rabies vaccination, all validated in the Spanish consulate in your home country. Outbreaks of African equine fever in 1988 and 1989 caused transport restrictions to be imposed on horse movements in some areas of Spain, including Andalucía.

CUSTOMS

Spanish customs officials are usually polite and unlikely to hassle travellers unless they have reason to believe they are wrongdoers. They are particularly on the lookout for drug smugglers at such ports as Algeciras and Málaga. EEC nationals can import 300 cigarettes or 75 cigars or 400 gm of tobacco products, 1.5 litres alcohol over 20 percent proof or 3 litres up to 22 percent and 5 litres of other wines, 3/8 litre of eau-de-cologne and 75 grammes of perfume.

Non-EEC nationals can import 200 cigarettes or 50 cigars or 250 gm of tobacco products, 1 litre of alcohol over 20 percent proof or 2 litres up to 22 percent and 2 litres of other wines, 1/4 litre of eau-de-cologne and 50 grammes of perfume. Irrespective of nationality you can also bring in duty free: two still cameras with 10 rolls of film each, one movie or video camera, a portable radio, a tape-recorder, a typewriter, golf clubs, tennis rackets, fishing gear, a bicycle, skis and two hunting weapons with 100 cartridges each.

PORTER SERVICE

Airport porters have set charges, often displayed, for handling baggage. Trolleys are available in bigger airports. Only more expensive hotels have porters available to carry your bags to your room.

RESERVATIONS

If you are travelling at peak periods, i.e. Christmas, Easter, July–August, and at long weekends, it is advisable to reserve seats and hotel accommodation well in advance. Within Spain fully-booked flights can delay you for a week, expecially at the end of July and the end of August when half the country appears to be on the move. This is also a bad time to attempt the Algeciras–Ceuta and Tangier crossing, as thousands of Moroccan immigrants will be queuing for the ferries.

EXTENSION OF STAY

If you wish to stay longer than three months, or six months in the case of North Americans, the simplest way is to make an excursion into neighbouring France, Portugal or Morocco and have your passport stamped again on re-entering Spain. However, you can also apply for a *permanencia*, an extension of your stay as a tourist for another three months.

If you know before travelling that you will be staying longer than the permitted time, it can save trouble to apply for the necessary visa at a Spanish consulate in your home country. Otherwise you are required to tangle with Spanish bureaucracy. You must visit a police station, where you will be required to show your passport, provide photos, and give evidence that you have the necessary funds to live without working in Spain.

Australians and New Zealanders wanting to stay longer than 30 days should obtain visas before coming as their stays cannot be extended.

ON DEPARTURE

Booking out time is noon in most hotels, but they will usually look after your luggage if your transport does not leave until later.

GETTING ACQUAINTED

GOVERNMENT AND ECONOMY

Since 1982, when it elected its own parliament for the first time, Andalucía has enjoyed a considerable degree of self-government as one of Spain's 17 autonomous regions. The Socialist Party dominates the regional government, known as the Junta de Andalucía. The 109 members of parliament, which sits in Seville, are elected for a four-year period.

Madrid retains overall control of such sectors as taxation, customs, defence, security and the judiciary, while Andalucía exerts important influence in agriculture, consumer protection, environment, health, urban planning, industry, roads, and tourism promotion. The region is split into eight provinces, each of which has a *diputación*, a provincial council composed of representatives of the municipalities. The Andalucían flag has three horizontal stripes, green, white and green.

Andalucía is Spain's most important agricultural region and agriculture continues to play a vital part in the economy, Traditional products such as olive oil, cereals and grapes have lost ground to new crops and new methods. Irrigation has been extended to new areas. Cotton, sunflowers, citrus fruits, sugar beet and rice are major crops. Strawberries have become a money-spinning export from Huelva and along the sheltered Mediterranean coast avocadoes, sweet potatoes, kiwi fruit and custard apples flourish. Fish-farming is also expanding fast.

Mining of copper, lead, silver and gold, which dates from ancient times, is declining but service industries are growing and the regional authorities are striving to attract high-tech industry.

Since 1960 there has been phenomenal growth in tourism, which has brought undreamed-of wealth to one of Spain's poorest areas. Thousands of Andalucíans depend directly or indirectly on this industry, particularly on the Costa del Sol in Málaga province. Apart from the annual influx of package-tour visitors, several hundred thousand North Europeans have permanent or semi-permanent residences on or near the Mediterranean coast. Foreigners have invested heavily in hotels and thousands of apartments and villas. The Atlantic coast and inland areas have also been affected by the tourist avalanche.

GEOGRAPHY AND POPULATION

Andalucía covers 34,700 sq. miles (87,000 sq. km), 17 percent of Spain's total area. Most of the 6.5 million inhabitants live on the coast or along the Guadalquivir river valley. The 410-mile (660-km) long Guadalquivir is the backbone of the region, draining a vast basin and providing water for power, irrigation and drinking. The alluvial sediments bordering the river provide fertile soil for a variety of crops.

North of the Guadalquivir, the hills of the Sierra Morena are a barrier to easy communication between Andalucía and the rest of Spain. To the south, the Cordillera Baetica runs from Gibraltar to Murcia, forming another higher barrier between the Guadalquivir basin and the Mediterranean coast. Mulhacén in the Sierra Nevada is the peninsula's highest mountain at 11,402 ft (3,478 metres) and the ranges bristle with dramatic crags. These sierras shield the coasts of Almería, Granada and Málaga from frost and snow.

TIME ZONES

Andalucía and the rest of Spain, except the Canary Islands, follow Continental time. For most of the year they are one hour ahead of the Canaries and Britain. Clocks go forward one hour in spring and back in October. When it is noon in Seville, it is 6 a.m. in New York, 3 a.m. in San Francisco, 8 a.m. in Buenos Aires, 5 a.m. in Mexico City, 7 p.m. in Hong Kong, and 9 p.m. in Melbourne.

CLIMATE

Andalucía's position at the southern edge of Europe gives it a privileged climate.

Summers are hot and winters generally mild. However, there are considerable variations due to the size of the region, its mountainous character and the fact that it is bordered by both the Atlantic and Mediterranean. Summers can be extremely hot in the interior with temperatures rising to 45° C (113° F) and even higher in the provinces of Seville and Córdoba. Almería has an extremely arid, desert-like climate. Snow covers the Sierra Nevada from November to June and frost is common in upland areas.

Weather in coastal areas is moderated by the sea and offshore breezes so that neither extremes of heat nor cold are experienced, except for a few weeks at the height of summer. Strawberries ripen in Huelva and Málaga in early February. Tropical fruits can be grown along the Mediterranean without the aid of greenhouses. The Levante wind has considerable influence, often blowing hard for days on the Cádiz coast and creating a persistent cloud over the Rock of Gibraltar. June to October are usually dry, except for sporadic torrential downpours. Heavy rain in the winter months is usually interspersed with brilliant sunshine. The best months to tour the region are in spring and autumn, when there are no climatic extremes.

CULTURE AND CUSTOMS

Isolated from the mainstream of European culture, differing in climate and temperament from the rest of Spain, conquered by a succession of invaders, Andalucía is unique in many ways, although the 20th century is bringing sharp changes.

Moorish, Oriental and Mediterranean influences, overlaid by Castilian and church domination, are clear in the people's character and customs. Worship of the Virgin reaches ecstatic heights in the hundreds of fiestas that mark the Andalucían year. Ancient customs and superstitions linger on in rural areas. In business and social life, personal relationships are all important. Andalucíans love to talk at all hours, in bars, cafés and restaurants. This is where you will meet them. Home is for the family. Although more emphasis is put these days on punctuality, the *mañana* philosophy has far from disappeared. Faster-moving European ways are bringing changes, but in the summer heat the siesta justifiably remains popular.

Andalucíans tend to rise late and eat late, compared to North Europeans. Lunch is usually at 2 p.m. or later and dinner can be any time after 9 p.m. Andalucían executives can be difficult to contact, perhaps because some follow a rigorous schedule on the lines of: 10 a.m., coffee time in the bar next to the office; 11 a.m., breakfast; noon, in conference; 1 p.m., taking a pre-lunch *aperitivo*; 2 p.m., time for *tapas*; 3–5 p.m., lunch; from 5 p.m., at the bullfight.

PHOTOGRAPHY

With its wide variety of landscapes and people, Andalucía is highly photogenic. There are virtually no restrictions on what you can photograph, although police may raise objections to being portrayed because of fears that terrorists could use the pictures to identify them. Most Andalucíans are very obliging if you wish to capture their image, but where possible ask permission and establish a relationship first. Nobody likes a camera thrust into his face by a stranger. Gypsies may be hostile and demand payment.

Unless you are using an all-automatic camera, double check exposure times with a good meter. The sub-tropical light is surprisingly strong and can lead to over-exposed pictures. Outdoors, you will seldom need fast film. Watch those whitewashed walls. They can confuse your meter. Avoid attempting portraits in mid-day sun as this gives a subject nasty shadows under eyes and chin, unless you use fill-in flash. Flash and tripods are often banned from churches and art galleries, unless you obtain special permission.

Bring enough film for your requirements. Most types of film are obtainable but tend to be costly, as is processing. Airport X-ray machines are claimed not to affect film, but ask security officials to hand-check film if it is particularly important to you. Don't put film in baggage intended for the hold.

Professionals should have a list of all equipment ready to show customs. Film crews must usually obtain permission to work in public places and some local authorities ask a fee.

WEIGHTS AND MEASURES

Spain has followed the metric system since 1871. Rainfall is measured by the number of litres falling per square metre. Land is calculated in square metres and hectares. One hectare equals 10,000 sq. metres or approximately 2.5 acres. Some traditional Spanish weights and measures are still in popular use. These include: *fanega* (6,460 sq. metres or 1.59 acres); *arroba* (11.5 kg); *quintal* (4 *arrobas* or 46 kg). Farmers sell wine and olive oil by the *arroba*, referring to a wine container with a capacity of 15 to 16 litres.

ELECTRICITY

In a few communities, the power may still be 110 or 125 volts, but almost everywhere today supplies 220 volts. British plugs do not fit Spanish sockets so British visitors should bring an adaptor. Wall sockets for shavers etc take plugs with two round pins.

BUSINESS HOURS

Shops usually open 9.30 or 10 a.m. to 1.30 p.m., opening again from 5 to 7.30 or 8 p.m. Large department stores and hypermarkets stay open from 10 a.m. to 9 or 10 p.m. Shops are closed on Sundays although newsagents are open on Sunday mornings. Government offices are usually open to the public between 9 a.m. and 1 p.m.

HOLIDAYS

There are a lot of them. Apart from national holidays, every region and every community has its own celebrations which usually fall on the most inconvenient day for a visitor. Remember also that if a holiday falls, for example, on a Thursday, Spaniards like to make a *puente* (bridge), meaning that they take Friday off too to create a long weekend. Many factories and offices, some restaurants and shops close during August when most of Spain is on holiday, including the government. It is a month to be avoided if you intend to do much more than lie on a beach.

NATIONAL HOLIDAYS

January 1: New Year's Day
January 6: Twelfth Night (Día de los Reyes)
March 19: San José*
Semana Santa (Holy Week): Easter Thursday (only in Andalucía), Good Friday. (Easter Monday is celebrated in all of Spain except Andalucía.)
May 1: Labour Day
May/June: Corpus Christi (moveable date)*
July 25: St. James's Day (Santiago)*
August 15: Assumption of the Virgin
October 12: Columbus Day, or Día del Pilar
November 1: All Saints' Day
December 6: Day of the Constitution
December 8: Immaculate Conception
December 25: Christmas Day
* In Andalucía these may be substituted for other local fiestas.

REGIONAL AND LOCAL HOLIDAYS

Almería: 25 August, 26 December.
Cádiz: Monday after Carnival week, 7 October (Virgen del Rosario). Algeciras: Monday after Carnival week, Monday after July fair.
Córdoba: 8 September (Virgen de la Fuensanta), 24 October (San Rafael).
Granada: 2 January (Día de la Toma), 1 February (San Cecilio).
Huelva: 3 August (Fiesta de la Colmena), 8 September (Virgen de la Cinta).
Jaén: 11 June (Virgen de la Capilla), 18 October.
Málaga: 8 September (Nuestra Señora de la Victoria). Estepona: 15 May (San Isidro). Fuengirola: 15 July (Virgen del Carmen), 7 October (Virgen del Rosario). Marbella: 12 June (San Bernabe). Mijas: 8 September (Virgen de la Peña). Nerja: 15 May (San Isidro). Torremolinos: 29 September (San Miguel).
Seville: 30 May (San Fernando).
Andalucía Day, 28 February, is celebrated throughout the region. In addition, each town has a further fiesta(s), usually in honour of its patron, when all businesses are closed. It is also likely you will encounter half-day opening only during Holy Week, particularly in Seville and Málaga, and during the major *ferias*, especially those of Córdoba, Jerez, Seville and Málaga.

RELIGIOUS SERVICES

Many non-Catholic churches have congregations in the region, particularly in areas where there are concentrations of expatriates. Contact church for details of services.
Anglican: Almería: Services in several locations, including Mojácar Roman Catholic Church.
Málaga/Costa del Sol: Nerja-Almuñecar, San Miguel Catholic Church, Nerja.
Málaga: St George's Church, Avda. de Pries 1, Málaga.
Torremolinos: Services at the Bodega, Apartamentos Bajondillo, Paseo Maritimo. (April–October).
Benalmadena–Costa: Residencia Hogar Marymar, Ctra N340.
Fuengirola: St Andrew's Church, Edificio Jupiter, Los Boliches, Fuengirola.
Mijas: Capilla San Sebastian, Mijas Pueblo.
Mijas Costa: Church of San Miguel.
Marbella: Virgen del Rocío Church, c. Linda Vista, San Pedro de Alcántara.
Estepona, San José Church.
Chaplains: Nerja, Rev. David Cherry, Frigiliana Tel: (952) 53 30 84. Málaga, Rev. Frank Ebbitt Tel: (952) 22 50 12. Eastern Costa del Sol, Rev. Ronald Matheson Tel: (952) 58 11 92. Western Costa del Sol, Rev. S. Elkington Tel: (952) 78 60 91.
Cádiz: Sotogrande, Catholic Chapel, Sotogrande School, Guadiaro.
Seville: Anglican Centre, Nick Drayson, Pelay Correa 4, 2°D 41010 Seville. Tel: (952) 33 93 47.
Christian Science: Marbella—Edificio Ami Galeria, c/. Valentuñana s/n.
Church of Jesús Christ of Latter-Day Saints: Fuengirola—Camino de Coin 34. Tel: (952) 46 49 90. Málaga - c/. Babel 1. Tel: (952) 35 23 83.
Church of Scotland: Fuengirola—Lux Mundi Ecumenical Centre, c/. Nueva 3. Tel: (952) 47 28 27.
Evangelical: Torremolinos—c/. Marañon 4. Fuengirola—International Evangelical Church, Edificio Maria del Carmen, Paseo Maritimo, Los Boliches. Also at Hotel El Puerto, Paseo Maritimo, Fuengirola.
Jehovah's Witnesses: Arroyo de la Miel—Kingdom Hall, Avenida Inmaculada Concepcion 26. Torremolinos—Kingdom Hall, Edificio Apolo, Avenida Sorolla Tel

(952) 38 86 82 (meetings in English). Fuengirola—Kingdom Hall, Edificio Eurola I, local 1, c/. Nuñez de Balboa Tel: ((952) 46 22 40. Marbella—Tel: (952) 77 04 68.

Jewish: Málaga—Duquesa de Parcent 3, 3rd floor. Torremolinos—Beth Minzi Synagogue, c/. Skal 13 (La Roca) Tel: (952) 38 39 52. Marbella—Beth-El Synagogue, Urbanización El Real.

Moslem: (Córdoba Province) Mosque, Ctra CNIV km 30, Pedro Abad. (Málaga) Marbella Mosque—Ctra N340, km 177,5.

Protestant: Marbella—Edificio Eliseo, Avenida Ricardo Soriano 48. Services in German.

Scottish Presbyterian: Fuengirola—Lux Mundi Ecumenical Centre, c/. Nueva 3. Tel: (952) 47 28 27.

Swedish Lutheran: Fuengirola—Edificio Tres Coronas, Avenida Jesús Santos Rein.

COMMUNICATIONS

MEDIA

National papers published in Madrid are available every morning. Dailies such as *Díario 16* and *ABC* have special Andalucían editions printed in Seville. At least one local daily is published in each of Andalucía's provincial capitals. They can be useful for finding out what events are scheduled and usually include emergency telephone numbers and transport information.

The foreign press is on sale by the afternoon of publication or the following morning. A number of English-language publications serve the large number of expatriates living along the Mediterranean coast.

Of the magazines, the longest established and most respected is *Lookout*, a glossy, Fuengirola-based monthly featuring practical information and well-researched articles about life in Spain. *Costagolf* is a monthly magazine devoted to the golfing scene.

Several free papers come out weekly, with details of doings in the expatriate community. They include *Sur* in English and *The Entertainer*. German publications include the monthly *Aktuelle* and the monthly *Solkysten* caters for Scandinavians.

Andalucía is served by the two national state-run television channels, an Andalucían channel, several private networks which started functioning in 1990, and cable television in many towns and villages. Satellites allow the beaming in of foreign programmes in English, Italian and other languages. Sky and Super Channel are among these. Gibraltar's English-language television is picked up along the Costa del Sol as are the colony's two radio stations. Most communities have their own FM radio stations in Spanish. In addition, Arabic speakers along the Mediterranean coast can tune to Algerian and Moroccan television.

POSTAL SERVICES

Usual opening times for the Correos (post office) are from 9 a.m. to 2 p.m., Monday to Friday, and 9 a.m. to 1 p.m., Saturday. In larger cities, main post offices have longer business hours. There are often long queues at the stamp counters, but stamps can also be bought in *estancos* (they advertise themselves with a "Tobacos" sign in yellow and brown). Within Europe all letters go by air. *Aerogramas* (special airmail letters) are also available at post offices. You can receive mail at post offices if it is addressed to *Lista de Correos* (equivalent to Poste Restante), followed by the place name. Remember that Spaniards have two surnames, that of their father first with their mother's tagged on after it. This can lead to confusion with foreign names. Thus, if a letter is addressed, for example, to James Robertson Justice, it will probably be filed under "R" rather "J".

TELEPHONE, TELEX AND FAX

Telex and fax facilities are available in main post offices or in the Oficinas de Telégrafos usually adjoining them. The telephone service has been modernised and it is possible to dial the world from the increasing number of public telephones. Look for a *cabina*. This is a telephone box marked with the legend "Conferencias urbanas, interurbanas e internacionales" (local, inter-city and international calls). Five, 25, 50 and 100 peseta coins are used. You cannot make reverse charge calls from a *cabina*, nor receive calls.

In tourist areas in season you will find temporary structures housing small exchanges. These are handy for long-distance calls as instead of fumbling with change you pay the operator afterwards. Bars also have telephones but make a surcharge. Restrict your calls from hotels as they often treble the charge.

AREA CODES

When calling a number in another province use the following prefixes: Almería 951, Cádiz 956, Córdoba 957, Granada 958, Huelva 955, Jaén 953, Málaga 952, Seville 954. When calling these regions from abroad, drop the 9. Note: Seville numbers are switching to seven digits, but are still often listed with only six digits. For local calls within the province, convert these numbers to seven digits by placing a 4 in front. Thus, if you want to call 61 01 22, you should dial 461 01 22.

INTERNATIONAL CALLS

Dial 07, wait for the high-pitched tone, dial international code for the country you require, e.g. to Britain: 07–44 + area code + number.

EMERGENCIES

SECURITY AND CRIME

Thefts from tourists and their cars have become common in recent years. Commonsense precautions should prevent your holiday being spoiled in this way. Cities, particularly Málaga and Seville, are black spots. Never leave anything of value in your car, including when parking near a beach. Don't leave cash or valuables unattended while you are swimming. When staying overnight, take all baggage into the hotel. If possible, park your car in a garage or a guarded car-park.

Particularly when driving into Seville, do not leave anything of value within sight. A favourite trick is to smash the windows of cars stopping at traffic lights, seize handbags and cameras and then take off on a motorbicycle. When walking, women should keep shoulder bags out of view if possible. Avoid badly-lit back streets at night in such quarters as Santa Cruz in Seville. Police patrols have been stepped up, but this area is a magnet for muggers, often working in twos and threes. Carry photocopies of your passport and other documents and leave the originals in the hotel safe.

If you are confronted do not resist, as thieves often carry knives. If robbed, remember that thieves usually want easily disposable cash. Check the nearest gutters, rubbish containers, toilets for your personal possessions; thieves swiftly toss away what they don't want.

Municipal police, who have limited powers and are mostly seen controlling traffic, wear blue uniforms and peaked caps. National police wear dark blue uniforms and berets. Both will assist you, but it is the national police who will take details of an offence and conduct any investigation. In smaller towns and rural areas, Civil Guards—in olive-green uniforms, but without the distinctive triocorn hat, recently discarded except for ceremonials—perform these duties. Few policemen speak anything but Spanish, but many national police stations (*comisarías*) now have report forms in several languages to aid tourists.

LOSS OF BELONGINGS

If you lose anything, report it to the municipal police, who will issue a certificate for any insurance claim. Lost property offices (*Oficina de Objetos Perdidos*) are usually located in town halls and railway stations. Lost passports should be reported to the nearest consulate. If you lose or have credit cards or travellers' cheques stolen go the nearest bank, or phone the emergency number issued with travellers' cheques.

MEDICAL SERVICES

Private clinics offering a range of medical services—some open 24 hours a day—are located in most towns of any size. Emergency services are also provided by *ambulatorios*, national health clinics run by Spain's Seguridad Social (social security system). Free medical attention is available if you are from EEC countries, which have reciprocal arrangements with Spain. Before leaving home, it is worth inquiring about this at your local government health department. As Seguridad Social facilities are often overstretched, visitors are also advised to take out private health insurance.

Farmacias (chemists) are well-stocked. They display lists of the duty chemists at night and on weekends.

The *Cruz Roja* (Red Cross) offers first aid services. Posts are along major highways.

EMERGENCY PHONE NUMBERS

Dial 091 for the Policia Nacional emergency 24-hour service.

ALMERIA

(area code 951):
Municipal police Tel: 092. Ambulance Tel: 23 48 79. First aid Tel: 23 07 12. Red Cross, Parque Nicolas Salmerón 14. Tel: 25 73 67. Roquetas municipal police Tel: 32 03 62, ambulance Tel: 48 24 12. Mojácar municipal police Tel: 47 83 50.

CADIZ

(area code 956):
Municipal police Tel: 22 67 10. First aid Tel: 21 10 53. Hospital Provincial, Campo del Sur, s/n. Tel: 21 23 51. Red Cross, Santa Maria de la Soledad 10. Tel: 27 76 70. Algeciras: Municipal police Tel: 66 01 55. Civil Guard Tel: 66 11 00. First aid Tel: 66 20 54.

CORDOBA

(area code 957):
Municipal police Tel: 47 20 00. First aid post Tel: 23 46 46. Ambulance Tel: 29 55 70. General Hospital Tel: 29 71 22. Red Cross, Paseo de la Victoria 4. Tel: 29 34 11.

GRANADA

(area code 958):
Municipal police Tel: 092. Civil Guard Tel: 062. Ambulance Tel: 20 20 24. First aid Tel: 22 12 63. Red Cross, Cuesta Escoriaza 8. Tel: 22 21 66.

HUELVA

(area code 955):
Municipal police Tel: 24 51 35. First Aid Tel: 25 38 00. Red Cross & ambulance, Avenida Suroeste s/n. Tel: 26 12 11.

JAEN

(area code 953):
Civil Guard Tel: 22 11 00. Municipal police Tel: 25 80 11. First aid Tel: 25 90 31; Red Cross, Carmelo Torres 1. Tel: 25 15 40. Jaén Provincial Hospital Tel: 22 26 50.

Province: Civil Guard, Baeza Tel: 74 01 06; Cazorla Tel: 72 00 80; Ubeda Tel: 75 01 02. Municipal police, Baeza Tel: 74 06 59; Cazorla Tel: 72 01 81; Ubeda Tel: 75 00 23. First aid, Andújar Tel: 50 12 59; Baeza Tel: 74 01 58; Cazorla Tel: 72 01 81; Linares Tel: 69 15 00; Ubeda Tel: 75 01 15.

MALAGA

(area code 952):
City: Municipal police Tel: 092. Civil Guard Tel: 39 19 00. First aid Tel: 29 03 40. Red Cross, Fernando Camino 2–4. Tel: 21 76 31. Carlos Haya Hospital Tel: 39 04 00. Fire Tel: 30 60 60.

Antequera: Civil Guard Tel: 84 01 06. Municipal police Tel: 84 11 91. First aid Tel: 84 44 11. Municipal hospital Tel: 84 44 11.

Estepona: National police Tel: 80 02 91. Municipal police Tel: 80 02 43. Civil Guard Tel: 80 10 87. First aid Tel: 80 06 83.

Fuengirola: Ambulance Tel: 47 31 57. First aid Tel: 47 31 57. Municipal police Tel: 47 31 57.

Mijas: Ambulance Tel: 48 59 00. Municipal police Tel: 48 50 67.

Marbella: Municipal police Tel: 092 (emergencies) & Tel: 77 31 94. Civil Guard Tel: 77 19 44 & (San Pedro) Tel: 78 00 37. First aid Tel: 77 29 49. Marbella Clinic Tel: 77 42 82.

Nerja: Municipal police Tel: 52 15 45.

Civil Guard Tel: 52 00 91. First aid Tel: 52 09 35.

Ronda: Civil Guard Tel: 87 14 61. Municipal police Tel: 87 13 69. First aid Tel: 87 15 40. Hospital Tel: 87 66 28.

Torremolinos: Municipal police, María Barrabino, 16. Tel: 38 14 22. National police, Calle Skal. Tel: 38 99 99. Ambulance Tel: 38 62 66. First aid, Ctra de Benalmadena. Tel: 38 64 84.

Vélez–Málaga: Municipal police Tel: 50 38 97. Civil Guard Tel: 50 01 48. First aid Tel: 50 04 76.

SEVILLE

(area code 954):

For calls within the province, place 4 in front of six-digit numbers.

Municipal police Tel: 092. First aid, Casa de Socorro, Jesús del Gran Poder, 34. Tel: 38 24 61. Ambulance Tel: 33 09 33. Hospital Universitario, Avda Dr Fedriani. Tel: 37 84 00. Lost property, Almansa, 21. Tel: 21 26 28.

LEFT LUGGAGE

For security reasons left luggage offices are practically non-existent but, on leaving, your hotel may look after your luggage for a few hours.

GETTING AROUND

MAPS

Michelin map 446, on a scale of 1:400,000 (1 centimetre to 4 kilometres), is the clearest road map of Andalucía. Guía Campsa includes maps, as well as details of sights, hotels and restaurants. Firestone T-29, 1:200,000, provides greater detail of the Costa del Sol and inland areas. Hikers and horse-trekkers will find most useful the military maps, scale 1:50,000, produced by Spain's Servicio Geográfico del Ejército. A handy map of the Sierra Nevada, 1:50,000, is published by the Federación Española de Montañismo.

FROM THE AIRPORT

Cheap bus services run from main airport to city centres and taxi drivers are authorised only to charge fixed rates. It is worth checking these before leaving the airport. Málaga airport is also served by an efficient train service, which runs between the provincial capital and Torremolinos and Fuengirola.

PUBLIC TRANSPORT

The chief Andalucían cities are linked by rail, although this can be a slow means of transport and more expensive than using buses. The nomenclature for train services can be confusing; *expresos* are speedier than the misleadingly-named *rápidos*, while *tranvías* and *ferrobuses* amble along, stopping at every station. Overnight trains, with sleeping compartments and couchettes, run between Algeciras, Málaga, Seville and Madrid.

Train fares are reasonable, but you pay supplements to travel on express trains. Eurail passes, sold only outside Europe, can be used in Spain, and within the country numerous discount schemes are available. Most of the reduced rates only apply on *Días Azules* ("blue days") i.e. off-peak days. Among the discounts are the: *Tarjeta dorada* for over-60s (foreigners must be resident in Spain); *Tarjeta jóven* for under-26s; *Tarjeta turística* for non-residents, issued for 8, 15 or 22 days; *Tarjeta familiar*, for families; there is also the *Chequetren*, a travel voucher giving a 15 percent discount, valid on any day.

In addition there is a variety of passes for rail travel in Europe including Spain: *Tarjeta Inter-Rail* for under-26s; Flexipass unlimited travel for 10 days during a month; and Eurail and Saverpasses for residents outside Europe.

Regular bus services run between Andalucía's cities and towns and this is a cheap and, generally, comfortable way to travel. Ask for the Estación de Autobuses.

Taxis are readily available in major centres and fares are reasonable. Fares are officially controlled; in urban areas fares are by meter, outside towns fixed rates apply. Extra charges are payable for journeys to and from airports.

PRIVATE TRANSPORT

Hire cars: Remember your international driving licence. Scores of car hire companies offer their services. Such international chains as Avis, Europcar and Hertz have airport offices, and offer collect and deliver service. A guide to price rates (1990): Ford Fiesta, one week, unlimited mileage, 6,000 pesetas a day. Smaller local companies are much cheaper and will arrange to meet you on arrival if you book beforehand.

Avis airport offices: Almería Tel: (951) 22 41 26/22 19 54. Córdoba Tel: (957) 47 68 62. Granada Tel: (958) 44 64 55. Jerez de la Frontera, Cádiz Tel: (956) 34 43 11/33 52 84. Málaga Tel: (952) 31 39 43/32 62 27. Seville Tel: (954) 51 43 15.

Europcar airport offices: Almería Tel: (951) 23 49 66. Córdoba Tel: (957) 23 34 60. Granada Tel: (958) 29 50 65/25 70 17. Jerez de la Frontera Tel: (956) 33 48 56/33 43 55. Málaga Tel: (952) 35 14 03/31 16 38. Seville Tel: 954) 67 38 39.

Hertz airport offices: Almería Tel: (951) 22 19 54 ext. 125. Córdoba Tel: (957) 47 72 43. Granada Tel: (958) 44 64 11 ext. 40. Jerez de la Frontera Tel: (956) 35 11 53/34 74 67. Málaga Tel: (952) 31 87 40/32 61 87. Seville Tel: (954) 51 47 20.

Advice for drivers: Driving in Spain is on the right, but often—on the part of Spanish drivers—in the centre of the road. The best advice is: be prepared to take evasive action at all times in the face of local devil-may-care attitudes. Civil Guard motorcycle patrols, out in force on holiday weekends, brook no nonsense and can administer heavy, on-the-spot fines for driving offences. Radar traps are common. Secondary roads have been much improved and can be much pleasanter to use than main highways, which are often clogged with heavy transport. Seat belts must be worn outside urban centres. Traffic from the right has priority unless otherwise signalled. The speed limit in built-up areas is 37 mph (60 kph), on main roads 62 mph (100 kph). Keep your eyes open at night for plodding mules and motorcycles without lights.

Mopeds, low-powered motorcycles, can be hired in main centres. They are ideal for short excursions, but make sure you are fully covered by insurance. Under Spanish law, you are only obliged to wear a crash helmet on higher-powered machines, but it is advisable to wear one anyway.

Cycling: Intense heat and precipitous mountain roads make cycling a means of transport reserved for the fit. Drivers do not give you much room as you pedal along. However, this is an ideal way to enjoy the beauty of Andalucía's scenery and to get off the beaten track cheaply without having to wait for local buses.

On foot: The sierras of the region are crisscrossed with forestry roads, footpaths and muletracks. With a good map, you can walk from village to village, camping or spending the night in inns far away from the usual tourist beat. Spring and autumn are the best times for hiking. In summer the heat strikes like a hammer and in winter heavy rain and snow can make progress impossible or at least uncomfortable. Some of the most striking mountain scenery is in the national park of Cazorla (Jaén) and in the sierras of Granada, Málaga and Cádiz provinces.

Hitchhiking: Hitchhikers require large doses of patience. It may not be difficult to get lifts along the coastal highways frequented by large numbers of tourists, but off the track you can be stranded for days. Hitching was never easy, but the increase in crime has made Spanish drivers more reluctant to pick up strangers, particularly travel-stained, long-haired backpackers. Women are advised to travel in male company.

STUDENTS

Under-26s can obtain reduced rates on rail travel for longer journeys by obtaining the *Tarjeta jóven* from RENFE. Students with proof that they are following courses at Spanish universities can obtain a card from RENFE, for 300 pesetas, giving them the right to lower fares. Some exhibitions and museums allow free entry to students, but they are unlikely to accept student cards from foreign universities. Student groups may be allowed entry at special rates if prior arrangements are made, e.g. to visit the Alhambra call the Patronato de la Alhambra in Granada tel: (958) 22 75 27.

Where to Stay

Spain may no longer be the bargain it once was but accommodation still offers good value. Where else can you stay in a ducal palace for under £20 a night? Hotels are officially rated from one to five stars. Five-star establishments are in the luxury category with all the comforts one would expect in a first-class hotel. Bear in mind that the rating has more to do with the amenities offered than the quality of the service.

The ratings do not take into account charm or friendly atmosphere. Small, family-run places in the lower categories can be more comfortable than large soulless establishments with gilded fittings and marble halls. Some amenities offered by large hotels may be a positive disadvantage—do you want a *discoteca* or bingo hall under your window or a rooftop nightclub above your bed? Independent travellers can find it disagreeable to stay in a hotel packed with tour groups.

Hotel prices are posted at the reception desk and behind your room door. IVA (value added tax) goes on top. There is a maximum and minimum price, but often the maximum rate is applied year round. There is no obligation to take breakfast or other meals, except at boarding houses. Breakfast, in any case, often consists of little more than coffee, bread and jam, and better value can be obtained in the nearest bar.

If the blue plaque at an establishment's door carries the sign "Hs", this signifies that it is a hostal. These also have star ratings but offer fewer facilities and are worth seeking out if you are on a tight budget. "HsR" signifies "hostal residencial", meaning it caters mainly to long-stay guests.

At the bottom of the market are the *pensión* (boarding house), the *fonda* (inn) and the *casa de huespedes* (guesthouse). These are small and spartan, but usually clean. They may not run to carpets or hot water and the beds may sag alarmingly. But most are perfectly adequate considering the low price.

Paradors are state-run hotels. Sometimes the service can be a little glum, but they are usually located in unrivalled positions, sometimes in modern buildings but often in old castles, palaces and convents.

Motels are not common in Spain, but you will find some on main highways. Thousands of apartments have been built in tourist areas and if you are planning to stay more than a few days it is worth renting one. In summer they are usually fully booked, but off-season it should be possible to negotiate a reasonable price.

Prices: In a *pensión*, expect to pay about 1,500 pesetas for a double room. In one and two-star *hostals*, prices will range from 1,500 to 3,500 pesetas. Hotel prices run roughly from 2,500 pesetas for a one-star establishment to 12,000 for a four-star. A double in a five-star hotel is usually in the 15,000 to 25,000-peseta bracket. *Paradors* charge 8,000 to 10,000 pesetas a double room.

HOTELS

Note: s/n in an address signifies *sin número* (no number); ctra means *carretera* (highway). Hotel names are in **bold** print.

ALMERIA

(area code 951):

Playaluz, Bahía el Palmeral s/n, (4 miles/ 6 km from Almería). Tel: 34 05 04. Four star. On edge of the sea. Sports facilities.

Costasol, Paseo Almería, 58. Tel 23 40 11. Three star. Good situation in the centre.

Torreluz II, Plaza Flores, 1. Tel: 23 47 99. Three star. Central.

In the province:

Near El Ejido: **Golf Hotel Almerimar**, Urb Almerimar. Tel: 48 09 50. Four star. Comfortable and tranquil. Golf, marina.

Mojácar: **Parador Reyes Católicos**, Playa de Mojácar. Tel: 47 82 50. Four star. A modern building, near beach.

San José, **Hotel San José**, Barriada San José, Nijar. Tel: 36 69 74. One star. Overlooks sea on pleasant bay. Closed 15 January–15 February.

In the province:
Laujar de Andarax: **Hotel Fernandez**, General Mola 4. Tel: 11 31 28. Moderately priced, homely, simple, in the centre of a small and quiet town. Good inland base.

Seron: **Hostal Caudrado**, Avda de Garcia Lorca 26. Tel: 42 00 81. Moderately priced. Country roadside hotel above large bar, good basic food.

Alhama de Almería: **Hotel San Nicolas**, Calle Banos s/n. Tel: 10 01 01. Medium priced, smart, old-fashioned spa hotel by hot thermal springs.

Sierra de Enix: Ctra de Yeserias, km 1. Tel: 34 29 13. More highly priced, but unbeatable views and situation in white hill village. Very comfortable.

CADIZ

(area code 956):
Cádiz: **Atlántico**, Parque Genovés 9. Tel: 21 23 01. Three star. State-run. On the bay.

Regio 11, Avda. Andalucía, 79. Tel: 25 30 09. Two star. Central.

Algeciras: **Reina Cristina**, Paseo de la Conferencia. Tel: 60 26 22. Four star. Stately old hotel with tropical gardens.

In the province:
Arcos de la Frontera: **Parador Casa del Corregidor**, Plaza de España s/n. Tel: 70 05 00. Splendid views. **Los Olivos**, San Miguel, 2. Tel: 70 08 11. Three star. Beautiful old Andalucían house. Good value. **El Convento**, Maldonado, 2. Tel: 70 23 33. One star. Tiny hotel with views over countryside. **Meson La Molinera**, Ctra Arcos–El Bosque km 6. Tel: 70 05 11. Pleasant location by lake.

Grazalema (Cádiz province): **Grazalema**, Ctra Olivar. Tel: 14 11 62. Two-star hostal. Modern. Mountain views.

Jerez de la Frontera: **Jerez**, Avda Alvaro Domecq, 35. Tel: 30 06 00. Five star. Tennis courts. Near fair ground.

Puerto de Santa María: **Los Cántaros**, Curva, 6. Tel: 86 42 42. Three star. Central.

San Roque: **Sotogrande**, Urb. Sotogrande, N340 km 132. Tel: 79 21 00. Five star. In luxury development. Full sports facilities.

Tarifa: **Dos Mares**, Ctra Cádiz–Málaga, km 78. Tel: 68 40 35. Two star. Closed January–March. On windsurfers' beach.

CORDOBA

(area code 957):
Parador Nacional Arruzafa, Avda de la Arruzafa, 33. Tel: 27 59 00. Fine views.

Maimonides, Torrijos, 4. Tel: 47 15 00. Three star. Near mosque.

Marisa, Cardenal Herrero, 6. Tel: 47 31 42. Two star. Opposite mosque. Reasonably priced.

In the province:
Montilla: **Don Gonzalo**, Ctra Madrid –Málaga km 447. Tel: 65 06 58. Three star. Convenient, modern highway hotel.

Palma del Río: **Hospederia San Francisco**, Avda Pío X11, 35. Tel: 64 41 85. Three-star hostal in a historic, converted monastery.

GRANADA

(area code 958):
Parador Nacional de San Francisco, Recinto de la Alhambra. Tel: 22 14 40. Within Alhambra. Once a Franciscan convent. Reservations essential.

Alhambra Palace, Peña Partida, 2. Tel: 22 14 68. Four star. Elaborate Moorish-style decor. Views over city.

Washington Irving, Paseo Generalife, 2. Tel: 22 75 50. Three star. Dignified old style.

Hostal América, Real de la Alhambra, 53. Tel: 22 74 71. Three-star hostal. Intimate, within Alhambra walls. Closed November–February.

California, Cuesta de Gomérez, 37. Tel: 22 40 56. Two-star hostal. Simple, inexpensive.

Sierra Nevada ski area: **Parador Nacional Sierra Nevada**, Ctra S. Nevada km 35. Tel: 48 02 00. **Nevasur**, Urb Sol y Nieve. Tel: 48 03 50. Closed June –November. Three star.

In the province:
Bubión (Alpujarras): **Villa Turística**, Barrio Alto. Tel: 76 31 11. Apartment hotel. Three star. Modern facilities in a village complex built in traditional Alpujarras style.

Capileira: **Meson Poqueira**, Dr Castillo, 6. Tel: 76 30 46. Clean, simple hostal.

Loja: **Finca La Bobadilla**, Ctra Loja –Seville. Tel: 32 18 61. Luxury, five-star hotel with all facilities, in heart of countryside. Top-rated restaurant. Champagne for breakfast and prices to match.

HUELVA

(area code 955):

Huelva: **Tartessos**, Avda Martín Alonso Pinzón, 13.Tel: 24 56 11. Three star. Centrally located.

Aracena: **Sierra de Aracena**, Gran Vía, 21. Tel: 11 07 75. Two star. Modern hotel.

Ayamonte: **Parador Costa de la Luz**, El Castillito. Tel: 32 07 00. Looks over Guadiana estuary towards Portugal.

Mazagón: **Parador Cristobal Colón**, Ctra Matalascañas. Tel: 37 60 00. Recently renovated. In tranquil, pine-shaded spot near sandy beach.

JAEN

(area code 953):

Jaén: **Parador Castillo de Santa Catalina**. Tel: 26 44 11. Castle with magnificent views over city and sierra.

Andujar: **Don Pedro**, Capitan Cortes, 5. Tel: 50 12 74. Three-star hostal.

Baeza: **Juanito**, Avda Arca del Agua, s/n. Tel: 74 00 40. Two star. Clean, functional.

Cazorla: **Parador El Adelantado**, 16 miles (26 km) from town. Tel: 72 10 75. In heart of sierra and park. **Sierra de Cazorla**, Ctra Sierra de Cazorla km. 2, La Iruela (just outside Cazorla town). Tel: 72 00 15. One-star hotel, with cheaper hostal attached. Restaurant, fine views.

Ubeda: **Parador Condestable Davalos**, Plaza Vázquez Molina, 1. Tel: 75 03 45. In 16th-century palace. **La Paz**, Andalucía, 1. Tel: 75 08 48. Comfortable, two-star hostal.

In the province:

Baeza: **Casa Juanito**, Avda Arca del Agua, s/n. Tel: 74 00 40. Plain, cheap and right on the main road, but central for the whole province. Good regional cooking.

La Iruela (Sierra de Cazorla): **Arroyo de la Teja**, Ctra del Tranco, 8. Tel: 72 02 11. Idyllically quiet and cheap country pension close to Cazoria.

Belmez de la Moraleda: **Hostal La Chopera**, Ctra 325, km 42. Tel: 39 40 06. Small, cheap and down to earth, one of the few places to stay in the Sierra Magina.

MALAGA

(area code 952):

Parador Nacional Gibralfaro, Monte de Gibralfaro. Tel: 22 19 02. Overlooking old fortress and city.

Las Vegas, Paseo de Sancha, 22. Tel: 21 77 12. Three star. Pool. Near bullring.

Los Naranjos, Paseo de Sancha, 35. Tel: 22 43 17. Three star.

Derby, San Juan de Dios, 1. Tel: 22 13 01. Two-star hostal. Central.

In the province:

Antequera: **Parador**, Paseo Garcia del Olmo, s/n. Tel: 84 02 61. **Manzanito**, Calvo Sotelo, 5. Tel: 84 10 23. One-star hostal.

Carratraca: **Hostal El Principe**, Antonio Rioboó, 9. Tel: 45 80 20. One-star hostal. Characterful old building.

Estepona: **Stakis Paraiso**, Urb El Paraiso, Ctra N340 km 167. Tel: 78 30 00. Four star. Between sea and mountain. **Caracas**, Avda. San Lorenzo, 50. Tel: 80 08 00. Two star. Modern. Comfortable.

Fuengirola: **Byblos Andaluz**, Mijas Golf, Apartado 138 (near Fuengirola). Tel: 47 30 50. Luxury five star. On golf course. **Las Palmeras Sol**, Paseo Marítimo, s/n. Tel: 47 27 00. Four star. **Florida**, Paseo Marítimo, s/n. Tel: 47 61 00. Three star.

Mijas: **Hotel Mijas**, Avda. de Mexico s/n. Urb. Tamisa, s/n. Tel: 48 58 00. Four star. Fine views.

Marbella: **Los Monteros**, Ctra N340 km 187. Tel: 77 17 00. Luxury five star. Golf course, riding. **Meliá Don Pepe**, Finca Las Merinas, Ctra N340. Tel: 77 03 00. Five star, amid gardens. **Puente Romano**, Ctra N340 km 176,7. Tel: 77 01 00. Five star. *Pueblo* style luxury. **Marbella Club**, Ctra N340 km 1178,2. Tel: 77 13 00. Four star. Gardens, private beach. **Las Fuentes del Rodeo**, Ctra N340, km 173. Tel: 81 40 17. Three star.

Nerja: **Parador Nacional**, El Tablazo, s/n. Tel: 52 00 50. Pool. Overlooking beach. **Nerja Club**, Ctra Almería, Km 293. Tel: 52 01 00. Three star. Tennis. **Portofino,** Puerta del Mar, 2. Tel: 52 01 50. One star. On Balcony of Europe, beach. Closed November–February. **Fontainebleau**, Alejandro Bueno, s/n. Tel: 52 09 39. Friendly two-star hostal. Popular with the British. **Las Chinas**, Plaza Capitán Cortés,14 Frigiliana, near Nerja. Tel: 53 30 73. Immaculate two-star hotel in picturesque village.

Ronda: **Reina Victoria**, Jerez 25. Tel: 87 12 40. Four star. Spacious old hotel. Majestic views. **El Tajo**, Doctor Cajal, 7. Tel: 87 62. 36. Two-star hotel for the budget-minded.

Torremolinos: **Castillo de Santa Clara**, Suecia, 1. Tel: 38 31 55. Four star. Handy for beaches. **Cervantes**, Las Mercedes, s/n. Tel: 38 40 33. Four star. Central. **Don Pedro**, Av. Lido, s/n. Tel: 38 68 44. Amid gardens by the main beach. Three star.

SEVILLE

(area code 954–see note under
Telephone re calls within province):
Alfonso X111, San Fernando 2. Tel: 22 28 50. Five star. Neo-Mudéjar decor.

Doña María, Don Remondo, 19. Tel: 22 49 90. Four star. Antiques and iron balconies. Opposite cathedral.

Fernando 111, San José, 21. Tel: 21 73 07. Three star. Near Santa Cruz quarter. Spacious, modern.

Murillo, Lope de Rueda, 7. Tel: 21 60 95. Two star. In the heart of Santa Cruz.

Simon, García de Vinuesa, 19. Tel: 22 66 60. One star. Central location, in 18th-century house with Andalucían patio.

Goya, Mateos Gago, 31. Tel: 21 11 70. Two-star hostal. Budget bargain near main sights.

In the province:
Parador Alcazar del Rey Don Pedro, Carmona (20 miles/33 km east of Seville). Tel: 14 10 10. Tranquil, Mudéjar-style building.

CAMPING

Andalucía has many open spaces and wilder areas where it is possible to camp. Fire risk is high so that extreme care should be taken with camp-fires. All fires may be banned during the dry season. Off-season you can find deserted beaches to pitch your tent. In summer, thousands of campers flock to the beaches, a trend the authorities have been trying to discourage because of the risk of pollution and health hazards. Andalucía has numerous officially-inspected camp sites. They are rated according to facilities as luxury, first, second, or third class. Some have supermarkets and restaurants attached. Camp-grounds in main tourist areas are too crowded for comfort in summer.

A full list of campsites is published in the camping guide (*Guía de Campings*) published by the Secretaria General de Turismo, available in most bookshops. Not all sites are open all the year, so it is advisable to phone beforehand. Site names are in **bold** print.

ALMERIA

(area code 951):
Almería: **La Garrofa**, Ctra N340 km.108. Tel: 23 57 70.

Adra: **La Sirena Loca**, Ctra N340 km 60. Tel: 40 09 20. **Las Gaviotas**, Ctra N340 km 58. Tel: 40 06 60. **La Habana**, Paraje La Habana, Ctra N340 km 64. **Las Vegas**, Paraje La Habana, N340 km 64.

El Ejido: **Mar Azul**, Playa San Miguel, Roquetas Road. Tel: 48 15 35.

Mojácar: **El Cantal de Mojácar**, Garrucha–Carboneras Road, Mojácar. Tel: 47 82 04.

San José: **Tau**, Bancalón de Cortijo de Sotillo, Barriada San José, Nijar.

Garrucha: **Las Palmeras**, Paraje La Esperusa. Naturist.

Vera: **Camping Almanzora**, Playa Vera, Ctra Garrucha–Palomares km 5. Tel: 45 65 75.

CADIZ

(area code 956):
Algeciras area: **Bahía**, Playa Rinconcillo, Ctra N340 km 109. Tel: 66 19 58. **Costa del Sol**, Ctra N340 km 108. Tel: 66 02 19. **San Roque**, Ctra N340 km 124. Tel: 78 01 00.

Barbate: **Caños de Meca**, Ctra Vejer–Caños km 10. Tel: 45 04 05.

Camaleón: **Playa de los Caños**, Ctra Vejer–Caños km. 13,3.

Conil: **Pinar Tula**, Rincón Juan Arías, Ctra CN340 km 20. Tel: 44 10 00. **Puerto de Santa María**, Ctra N340 km 124. Tel: 86 17 49.

Rota: **Punta Candor**, Ctra Chipiona –Rota km 13. Tel: 81 33 03.

Tarifa: **Paloma**, Ctra N340 km 70. Tel: 68 42 03. **Rio Jara**, Ctra N340 km 80. Tel: 68 42 79. **Torre de la Peña I**, Ctra N340 km 76,5. Tel: 68 49 03.

CORDOBA

(area code 957):

Córdoba: **Campamento Municipal**, Avda del Brillante 50. Tel: 27 50 48. **Cerca del Lagartijo**, Ctra Madrid–Cádiz km 398. Tel: 25 04 26.

Santaella: **La Campiña**, Ctra Aldea Quintana–Santaella km 11. Tel: 31 33 48.

HUELVA

(area code 955):

Near the city: **Las Vegas**, Ctra Huelva–Punta Umbria km 7, Aljaraque. Tel: 31 81 41. **Catapum**, Ctra El Rompido-Punta Umbria km 3, El Rompido. Tel: 39 01 65.

Aracena: **Aracena-Sierra**, Ctra N433.

Matalascañas: **Rocío Playa**, Ctra Huelva–Matalascañas km 45. Tel: 43 02 38.

Mazagón-Moguer area: **Doñana Playa**, Ctra Huelva–Matalascañas km 28,8. Tel: 37 68 21. **Fontanilla Playa**, Playa Mazagón. Tel: 37 63 27. **Playa de Mazagón**, Cuesta de la Barca, Ctra Huelva–Mataslascañas. Tel: 37 62 08.

Punta Umbria: **Pinos del Mar**, Ctra Punta Umbria–Huelva km 23. Tel: 31 08 12. Open June-September.

GRANADA

(area code 958):

Near city: **Sierra Nevada**, Ctra Madrid. Tel: 27 09 56. **Los Alamos**, Ctra Granada –Málaga km 439. Tel: 27 57 43. **El Ultimo**, Camino Huetor Vega 22. Tel: 12 30 69. **Zubia**, Reina Isabel, Ctra Granada–la Zubia km 5. Tel: 59 00 41.

Almuñecar: **El Paraiso**, Ctra Málaga –Almería km 334. Tel: 63 23 70. **La Herradura**, Paseo Marítimo Andres Segovia, La Herradura. Tel: 64 00 56.

Castell de Ferro: **Huerta Romero**, Paseo Marítimo. Tel: 64 64 53. **Las Palmeras**, Ctra N340. Tel: 64 61 30. **El Sotillo**, Playa de Castell de Ferro. Tel: 64 60 78.

Motril: **Don Cactus**, Ctra Motril –Almería km 11, Carchuna. Tel: 62 31 09.

Salobreña: **El Peñon**, Paseo Marítimo de Salobreña. Tel: 61 02 07.

JAEN

(area code 953):

Andujar: Ctra Madrid–Cádiz km 322. Tel: (955) 50 07 00.

Cazorla and Segura park: **Chopera de Coto Rios**, Ctra Cazorla–Coto Rios km 21, Coto Rios. Tel: 72 13 69. **Fuente de la Pascuala**, Ctra Cazorla–Coto Ríos km 22. Tel: 72 12 28. **Llanos de Arana**, Ctra Cazorla–Coto Ríos km 20. Tel: 72 09 39. **El Estanque**, Ctra CNIV km 260, Santa Elena. Tel: 62 30 93.

MALAGA

(area code 952):

Málaga: **Balneario del Carmen**, Ctra Almería–Málaga km 249. Tel 29 00 21.

Estepona: **La Chimenea**, Ctra N340 km 162. Tel: 80 04 37.

Fuengirola: **La Rosaleda**, Ctra N340 km 211. Tel: 46 01 91. **Fuengirola**, Ctra N340 km 267. Tel: 47 41 08.

Marbella: **La Buganvilla**, Ctra N340 km 188. Tel: 83 19 73. **Marbella 191**, N340 km 184.

Manilva: **Chullera**, Ctra N340 km 142. Tel: 89 01 96.

Mijas–Costa: **La Debla**, Ctra N340 km 200. **Calazul**, N340 km 200. Tel: 49 32 19. **El Castillo**, Ctra N340 km 207. Tel: 47 38 27. **Los Jarales**, Ctra N340 km 197. Tel: 83 02 35.

Torre del Mar: **Paseo Marítimo**. Tel: 54 02 24. **Valle Niza**, Ctra N340 Málaga Km 269. Tel: 51 31 81.

Torremolinos: Ctra N340 Km 228. Tel: 38 26 02.

SEVILLE

(area code 954):

Ctra Madrid–Cádiz, km 534. Tel: 51 43 79. 6 km out. **Club de Campo**, Ctra Madrid–Cádiz, km 554. Tel: 72 02 50. 12 km out. **Villsom**, Ctra Madrid–Cádiz, km 555. Tel: 72 08 28. Near Club de Campo.

YOUTH HOSTELS

It is advisable not to turn up on spec as some youth hostels only open part of the year or may be undergoing restoration. Telephone numbers not yet available for some new hostels.

Almería (area code 951):
Almería: Angel Jover 10. Tel: 24 31 55.
Garrucha: Marques de Chavarri. Tel: 46 01 52.

Cádiz (area code 956):
Algeciras: Parque Natural Los Canutos s/n. Jerez: Avda Carrero Blanco 30. Tel: 34 28 90.

Córdoba (area code 957):
Córdoba: Plaza Juda Levi s/n.

Granada (area code 958):
Granada: Camino de Ronda 171. Tel: 27 26 38. Sierra Nevada (Monachil): Urbanización Sol y Nieve, Pradollano. Tel: 48 03 05. Viznar: Retiro Camino Fuente Grande. Tel: 49 03 07.

Huelva (area code 955):
Huelva: Avda Marchena Colombo 22.

Jaén (area code 953):
Jaén: Ctra de Andalucía, Glorieta de Blas Infante. Tel: 22 02 98. Cazorla: Plaza Mauricio Martinez 6. Tel: 72 03 29.

Málaga (area code 952):
Málaga: Plaza Pio XII. Tel: 30 85 00. Torremolinos: Avda Carlota Alessandri 127. Tel: 38 08 82. Marbella: Trapiche 2. Tel: 77 14 91. Archidona: Plaza Ochavada 1. Tel: 71 42 29. Cortes de la Frontera: Ctra Estación. Tel: 15 40 74.

Seville (area code 954):
Seville: Isaac Perál 2. Tel: 61 31 50. Constantina: Cuesta Blanca s/n. Tel: 88 10 54.

FOOD DIGEST

WHERE TO EAT

It is not necessary to step into a restaurant to eat well in Andalucía. Fast food was a part of Spanish culture when the hot dog was hardly more than a puppy. *Tapas*, tasty snacks varying from grilled birds to stewed tripe and chick peas, are served in thousands of bars. Sometimes they come automatically with the drink. Sometimes you have to order them and pay extra. If you want more, you can ask for a *ración* (plateful), or *media ración* (half plateful). In many bars calling themselves cafeterias, you can order a *combinado*. This is usually a variation on pork chop, fried eggs, ham, salad and chips. Even the smallest village usually has a bar serving *tapas* or a *fonda* (inn) serving simple set meals at budget prices.

But Andalucía also offers a vast range of good restaurant eating to suit all pockets and tastes. Efforts have been made to develop regional dishes and resuscitate Moorish recipes. The greatest variety of restaurants is to be found along the Costa del Sol, where you can try everything from Vietnamese cuisine to Lebanese. Only a brief selection of these eating places is listed here.

Restaurants usually offer a *menú del día*, a three-course meal, including wine, at an economical price. Note also that on the Atlantic and Mediterranean coasts you can eat well on the beaches in restaurants known as *chiringuitos* and *merenderos*. Some of these have become quite sophisticated, with prices to match. Others remain simple, with the best bet probably being "fish of the day".

Price guide: B is for budget (under 1,500 pesetas per person for a three course meal, not including wine), M for moderate (1,500 to 3,500 pesetas), and E for expensive (more than 3,500 pesetas). Moderate to expensive restaurants usually accept at least one credit card. Cheaper establishments prefer cash.

ALMERIA

(area code 951):

Almería: **Anfora**, González Galbín 25. Tel: 23 13 74. Open: 1.30–3.45 p.m., 9–midnight. Closed: Sunday, holidays, 17–31 July. Amex, Master, Visa. Imaginative cooking, international dishes. (M)

Club de Mar, Muelle, 1. Tel: 23 50 48. Open: 1–4 p.m., 8–11 p.m. Amex, Visa. Seafood by the port. (M)

In the province:

Aguadulce: **Mesón El Abuelo**, Del Alamo. Tel: 34 16 53. Open: 11.30 a.m.–midnight. Closed: Tuesday (winter). Eurocard, Visa. Traditional Spanish. (M); **Mesón del Carmen**, Ctra de Málaga, Venta Victorino, 35. Tel: 34 00 55. Open: 1.30–5 p.m., 7–12.30 p.m. Closed: Monday. Diners, Master, Visa. National, international. (M)

Mojácar: **El Palacio**, Plaza del Caño s/n. Tel: 47 82 79. Open: 8–11 p.m. Closed: Thursday, November and February. Master, Visa. International, national dishes. (M)

CADIZ

(area code 956):

Cádiz: **El Faro**, San Felix, 15. Tel: 21 10 68. Open: 1–4 p.m., 8 p.m.–midnight. Amex, Master, Visa. Recommended for its quality seafood. (M).

Ventorillo del Chato, Ctra de San Fernando, km 647. Tel: 25 00 25. Open: 1–5 p.m., 8 p.m.–midnight. Closed: Sunday, in winter Sunday night. Amex, Master, Visa. Bull's tail is the speciality. (M).

Achuri, Plocia, 15. Tel: 25 36 13. Open: 1–4 p.m., 7 p.m.–midnight. Closed: evenings of Sunday, Tuesday, Wednesday. Visa. Basque dishes. (M)

In the province:

Algeciras: **Mesón El Copo**, Ctra Cádiz-Málaga, Palmones, Los Barrios. Tel: 67 77 10. Amex, Master, Visa. Open: 1–5 p.m., 8 p.m.–midnight. Closed: Sunday. Seafood. (M). **Los Remos**, Finca Villa Victoria, Ramal La Linea-Gibraltar km 2, Campamento San Roque. Tel: 76 08 12. Closed: Sunday night, except August. Amex, Master, Visa. Delicious seafood served in style in a magnificent colonial house. (E).

Arcos de la Frontera: **El Convento**, Mal-donado, 2. Tel: 70 23 33. Open: 1–4 p.m., 8–11 p.m. Master, Visa. Pleasant, family-run. Near top of the town adjoining a convent. (M); **Mesón del Brigadier**, Lago de Arcos. Tel: 70 10 03. Open: noon–4.30 p.m., 8 p.m.–midnight. Amex, Visa. Regional food, fine lake views. (M).

Barbate: **Gadir**, Padre Castrillon, 15. Tel: 43 08 00. Open: 1–4 p.m., 8 p.m.–midnight. Closed: Tuesday, and November–March. Amex, Visa. Basque dishes. (M).

Jerez de la Frontera: **La Mesa Redonda**, Manuel de la Quintana, 3. Tel: 34 00 69. Closed: Sunday, holidays and August. Amex, Visa. Impeccably served regional dishes in a comfortable location. (M-E).

Puerto de Santa María: **Alboronia**, Santo Domingo, 24. Tel: 85 16 09. Open: 2–4 p.m., 9 p.m.–midnight. Closed: Saturday lunch, Sunday and January. Dinner only in summer. Amex, Master, Visa. Imaginative cuisine in an old Andalucían house with garden.(M). **Casa Flores**, Ribera del Río, 9. Tel: 86 35 12. Open: 1–11 p.m. Noted for seafood. (M). **La Goleta**, Ctra Rota km 0.75. Tel: 85 22 56. Open: 11 a.m.–5 p.m., 7 p.m.–12.30 a.m. Closed: Monday, 1–15 November. Amex, Master, Visa. Fresh seafood in pleasant villa setting. (M).

CORDOBA

(area code 957):

El Caballo Rojo, Cardenal Herrero, 28. Tel: 47 53 75. Open: 1–4.30 p.m., 8.30 p.m.–midnight. Amex, Diners, Master, 6,000, Visa. Classic Córdoban and Mozarabic dishes in heart of the old quarter. (E).

El Churrasco, Romero, 16. Tel: 29 08 19. Open: 1–4 p.m., 8 p.m.–midnight. Closed: Thursday and August. Amex, Diners, Master, 6,000, Visa. Meat dishes. (M).

Castillo de Albaida, Ctra de Trassierra, Km 4.5. Tel: 27 34 93. Open: 1–4 p.m., 8 p.m.–midnight. Closed: 24 December. Amex, Diners, Master, 6,000, Visa. Outside city. Regional dishes. (M).

In the province:

Palma del Río: **Hospedería San Francisco**, Avda Pío X11, 35. Tel: 64 41 85. Closed: Sunday evenings and 1–15 August. Amex, Master, Visa. Basque, Moorish dishes in restored monastery. (M).

Montilla: **Las Camachas**. An old rambling, roadside restaurant where the landed gentry of the wine district dine out. Sturdy, good food. Montilla wines on sale.

GRANADA

(area code 958):

Baroca, Pedro Antonio de Alarcón, 34. Tel: 26 50 61. Open: 1.30–4 p.m., 9–11.30 p.m. Closed: Sunday and August. Amex, Master, Visa. International. (M).

Sevilla, Oficios, 12. Tel: 22 12 23. Open: 1–4.30 p.m., 8–11.30 p.m. Closed: Sunday night. Amex, Master, 6,000, Visa. Regional. (M)

Mesón Antonio, Ecce Homo, 6. Tel: 22 95 99. Open: 2–3.30 p.m., 9–10.30 p.m. Closed: Sunday and July–August. Home cooking in an intimate atmosphere. (M)

Los Manueles, Zaragoza, 2. Tel: 22 34 15. Open: 1–4.30 p.m., 7.30 p.m.–midnight. Tiled traditional. Granada dishes. (M)

Mirador de Morayma, Callejón de las Vacas 2, Albaicin (opposite road to Sacromonte). Tel: 22 82 90. Open: 1.30–3.30 p.m., 8.30–11 p.m. Closed: Sunday night and Monday. Amex, Visa. Local dishes. Views of Alhambra. Summer dining in patio. (E).

In the province:

Alpujarras: **Teide**, Bubion. Tel: 76 30 37. Closed: Tuesday. Local dishes. (B); **Casa Ybero**, Parra, 1, Capileira. Tel: 76 30 06. Open: 1–3.30 p.m., 9–11 p.m. Closed: Sunday night and Monday. Visa. Local dishes. (B)

Almuñecar: **Cotobro**, Bajada del Mar, 1 Playa del Cotobro. Tel: 63 18 02. Open: 1–4 p.m., 7.30–11 p.m. Closed: Monday and mid-November to 6 December. In summer dinner only. French and international cuisine. Best to reserve. (M)

Durcal: **El Molino**, Camino de las Fuentes, Paraje de la Isla, Durcal (15 miles/25 km, from Granada, off Motril road). Tel: 78 02 47. Open: 2–4 p.m., 8.30–11 p.m. Closed: Sunday and holiday nights, and Monday. Andalucían Gastronomic Research Centre and cooking school. Gastronomic adventures in a 200-year-old mill. Traditional Andalucían dishes. (M)

Gualchos (17 km from Motril): **La Posada**, Plaza Constitución, 9. Tel: 64 60 34. Open: 1–3.30 p.m., 7.30–11.30 p.m.

Closed: Monday and November–February. Located in a fine old house in small village. Tastefully prepared imaginative food. In the same building is a small, tranquil hotel. (M); **La Finca**, Hotel La Bobadilla, Ctra Loja-Seville. Tel: 32 18 61. Open: 1.30–5 p.m., 8–12 p.m. Amex, Master, Visa. First-class international cuisine. (VE); **Riofrio**, on Málaga-Granada road N342, 3 miles (5 km) west of Loja: several restaurants serving fresh trout from adjacent hatchery. (B)

Motril: **Los Balandros**, Torrenueva. Tel: 83 57 40.

HUELVA

(area code 955):

Huelva: **Las Candelas**, Ctra Punta Umbria, Aljaraque crossroads. Tel: 31 83 01. Open: 1–4 p.m., 8 p.m.–midnight. Closed: Sunday. Amex, Master, Visa. Good value and fresh seafood and meat dishes. (M)

La Cazuela, Garcí Fernández, 5. Tel: 25 80 96. Open: 1–4 p.m., 8 p.m.–midnight. Closed: Sunday night and second fortnight in June. Amex, Master, Visa. Basque and Andalucían cooking. (M)

Los Gordos, Carmen, 14. Tel: 24 62 66. Open: 1–4 p.m., 8.30 p.m.–midnight. Closed: Saturday night and Sunday. Amex, Master, Visa. First-rate shellfish and pork dishes. (M)

In the province:

Aracena: **Casas**, Colmenitas 41. Tel: 11 00 44. Open: noon–5 p.m. Visa. Famed for its regional ham and pork dishes. (M)

El Rompido: **El Caribe 11**, Virgen del Carmen, 18. In the heart of a fishing community. Ultra-fresh seafood at very reasonable prices. (B-M)

Moguér: **La Parrala**, Plaza Monjas, 22. Tel: 37 04 52. Open: 11 a.m.–5 p.m., 7 p.m.–midnight. No cards. Agreeable family-run restaurant with good seafood. (B)

JAEN

(area code 953):

Jaén: **Mesón Vicente**, Arco del Consuelo, 1. Tel: 26 28 16. Open: 1–4 p.m., 8.30–11 p.m. Closed: Sunday. Visa. Popular for its tasty regional food. (M)

Andújar: **Don Pedro**, Gabriel Zamora, 5. Tel: 50 12 74. Open: noon–4 p.m., 8 midnight. Amex, Master, Visa. Game, in season. Reasonably priced. (M)

Baeza: **Juanito**, Paseo Arca del Agua, s/n. Tel: 27 09 09. Closed: Sunday night and last fortnight November. Amex, Master, Visa. Regional dishes are a speciality. (M).

Cazorla: **Cueva de Juan Pedro**, near Santa María Church. Tel: 72 12 25. Meat grilled on an open fire. (B)

MALAGA

(area code 952):

Thousands of restaurants cater to the millions of tourists visiting annually. New ones open as fast as old ones close. This is only a small selection of those which have showed stamina as well as quality.

Málaga: **El Cabra**, Copo, 21 (Pedragalejo). Tel: 29 15 95. Open: 9 a.m.–2 a.m. Visa. By sea. Fish. (M)

Antonio Martín, Paseo Marítimo, s/n. Tel: 22 21 13. Open: 1–4 p.m., 8 p.m.–midnight. Closed: Sunday night in winter. Amex, Master, Visa. Fish. (M)

Casa Pedro, Playa de El Palo. Tel: 29 00 13. Open: 1–4.15 p.m., 8–11.45 p.m. Closed: Monday night and November. Amex, Master, Visa. Popular beach eating place. Paella, sardines. (M)

Refectorium, Cervantes, 8. Tel: 21 89 90. Also in Avda. Juan Sebastian Elcano, El Palo. Tel: 29 45 93. Open: 1.30–4.30 p.m., 8 p.m.–midnight. Closed: Sunday (El Palo-Mon). Amex, Visa. Traditional dishes. (M)

Taberna del Pintor, Maestranza, 6. Tel: 21 53 15. Open: 12.30–4 p.m., 8.30 p.m.–midnight. Closed: Sunday. Amex, Master, Visa. Businessmen´s favourite, meat dishes. (M).

Tormes, San José, 2. Open: 1–5 p.m. Solid, simple fare. (B)

In the province:

Antequera: **Chaplin**, San Agustin, 3. Tel: 84 30 34. Open: 1–4 p.m., 8 p.m.–midnight. Amex, Master, Visa. Regional. (B); **Lozano**, Poligono Industrial. Tel: 84 03 96. Open: 8.30 a.m.–midnight. Amex, Diners, Visa. Regional. (B)

El Chorro area: **El Oasis**. Overlooking one of Guadalhorce reservoirs. Barbecued meat. (B-M)

Ronda: **Don Miguel**, Villanueva, 4, Ronda. Tel: 87 10 90. Open: 12.30–4 p.m.,

7.30–11 p.m. Closed: Tuesday p.m., also Sunday, June–September; Tuesday night and Wednesday, October–May; 15 January–15 February. Amex, Master, Visa. National and regional cooking, spectacular views over the gorge. (M); **Mesón Santiago**, Marina, 3. Tel: 87 15 59. Open: 1–4 p.m. Master, Visa. Traditional. (M)

On the coast:

Estepona: **Costa del Sol**, Calle San Roque. Tel: 80 11 01. Open: 12–4 p.m. (except Monday), 7 p.m.–midnight. Closed: Sunday. Amex, Visa, Master. A French bistro offering excellent value. (M)

Fuengirola: **La Baraka**, Edificio Saturno, Paseo Marítimo, 10. Tel: 47 14 95. Open: lunch and 6.30 p.m.–1 a.m. Closed: Wednesday (winter). French specialities and pizza. All cards. (M); **Mesón El Castellano**, Camino de Coín, 5. Tel: 46 27 36. Open: 12–4 p.m., 7–11.30 p.m. Closed: Saturday lunch. Amex, Master, Visa. Authentic Castilian roasts. (M); **Portofino**, Edificio Perla, 1, Paseo Marítimo. Tel: 47 06 43. Open: 1–3.30 p.m., 7–11 p.m. Closed: Monday. Dinner only, June–August. Major cards. Popular seafront restaurant serving international and Italian dishes. (M)

Marbella: **Hostería del Mar**, Avda de Canovas del Castillo, 1A. Tel: 77 55 81. Open: 7.30 p.m.–midnight. Closed: Sunday. Amex, Master, Visa. Spanish-international food in an intimate villa atmosphere. (E); **La Fonda**, Plaza Santo Cristo 9. Tel: 77 25 12. Open: 8 p.m.–midnight. Closed: Sunday except August. Amex, Visa. Impeccable service in an elegant atmosphere. Booking essential. (VE); **La Freiduria**, Trapiche, 24. Tel: 77 26 81. Open: 1–4 p.m., 8 p.m.–midnight. Closed: Wednesday. Good seafood at reasonable prices (B); **La Meridiana**, Camino de la Cruz, near mosque. Tel: 77 61 90. Open: 1.30–3.30 p.m. Wednesday–Sunday winter only, 8.30 p.m.–midnight daily. Stylish, sophisticated. One of Marbella's top eating spots. (VE); **Mesón del Pasaje**, Pasaje 5. Tel: 77 12 61. Open: 1–3 p.m., 7.30 p.m.–12.30 a.m. Dinner only in summer. Closed: Thursday and 15 November–15 December. Eurocard, Master, Visa. Good value pasta, meat dishes, seafood. Booking recommended. (M)

Nerja: **Casa Luque**, Pl. Cabana, 2. Tel: 52 10 04. Open: 1–4 p.m., 7 p.m.–midnight.

Closed: Thursday. Visa, Master. National, international dishes. (M); **Haveli**, Almirante Ferrandiz, 44. Tel: 52 22 92. Open: 1–3 p.m., Saturday, Sunday, Tuesday and 7–12.30 p.m. (7–11 p.m. winter). Visa, Master. Indian Tandoori. (M); **Pepe Rico**, Almirante Ferrandiz, 28. Tel: 52 02 47. Open: 7.30–10 p.m. Closed: Thursday and 1 November–20 December. Amex, Diners, Visa, Master. International. (M); **Portofino**, Puerta del Mar, 2. Tel: 52 01 50. Open: 1–3 p.m., 8–10 p.m. Closed: 15 November–15 December. Master, Visa. French, Italian. (M)

Torremolinos: **Frutos**, Ctra de Cádiz, km 235 (next to Los Alamos petrol station). Tel: 38 14 50. Open: 1–4 p.m., 8 p.m.–midnight. Closed: Sunday p.m. in winter. Amex, Master, Visa. Traditional Spanish style. (M); **Marrakech**, Ctra de Benalmadena. Tel: 38 21 69. Open: 12.30–4.30 p.m., 7.30 p.m.–midnight. Closed: Sunday and Tuesday. Moroccan food in an exotic setting. (M); **El Roqueo**, Carmen, 35, La Carihuela. Tel: 38 49 46. Open: 1–4 p.m., 7 p.m.–midnight. Closed: Tuesday and November. Amex, Master, Visa. Popular, possibly the best of the many seafood establishments on the Carihuela beach. (M); **Ventorillo de la Perra**, Avda de la Constitución, s/n. Arroyo de la Miel. Tel: 44 19 66. Open: 1–4 p.m., 8 p.m.–midnight. Closed: Monday and November. Major cards. Málaga and Spanish specialities in old country house. (M)

SEVILLE

(Convert phone numbers to 7 digits by placing 4 in front when dialling within the province, dial 954 from outside): **La Dorada**, Virgen de Aguasantas, 6. Tel: 45 51 00. Open: 1–4 p.m., 8 p.m.–midnight. Closed: Sunday and August. Amex, Visa. Fish specialities. (E)

El Ancora, Virgen de la Huerta, s/n, Los Remedios. Tel: 27 38 49. Open: 1–5 p.m., 8 p.m.–1 a.m. Amex, Master, Visa. Fresh fish. (M)

Don Raimundo, Argote de Molina, 26. Tel: 22 33 55. Open: 12–4 p.m., 7 p.m.–midnight. Closed: Sunday nights. Amex, Diners, Master, Visa. Andalucía food. (M)

La Albahaca, Pl. Sta. Cruz, 12. Tel: 22 07 14. Open: 1–4 p.m., 8 p.m.–midnight. Closed: Sunday. Amex, Master, Visa. Elegant. (E).

Río Grande, Betis 70. Tel: 27 39 56. Open: 1–5 p.m., 8 p.m.–midnight. Amex, Master, Visa. Terrace on river. (M)

Trastevere, Salado, 6, Barrio Los Remedios. Tel: 27 14 36. Good pizzas. (B)

El 3 de Oro, Sta. María de la Blanca, 34. Tel: 22 27 59. Open: 8 a.m.–4.30 p.m., 8–11.30 p.m. Closed: Saturday. Self service. Mecca for budget travellers. (B)

THINGS TO DO

WHAT TO SEE

ALMERIA

Alcazaba: built by the caliph of Córdoba Abd-er-Rahman II. Open: 10 a.m.–2 p.m., 4–8 p.m. summer, winter 9 a.m.–1 p.m., 3–7 p.m.

Cathedral: built in the 17th century, Open: 8 a.m.–noon, 5–8 p.m.

Centro de Rescate de Fauna Sahariana (rescue centre for endangered Sahara species): This is located near the gypsy quarter, at the rear of the Alcazaba. Visits by previous arrangement.

In the province:

From Almería, visit the **filmsets** in desert scenery near Tabernas (20 miles/33 km), where spaghetti Westerns were once churned out. Stuntmen put on special performances at Mini Hollywood. The **Plataforma Solar** (solar energy research station), near Tabernas, can also be visited, tel: (951) 36 50 15 for times. Nijar (17 miles/28 km) is a centre for **pottery and blanket weaving,** not far from the rocky, little-developed coast east of Cabo de Gata. The hilltop resort of Mojácar is growing fast. Castle connoisseurs should visit **Velez Blanco** (100 miles/167 km from Almería), where there is an impressive 16th-century fortress.

CADIZ

Cathedral: Composer Manuel de Falla is buried in this neoclassic structure. Open: 5.30–7.30 p.m., Saturday 9.30–10.30 a.m., 5.30–8 p.m., Sunday 11 a.m.–1 p.m.

San Felipe Neri church: Spain's first constitution was signed here in 1812. Open: noon–2 p.m., 5–9 p.m. Closed: fiestas and July.

In the province:

Jerez (22 miles/36 km) floats on sherry. Visit the *bodegas*, open mornings during the week. The "**dancing horses of Andalucía**" of the Escuela Andaluza del Arte Ecuestre, Recreo de las Cadenas, Avda Duque de Abrantes, train every morning and have public performances on Thursdays at 11 a.m.

Arcos de la Frontera (50 miles/80 km) is a superbly situated medieval town, atop a hill overlooking the Guadalete river. Worth seeing are the town hall and the church of San Pedro Apostol with works by Zurburan, Pacheco and Rivera.

Tarifa (63 mile/101 km) offers Europe's finest windsurfing beaches and a hydrofoil service across the Straits of Gibraltar to Tangier. The ancient **Castillo Guzman el Bueno** is open for visits 9.30 a.m.–1.30 p.m., Friday and Saturday.

CORDOBA

Mosque: One of the great architectural treasures left by the Moors. A 16th-century cathedral stands at its centre. Open: 10.30 a.m.–1.30 p.m. (all year), 3.30–5.30 p.m. (winter), 5–7 p.m. (summer).

Alcázar of the Christian Kings: 14th-century palace-fortress. Open: 9 a.m.–1.30 p.m., 5–8 p.m. Gardens floodlit May–September, 10 p.m.–midnight. Closed: Monday.

Synagogue: Calle Judio. Open: 10 a.m.–2 p.m. Afternoon, 6–8 p.m. May–September, 5–7 p.m. October –April. Sunday and holidays, 10 a.m.–1.30 p.m. Closed: Monday.

Museo Municipal del Arte Taurino (bullfight museum): In the Judería (old Jewish quarter). Open: 9.30 a.m.–1.30 p.m. 4–7 p.m. Closed: Monday.

Torre de la Calahorra: ancient guard tower on river. Multivision historical show:

Open: 9.30 a.m.–2 p.m., 5–7.30 p.m. Closed: Sunday evening and Monday.

Palace of Viana: Plaza Don Gome, 2. Palatial mansion with 14 patios. Open: October–May, 10 a.m.–1 p.m., 4–6 p.m. Sunday and holidays, 10 a.m.–2 p.m. June–September, 9 a.m.–2 p.m. Closed: Wednesday.

Archaeological Museum: Pl. Jeronimo, Paez, 7. Open: May–September, 10 a.m.–2 p.m., 5–8 p.m. October–April 10 a.m.–2 p.m., 5–7 p.m. Sunday 10 a.m.–1.30 p.m. As of January, 1990, the museum was closed for repair work.

Museum of Julio Romero: Pl. Potro. Open: 10 a.m.–1.15 p.m., 5–6.45 p.m. Fiestas 10 a.m.–1.45 p.m. Closed: Monday. Work of Córdoba artist. As of January, 1990, the museum was closed for repairs.

In the province:

Medina Azahara: On the edge of the Sierra Morena, overlooking the Guadalquivir valley (6 miles/9 km west of Córdoba) the splendours of this palace city of the Caliphs are being restored. Open: May–September, 10 a.m.–1 p.m., 6–8 p.m. October–April, 10 a.m.–2 p.m., 4–6 p.m. Sunday and holidays 10 a.m.–1.30 p.m. Closed: Monday.

GRANADA

Alhambra and Generalife: Largely dating from the 14th century, the Alhambra marks the peak of sophisticated Moslem architecture in Spain. The Generalife with its terraced water gardens was the summer palace. Open: winter 10.30 a.m.–8.30 p.m., summer 9 a.m.–6 p.m. Interior floodlit, summer Tuesday, Thursday and Saturday 10–12 p.m., winter Saturday 8–10 p.m.

Cathedral and Royal Chapel (tombs of the Catholic Monarchs): Open: 10.30–1.30 p.m. (all year), 3.30–6 p.m. (winter), 4–7 p.m. (summer).

La Cartuja Monastery (baroque grandeur): Visiting times as for cathedral.

San Jeronimo Monastery (Renaissance splendour): Visiting times as for cathedral.

Albaicin (Arab for Falconers' Quarter): The old Moorish quarter, straggling over a hill opposite the Alhambra. For the finest views of Alhambra and the Sierra Nevada, visit the terrace of San Nicolas Church.

Corral de Carbón: Oldest Moorish relic. Used as inn and storage place, later as theatre. Now showplace for handicrafts. Normal shop hours.

Palacio de la Madraza: Calle Oficios, opposite Royal Chapel. Once a Moorish university, now a cultural centre.

In the province:

Casa-Museo Federico Garcia Lorca: Calle Poeta Garcia Lorca, 4 in the village of Fuentevaqueros (12miles/20 km, from Granada, north of the Málaga highway). Birthplace of the poet converted into a museum. Guided visits from 10 a.m.–1 p.m., on the hour, and at 4, 5 and 6 p.m. (later in summer). Closed: Monday.

Federico García Lorca memorial park: 6 miles (9 km) from city, between Viznar and Alfacar, where the Granada poet was executed in August 1936.

Santa Fé: West of Granada on Málaga highway, town built where Christian forces camped during siege of Granada. Here Ferdinand and Isabel agreed to back Columbus´s voyage of discovery.

Sierra Nevada: Solynieve ski resort, 20 miles (33 km) from Granada. Season December to May, 31 miles (50 km) of marked runs, cross country routes, ski school. Cable car to top of Veleta peak (11,130 ft/3,395 metres), magnificent views of sierras and towards Mediterranean. Paved road, highest in Europe, open in summer to Veleta from where the track continues south to Alpujarras.

Alpujarras: A beautiful mountainous region on the southern fold of the Sierra Nevada, is worth visiting, as is the district around Guadix, where thousands of people live in caves.

HUELVA

Monument to Christopher Columbus: Punta del Sebo. Gift from the United States in honour of the discoverers of America, sculpture by Gertrude Vanderbilt Whitney.

Barrio Reina Victoria: relic built by British-owned Río Tinto mining company.

Alto de Conquera: Residential neighbourhood commanding views of town and surrounding marshlands.

La Rábida (near Huelva): 14th-century Franciscan monastery in Andalucían-

Mudéjar style where Columbus obtained support for his expedition to America. Open: 10 a.m.–1 p.m., 4–7 p.m. Closed Monday.

In the province:

Palos de la Frontera: Columbus started his voyage from here and provisioned his ships with water from La Fontanilla well.

Moguer: Home of poet Juan Ramón Jiménez, Nobel prize-winner. Open: 10 a.m.–2 p.m., 4–8 p.m. Columbus prayed in 14th-century Santa Clara convent.

Coto Doñana: guided visits to the park interior are by four-wheel-drive vehicle, twice daily and last four hours—places reserved at Parque Nacional Doñana, Reception Centre, Acebuche, near park entrance on Almonte-Matalascañas road (Huelva 32 miles/51 km), tel: (955) 43 04 32. Open: 8 a.m.–7 p.m., except Monday. Information centres at La Rocina, near El Rocío tel: (955) 40 61 40. Open: 9.30 a.m.–1.30 p.m., 4–7 p.m. and the Palacio del Acebron (4 miles/6 km from the Rocina centre). Open: 8 a.m.–7 p.m.

Aracena (67 miles/108 km): castle built by the Knights Templar with panoramic views. Gruta de las Maravillas cave system with 12 chambers and 6 underground lakes. Open: 1 a.m.–6 p.m. (winter), 11 a.m.–7 p.m. (summer).

Jabugo (70 miles/113 km): centre of ham curing industry. Visits to ham curers, Cooperativa Sánchez Romero, Carvajal Jabugo SA. Open: 10 a.m.–1 p.m.

Ayamonte (37 miles/60 km): Fishing village on River Guadiana, boundary between Spain and Portugal. Bridge being built to replace ferry service to Vila Real de San Antonio on Portuguese bank.

JAEN

Santa Catalina castle (housing *parador*): commands impressive views of town and surrounding olive groves. Cathedral, main chapel holds the relics of the Santo Rostro. Open: 8.30 a.m.–1.30 p.m., 4.30–7 p.m.

Arab baths: in the Palacio de Villardompardo, most important Arab baths surviving in Spain. Tel: (953) 26 21 11 for visit.

Provincial Museum: Paseo Estación. Open: 10 a.m.–2 p.m., 4–7 p.m.. Closed: Monday and holidays.

In the province:

Baeza (30 miles/48 km), **Jaén Gate**: Villalar victory arch, Renaissance-style university where Antonio Machado once taught, cathedral reconstructed in the 16th century.

Ubeda (35 miles/56 km), **churches of Santa María**, **San Pablo** and **Salvador**: The old town hall and Santiago hospital. **Archaeological Museum**, Cervantes 6. Open: 9.30 a.m.–1.30 p.m., 4–7 p.m. except Monday.

Cazorla (65 miles/104 km), **Museum of Popular Art and Customs**: Castillo de la Yedra. Open: 9 a.m.–1 p.m.

Cazorla and Segura Natural Park: source of Guadalquivir, wild life, trout hatchery. Museum and guidance centre at Torre Vinagre, Ctra del Tranco km 18. Open: 11 a.m.–2 p.m., 5–8 p.m. Park guide service, Quercus Cooperative, at Torre Vinagre and Juan Domingo, 2 Cazorla. Tel: (953) 72 01 15.

MALAGA

Cathedral: 16th-century building with baroque choir, the work of Pedro de Mena. Open: 10 a.m.–1 p.m., 4–5.50 p.m.

Alcazaba: Moorish fortress with Archaeological Museum. Open: Summer, 11 a.m.–1 p.m., 5–8 p.m.; winter, 10 a.m.–1 p.m., 4–7 p.m. Sun, 10 a.m.–2 p.m. Roman theatre near the entrance. Repair work began in 1990.

Gibralfaro Castle: above the Alcazaba, commanding magnificent views of city and Mediterranean.

Museo de Bellas Artes: San Agustín, 6. Works by Ribera, Murillo, Zurbarán and others in old palace. Open: 10 a.m.–1.30 p.m., 5–8 p.m. (summer), 4–7 p.m. (winter). Closed: Sunday afternoon and Monday.

Museo de Artes Populares: Pasillo de Santa Isabel, 7. Local crafts and traditions housed in 17th-century inn. Open: 10 a.m.–1.30 p.m., 5–8 p.m. (summer), 4–7 p.m. (winter). Closed: Sunday afternoon, Monday and holidays.

Pablo Picasso Foundation: located in the house where the painter was born, 16, Plaza de la Merced. Centre for Picasso research, also promotes contemporary art. Organises lectures on various aspects of Picasso's life and work, and "Octubre Picassiano" to celebrate painter's birth, with exhibitions and events. Entry free. Open: 10 a.m.–2 p.m., 5–8 p.m. Tel: (952) 28 39 00.

In the province:

Antequera (35 miles/57 km): **Dolmens— Cueva de Menga**, Bronze-age burial site, almost 1 mile (1 km) from town centre on Granada road. Open: 10 a.m.–1 p.m., 2–6 p.m. winter, 4–8 p.m. summer. **Cueva de Viera** nearby. Open: 10 a.m.–1 p.m. (summer and winter), 3–5 p.m. (winter), 5–7 p.m. (summer).

Romeral dolmen (4 miles/6 km): near junction Granada road and bypass to Córdoba, apply at Fabrica de Azucar (sugar factory). Open: 10 a.m.–1 p.m. (winter and summer), 3–5 p.m. (winter), 5–7 p.m. (summer).

Municipal Museum, Palace of Najera, Plaza Coso Viejo: Open: 10 a.m.–1.30 p.m., Sunday 11 a.m.–1 p.m. Closed: Monday.

Colegiata de Santa María la Mayor: Renaissance monument.

Puerta de Arco de los Gigantes: erected 1585.

El Chorro (38 miles/60 km, northwest of Málaga): dramatic chasm, through which passes the Guadalhorce River.

Cueva de Nerja (35 miles/56 km): home of prehistoric man, spectacular rock formations. Open: 10 a.m.–1.30 p.m., 4–7 p.m. except May–September, 9.30 a.m.–9 p.m.

Ronda (76 miles/122 km, from Málaga): **El Tajo** (chasm) spanned by 18th-century bridge Puente Nuevo, **Palacio de Salvatierra**, **Casa del Rey Moro**, **Arab Baths** (Open: 10 a.m.–1 p.m., 4–7 p.m.. Closed: Sunday p.m. and Monday). **Plaza de Toros**: oldest bullring in Spain. Open: 10 a.m.–6 p.m.

Ronda la Vieja (12 miles/20 km, from Ronda): Roman ruins, theatre.

Cueva de la Pileta (17 miles/27 km, from Ronda): prehistoric cave paintings.

In Cádiz province: **Setenil** (11 miles/18 km, north of Ronda): streets built under rock; **Grazalema** (20 miles/31 km): wild mountain scenery, *pinsapo* (pine) forest; **Zahara** (22 miles/35km): Arab castle.

346

SEVILLE

Cathedral and Giralda tower: Colossal 15th-century Gothic building. Many art treasures. Tombs of King Ferdinand the Saint and Pedro the Cruel. Giralda, 12th-century Arab minaret, can be climbed for views. Open: 11 a.m.–6 p.m. Monday–Friday, 11 a.m.–4 p.m. Saturday, 2–4 p.m. Sunday. School groups 2–4 p.m. Closed: holidays.

Reales Alcázares: 11th-century Mudéjar palace. Fine gardens. Open: 9 a.m.–12.45 p.m., 3–5.30 p.m. Saturday, Sunday and holidays 9 a.m.–1 p.m.

Torre del Oro (Tower of Gold): Moorish-built, houses Maritime Museum. Open: 10 a.m.–2 p.m. Sunday and holidays, 10 a.m.–1 p.m. Closed: Monday.

Archives of the Indies: Avda de la Constitución. Contains historic documents relating to conquest of New World. (Researchers, tel: (954) 22 51 58). Open: 10 a.m.–1 p.m. Monday–Friday.

Casa Pilatos: Mudéjar-Renaissance mansion. Open: 9 a.m.–6 p.m.; upper floor, 10 a.m.–1.30 p.m., 4–6.30 p.m. Closed: Saturday afternoon, Sunday.

María Luisa Park: Pleasant park with interesting buildings from 1929 Iberoamerican Exhibition.

Museo de Bellas Artes (Fine Arts Museum): Plaza del Museo, 9. Works by Murillo and Ribera. Open: 10 a.m.–2 p.m., 4–7 p.m. Closed: Saturday and Sunday afternoon, Monday.

La Macarena church: Contains one of Seville´s most venerated Virgins. Open: 8 a.m.–1 p.m., 5–9 p.m. Treasury open: 9.30 a.m.–12.30 p.m., 5.30–7.30 p.m.

Ayuntamiento (Town Hall): Striking Renaissance-style building.

Tobacco Factory: Now part of the university.

River Guadalquivir cruises (in summer as far as Sanlucar): Quayside next to Torre del Oro. Tel: (954) 12 19 34 and 21 38 36 for details.

In the province:
Carmona (21 miles/33km): Girdled by ancient walls, town of fine old buildings, churches. **Roman necropolis**, open 10 a.m.–2 p.m., 4–6 p.m., closed Monday and holidays.

Ecija (54 miles/87 km): **"town of steeples"**, many beautiful churches and mansions (Palacio de los Marqueses de Peñaflor, Palacio de los Condes de Valverde), remains of Roman amphitheatre and necropolis.

Itálica (6 miles/9 km): Streets, amphitheatre, mosaics in Roman town, **birthplace of Hadrian**. Open: 9 a.m.–6.30 p.m., October–February 9 a.m.–5 p.m. Sunday 9 a.m.–3 p.m. Closed: Monday.

TRAVEL PACKAGES

Tour operators offer hundreds of possibilities for all-in holidays in Andalucía, usually based on the Costa del Sol. From the coast, numerous excursions are possible, taking in the better-known sights of the region. Day trips include Granada, Seville, Ronda and Tangiers. Two-day trips to the natural splendours of the Alpujarras and Cazorla are also available.

A five-day all-in tour of Andalucía, including the major cities, costs from 42,000 pesetas. A train ride in the grand style of the Orient Express is offered by the Al-Andalus Expreso. Operating May–October, this de luxe train visits Seville, Córdoba, Granada and Málaga, with option of visit to Jerez (from 85,000 pesetas). See sport for details of horse-trekking tours.

Tourist guides: Tourist information offices can put you in touch with official guides.

SPAS

Andalucía has a number of *balnearios* (spas) where the waters have medicinal properties. Usually open from June to October, these are tranquil spots with doctors on hand to offer advice. Among the spas are establishments at Alhama de Granada and Lanjarón (Granada province), Carratraca and Tolox (Málaga), and Marmolejo (Jaén).

CULTURE PLUS

Granada's events guide, *Guía Cultural y de Ocio*, published fortnightly in Spanish and English, gives useful information about cultural events. Seville has two useful entertainment guides, *El Giraldillo*, and the *Guía de Ocio*. On the Costa del Sol, numerous publications, some free, offer information about what's on. *Lookout* Magazine has details about theatre, sport, films in English, club events.

THEATRE AND MUSIC

Córdoba's orchestra (Orquesta Ciudad de Córdoba) gives concerts in the conservatory of music. The Gran Teatro, recently restored, stages opera, ballet, classical music and pop concerts. Check tourist office or local press for details of performances.

Granada: Classical music concerts in the Auditorio Manuel de Falla, Paseo de los Martires, Alhambra. Tel: (958) 22 82 88.

Málaga: The Orquesta Sinfónica de Málaga, gives concerts in the Teatro Cervantes, Ramos Martín 2. Tel: (952) 22 44 00. Plays and opera productions are also staged in this theatre. Marbella's ballet troupe, Ballet Ciudad de Marbella, gives performances in the municipal auditorium, Parque de la Constitución. The Salon Varietes in Fuengirola stages productions in English, musicals, drama and at Christmas a pantomime. Information: Salon Varietes, Emancipación 30, Fuengirola. Tel: (952) 47 45 42. Internationally known performers such as Stevie Wonder, Paul Simon and Tina Turner feature in summer pop concerts in Málaga and (more often) Marbella.

Seville: The Bética Filarmónica de Sevilla gives concerts in the music conservatory, c/. Jesús del Gran Poder. Drama, flamenco and concerts are staged in the Lope de Vega Theatre. Seville has two financial institutions which promote cultural activities, exhibitions and concerts. Information appears in local press or direct from organisers: El Monte (Caja de Ahorros de Sevilla), Tel: (954) 21 37 44, concerts in the Salón de Actos, Pasaje Villasis; and the Caja San Fernando, Salón de Actos, Chicarreras.

DIARY OF EVENTS

The following is a list of some of the more important or interesting festivals and events in the region. As dates vary each year, it is advisable to check with the organisers or local tourist office for exact details.

CADIZ

April: Jerez, World Motorcycling Championship at Jerez race track.

May: Jerez, Jerez Horse Fair. Display of horses and horsemanship. Information: (956) 34 76 63.

August: Sanlucar de Barrameda. Horse races along the beach.

August: Sotogrande, International Polo Competition. Matches throughout the month to dispute three trophies.

August: Jerez, International Flamenco Contest.

September: Cádiz, Atlantic Film Festival. Retrospectives, documentaries and new films from international participants. Information: (956) 21 23 91.

September/October: Jerez, Tío Pepe Formula I Grand Prix, Jerez race track.

December: Jerez, National Flamenco Guitar Contest.

CORDOBA

May: Córdoba, International Sierra Morena Rally. Gruelling motorcycle race through heart of the Sierra Morena. Information: (957) 47 37 11.

July: Córdoba, Guitar and Dance Courses. Courses in flamenco, classical guitar and dance, organised by the Centro Flamenco Paco Peña, Plaza del Potro 15, 14002 Córdoba.

July–October: Córdoba, International Guitar Festival. Performances of flamenco and classical guitar. Information from the town hall: (957) 47 93 29.

GRANADA

January: Almuñécar, Andres Segovia International Classical Guitar Competition. Information from Almuñécar town hall.

May: Granada, International Drama Festival. Showcase for most innovative international theatre productions. Information from festival office: Palacio de la Madraza, c/. Oficios 14, Granada 18001. Tel: (958) 22 84 03.

June/July: Granada, Manuel de Falla Music Course. Principally intended for music students, also recitals.

June/July: Granada, International Festival of Music and Dance. One of Spain's leading festivals offers a varied programme of music and dance by national and international companies. Concerts in the Auditorio Manuel de Falla and the Palacio Carlos V in the Alhambra, dance in the Generalife. Information from the festival office: Gracia 21–4, 18002 Granada. Tel: (958) 26 74 42–45.

July: Granada, Romantic Concerts. Classical music concerts in the unusual setting of the Carmen de los Martires, near the Alhambra.

November: Granada, Granada International Jazz Festival. Emphasis on modern jazz. Information from town hall: Tel: (958) 22 35 73.

HUELVA

November/December: Huelva, Iberoamerican Film Festival. Dedicated to films from Latin America. Information: Hotel Tartessos, Avenida Martín Alonso Pinzón 13, Huelva. Tel: (955) 24 56 11.

MALAGA

February: Ruta Ciclista Vuelta a Andalucía—Cycle race covering most of the provinces of Andalucía.

July: Málaga, International Theatre Festival. Showcase for productions by international companies.

July/August: Nerja International Dance and Music Festival. Performances of classical musical and ballet in the Nerja Caves.

September: Ronda, International Folklore Gala. Performances of folkloric dancing by international groups. Information:

Asociacion Cultural Folklorica Abdul-Beka, c/. Virgen de la Paz s/n, Ronda. Tel: (952) 87 23 10.

November: Ronda, Week of International Scientific Film. Dedicated to investigative and informative films not usually on release for public viewing. Information: Centro de Medios de la Caja de Ahorros de Ronda. Tel: (952) 30 68 94.

SEVILLE

February/March: Seville, Ancient Music Festival. Music from Romantic, Gothic and early baroque periods played on original or replica instruments. Information from town hall: (954) 21 88 83.

April: Seville, Antiques fair. Exhibitors from all over Spain. Information: Palacio de Exposiciones y Congresos, Recinto Ferial, Polígono Aeropuerto, Seville Este. Tel: (954) 67 51 40.

May/June: Cita en Sevilla. Cultural festival with classic and avant garde theatre and dance, exhibitions and music from pop, rock, to jazz and blues. Information from town hall: (954) 21 88 83.

July: Italica, International Festival of Theatre and Dance. Contemporary dance and classical ballet by prestigious international companies. Held in the Roman amphitheatre. Information: Fundación Luis Cernuda, Diputación Provincial de Sevilla. Tel: (954) 21 77 22.

September: Biannual Flamenco Festival. Held every two years (1990, 1992, etc). Lasts throughout the month and represents the best in flamenco. Information from town hall. Tel: (954) 21 88 83.

November: Seville, International Jazz Festival. Information from organisers: Avenida de la Constitución 24, Pasaje de los Seises, 41001 Sevilla. Tel: (954) 21 77 22.

ARCHITECTURE

Andalucía has magnificent examples of Renaissance and baroque architecture and the massive Seville Cathedral is one of the last great structures to be built in the Gothic style. But the Moorish influence is the most remarkable aspect of the region. From the golden age of the Caliphate come the horseshoe-shaped arches, ornamented brickwork, and cupolas which characterise such monuments as Medina Azahar and the Córdoba Mosque.

Later, austere Almohad builders created structures like Sevilla's Giralda minaret. And in the sophisticated era of the Nasrids, lacey stucco, glazed tiles, flowing calligraphy and bubbling water were used to create the dreamy, ethereal beauty of Granada's Alhambra. The intermingling of cultures produced Mudéjar architecture, produced by Moslems under Christian rule, and Mozarabic architecture, Moorish-influenced Christian styles.

Although modern high-rises of little merit have spread across the region, many communities still inhabit dwellings little changed in centuries. Red-tiled roofs, whitewashed walls and wrought-iron grills and balconies are common. In Cádiz province, several dwellings are often to be found around a central *patio* known as a "corral". Córdoba's and Sevilla's grand old houses pride themselves on their flower-decked *patios*. In Granada, the "carmen"—a house with a garden and high walls around it—keeps intruders at bay. In Almería, flat-roofed dwellings whisper of Africa.

NIGHTLIFE

BARS

Spaniards like nothing better than to drink and talk until the early hours. All cities have at least one bar area which comes to life in the evening. The *tapeo* is an accepted custom, in which you move between bars, sampling with every drink a different *tapa*, the tasty titbits that can run from grilled shrimps to stewed tripe. Remember in all bars and cafés it is cheapest to drink at the counter. If you sit at a table, the price goes up—and up again if you take a drink on a terrace. Some bars offer live music, in which case you will pay extra. Bars advertising themselves as "pubs" are nothing like the English version. They are usually dimly lit, with over-stuffed furniture, and favoured by the trendy young. Prices are higher than in a down-to-earth bar. An "American bar" is one where the staff is female or there are hostesses, i.e. expect to be ripped off.

Seville is justifiably renowned for its bars. They vary from traditional seedy to elegantly modern and offer a vast range of excellent *tapas*. Examples: **Casa Morales**, García de Vinuesa, 11. Old *bodega*, huge barrels, reeking of atmosphere; **El Rinconcillo**, Gerona, 42. Founded 1670. Tiles, beams, wine from barrel; Abades, Abades, 13 (Santa Cruz). Elegant *patio* in stylish house, classical music, frequented by upwardly mobile *sevillanos*. **La Carboneria**, Levies, 18. Former palace, then coal merchants. Lively hang out for young artists, musicians. There are many more, particularly in the Triana quarter, but watch your valuables when doing a night crawl.

NIGHTCLUBS

Full-fledged nightclubs are few and far between. If you are looking for a Folies Bergeres-type extravaganza, the Casino Torrequebrada near Málaga is probably the best bet (*see Gambling*). Restaurants and cafes often put on live entertainment. "Sexy shows" usually feature strippers. Remember that a "sala de fiestas" may not be a genuine nightclub. Many establishments use this name when they are in fact brothels, or bars where prostitutes make their contacts. You will often see them on the fringes of towns, signalled with gaudy lighting.

DISCOS

These come in all varieties, for teenagers, the upwardly mobile, jetsetters and just the young-at-heart. This season's "in" place may be "out" by the time you arrive. Entry price is usually from 600 pesetas. Worth investigating :

Córdoba: Contactos, Eduardo Dato 8; Saint Cyr, Eduardo Lucena 4; Zahira, Conde de Robledo 1.

Granada: Granada 10, Carcel Baja 13; Oh Granada, Doctor Guirao Gea s/n; Perkussion, Plaza de Gracia 9 (next to Multicines); Krokis, Santa Barbara 3.

Málaga: Main centres are along the Costa del Sol in Torremolinos/Benalmádena-Costa, Marbella and Puerto Banus. In Málaga—Duna, Avenida Juan Sebastian Elcano, Pedregalejo; Extasis, Plaza de Reding, Malagueta; H2O, c/. Fernando Camino, Malagueta. In Torremolinos—Piper's, Avenida Palma de Mallorca; Borsalino Palace, Ctra Cádiz; No. 1, Avenida Carlota Alessandri. In Marbella—Jimmy's, Marbella Club Hotel; Kiss, Avenida Ricardo Soriano; Olivia Valere, Puerto Banús; Pepe Moreno, Ctra Cádiz km 186.

Seville: Mostly in the Remedios district across the river. Disco FM, Avenida Garcia Morato s/n; Rio, Betis 67; Groucho, Federico Sánchez Bedoya 20; Piruetas, Asunción 3.

<hr>

FLAMENCO

Not all the best performers are earning millions in New York, contrary to what you may have heard. Even so, you will be fortunate to come across a top-quality authentic flamenco performance. Often it is cheapened to make it more palatable for popular taste. The best performances come spontaneously, when a singer is moved by emotion rather than money and that is unlikely to happen before a crowd of tourists.

Flamenco festivals are held throughout Andalucía, sometimes lasting all night. Purists are contemptuous of the shows staged for tourists in the caves of Sacromonte, Granada's gypsy quarter. Visiting one of the caves can be a memorable experience, but you may well feel ripped off. Places where you can see reasonable-quality commercial flamenco include: in Granada, El Corral del Príncipe, Campo de Príncipe s/n; El Curro, Lavadero de las Tablas, tel: (958) 28 35 37; La Reina Mora, Mirador de San Cristobal. In Seville, Tablao Flamenco de Curro Vélez, Rodo 7, tel: (954) 21 64 92; El Patio Sevillano, Paseo Colón 11, tel: 22 20 68; Los Gallos, Plaza Santa Cruz 11, tel: (954) 21 69 81. Advance bookings are highly recommended.

<hr>

GAMBLING

Gambling is a national pastime in Spain. People of all ages pour their cash into "tragaperras", the slot machines found in many bars. Every week during the soccer season there is the "Quiniela", football pool. Vast sums are gambled on the frequent lotteries, run by the state or ONCE, the organisation for the blind.

Andalucía has three casinos. Passports or national identity cards must be shown, "correct" dress is expected and an entry fee is payable.

Casino Torrequebrada, Ctra N340 km 226, Benalmádena Costa, Málaga. Tel: (952) 44 25 45. Also has restaurant/bar, nightclub, disco and cinema.

Casino Nueva Andalucía, Hotel Andalucía Plaza, Nueva Andalucía, Marbella, Málaga. Tel: (952) 78 08 00. Jetsetters' favourite.

Casino de Bahía de Cádiz , Ctra Madrid-Cádiz km 650,3, Puerto de Santa María, Cádiz. Tel: (956) 86 20 42. Also has restaurant, disco, cinema, nightclub.

SHOPPING

Shops are generally open 9.30/10 a.m. to 1/1.30 p.m. and 4.30/5 p.m. to 8/8.30 p.m. Monday to Friday, mornings only on Saturday. The larger department stores such as El Corte Inglés and Galerías Preciados do not usually close at midday.

El Corte Inglés has become a Spanish institution, offering a vast range of products, as well as a service for foreign tourists and export facilities.

Purchases worth making anywhere in Spain include qood-quality leather goods, Havana and Canary Islands cigars, porcelain statuary, cultured pearls, bargain-priced alcohol, virgin olive oil, saffron and craftware. Andalucía offers a variety of handmade products, including intricate fans, embroidery, finely-tooled leather goods, earthenware pottery, baskets, Seville tiles, silver jewellery, and rugs. Some of the finest guitars are made in Granada and Seville.

Visitors can claim back tax (IVA) on

purchases, but each item must have a value of over 52,800 Pesatas. Shops should have the forms to fill in. The tax refund will normally be sent to your home address, except for travellers leaving via Málaga airport, who can claim the refund immediately from the office of the Banco de España in the airport terminal.

ALMERIA

The commercial centre is around the Paseo de Almería, Puerta de Purchena, Obispo Orbera, and Calle de las Tiendas.

Principal buys are in handicrafts: Ceramics and pottery (from Albox, Nijar, Sorbas and Vera); basketwork (from Almería, Alhabia and Nijar); *jarapas*, rugs made with rags and strips of cotton (from Nijar, Huercal Overa and Berja); bedspreads and blankets from (Albox, Berja and Macael); marble objects from Macaél.

CADIZ

The main shopping area is in the warren of streets near the cathedral.

What to buy: Sherry from Jerez and Puerto de Santa María (such as Harveys, Williams and Humbert, Pedro Domecq and Osborne, well known to the British market); dolls from doll factory in Chiclana (Fabrica de Muñecas Marin, Rivero 16. Tel: (956) 40 06 67); fine leather from Ubrique; carpets from Arcos de la Frontera; capes and ponchos from Grazalema; guitars from Algodonales; wickerwork from Jerez; saddlery from Olvera.

CORDOBA

For general shopping in the city the main area lies between the streets Gondomar, Tendillas and Ronda de los Tejares. Of the various markets, the most interesting is on Saturday and Sunday mornings in the Plaza Corredera. Handicrafts can be bought at the municipal handicrafts market (Zoco Municipal de Artesanía) behind the bullfighting museum.

What to buy: Silver filigree jewellery, for which Córdoba is particularly noted; Montilla wines (*Bodegas* in Montilla, 28 miles/46 km from Córdoba); *anís* liquor from Rute (Anís Machaquito, Anís De Raza); ceram-

ics, Lucena pottery with geometric green and yellow design, and *botijos* (2-spouted drinking pitchers) from La Rambla; leatherwork; decorative metalwork in copper, bronze and brass (from Espejo and Castro del Río).

GRANADA

Main shopping area: around Recogidas, Acera de Darro, Gran Vía and Reyes Católicos and the maze of surrounding streets. Granada offers some excellent handicrafts, many incorporating techniques and designs handed down from the Arabs. You will find a large range of handmade articles in the Alcaiceria (old Arab silk market), near the cathedral, and the handicrafts market in the Corral del Carbón, Mariano Pineda.

What to buy: Foodstuffs—cured mountain hams from the Alpujarras; pottery, most typical is Fajalauza with distinctive blue and green design originally from the Albaicín; leather, especially embossed leatherwork; marquetry (technique of inlaying wood with bone, ivory, mother of pearl and other woods) chests, chess boards, small tables; metal craftwork, lanterns made to traditional Moorish designs; textiles—rugs, cushions, bedspreads from the Alpujarras; hand-made guitars, several workshops on the Cuesta de Gomerez leading to the Alhambra; silver filigree jewellery.

HUELVA

What to buy: Cured hams from Jabugo; white wine from the Condado de Huelva; pottery (from Aracena and Cortejana); rugs from Ecinasola; embroidery (from Aracena, Alosno and Puebla de Guzmán); handmade leather boots (Valverde de Camino).

JAEN

What to buy: Glass and ceramics (from Andújar, Bailen and Ubeda); carpets and wickerwork (from Ubeda, Jaén and Los Villares); forged iron objects and lanterns (Ubeda); guitars (Marmolejo).

MALAGA

The main shopping area in the city is centred around the streets Larios, Nueva,

Granada, Caldereria and adjacent streets, and also in Avenida de Andalucía where there is an El Corte Ingles. On the outskirts of Málaga are shopping complexes, the biggest if not the best being Los Patios.

The towns along the Costa del Sol also offer a variety of street markets, colourful though not necessarily the place to find a bargain.

Market timings are as follows: Monday, Marbella; Tuesday, Fuengirola and Nerja; Wednesday, Estepona; Thursday, Torremolinos and San Pedro de Alcántara; Friday, Arroyo de la Miel and Benalmádena *pueblo*; Sunday, Estepona port and Málaga (by the football stadium).

What to buy: Leather goods at factory prices; Málaga wine; Pottery and ceramics (from Málaga, Ronda, Vélez Málaga and Coín); embossed copper (Málaga); castanets (Alora); guitars (Málaga and Ronda); basketry (Vélez Málaga, Benamocarra); rugs from Mijas (can be made to order).

SEVILLE

For general shopping go to the area behind the El Salvador church; for clothes, Sierpes, Campana, O'Donnell and Velázquez; department stores around Plaza del Duque, and the streets O'Donnell and Velázquez. Seville also has a number of street markets selling handicrafts and bric-a-brac—daily handicraft market in the Mercado del Postigo; Wednesday and Thursday, handicrafts in c/. Rioja and c/. Magdalena, Friday and Saturday in the Plaza del Duque; Thursday, secondhand, antiques in c/. Feria; Sun, antiques and secondhand in Alameda de Hércules, and also Parque Alcosa.

What to buy: Antiques around the streets Mateos Gago, Placentines and Rodrigo Caro; ceramics and tiles from Santa Ana (factory in Triana) and La Cartuja de Sevilla (factory at Ctra de Merida km 529, tel: (954) 39 28 54); saddlery and leather items, boots and chaps; fashion, Seville's own designers Victorio and Lucchino have showroom at Sierpes 87; fans and castanets.

COMPLAINTS

From August 1990 it became a statutory requirement for all businesses dealing with the public (hostelry, garages, transport, shops, etc) to have a complaints book (*Libro* or *hoja de reclamaciones*). Any complaint is registered in the book and sent to the local authority. Any receipts should be attached to the claim. You can take your complaint to the town hall or the Consumer Advice Office (Oficina de Información al Consumidor) if one exists.

Consumer Advice Offices:

Almería, Avenida de Pablo Iglesias 25-1-A. Tel: (951) 25 27 44.

Cádiz, Plaza de San Juan de Dios. 25 06 60. Algeciras, Avenida Fuerzas Armadas 34. Tel: (956) 66 18 21.

Córdoba, Gran Capitán 6. Tel: (957) 47 44 29.

Granada, Gran Capitán 24.

Málaga, Town Hall, Avenida de Cervantes, Tel: (952) 77 02 45. Estepona, Villa s/n, Tel: (952) 80 12 52. Fuengirola, Avenida Suel (in market building.) Arroyo de la Miel, Luis Flores 1, Tel: (952) 44 19 84.

Seville, Avenida de Portugal 2. Tel: (954) 23 39 79.

SPORTS

GOLF

Southern Spain, particularly the Costa del Sol, is a golfer's paradise. Apart from the clubs listed, many more courses are in the planning stage or nearing completion.

ALMERIA

(area code 951):

Golf Almerimar, Golf Hotel Almerimar, El Ejido. 18 holes. Tel: 48 09 50.

Golf Playa Serena, Urbanización Playa Serena, Roquetas de Mar. 18 holes. Tel: 32 20 55.

Cortijo Grande Golf Club, Cortijo Grande, Turre (near Mojácar). 18 holes. Tel: 47 91 64.

CADIZ

(area code 956):

Costa de la Luz, Ctra N340, km 16, Chiclana. 9 holes. Tel: 40 67 19.

La Cañada, Carretera s/n, Guadiaro. 9 holes. Tel: 79 50 48/79 56 85.

San Roque Golf Club, San Roque. Tel: 79 21 00.

Sotogrande Golf Club, Urbanización Sotogrande, Ctra N340 km 133, Sotogrande. Two courses 18 holes and 9 holes. Tel: 79 20 50/1.

Valderrama, Ctra N340 km 132, Sotogrande. 18 holes. Tel: 79 27 72.

Vista Hermosa, Puerto de Santa María. Tel: 85 00 11.

CORDOBA

(area code 957):

Los Villares, 5 miles (9 km) from Córdoba. 18 holes. Tel: 35 02 08.

Pozoblanco: San Gregorio 2, Pozoblanco. 9 holes. First municipal golf course in Spain.

GRANADA

(area code 958):

Granada Golf Club, Las Gabias, Granada. 18 holes. Tel: 26 75 49.

Los Moriscos, Motril. 9 holes. Tel: 60 04 12.

HUELVA

(area code 955):

Bellavista, Ctra de Aljaraque km 6. 9 holes. Tel: 31 80 83.

Golf Rústico El Higueral, El Rompido. 9 holes. Tel: 24 93 18.

JAEN

(area code 953):

La Garza, Colónia Ermita 2, Linares. 9 holes. Tel: 69 35 90.

MALAGA—
INCLUDING THE COSTA DEL SOL

(area code 952):

Aloha Golf, Nueva Andalucía, Marbella. 27 holes. Tel: 81 23 88.

Atalaya Park, Ctra Benahavis km 0,7,

Estepona. 18 holes. Tel: 78 18 94.

Coto La Serena, Ctra N340 km 163,4, Estepona. 9 holes.

Las Brisas, Nueva Andalucía, Marbella. 18 holes. Tel: 81 08 75.

El Candado, Urb El Candado, El Palo, Málaga. 9 holes. Tel: 29 46 66.

Golf La Duquesa, Urbanización El Hacho, Sabinillas–Manilva. 9 holes. Tel: 89 04 25.

Guadalmina, Guadalmina Alta, San Pedro de Alcantara. Tel: 78 13 77, two courses Guadalmina Norte and Guadalmina Sur, each 18 holes.

Club de Campo de Málaga, 4 km de Torremolinos. 18 holes. Tel: 38 11 20.

Mijas, 1 mile (3 km) from Fuengirola. Tel: 47 68 43., two courses Los Lagos and Los Olivos each 18 holes.

Los Naranjos, Ctra N340 km 174, Marbella. 18 holes. Tel: 81 52 06.

Golf El Paraiso, N340 km 173, Estepona. 18 holes. Tel: 78 30 00.

Los Moriscos Club de Golf, Motril (Granada). 9 holes. Tel: (958) 60 04 12.

La Quinta, Ctra de Ronda km 3,5, San Pedro de Alcántara. 18 holes. Tel:78 38 16.

Golf Río Real, Ctra N340 km 185. 18 holes. Tel: 77 37 76.

Golf Torrequebrada, Benalmádena–Costa. 18 holes. Tel: 44 27 42.

SEVILLE

(area code 954):

Pineda, Avenida de Jerez s/n, Sevilla. Tel: 61 33 99/61 14 00.

Las Minas Golf, Ctra Isla Mayor km 0,800, Aznalcazar. Tel: 75 05 71.

HORSE-RIDING AND TREKKING

Riding is available for all levels, instruction for beginners, renting by hour, to treks through the sierras.

CADIZ

(area code 956):

Valderrama stables (behind Hotel Sotogrande), Sotogrande. Lessons, ponies for children, rental, treks. Tel: 79 20 60; Almoguera stables, Los Barrios. Lessons, rental, day excursions. Tel: 66 00 00; Finca Bordalla, Jimena de la Frontera. Daily rides, and

2 and 6-day treks. Tel: 64 05 59; Sotogrande complex, Urbanización Sotogrande. Polo available; Arcos de la Frontera, treks into surrounding sierra arranged through tourist office, Cuesta de Belen s/n. Tel: 70 22 64; Royal Andalucían School of Equestrian Art, Avenida Duque de Abrantes s/n, Recreo de las Cadenas, Jerez. Lessons. Tel: 33 41 98.

CORDOBA

(area code 957):
Club Hípico, Ctra Trassierra (2 miles/3 km, from Córdoba). Tel: 27 16 28.

GRANADA

(area code 958):
El Picadero, English Riding School La Ribera, Almuñecar. Tel: 63 07 39; Internado Emilio Muñoz, Cogollos Vega. Classes. Tel: 42 80 36; Real Sociedad Hípica, Hipodromo del Zaidin, Fontiveros 40. Riding school within the Zaidin race track. Tel: 11 09 20; Sierra Trails, Bubión, Alpujarras. 2 and 3-day treks in the Alpujarras, hourly rides. Tel: 76 30 38.

FISHING

Offshore fishing: boats can often be hired at marinas. Some excursions are available, particularly for shark fishing. Inland fishing: It is possible to catch tench, carp, pike, black bass and trout. Legislation varies from province to province with regards licences, so it is advisable to check details with local tourist offices.

HUNTING

You are legally entitled to import two hunting guns with 100 cartridges. It is advisable to contact the Hunting Federation (Federación Española de la Caza, Avenida Reina Victoria 72, Madrid. Tel: (91) 253 90 17) for details of licences, restrictions and seasons, as some species are protected and others have a quota ceiling.

For the serious, hunting is available in controlled areas and state-run game parks such as Cazorla in Jaén where it is possible to hunt wild goat (*capra hispanica*), deer or wild boar. Organised parties, known as "monterias", take part in shoots in the Sierra Morena (Jaén and Córdoba provinces), where deer and boar abound.

LAWN BOWLS

Lawn bowls is fairly new to the south of Spain, but the number of greens is increasing and international competitions are staged on the Costa del Sol: **Aloha Superbowl**, Nueva Andalucía, Marbella, Málaga. Tel: (952) 81 33 92; **Miraflores Lawn Bowls Club**, Miraflores Sports Centre, Mijas–Costa, Málaga. Tel: (952) 83 35 89.

TENNIS

There are too many tennis clubs in the region to list them all. A number have outstanding facilities, including tuition in some cases by ex-international champions e.g:
Lew Hoad's Tennis Ranch, Ctra Mijas–Fuengirola, Málaga. Tel: (952) 47 48 58.
El Madroñal Tennis Club, San Pedro de Alcantara, Marbella, Málaga. Tel: (952) 78 09 90.
Los Monteros Tennis Club, Hotel Los Monteros, Ctra N340, Marbella, Málaga. Tel: (952) 77 17 00.
Puente Romano Tennis Club, Hotel Puente Romano, Ctra N340, Marbella, Málaga. Tel: (952) 77 01 00.

SKIING

There is skiing in the Sierra Nevada 20 miles (32 km) from Granada, the southernmost ski slope in Europe. The slopes are between 7,000 ft (2,100 metres) and 11,000 ft (3,390 metres) above sea level, with 21 ski runs of varying difficulty and 18 lifts.

Facilities include equipment to rent, instruction including a special school for children, first aid and rescue service and emergency clinic. The Solynieve complex offers a variety of accommodation and *après ski* entertainment. General information: (958) 48 05 00/48 05 04/48 05 08. Weather information, snow report (958) 48 01 53.

WATERSPORTS

Facilities for sailing, windsurfing, scuba diving, waterskiing and sub aqua diving are available on the Atlantic and Mediterranean coasts.

MARINAS

Almería: Almerimar Marina, El Ejido. Tel; 48 01 34; San Jose Marina, Nijar.

Cádiz: Puerto Sherry, Puerto de Santa María; Puerto de la Albufera de Barbate, Barbate; Puerto Sotogrande. Tel: 79 00 00; Arcos Lake, for protected sailing.

Granada: Puerto de Motril. Tel: 64 03 50; Puerto de Marina del Este, Almuñecar. Tel: 60 00 37.

Huelva: Punta Umbria; Huelva; El Rompido; Ayamonte; Isla Cristina.

Málaga: El Candado, Málaga; Marina Benalmádena. Tel: 44 29 44/44 13 44; Puerto de Fuengirola; Puerto Cabopino, Marbella. Tel: 83 19 75/83 30 39; Puerto Deportivo Marbella. Tel: 77 25 04/777 43 76; Puerto Banus, Marbella. Tel: 78 33 50/78 66 58; Puerto Deportivo Estepona. Tel: 80 18 00; Puerto de la Duquesa, Manilva. Tel: 89 01 00/89 03 00.

Seville: Club Nautico de Sevilla, Avenida Tablada s/n. Tel: 45 03 10, offers sailing on the river.

WINDSURFING

Many beaches have schools and rent equipment. The best area is near Tarifa, Cádiz. The good winds attract surfers from all over Europe and a variety of competitions are held throughout the year.

SCUBA AND SUB-AQUA DIVING

The rocky shoreline around much of the coast offers plenty of scope for underwater exploring and fishing. If you swim any distance from the shore, you are required to tow a marker buoy. A diving school near Almuñecar (Granada), runs scuba courses: Edificio Rosa Nautica, La Herradura, Almuñecar. Tel: (958) 64 01 25.

Best areas for diving are:

Almería: Cabo de Gata, Las Negras, La Isleta, San José and Morrón de los Genoveses, where international underwater fishing competitions have been held.

Cádiz: North of Tarifa, especially for underwater fishing.

Granada: La Herradura and west toward Málaga.

Málaga: from Nerja east toward Granada coast.

Soccer and basketball are Spain's most popular spectator sports. Andalucía's leading soccer teams are Betis and Sevilla (both of Seville), Cádiz and Málaga. Games usually start at 5 p.m. on Sundays. Basketball attracts a fanatical following. Several of Andalucía's leading teams are sponsored by local savings banks.

You will not find bullfighting reported in the sports pages as it is classed as an art. Andalucía is the womb of this controversial struggle between man and beast and the town of Ronda is regarded as the cradle of modern bullfighting. Many of Spain's top *matadors* come from the region and many of the most-respected fighting bulls. There are occasional charity fights in winter, but the season really gets under way at Easter and with the series of *corridas* during the Seville Fair.

Seville's Maestranza bullring is the most important arena. Daily fights are held during the fairs in other towns, throughout the summer. Six bulls are killed during a *corrida*, which usually starts at 6 p.m. Tickets are expensive, particularly if you want to be in the shade ("Sombra") and near the *barrera*, the ringside. Cheaper tickets are sold for "Sol", the seating on the sunny side of the stadium. In a number of communities, bullruns are held through the streets during local festivities.

LANGUAGE

Even a few words of Spanish are worth learning, as your efforts will be appreciated. Pronunciation is phonetic, but Andalucían speech—particularly among rural-dwellers—can baffle anybody. However, youngsters usually know a few words of English learned in school.

In the main cities you will always find somebody who knows German, French or

English, often because he or she has spent years abroad as an exile or as an emigrant worker. In tourist areas, particularly on the Costa del Sol, English or German is sometimes more useful than a knowledge of *castellano* (i.e. the Spanish originating in Castile). The Andalucían accent is markedly different from that of Central and Northern Spain and is closer to that heard in Latin America. Andalucíans speak more musically than Castilians and often drop consonants from their words. "C" (as in "cielo") and "z" (as in "caza") are usually pronounced like an "s" rather than a "th" as is the custom in Madrid. In contrast, you will sometimes here a word like "eso" pronounced "etho".

Numerous private language schools offer Spanish courses in Andalucía and there are a number of special summer courses. Málaga University runs a Hispanic Studies course for foreigners starting each autumn. Facultad de Filosofia y Letras, San Agustín, 4, Málaga. Tel: (952) 21 40 07.

USEFUL PHRASES

Good morning: *Buenos días*.
Good afternoon: *Buenas tardes*.
Good night: *Buenas noches*.
Goodbye: *Adiós* or *Hasta luego*.
How are you?: *Qué tal?* or *Cómo está?*
Please: *Por favor*.
Thank you: *Gracias*.
How much is it?: *Cuánto es?*
Where is the post office, railway station, police station, the toilet?: *Donde está (están) el correos, la estación de ferrocarril, la comisaría, los servicios?*
I would like a double (single) room: *Querría una habitación doble (individual)*.
What time is it?: *Qué hora es?*
It is two o'clock: *Son las dos*.
When does the bus to Granada leave?: *A qué hora sale el autobús para Granada?*
Today: *Hoy*.
Tomorrow: *Mañana*.
Yesterday: *Ayer*.
Breakfast: *Desayuno*.
Lunch: *Almuerzo*.
Dinner: *Cena*.
The bill: *La cuenta*.
1: *uno*.
2: *dos*.
3: *tres*.
4: *cuatro*.
5: *cinco*.
6: *seis*.
7: *siete*.
8: *ocho*.
9: *nueve*.
10: *diez*.
20: *veinte*.
50: *cincuenta*.
100: *cien*.
1,000: *mil*.

Commonly used Spanish words:
abierto: open.
aficionado: enthusiast; amateur (player).
alcazaba: castle.
alcázar: fortress, royal palace.
baile: dance.
balneario: spa.
barrio: quarter (of a city).
bodega: wine cellar.
calle: street.
campo: countryside, field.
cerrado: closed.
chico, chica: boy, girl.
corrida: bullfight.
cortijo: farmhouse.
cura: priest.
chiringuito: beach bar-restaurant.
churros: fried batter, eaten for breakfast.
entrada: entrance.
feria: annual fair.
finca: farm.
fino: dry sherry.
gitano: gypsy.
gracia: charm, attractiveness, wit.
jamón serrano: mountain-cured ham.
latifundio: large estate.
machismo: cult of masculine toughness.
matador: killer, bullfighter.
morisco: Moslem turned Christian.
mozárabe: culture developed by Christians under Moslem rule.
mudéjar: Moslem art in Christian-occupied territory.
novillero: beginner bullfighter.
novio, novia: fiance, fiancée.
paso: religious float.
patio: courtyard.
piropo: flirtatious compliment.
playa: beach.
plaza de toros: bullring.
pueblo: village, town.
rejoneador: bullfighter on horseback.
romería: religious pilgrimage.

salida: exit.
Semana Santa: Holy Week.
semáforos: traffic lights.
sevillana: lively flamenco song and dance.
tablao: flamenco night club.
tajo: steep cliff.
tapa: snack.
vendimia: grape harvest.
venta: inn.
vino tinto: red wine.

FURTHER READING

Although Spain did not figure in the Grand Tour of the early tourists, from the 19th century it attracted a succession of foreign travellers in search of the "exotic". Andalucía in particular awakened their interest. Théophile Gautier, Hans Christian Andersen and Washington Irving were among those to visit the region and their comments make fascinating reading.

Ian Robertson aptly titled his book on the succession of English travellers *Los Curiosos Impertinentes* (the impertinent inquisitive ones). These impertinent English included Henry Swinburne, Joseph Townsend, and Richard Ford. Ford did most to awaken interest in the region with witty and shrewdly-observed accounts of his travels between 1830 and 1833. This century Gerald Brenan, who lived much of his life in Andalucía, stands out as a writer whose great affection for the region did not diminish his critical faculties.

Baird, David: *Inside Andalucía—A Travel Adventure in Southern Spain* (Lookout Publications, Fuengirola, Málaga, 1988), informative account of Andalucía and its people, profusely illustrated.

Borrow, George: *The Bible in Spain* (first published 1842), eccentric, opinionated and entertaining.

Boyd, Alastair: *The Road from Ronda* (Collins, 1969), vivid account of a horse-ride through the Serrania de Ronda.

Brenan, Gerald: *South from Granada* (Cambridge University Press, 1988), classic account of life in a remote Granada village; *The Face of Spain* (Penguin, 1987), Brenan's grim view of an impoverished post-war Spain.

Burckhardt, Titus: *La Civilización hispano-árabe* (original title Die maurische Kultur in Spanien, 1970 Verlag Georg D.W. Callwey, Munich), (Alianza Editorial, Madrid, 1977), about Moorish culture.

Caro Baroja, Julio: *Los Moriscos del Reino de Granada* (Ediciones Istmo, Madrid, 1985), one of Spain's foremost historians relates the last days of the Moors of Granada.

Collins, Larry, and Dominique Lapierre: *Or I'll Dress You in Mourning* (Simon & Schuster), brilliant insights into Spain's post-Civil War hardships which moulded the Andalucían matador El Cordobés.

Ford, Richard: *Handbook for Travellers in Spain* (Centaur Press, 1966) and Gatherings from Spain (Dent Everyman, 1970), accounts of Spanish travels last century.

Fraser, Ronald: *The Pueblo*: A Mountain Village in Spain (Pantheon), villagers of Mijas tell their own story; *In Hiding*: The Life of Manuel Cortes (Penguin, 1982), how a village mayor stayed hidden for 30 years for fear of execution.

Gibson, Ian: *The Assassination of Federico García Lorca* (Penguin, 1983), banned in Franco's Spain because it revealed the truth about Lorca's death; *Federico García Lorca*: A Life (Faber & Faber, 1989), award-winning, deeply researched biography.

Irving, Washington: *Tales of the Alhambra* (Miguel Sánchez, Granada), legends and colourful view of Granada last century.

Josephs, Allen: *White Wall of Spain* (Iowa State University Press), fascinating examination of Andalucía's roots and the creation of a unique culture.

Lee, Laurie: *As I Walked Out One Midsummer Morning* (Penguin, 1983), heady, romantic young man's vision of pre-Civil War Spain; *A Rose for Winter* (Penguin, 1983), Lee's post-war return to Andalucía.

Lévi-Provencale, Evariste: *Histoire de l'Espagne musulmane*. Three volumes. Erudite history of Spain under the Moors.

Mendel, Janet: *Cooking in Spain* (Lookout Publications, Fuengirola, Málaga), details of many typical Andalucían dishes.

Mitchell, David: *Here in Spain* (Lookout Publications, Fuengirola, Málaga), the country viewed through the eyes of foreign travellers through the centuries.

Ortega y Gasset, José: *Teoría de Andalucía, in Andalucía Sueño y Realidad*, with María Zambrano (Editoriales Andaluzas Unidas), insights into the Andalucían character.

Pitt-Rivers, Julian A.: *The People of the Sierra* (Weidenfield & Nicolson, 1954), social anthropologist's dissection of a remote mountain community.

Pohren, D.E.: *The Art of Flamenco* (Musical New Services Ltd., 1984), the *aficionado's* bible, and *A Way of Life* (Society of Spanish Studies, Madrid, 1980), colourful, humorous account of a disappearing Andalucían lifestyle.

Robertson, Ian: *Los Curiosos Impertinentes* (published in Spanish by Serbal, 1988), English travellers' adventures in and comments on Spain between 1760 and 1855.

Schulten, Adolph: *Tartessos* (Espasa-Calpe, Madrid), controversial attempt to establish the site of Tartessos near the mouth of the Guadalquivir.

Woolsey, Gamel: *Death's Other Kingdom* (Virago Press, 1988). Vivid account of outbreak of Civil War by American poet, the wife of Gerald Brenan.

Los Andaluces (Ediciones Istmo, Madrid, 1980), collection of wide-ranging essays on the people, their history, economy and culture to the present day.

Los Toros en Andalucía (Arguval, Málaga), large format, for bullfight *aficionados*, history, statistics, personalities, superstitions of the *corrida*.

Anybody interested in probing deeper into Andalucían history and culture is recommended to check some of the titles issued recently by Spanish publishers in the region. Details of the publishers and their works can be obtained from Asociación de Editores de Andalucía, Héroe Sostoa, 122 29002 Málaga. Tel: (952) 318784.

USEFUL ADDRESSES

ALMERIA

(area code 951):

Tourist information: Hermanos Machado 4, Edificio Multiple. Tel: 23 47 05; also at Ctra N340, 1 mile (2 km) west of city. Tel: 23 48 59. Airport office: Tel: 22 19 54.

Iberia: Paseo de Almería, 42. Information: Tel: 23 84 11.

Airport: 5 miles (8 km) from centre.

RENFE (train) station: Tel: 25 11 35. Information: Alcalde Muñoz, 1. Tel: 23 12 07.

Bus station: Plaza de Barcelona. Tel: 22 18 88.

Boats to Melilla: Transmediterranea, Parque Nicolas Salmerón 26. Tel: 23 61 55.

Post office, Plaza Casinello.

CADIZ

(area code 956):

Tourist information: Calderón de la Barca, 1. Tel: 21 10 53.

Iberia: Almirante Lobo, 3. Tel: 22 89 01.

Train station: Plaza de Sevilla. Tel: 25 43 01.

Bus station: Plaza de la Hispanidad, 1. Tel: 22 42 71.

Teletaxi: Tel: 27 67 35. Post office: Plaza de Topete. Tel: 21 39 45.

Algeciras: Tourist information, Avda de la Marina s/n. Tel: 60 09 11.

Bus stations: Portillo (for Costa del Sol), Avda Virgen del Carmen, 15. Tel: 65 10 55; Comes (for Cádiz, Seville), San Bernardo, 1.

RENFE: Estación de Ferrocarriles. Tel: 65 11 55.

Boats to North Africa: Transmediterranea, Recinto del Puerto. Tel: 66 75 10.

Radio taxis: Tel: 65 55 12.

Post office: Primo de Rivera, 4. Telephones: Prim, 5.

Jerez de la Frontera: Tourist information,

Alameda Cristina 7. Tel: 33 11 50.

Puerto de Santa María: Tourist information, Guadalete s/n. Tel: 86 31 45. Ferry to Cádiz, summer service from quay.

CORDOBA

(area code 957):

City Council tourist office: Plaza de Juda Levi, Judería. Junta de Andalucía tourist information bureau: Torrijos 10 (Palacio de Congresos). Tel: 47 12 35.

Train station: Tel: 47 93 02. Reservations: Ronda de los Tejares, 10. Tel: 47 58 84.

Iberia: Ronda de los Tejares, 3. Tel: 47 26 95.

Airport: 4 miles (6 km) from centre.

Buses: Alsina Graells (for Málaga, Granada, Badajóz) Avda de Medina Azahara, 29. Tel: 23 27 34.

Ureña (for Jaén, Seville): Avda Cervantes, 22. Tel: 47 23 52.

Taxi stands: Tendillas. Tel: 47 02 91; Gran Capitán. Tel: 41 51 53; Colón. Tel: 47 13 06; Puerta de Almodovar. Tel: 29 09 47.

Post office: Cruz Conde, 15. Tel: 47 82 67.

GRANADA

(area code 958):

Municipal tourist office: Libreros 2. Tel: 22 59 90; also Plaza Mariana Pinea 10, bajo. Tel: 22 66 88. Junta de Andalucía tourist office: Casa de los Tiros, Plaza del Padre Suarez. Tel: 22 10 22.

Iberia: Pl Isabel la Católica, 2. Reservations: Tel: 22 37 37.

Airport: 11 miles (18 km) from centre.

Buses: Alsina Graells (services to Andalucían cities) Camino de Ronda, 97. Tel: 25 13 50; Bacoma (services to Madrid, Alicante, Valencia and Barcelona) Avda de Andaluces, 10. Tel: 28 18 83. Bus to Sierra Nevada: daily at 9 a.m. from Puerta Real. Returning at 5 p.m. Autocares: Bonal. Tel: 27 31 00.

RENFE: Avda Andaluces, s/n. Tel: 27 12 72.

Taxis: Tel: 20 14 61.

Post office, Puerta Real. Tel: 22 48 53.

HUELVA

(area code 955):

Tourist office: Vazquez Lopez 5, Huelva.

Tel: 25 74 03.

RENFE station: Avenida de Italia. Tel: 24 66 66.

Bus station: Avenida de Portugal 9. Tel: 25 69 00.

Iberia: Almirante Lobo 2. Tel: 22 89 01. Reservations: Tel: 21 88 80.

Teletaxi: Tel: 25 00 22.

Post Office: Avda de Italia s/n. Tel: 24 91 84.

JAEN

(area code 953):

Tourist information: Arquitecto Berges, 1, Jaén. Tel: 22 27 37.

Rail station: Jaén. Tel: 25 56 07; Andújar. Tel: 50 05 70.

Bus station: Jaén, Plaza Coca de la Piñera. Tel: 25 01 06.

Iberia: Jaén. Tel: 22 75 92.

Tourist information: Baeza, Plaza del Populo s/n. Tel: 74 04 44; Cazorla, Martinez Delgado, 1. Tel: 72 00 00; Ubeda, Bajos del Ayuntamiento. Tel: 75 08 97.

Bus stations: Baeza, Avda Puche y Pardo,1. Tel: 25 50 14; Ubeda, San José s/n. Tel: 75 18 35.

Rail station: Cazorla. Tel: 72 07 00; Ubeda 69 46 14.

MALAGA

(area code 952):

Tourist information: Marques de Larios, 5. Tel 21 34 45; Also at airport, terminal nacional. Tel: 31 20 44; terminal internacional. Tel: 31 60 00 ext: 5433. Airport 5 miles (8km).

Iberia and flight information: Tel: 32 20 00. Iberia city office, Molina Lario, 13. Tel: 22 76 00. Aviaco, 31 39 92.

British Airways: (airport) Tel: 23 06 23.

Ferry: to Melilla, Aucona, Juan Diaz, 1. Tel: 22 43 91.

RENFE station: Cuarteles. Tel: 31 25 00; information & tickets, Strachan, 2. Tel: 21 31 22.

Bus station: Paseo de los Tilos. Tel: 35 00 61.

Radio taxis: Tel: 32 79 50/32 80 62.

Post Office: Avda de Andalucía. Phone office: Molina Larios (near cathedral).

Antequera: tourist information, Palacio de Najera. Tel: 84 21 80.

RENFE: Tel: 84 28 60.

Post Office: Najera, s/n. Tel: 84 20 83.

Benalmádena–Costa: tourist information: Ctra N340 km 227, Benalmádena Costa, also at Castillo Bil Bil, Ctra N340. Tel: 44 24 94.

Estepona: Tourist information, Paseo Maritimo Jorge Manrique s/n. Tel: 80 09 13.

Bus station: Empresa Portillo, Avda de España. Tel: 87 22 62.

Taxi: Tel: 80 29 00.

Post office: Calle Sonsoles.

Fuengirola: Tourist information, Parque de España. Tel: 47 61 66.

Bus station: Av Ramón y Cajal. Tel: 47 40 86.

Regular trains to Málaga.

Taxis: Tel: 47 50 41.

Post office: Ramón y Cajal, s/n.

Marbella: tourist information, Miguel Cano, 1. Tel: 77 14 42.

Iberia: Paseo Maritimo, Complejo Marbella 2000. Tel: 77 02 84; reservations Tel: 77 30 82. KLM: Alonso de Bazán, 8. Tel: 82 01 50.

Bus station: Avda Ricardo Soriano. Tel: 77 21 92/77 21 35.

Radio taxis: Tel: 77 00 53.

Post office: Calle Alvaro de Bazán.

Nerja: tourist information, Puerta del Mar, 4, Nerja. Tel: 52 15 31.

Bus station: Nerja–La Ermita. Tel: 52 15 04.

Taxi rank: Nerja. Tel: 52 05 37.

Post office: Almirante Ferrandiz, 6. Tel: 52 17 49.

Ronda: Tourist information, Plaza de España,1, Ronda. Tel: 87 12 72.

Bus station: Ronda. Tel: 87 22 62.

Railway station: Ronda. Tel: 87 16 73.

Torre del Mar: Tourist information, Av. de Andalucía, 92-A. Tel: 54 11 04.

Bus station, Calle del Mar. Tel: 54 09 36.

Torremolinos: Tourist information, Calle Guetaria, La Nogalera. Tel: 38 15 78.

Bus station: Calle Hoyo. Tel: 38 09 65.

Trains: regular services along coast and to airport from town centre.

Iberia Airlines: Guetaría, Local 411 and 413. Tel: 38 24 00; British Airways: Airport Tel: 23 06 23; SAS: Pasaje Pizarro, 8. Tel: 38 06 27; KLM: Airport, Tel: 31 36 42; Lufthansa: La Nogalera. Tel: 38 29 44; Swissair: La Nogalera, 410. Tel: 38 76 55.

Taxis: Tel: 38 21 52/38 10 30.

Torremolinos Congress and Exhibition Hall and Provincial Tourist Promotion Board: Tel: 38 57 31.

Post office: Avenida Palma de Mallorca. Tel: 38 45 18.

Torrox–Costa: Tourist Information, Centro Internacional, Bloque 79. Tel: 53 02 25.

Bus station: Avda de Cómpeta. Tel: 53 81 70.

Vélez–Málaga: Tourist information, Pl. de España. Tel: 50 01 00.

Bus station: Calle Renidero. Tel: 50 17 31.

Taxi rank: Tel: 50 00 88.

Post office: Pl. San Roque. Tel: 50 01 43.

SEVILLE

(area code 954):

Tourism office: Avda de la Constitución, 21. Tel: 22 14 04; Municipal tourism office: Paseo de las Delicias. Tel: 23 44 65.

Iberia: Almirante Lobo, 1. Information Tel: 51 06 72. Reservations Tel: 21 88 00. San Pablo Airport: 7 miles (12 km). Tel: 51 61 77.

Buses: Main station, Manuel Vazquez Sagastizabal s/n. Tel: 41 88 11; Estación Empresa Damas, Segura, 16 (for Huelva, Rocío). Tel; 22 22 72. Estación Empresa la Estrella, Arenal 3. Tel: 22 58 20 (for Badajoz).

RENFE office: Zaragoza, 29. Tel 441 41 11. Reservations Tel: 21 79 98; Rail station Plaza de Armas (for Córdoba, Madrid, Barcelona). Tel: 22 18 28; Estación San Bernardo (for Cádiz). Tel: 41 43 60.

Radio taxi: Tel: 58 00 00.

Post office: Avda de la Constitución, 32. Tel: 22 58 20.

CONSULAR OFFICES

ALGECIRAS

(area code 956):

Belgium: Hotel Playa de la Luz, Rota. Tel: 810500.

Britain: Fuerzas Armadas, 11. Tel: 661600.

Denmark: Paseo de la Conferencia, 11. Tel: 603600.

France: Calle Nicaragua. Tel: 654205.

Netherlands: Calle Teniente Maroto. Tel: 656900.

Norway: Avenida Virgen del Carmen, 29. Tel: 667511.
Sweden: Alfonso X1, 10. Tel: 661883.

CADIZ

(area code 956):
Belgium: Hotel Playa de la Luz, Rota. Tel: 810500.
Denmark, Finland, Norway, Sweden: Alameda Apodaca 21. Tel: 221364.
France: Antonio López 10. Tel: 223284.
Italy: Ancha 8, entresuelo izquierda. Tel: 211715.
Netherlands: Plaza Tres Caravelas 5. Tel: 276326.

ALMERIA

(area code 951):
Denmark, Finland: Alvarez de Castro 34. Tel: 238275.
Finland: Lopez Falcon 6. Tel: 230481.
France: Avenida Cabo de Gata 81. Tel: 239011.
Netherlands: Paseo de Almería 73. Tel: 238275.
Sweden: Dr. Arriez Pacheco 2. Tel: 250033.
West Germany: Hotel Satelite Park, Aguadulce. Tel: 340555/3418143.

CORDOBA

(area code 957):
France: Manuel Sandoval 4–2. Tel: 472314.
Sweden: Ctra NIV km 388. Tel: 310200.

GRANADA

(area code 958):
Belgium: Recogidas 66, 1-A. Tel: 251631.
Italy: Dr Martin Lagos 6–3C. Tel: 261361.
West Germany: Avenida de la Constitución 20–2, Edificio Piramide. Tel: 293352.

HUELVA

(area code 955):
France: Rico 53, 1. Tel: 245350.
Finland, Avenida Martin Alonso Pinzon 14. Tel: 249583.
Netherlands, Plaza San pedro 12. Tel: 240651.
Norway, Sweden and Denmark, Santo Domingo de la Calzada. Tel: 253577.

MALAGA

(area code 952):
Austria: Occidente,1, Benalmádena–Costa. Tel: 443952.
Belgium: Compositor Lehmberg Ruiz, 5. Tel: 392003.
Canada: Edificio Horizonte, Plaza de la Malagueta, 3. Tel: 223346.
Denmark: Blasco de Garay, 3. Tel: 226373.
Finland: Blasco de Garay, 3. Tel: 212435.
France: Duquesa de Parcent, 8. Tel: 214888.
Great Britain: Duquesa de Parcent, 3. Tel: 217571.
Ireland: Avenida de los Boliches, Fuengirola. Tel: 475108.
Italy: Palestina, 3. Tel: 306150.
Morocco: Avda de Andalucía, 63. Tel: 329950l67.
Netherlands: Alameda de Colón, Pasaje Linaje 3, portal 2,4D. Tel: 279954.
Norway: Blasco de Garay, 5–3º. Tel: 210331.
Sweden: Alameda de Colón 9. Tel: 21 56 62/ 215668.
Switzerland: Puerta del Mar, 8. Tel: 217266.
United States: Complejo Sol Playa, portal 6, apartmento 5B, Martinez Catena, Fuengirola. Tel: 474891.
West Germany: Paseo del Limonar, 28. Tel: 22 78 66.

SEVILLE

(area code 954):
Austria: Marqués de Paradas 26. Tel: 222162.
Belgium: Avenida San Francisco Javier 20A–3. Tel: 647061.
Britain: Plaza Nueva, 8. Tel: 228875.
Canada: Avenida de la Constitución 30. Tel: 229413.
Denmark, Norway, Sweden: Avda Reina Mercedes, 25.–1B. Tel: 611489.
Finland: Adriano 45. Tel: 4225079.
France: Plaza de Santa Cruz, 1. Tel: 222897.
Italy: Avenida de la Constitución 30. Tel: 227774.
Netherlands: Gravina, 55. Tel: 228750.
United States: Paseo de las Delicias, 7. Tel: 231885.
West Germany: Ramón de Carranza, 22. Tel: 457811.

Gibraltar is one of the last relics of the British Empire. Connoisseurs of anachronisms and quirks of history will find the tiny colony of interest. One-third of the 30,000 population on the Rock, a limestone mass rising to 1,396 ft (426 metres), is composed of British servicemen and their families. But the garrison town atmosphere is being reduced as Britain cuts back on its military presence.

The permanent population is a mixture of Spanish, Moroccan, Jewish, Maltese and Genoese, who speak both English and Spanish although English is the official language. They resolutely oppose Spain's desire to absorb the 2 sq. mile (5.8 sq. km) peninsula. A democratically-elected House of Assembly led by a Chief Minister rules the colony.

The Rock's name derives from the Berber warrior Tarik who landed there in AD 711, hence Jebel Tarik (Mount Tarik). Spain held the Rock until in 1704, during the War of the Spanish Succession, an Anglo-Dutch fleet captured it. General Franco tried to force sovereignty to be transferred to Spain by closing the frontier. But his blockade only succeeded in making the Gibraltarians more stubbornly British. Today the colony has become a tourist attraction and is a growing off-shore financial centre.

GETTING THERE

BY AIR

Gibraltar airport offers handy access to the western end of the Costa del Sol. It is served by three commercial airlines—British Airways, GB Airways and Air Europe. Coach services are available for passengers travelling to and from the Costa del Sol.

Airport information. Tel: 75984.

GB Airways, Cloister Building, Irish Town. Tel: 79200: Gibraltar–London (Gatwick) flights daily; Gibraltar–Manchester 2 flights weekly (Thursday and Sunday); Gibraltar–Tangier (flight time 20 min.) flights Monday–Friday; Gibraltar–Casablanca 1 flight weekly (Tuesday).

Air Europe, 238 Main Street. Tel: 76028: Gibraltar–London (Gatwick) flights daily; Gibraltar–Manchester 1 flight weekly (Sunday).

BY SEA

A ferry service runs to the Moroccan port of Tangier throughout the year, five times a week in summer, four times in winter. In summer there is also a weekly crossing to Mdiq. Information from Seagle Travel. Tel: 76763.

BY ROAD

The only road access to Gibraltar is via the border with Spain at the crossing with La Linea. The border, known as La Verja, is open 24 hours.

TRAVEL ESSENTIALS

VISAS AND PASSPORTS

Immigration Control, Waterport Police Station, 124 Irish Town. Tel: 71543.

EEC nationals may present a valid passport or national identity card. Spaniards are required to show a passport. Visas are required from nationals of Eastern Bloc countries, Argentina, Libya, Russia, certain Near and Middle Eastern countries and all stateless persons. Visas are issued by British Visa issuing posts on Gibraltar's behalf and are usually for a single entry, maximum period of three months.

MONEY MATTERS

Official currency is the Gibraltar pound, which is on a par with the pound Sterling. UK and Gibraltar notes circulate freely, but

Gibraltar notes are not exchangeable outside Gibraltar. UK coinage is legal tender, although the colony has introduced its own coins. There are no restrictions on either bringing in or taking money out of Gibraltar.

Banking hours are generally 9/9.30 a.m.–3.30 p.m (Monday–Thursday), 9/9.30 a.m.–4.30 p.m (Friday), with variation during summer trading (July–mid September). Most banks are centred around Main Street or Line Wall Road. Although there are Barclays, Lloyds and National Westminster banks, UK account holders should not automatically assume that cash cards and current account cheque books are valid for use in Gibraltar. Barclays and National Westminster will cash UK cheques on presentation of a bankers guarantee card, while only the National Westminster cash card is valid for use in the Gibraltar cash dispenser.

Travellers holding travellers' cheques or wishing to draw cash on credit cards should check with the relevant agent as banks/foreign exchange bureaux and travel agents do not work with all cards. Access is represented by Banque Indosuez, 206/210 Main Street (tel: 75090), Visa by Barclays Bank with branches at 84-90 Main Street, 217 Main Street and 83-87 Irish Town (tel: 78565), American Express by National Westminster Bank, 57 Line Wall Road (tel: 77737). Bland Travel, Cloister Building, Irish Town will also cash Amex travellers cheques. Outside banking hours, travellers' cheques can be cashed at exchange bureaux and some hotels.

CUSTOMS

Gibraltar Customs, Custom House, Waterport. Tel: 78879.

Duty free allowance is available for people entering Gibraltar who have not been in Gibraltar during the previous 24 hours. Other than general items, these items are not allowed to persons under 17 years of age.

Tobacco products: 200 cigarettes or 50 cigars or 250 gm of smoking tobacco. Alcohol: 1 litre of spirits, liqueur or cordial or 2 litres of fortified or sparkling wine or 2 litres of still wine. Perfume: 50 grammes of perfume and 0.25 litres of toilet water.

GETTING ACQUAINTED

WEIGHTS AND MEASURES

Gibraltar officially uses the metric system, i.e. kilogramme and gramme for weights, litre for liquid measures, and metre and centimetre for measurements.

ELECTRICITY

Electricity supply is the same as the UK, i.e. 240 volts, single phase 50 Hz for domestic use and 415 volts, 3 phase, 50 Hz for high power. Electric plugs are the same as for the UK, 13 amp, 3 flat pin. Electrically-powered items bought in UK are compatible.

RELIGIOUS SERVICES

A complete list of places of worship in Gibraltar is available from the Tourist Office. A guided tour of the churches is run once a week starting from the Tourist Office.

Church of England, Cathedral of the Holy Trinity, Cathedral Square. Tel: 75745.

Bethel Christian Fellowship, 95 Main Street. Tel: 75398.

Church of Scotland, Church of St. Andrews, Governors Parade. Tel: 77040.

Evangelical Church of Gibraltar, 6/13 Parodys Pasage. Tel: 71829.

Pentecostal Church, 95 Main Street. Tel: 75398.

Quakers, P.O. Box 349. Tel: 76849.

Shaar Hashamayim Synagogue, 47 Engineer Lane. Tel: 78069, 73816; Nefussot Yehuba Synagogue, Line Wall Road. Tel: 76477; Etz Hayim Synagogue, Irish Town; Abudar Ham Synagogue, Parliament Lane.

Wesley Methodist Church, 297 Main Street. Tel: 77491.

Gibraltar Mosque, Casemates Square.

Details of services appear in The Gibraltar Chronicle (Jewish services in the Friday edition, Christian services in Saturday's).

COMMUNICATIONS

MEDIA

Gibraltar has its own TV station and two radio stations all broadcasting in English.

GBC Television: Daily broadcasts, 7 p.m.–midnight. Monday-Friday, 5.50 p.m.––midnight Saturday, 1.30 p.m.–midnight Sunday.

GBC Radio: 206m medium wave. Broadcasts 6.45 a.m.–midnight in English, except 2–4 p.m. when programme is in Spanish.

BFBS Gibraltar (British Forces Broadcasting Service)—on FM (VHF). There are two stations: BFBS 1 broadcasting music and sport and BFBS 2 broadcasting theatre, current affairs, comedy and music.

Gibraltar has several English-language newspapers the most important being *The Gibraltar Chronicle*, founded in 1801. Other publications include *The Democrat*, *The· Gibraltar Post*, *Panorama* and *The People*.

POSTAL SERVICES

The main branch of the Post Office is at 104 Main Street, with two sub-Post Offices at Sand Hill and Glacis Estate. Opening hours are 9 a.m.–1 p.m. and 2–5 p.m. Monday–Friday and 10 a.m.–1 p.m. Saturday, with variation during summer. Post boxes are red with a black base. Letters can be received at the Post Office using the address of Poste Restante, Gibraltar, and can be collected on presentation of passport.

Gibraltar stamps are of great interest to collectors and the main Post Office has a philatelic counter for first day covers, gift packs and previous issues, also available by post from Philatelic Bureau, P.O. Box 5662, Gibraltar.

TELEPHONE AND TELEX

There is International Direct Dialling for all countries. The International Access prefix for all countries is 00 (except Spain), followed by the country code, the province/town prefix and finally the subscribers number, e.g. to phone London 00-44 (UK code)—1 (London code) + subscribers' number. To phone Spain, only the province code + subscribers' number are required e.g. to Málaga 952 + number.

Calling Gibraltar from Spain, dial first 9567, except when you are in Cádiz province when you only need to dial 7 + subscribers' number. To phone Gibraltar from other countries, use the international access prefix + 350 (country code for Gibraltar). Operator-connected telephone booths are available on the ground floor of City Hall at the rear of John Mackintosh Square.

Telegrams, telexes and faxes can be sent from the offices of Cable and Wireless. Main office is at 25 South Barracks Road and branch at 60 Main Street. Open: 9 a.m.–5 p.m. Monday–Friday.

MEDICAL SERVICES

UK residents are entitled to free medical treatment provided they have a temporary address in Gibraltar. Other EEC nationals may receive free treatment on presentation of form E111.

St Bernard's Hospital—enquiries: tel: 79700, casualty: 73941. Health Centre, Casemates Square, tel: 78337. Open: 9.15 a.m.–5.30 p.m. Monday–Friday, 9 a.m.–1 p.m. Saturday.

GETTING AROUND

DOMESTIC TRAVEL

Driving is on the right side of the road. A current UK or EEC license is valid, other nationals need be in possession of an International Driving Licence obtained in their home country. There are no parking meters in Gibraltar, but fines are imposed for dangerous or illegal parking. Car clamps are also used and cars may be towed away. Gibraltar is small enough to manage without your own transport, although there are local and international car hire companies.

PUBLIC TRANSPORT

There are about 112 licensed taxis, with ranks in the town centre and at the airport and frontier, although phone reservations can be made by calling Gibraltar Taxi Association, 12 Cannon Lane, tel: 70027. Fares are not metered but rates are fixed and should be on display at ranks and in the taxi itself. There are surcharges for calls made via the office and from midnight–7 a.m. Some taxis offer tours of the Rock; look for a sign on the windscreen saying City Service.

Three bus companies operate services around Gibraltar. Information on routes available from the Tourist Office.

COMPLAINTS

The Consumer Protection Office in Library Street (Tel: 78136) deals with consumer complaints.

WHERE TO STAY

Accommodation in Gibraltar tends to be more expensive than in Spain.

Rock Hotel, Europa Road. Tel: 73000. The colony's top spot. In 9 acres (3.60 hectares) of gardens, with fine views.

Holiday Inn, 2 Governor St. Tel: 70500. Modern, with pool, near centre of town.

Bristol Hotel, 10 Cathedral Square. Tel: 76800. Pleasant old hotel, central.

Montarik Hotel, Main Street. Tel: 75566. Near the shops.

FOOD DIGEST

Da Paolo, Marina Bay. Tel: 76799. Lunch 12.30–3 p.m., dinner 7.30–11.15 p.m. Closed: Sunday. Major cards. Spanish, international. (M)

Spinning Wheel, 9 Horse Barrack Lane. Tel: 76091. Open: 12.30–3 p.m., 8–11 p.m. Closed: Saturday lunch and Sunday. Amex, Visa. Comfortable. International cuisine. Booking advisable. (M)

Strings, 44 Cornwall Lane. Tel: 78800. Open: 1–3 p.m., 8–11 p.m. Closed: Monday, lunch Saturday and Sunday. English/Moroccan food. No credit cards. (M)

Pub food: Royal Calpe, 176 Main Street. Tel: 75980. Open: 12 a.m.–3 p.m. Closed: Sunday. No credit cards. Reasonable prices.

THINGS TO DO

St Michael's Cave: The entrance chamber to the main cave has been converted to an auditorium for live concerts. There is a twice daily *son et lumiére* show. Lower cave has an underground lake, tours of which can be arranged through the Tourist Office.

Galleries: The Galleries were hewn out of solid rock in 1782 to make gun emplacements high up on the north face of the rock. Wonderful views of the airfield and harbour. Upper galleries open 10 a.m.–7 p.m. summer, 10 a.m.–5.30 p.m. winter.

Cable Car: From the top there are views of Africa and the Bay of Gibraltar. Half way up, stop at the Apes' Den (colony of tailless monkeys, the only breed living wild in Europe). Lower station in Grand Parade. Leaves every 10 minutes Monday-Saturday.

Europa Point: The 144-year old lighthouse is at the most southerly point of Gibraltar. Nearby shrine to Our Lady of Europa, venerated by sailors.

Changing of Guard: Once a month in front of the Governor's Residence on Main Street. For security reasons details are in local press only one week before the event.

Ceremony of the Keys: Celebrates the traditional locking of the Fortress Gates at Landport and the return of the keys to the safe custody of the Governor. Held three times a year in Casemates Square. Details published in local press one week before.

Excursions: Dolphin Safaris leave from Sheppard's Marina. Trips daily except Sunday combine sea views of Rock.

Gibraltar Museum: Represents history of Gibraltar from Stone Age to present. Open 10 a.m.-6 p.m. Monday-Friday, 10 a.m.-2 p.m. Saturday, closed Sunday.

Disco: Penelope's, 8 Corral Road, opens around 10.30 p.m. A popular spot, burrowing under the old ramparts.

DIARY OF EVENTS

Exact dates and details of events are available from the Tourist Office.

May: May Festival. Drama, music and dance events. Includes the Gibraltar Flower Show and the Miss Gibraltar Contest.

July: International Festival of Music and Performing Arts. Includes a gala night at St Michael's Cave, fitted out as an auditorium.

16 October: Trafalgar Day. Ceremony at the Trafalgar Cemetery, an old military cemetery and the site of the graves of the men killed in the famous sea battle.

November/December: Drama Festival. A week of drama performances at Ince's Hall.

SHOPPING

Shopping hours are generally 9/9.30 a.m.–1 p.m. and 3–7 p.m.

Commercial centre is focused on Main Street and Irish Town where there is an array of bazaars plus branches of Liptons food store, Marks and Spencer, British Home Stores. There are also new shopping complexes at Marina Bay and Sheppard's Marina. On Fridays and Saturdays there is a street market in Cannon Lane, and on Fridays an arts and crafts market at the Boulevard behind the Piazza. Worth buying: watches, jewellery, electrical goods, perfume, tobacco, spirits and cashmere. Prices are cheaper than in Spain, although the difference has narrowed.

GAMBLING

Gibraltar has a weekly lottery every Monday, with special prizes in June and at Christmas. Tickets from shops and kiosks in town centre. Turf accountants take bets for English horse and greyhound racing.

Gibraltar Casino, 7 Europa Road. Bingo, roulette, blackjack. Entry fee payable and you need your passport.

USEFUL ADDRESSES

Tourist information, Cathedral Square. Tel: 76400 & Piazza, Main Street. Tel: 75555. Airport (Gibraltar Airways) Tel: 75984. St Bernards Hospital Tel: 79700. Health Centre, Casemates Square. Tel: 77003. Ambulance Tel: 199. Police Tel: 72500, emergency calls Tel: 199. Post Office, 104 Main Street. Taxis Tel: 70027.

CONSULATES

Belgium, 47 Irish Town. Tel: 78564.
Denmark, Cloister Building, Market Lane. Tel: 72735.
Finland, 20 Line Wall Road. Tel: 74813.
France (Consular Office), 2nd floor, 209 Main Street. Tel: 78830.
Israel, 3 City Mill Lane. Tel: 75955.
Italy, 12 College Lane. Tel: 78123.
Netherlands, (Consul), 2-6 Main Street, Tel: 79220; (Vice Consul), 65 Irish Town Tel: 78305.
Norway, 315 Main Street. Tel: 74755.
Sweden, Cloister Building, Irish Town. Tel: 79200.

CREDITS

INDEX

D

E

F

G

H

I

A
B

D
E
F
G
H
I
J
a
b

d
e
f
g
h
i
j
k
l